PENGUIN B...

THE ACTOR'...
OF SCENES FROM NEW...

ERIC LANE is a playwright, director, and editor. His plays *Dancing on Checkers' Grave* and *So Slow It Whirls* have been produced in New York. *Blue Christmas* and *Jersey Bounce* have received staged readings at the 92nd Street Y and Riverwest Theatre. He is co-founder of "Orange thoughts" poetry theatre, which has performed in the Poets and Writers Series at LaMama. Mr. Lane is an honors graduate of Brown University. For his television work on "Ryan's Hope," he received a Writers Guild Award.

NINA SHENGOLD edited *The Actor's Book of Contemporary Stage Monologues* for Penguin Books. She received the ABC Playwright Award and the L.A. Weekly Award for her play *Homesteaders*, which has been produced by many regional theatres including the Long Wharf and Capital Rep. Her one-act plays *Finger Food* and *Women and Shoes*, originally commissioned by the Actors Theatre of Louisville, have been staged at the Ark Theatre and Manhattan Punchline. Ms. Shengold is currently an executive story editor for the ABC series "Hothouse." She is a graduate of Wesleyan University and has been a guest artist in playwriting at Skidmore College and Virginia Polytechnic Institute.

THE
ACTOR'S BOOK
OF
SCENES
FROM
NEW PLAYS

EDITED BY
Eric Lane and Nina Shengold

A SMITH AND KRAUS INC. BOOK
PENGUIN BOOKS

PENGUIN BOOKS
Published by the Penguin Group
Viking Penguin Inc., 40 West 23rd Street, New York, New York 10010, U.S.A.
Penguin Books Ltd, 27 Wrights Lane, London W8 5TZ, England
Penguin Books Australia Ltd, Ringwood, Victoria, Australia
Penguin Books Canada Ltd, 2801 John Street, Markham, Ontario, Canada L3R 1B4
Penguin Books (N.Z.) Ltd, 182–190 Wairau Road, Auckland 10, New Zealand

Penguin Books Ltd, Registered Offices: Harmondsworth, Middlesex, England

First published in Penguin Books 1988
Published simultaneously in Canada

3 5 7 9 10 8 6 4 2

Copyright © Smith and Kraus Inc., 1988
All rights reserved

LIBRARY OF CONGRESS CATALOGING IN PUBLICATION DATA
The Actor's book of scenes from new plays / edited by Eric Lane and
Nina Shengold.
p.   cm.
"A Smith and Kraus Inc. book."
ISBN 0 14 01.0487 9
1. Acting.   2. American drama—20th century.   3. English
drama—20th century.   I. Lane, Eric.   II. Shengold, Nina.
PN2080.A286 1988
792'.028—dc19   87-33389

Printed in the United States of America
Set in Caledonia
Designed by Robert Bull

Grateful acknowledgment is made for permission to reprint excerpts from the following plays:

Am I Blue by Beth Henley. Copyright 1982 by Beth Henley. All inquiries concerning rights (other than stock and amateur rights) should be addressed to Gilbert Parker, c/o William Morris Agency, Inc., 1350 Avenue of the Americas, New York, NY 10019. The stock and amateur production rights are controlled exclusively by the Dramatists Play Service, Inc., 440 Park Avenue South, New York, NY 10016.

The Art of Dining by Tina Howe. Copyright 1980 by Tina Howe. Used by permission of Flora Roberts, Inc. a/a/f Tina Howe.

Asian Shade by Larry Ketron. Copyright 1983 by Larry Ketron. All inquiries concerning rights (other than stock and amateur rights) should be addressed to Gilbert Parker, c/o William Morris Agency, Inc., 1350 Avenue of the Americas, New York, NY 10019. The stock and amateur production rights are controlled exclusively by the Dramatists Play Service, Inc., 440 Park Avenue South, New York, NY 10016.

Betrayal by Harold Pinter. Copyright © 1978 by H. Pinter Limited. By permission of Judy Daish Associates Ltd.

Beyond Therapy by Christopher Durang. Copyright © 1983 by Christopher Durang. All inquiries concerning rights should be addressed to Helen Merrill, 435 West 23rd Street, New York, NY 10011.

Danny and the Deep Blue Sea by John Patrick Shanley. Copyright 1984 by John Patrick Shanley. By permission of Jeannine Edmunds, Artists Agency, Inc., 230 West 55th Street, New York, NY 10019.

A Different Moon by Ara Watson. By permission of the playwright. Copyright © 1983 by Ara Watson.

Domino Courts by William Hauptman. Copyright © 1977 by William Hauptman. Reprinted by permission of Samuel French, Inc.

the dreamer examines his pillow by John Patrick Shanley. Copyright 1987 by John Patrick Shanley. By permission of Jeannine Edmunds, Artists Agency, Inc., 230 West 55th Street, New York, NY 10019.

Edmond by David Mamet. Copyright © 1983 by David Mamet. Reprinted by arrangement with Grove Press, Inc.

Entertaining Mr. Sloane by Joe Orton. Copyright © 1964 by Joe Orton. Reprinted by permission of Grove Press, a division of Wheatland Corporation.

FOB by David Henry Hwang. © 1982 by David Henry Hwang.

Getting Out by Marsha Norman. © Copyright 1978, 1979 by Marsha Norman. Reprinted by permission of William Morris Agency, Inc., on behalf of Marsha Norman.

ACKNOWLEDGMENTS

We'd like to thank the following people for their help and support: Laurie Alberts, Alan Amtzis, David Babcock, Mary Barber, Lynn Bernstein, Laura Harrington, Ken Mueller, Tina Newton, Sarah Noll, Mary Portser, Jeff Sweet, David Van Biema, Shelley Wyant, and most of all, Marc Helman.

We'd also like to thank the playwrights for their generous contributions to this collection.

C O N T E N T S

SCENES FOR TWO WOMEN

SCENES FOR TWO MEN

INTRODUCTION

While editing this book, we had an opportunity to read several hundred plays from sources as varied as Off Broadway, regional theatre, fringe theatre in London, and South Africa. Ultimately, we selected scenes from recent plays, many by younger playwrights whose works are being anthologized here for the first time. Scenes by more widely recognized playwrights were selected from their less-well-known plays.

All these scenes provide a strong, clear challenge to actors. There are parts for actors of every age range, though the majority are geared toward younger actors. Although there are scenes specifically written for minority actors, we encourage readers to choose whatever roles they identify with, and we hope that theatres will begin and continue to cast minority actors more imaginatively.

For each scene, you will find a brief introduction that sets up the given circumstances, characters, and, where appropriate, the tone or style of the piece. We tried to choose scenes that are self-contained and have a clear dramatic build. We encourage actors, after choosing a scene, to go out and read the entire play. For that purpose, publishers' names are included along with each scene.

There is incredible joy and excitement taking place in contemporary theatre. We hope this book begins to capture that.

—Eric Lane and Nina Shengold
March 1988

SCENES FOR

ONE MAN AND ONE WOMAN

Am I Blue

Beth Henley

Characters: John Polk (17), Ashbe (16)
Setting: New Orleans French Quarter: Street, bar, Ashbe's
  apartment
Premiere: Circle Repertory Company, New York City, 1982
Publisher: Dramatists Play Service, Inc.

It is around 10:00 P.M. on a rainy blue bourbon night in
the New Orleans French Quarter. John Polk sits alone at a
table in a sleazy bar. He is a bit overweight and awkward. In
two hours it will be his eighteenth birthday. He belongs to a fraternity at school. Membership in the frat has not solved all his
problems, as he had been told it would. He is slightly drunk.

Ashbe enters wearing a flowered plastic rain cap, red ga-
loshes, a butterfly barrette and jeweled cat-eye glasses. She
carries a bag full of stolen goods. She sits at John Polk's table
and hides under his raincoat because she is afraid the manager
from the Screw Inn may have seen her take two ashtrays.
Ashbe sees herself as a modern-day Robin Hood, telling John
Polk she plans to give the goods away to a neighbor.

Before sitting, she saw John Polk hide a red-and-black card
in his pocket. It's from the whorehouse down the block, where
he has a midnight appointment. John Polk and Ashbe are
thrown out of the bar for being underage. It is raining. John
Polk still has two hours to kill and needs to get drunk. He
reluctantly accepts Ashbe's invitation to her apartment.

ASHBE: A lot of jerks live around here. Come on in. (*She opens
the door. Lights go up on the living room of a run-down
apartment in a run-down apartment house. Besides being
merely run-down the room is a malicious pig sty with colors,
paper hats, paper dolls, masks, torn up stuffed animals, dead
flowers and leaves, dress up clothes, etc., thrown all about.*)
My bones are cold. Do you want a towel to dry off?

JOHN POLK: Yes, thank you.

ASHBE: (*She picks a towel up off of the floor and tosses it to him.*) Here. (*He begins drying off, as she takes off her rain things, then she begins raking things off the sofa.*) Please do sit down. (*He sits.*) I'm sorry the place is disheveled, but my father's been out of town. I always try to pick up and all before he gets in. Of course he's pretty used to messes. My mother never was too good at keeping things clean.

JOHN POLK: When's he coming back?

ASHBE: Sunday, I believe. Oh, I've been meaning to say—

JOHN POLK: What?

ASHBE: My name's Ashbe Williams.

JOHN POLK: Ashbe?

ASHBE: Yeah, Ashbe.

JOHN POLK: My name's John Polk Richards.

ASHBE: John Polk? They call you John Polk?

JOHN POLK: It's family.

ASHBE: (*Putting on socks.*) These are my favorite socks, the red furry ones. Well here's some books and magazines to look at while I fix you something to drink. What do you want in your rum?

JOHN POLK: Coke's fine.

ASHBE: I'll see do we have any. I think I'll take some hot Kool-Aid myself. (*She exits to the kitchen.*)

JOHN POLK: Hot Kool-Aid?

ASHBE: It's just Kool-Aid that's been heated, like hot chocolate or hot tea.

JOHN POLK: Sounds great.

ASHBE: Well, I'm used to it. You get so much for your dime it makes it worth your while. I don't buy pre-sweetened, of course, it's better to sugar your own.

JOHN POLK: I remember once I threw up a lot of grape Kool-Aid when I was a kid. I've hated it every since. Hey, would you check on the time?

ASHBE: (*She enters carrying a tray with several bottles of food coloring, a bottle of rum, and a huge glass.*) I'm sorry we don't have Cokes. I wonder if rum and Kool-Aid is good?

Oh, we don't have a clock either. (*She pours a large amount of rum into the large glass.*)

JOHN POLK: I'll just have it with water then.

ASHBE: (*She finds an almost empty glass of water somewhere in the room and dumps it in with the rum.*) Would you like food coloring in the water? It makes a drink all the more aesthetic. Of course, some people don't care for aesthetics.

JOHN POLK: No thank you, just plain water.

ASHBE: Are you sure? The taste is entirely the same. I put it in all my water.

JOHN POLK: Well—

ASHBE: What color do you want?

JOHN POLK: I don't know.

ASHBE: What's your favorite color?

JOHN POLK: Blue, I guess. (*She puts a few blue drops into the glass—as she has nothing to stir with, she blows into the glass, turning the water blue.*) Thanks.

ASHBE: (*Exits. She screams from the kitchen.*) Come on, say come on cat, eat your fresh good milk.

JOHN POLK: You have a cat?

ASHBE: (*Off.*) No.

JOHN POLK: Oh.

ASHBE: (*She enters carrying a tray with a cup of hot Kool-Aid and Cheerios and colored marshmallows.*) Here are some Cheerios and some cute little colored marshmallows to eat with your drink.

JOHN POLK: Thanks.

ASHBE: I one time smashed all the big white marshmallows in the plastic bag at the grocery store.

JOHN POLK: Why did you do that?

ASHBE: I was angry. Do you like ceramics?

JOHN POLK: Yes.

ASHBE: My mother makes them. It's sort of her hobby. She is very talented.

JOHN POLK: My mother never does anything. Well, I guess she can shuffle the bridge deck okay.

ASHBE: Actually, my mother is a dancer. She teaches at a school in Atlanta. She's really very talented.

JOHN POLK: (*Indicates ceramics.*) She must be to do all these.

ASHBE: Well, Madeline, my older sister, did the blue one. Madeline gets to live with Mama.

JOHN POLK: And you live with your father.

ASHBE: Yeah, but I get to go visit them sometimes.

JOHN POLK: You do ceramics too?

ASHBE: No, I never learned . . . but I have this great pot-holder set. (*Gets up to show him.*) See I make lots of multi-colored potholders and send them to Mama and Madeline. I also make paper hats. (*Gets material to show him.*) I guess they're more creative but making potholders is more relaxing. Here would you like to make a hat?

JOHN POLK: I don't know, I'm a little drunk.

ASHBE: It's not hard a bit. (*Hands him material.*) Just draw a real pretty design on the paper. It really doesn't have to be pretty, just whatever you want.

JOHN POLK: It's kind of you to give my creative drives such freedom.

ASHBE: Ha, ha, ha, I'll work on my potholder set a bit.

JOHN POLK: What time is it? I've really got to check on the time.

ASHBE: I know. I'll call the time operator. (*She goes to the phone.*)

JOHN POLK: How do you get along without a clock?

ASHBE: Well, I've been late for school a lot. Daddy has a watch. It's 11:03.

JOHN POLK: I've got a while yet.

ASHBE: (*Twirls back to her chair, drops, and sighs.*)

JOHN POLK: Are you a dancer too?

ASHBE: (*Delighted.*) I can't dance a bit, really. I practice a lot is all, at home in the afternoon. I imagine you go to a lot of dances.

JOHN POLK: Not really, I'm a terrible dancer. I usually get bored or drunk.

ASHBE: You probably drink too much.

JOHN POLK: No, it's just since I've come to college. All you do there is drink more beer and write more papers.

ASHBE: What are you studying for to be?

JOHN POLK: I don't know.

ASHBE: Why don't you become a rancher?

JOHN POLK: Dad wants me to help run his soybean farm.

ASHBE: Soybean farm. Yikes, that's really something. Where is it?

JOHN POLK: Well, I live in the Delta, Hollybluff, Mississippi. Anyway, Dad feels I should go to business school first; you know, so I'll become, well, management minded. Pass the blue.

ASHBE: Is that what you really want to do?

JOHN POLK: I don't know. It would probably be as good as anything else I could do. Dad makes good money. He can take vacations whenever he wants. Sure it'll be a ball.

ASHBE: I'd hate to have to be management-minded. (*John Polk shrugs.*) I don't mean to hurt your feelings but I would really hate to be a management mind. (*She starts walking on her knees, twisting her fists in front of her eyes, and making clicking sounds as a management mind would make.*)

JOHN POLK: Cut it out. Just forget it. The farm could burn down and I wouldn't even have to think about it.

ASHBE: (*After a pause.*) Well, what do you want to talk about?

JOHN POLK: I don't know.

ASHBE: When was the last dance you went to?

JOHN POLK: Dances. That's a great subject. Let's see, oh, I don't really remember it was probably some blind date. God, I hate dates.

ASHBE: Why?

JOHN POLK: Well, they always say that they don't want popcorn and they wind up eating all of yours.

ASHBE: You mean, you hate dates just because they eat your popcorn? Don't you think that's kind of stingy?

JOHN POLK: It's the principle of the thing. Why can't they just say, yes, I'd like some popcorn when you ask them. But, no, they're always so damn coy.

ASHBE: I'd tell my date if I wanted popcorn. I'm not that immature.

JOHN POLK: Anyway, it's not only the popcorn. It's a lot of little things. I've finished coloring. What do I do now?

ASHBE: Now you have to fold it. Here . . . like this. (*She explains the process with relish.*) Say, that's really something.

JOHN POLK: It's kind of funny looking. (*Putting the hat on.*) Yeah, I like it, but you could never wear it anywhere.

ASHBE: Well, like what anyway?

JOHN POLK: Huh?

ASHBE: The things dates do to you that you don't like, the little things.

JOHN POLK: Oh, well just the way they wear those false eye lashes and put their hand on your knee when you're trying to parallel park, and keep on giggling and going off to the bathroom with their girlfriends. It's obvious they don't want to go out with me. They just want to go out so that they can wear their new clothes and won't have to sit on their ass in the dormitory. They never want to go out with me. I can never even talk to them.

ASHBE: Well, you can talk to me and I'm a girl.

JOHN POLK: Well, I'm really kind of drunk and you're a stranger . . . well, I probably wouldn't be able to talk to you tomorrow. That makes a difference.

ASHBE: Maybe it does. (*A bit of a pause and then extremely pleased by the idea she says.*) You know we're alike because I don't like dances either.

JOHN POLK: I thought you said you practiced . . . in the afternoons.

ASHBE: Well, I like dancing. I just don't like dances. At least not like—well, not like the one our school was having tonight . . . they're so corny.

JOHN POLK: Yeah, most dances are.

ASHBE: All they serve is potato chips and fruit punch, and then this stupid baby band plays and everybody dances around thinking they're so hot. I frankly wouldn't dance there. I would prefer to wait till I am invited to an exclusive ball. It doesn't really matter which ball, just one where they have huge, golden chandeliers and silver fountains, and serve delicacies of all sorts and bubble blue champagne. I'll arrive in a pink silk cape. (*Laughing.*) I want to dance in pink!

JOHN POLK: You're mixed up. You're probably one of those people that live in a fantasy world.

ASHBE: I do not. I accept reality as well as anyone. Anyway, you can talk to me remember. I know what you mean by the kind of girls it's hard to talk to. There are girls a lot that way in the small clique at my school. Really tacky and mean. They expect everyone to be as stylish as they are and they won't even speak to you in the hall. I don't mind if they don't speak to me, but I really love the orphans and it hurts my feelings when they are so mean to them.

JOHN POLK: What do you mean—they're mean to the orpheens? (*Notices pun and giggles to self.*)

ASHBE: Oh, well, they sometimes snicker at the orphans' dresses. The orphans usually have hand-me-down drab ugly dresses. Once Shelly Maxwell wouldn't let Glinda borrow her pencil, even though she had two. It hurt her feelings.

JOHN POLK: Are you best friends with these orphans?

ASHBE: I hardly know them at all. They're really shy. I just like them a lot. They're the reason I put spells on the girls in the clique.

JOHN POLK: Spells, what do you mean, witch spells?

ASHBE: Witch spells? Not really, mostly just voodoo.

JOHN POLK: Are you kidding? Do you really do voodoo?

ASHBE: Sure, here I'll show you my doll. (*Goes to get doll, comes back with straw voodoo doll. Her air as she returns is one of frightening mystery.*) I know a lot about the subject. Cora she used to wash dishes in the Moonlight Cafe, told me all about voodoo. She's a real expert on the subject, went to all the meetings and everything. Once she caused a man's throat to rot away and turn almost totally black. She's moved to Chicago now.

JOHN POLK: It doesn't really work. Does it?

ASHBE: Well, not always. The thing about voodoo is that both parties have to believe in it for it to work.

JOHN POLK: Do the girls in school believe in it?

ASHBE: Not really, I don't think. That's where my main problem comes in. I have to make the clique believe in it, yet I have to be very subtle. Mainly, I give reports in English class or Speech.

JOHN POLK: Reports?

ASHBE: On voodoo.

JOHN POLK: That's really kind of sick, you know.

ASHBE: Not really. I don't cast spells that'll do any real harm. Mainly, just the kind of thing to make them think—to keep them on their toes. (*Blue drink intoxication begins to take over and John Polk begins laughing.*) What's so funny?

JOHN POLK: Nothing. I was just thinking what a mean little person you are.

ASHBE: Mean! I'm not mean a bit.

JOHN POLK: Yes, you are mean— (*Picking up color.*) and green too.

ASHBE: Green?

JOHN POLK: Yes, green with envy of those other girls; so you play all those mean little tricks.

ASHBE: Envious of those other girls, that stupid, close-minded little clique!

JOHN POLK: Green as this marshmallow. (*Eats marshmallow.*)

ASHBE: You think I want to be in some group . . . a sheep like you? A little sheep like you that does everything when he's supposed to do it!

JOHN POLK: Me a sheep—I do what I want!

ASHBE: Ha! I've known you for an hour and already I see you for the sheep you are!

JOHN POLK: Don't take your green meanness out on me.

ASHBE: Not only are you a sheep, you are a NORMAL sheep. Give me back my colors! (*Begins snatching colors away.*)

JOHN POLK: (*Pushing colors at her.*) Green and mean! Green and mean! Green and mean! Etc.

ASHBE: (*Throwing marshmallows at him.*) That's the reason

you're in a fraternity and the reason you're going to manage your mind, and dates—you go out on dates merely because it's expected of you even though you have a terrible time. That's the reason you go to the whorehouse to prove you're a normal man. Well, you're much too normal for me.

JOHN POLK: Infant bitch. You think you're really cute.

ASHBE: That really wasn't food coloring in your drink, it was poison! (*She laughs, he picks up his coat to go and she stops throwing marshmallows at him.*) Are you going? I was only kidding. For Christ sake it wasn't really poison. Come on, don't go. Can't you take a little friendly criticism?

JOHN POLK: Look, did you have to bother me tonight? I had enough problems without—(*Phone rings. Both look at phone, it rings for the third time. He stands undecided.*)

ASHBE: Look, wait, we'll make it up. (*She goes to answer phone.*) Hello—Daddy. How are you? . . . I'm fine . . . Dad, you sound funny . . . what? . . . Come on, Daddy, you know she's not here. (*Pause.*) Look, I told you I wouldn't call anymore. You've got her number in Atlanta. (*Pause, as she sinks to the floor.*) Why have you started again? . . . Don't say that. I can tell it. I can. Hey, I have to go to bed now, I don't want to talk anymore, o.k.? (*Hangs up phone, softly to self.*) Goddamnit.

JOHN POLK: (*He has heard the conversation and is taking off his coat.*) Hey, Ashbe— (*She looks at him blankly, her mind far away.*) You want to talk?

ASHBE: No.

The Art of Dining
Tina Howe

Characters: Elizabeth Barrow Colt (30s), David Osslow (mid-50s)

Setting: The Golden Carousel, an intimate, elegant restaurant
   on the New Jersey shore
Premiere: New York Shakespeare Festival, New York City,
   1979
Publisher: Avon Books (in *Three Plays by Tina Howe*)

A young couple, Ellen and Cal, have recently opened the
restaurant of their dreams. On this raw, freezing day in November, three different parties have made reservations. Publisher David Osslow, "a man with a glowing appetite and
glowing literary taste," has asked the writer Elizabeth Barrow
Colt to meet him for dinner. Elizabeth is nearsighted, hys-
terically timid, and terrified of food. This is their first en-
counter, and it began with the stricken Elizabeth spilling a
bowl of soup in her lap. The waiter has just brought her a new
bowl of soup.

ELIZABETH BARROW COLT: (*Her shoulders giving way, looks
   at it.*) Oh dear.
   (*A slight pause.*)
DAVID OSSLOW: Elizabeth, I'd like to publish your short sto-
   ries.
ELIZABETH BARROW COLT: (*Looking into the soup, stunned.*)
   Oh my.
DAVID OSSLOW: They're wonderful.
ELIZABETH BARROW COLT: Mercy!
DAVID OSSLOW: What did you say?
ELIZABETH BARROW COLT: (*Softly.*) I don't know what to
   say. . . .
DAVID OSSLOW: . . . really wonderful!
ELIZABETH BARROW COLT: I never imagined . . . (*Starts
   fishing around in her pocketbook.*)
DAVID OSSLOW: You're incredibly gifted. . . .
ELIZABETH BARROW COLT: Oh no, I'm . . . (*Pulls out her
   lipstick, lowers her head, and sneaks on a smear, hands
   shaking. Suddenly she drops the lipstick. It falls into her
   soup with a splash.*) Oh no!

DAVID OSSLOW: What was that?

ELIZABETH BARROW COLT: (*Dives for it.*) Oh nothing, I just dropped my lipstick. . . .
　(*She repeatedly tries to retrieve it with her spoon, but it keeps splashing back down into her soup. She finally gives up, fishes it out with her hands, and drops it into her purse.*)

DAVID OSSLOW: Don't you like the soup?

ELIZABETH BARROW COLT: (*Hunched over her pocketbook.*) Oh yes, it's . . .

DAVID OSSLOW: It looks delicious.

ELIZABETH BARROW COLT: (*Staring at it.*) Yes, it's very nice.

DAVID OSSLOW: I've always loved French Provincial. ELIZABETH BARROW COLT: Would you like it?
. . . I'm sorry. . . . I . . .
　(*A pause.*)

ELIZABETH BARROW COLT: OH, YOU HAVE IT!

DAVID OSSLOW: No, really, I . . .

ELIZABETH BARROW COLT: (*Picks up the bowl with trembling hands and starts lifting it across the table to him, her spoon still in it.*) I want you to have it!

DAVID OSSLOW: *Careful!*

ELIZABETH BARROW COLT: (*Giddy, the soup sloshing wildly.*) I never have soup!

DAVID OSSLOW: *Look out!*

ELIZABETH BARROW COLT: In fact, I hardly ever have dinner, either!

DAVID OSSLOW: Really, I . . .

ELIZABETH BARROW COLT: (*Sets it down in front of him, spilling some.*) THERE!

DAVID OSSLOW: (*Looks at it. Weakly.*) Well, thank you.

ELIZABETH BARROW COLT: (*Incredibly relieved, looks at him and sighs.*)

DAVID OSSLOW: (*Picks up her spoon and dips it into the soup.*)

ELIZABETH BARROW COLT: This is nice.

DAVID OSSLOW: (*Starts eating it.*)

ELIZABETH BARROW COLT: How is it?

DAVID OSSLOW: Very good. Would you like a taste?

ELIZABETH BARROW COLT: Oh, no thank you!
  (*A silence.*)

DAVID OSSLOW: Do you cook at all?

ELIZABETH BARROW COLT: Oh no.

DAVID OSSLOW: (*Reaches a spoonful of soup across the table
  to her.*) Come on, try some.

ELIZABETH BARROW COLT: (*She tastes it.*) My mother didn't
  cook either.

DAVID OSSLOW: Now isn't that good?
  (*Gives her another taste.*)

ELIZABETH BARROW COLT: Mmmmmmmm . . . (*Quickly
  wipes her mouth with her napkin.*)

DAVID OSSLOW: (*Takes a taste himself.*) My mother was a
  great cook.

ELIZABETH BARROW COLT: She didn't know how. She grew
  up with servants.

DAVID OSSLOW: Her Thanksgiving dinners! . . .

ELIZABETH BARROW COLT: We had a cook. Lacey. She was
  awful and she smelled.

DAVID OSSLOW: I cook every once in a while.

ELIZABETH BARROW COLT: We all hated her. Especially my
  mother.

DAVID OSSLOW: My wife is a great cook! Some night you'll
  have to come over for dinner!
  (*He settles into his soup, eating with less and less relish as
  her story progresses.*)

ELIZABETH BARROW COLT: In fact, when I was young I never
  even saw my mother in the kitchen. The food just appeared
  at mealtime as if by magic, all steaming and ready to eat.
  Lacey would carry it in on these big white serving platters
  that had a rim of raised china acorns. Our plates had the
  same rim. Twenty-two acorns per plate, each one about the
  size of a lump of chewed gum. When I was very young I
  used to try and pry them off with my knife. . . . We ate every
  night at eight o'clock sharp because my parents didn't start
  their cocktail hour until seven, but since dinner time was
  meant for exchanging news of the day, the emphasis was

always on talking . . . and not on eating. My father bolted his food, and my mother played with hers: sculpting it up into hills and then mashing it back down through her fork. To make things worse, before we sat down at the table she'd always put on a fresh smear of lipstick. I still remember the shade. It was called "Fire and Ice" . . . a dark throbbing red that rubbed off on her fork in waxy clumps that stained her food pink, so that by the end of the first course she'd have rended everything into a kind of . . . rosy puree. As my father wolfed down his meat and vegetables, I'd watch my mother thread this puree through the raised acorns on her plate, fanning it out into long runny pink ribbons. . . . I could never eat a thing. . . . "WAKE UP, AMERICA!" she'd trumpet to me. "You're not being excused from this table until you clean up that plate!" So, I'd take several mouthfuls and then when no one was looking, would spit them out into my napkin. Each night I systematically transferred everything on my plate into that lifesaving napkin. . . .

DAVID OSSLOW: Jesus Christ.

ELIZABETH BARROW COLT: It's amazing they never caught on.

DAVID OSSLOW: (*Lights a cigarette and takes a deep drag.*)

ELIZABETH BARROW COLT: I mean, you'd think Lacey would have noticed the huge bundles of half-chewed food I left in my chair. . . .

DAVID OSSLOW: I have never had trouble eating!

ELIZABETH BARROW COLT: We used cloth napkins, after all. They were collected after each meal.

DAVID OSSLOW: I can always eat, no matter where I am!

ELIZABETH BARROW COLT: We had a fresh one each evening.

DAVID OSSLOW: Believe me, I could use a little of your problem. . . .

ELIZABETH BARROW COLT: Lacey washed and ironed them.

DAVID OSSLOW: That is, if you call not eating a problem.

ELIZABETH BARROW COLT: To launder them, she had to dump the food out.

DAVID OSSLOW: (*Patting his stomach.*) I should have such problems!

ELIZABETH BARROW COLT: She must have noticed. I left so much, at least a pound. . . .

DAVID OSSLOW: I'm so bad, I start thinking about my next meal before I've even finished the one I'm eating!

ELIZABETH BARROW COLT: I wonder what she thought? If she was hurt that I could never get it down . . .

DAVID OSSLOW: Now *that's* serious! . . .

ELIZABETH BARROW COLT: I lived in constant fear that she'd tell my parents. You see I was terribly underweight. . . .

DAVID OSSLOW: I love to eat!

ELIZABETH BARROW COLT: Or worse, that she'd sneak into my room some night, lugging all those bulging napkins . . . and spill everything out . . . from one end of my bed to the other . . . and *force* me to eat it . . .

DAVID OSSLOW: I've always loved to eat. . . . It will be the death of me. . . . Every time I see my doctor, he says the same thing. He says, "David, you've got to lose some of that weight!"

(*A silence.*)

ELIZABETH BARROW COLT: I used to bite my nails. I think it was because I was so hungry all the time.

DAVID OSSLOW: (*Hands her back her empty soup bowl.*) Thank you, it was delicious.

ELIZABETH BARROW COLT: (*Hiding her hands.*) I still bite them sometimes. (*A silence. She looks around the room, a sigh.*) This is wonderful.

(*Another silence.*)

DAVID OSSLOW: Oh! I forgot to return your spoon!

(*He hands it to her, covering her hand with both of his.*)

ELIZABETH BARROW COLT: (*Grasps it, turns it gently in her hands, sneaks it up against her cheek for a moment . . . and then drops it into her pocketbook.*) I can't believe this is happening.

(*The lights fade . . .*)

Asian Shade

Larry Ketron

Characters: Tom (19), Kaylene (21)
Setting: A lakeside cabin in East Tennessee, 1967–68
Premiere: WPA Theatre, New York City, 1983
Publisher: Dramatists Play Service, Inc.

It is June 1967, and Tom and Ernie are going to Vietnam. They have finished Basic Training and now have a one-week furlough before they go overseas. Neal, a World War II veteran, gives the two boys the use of his lakeside cabin so they can escape from their sentimental families and "raise a little hell." They spend a large part of the week with two local girls, Casey and Jean, roasting hot dogs, swimming, and trying to stave off their fears about going to war. Neal tells them that a World War II buddy of his can pull a few strings and change their posting to Fort Ord, California. The boys are initially dubious, but as their departure gets closer, they cling more and more to this hope. When it turns out that Neal's contact has retired from the service and can't do them a bit of good, the boys are devastated. Neal is mortally embarrassed, and promises them he'll do something good for them when they come back.

This scene, the play's last, takes place one year later. Tom has come back from the war alone; Ernie is dead. Neal brings Tom out to visit the cabin, leaving him there with his daughter, Kaylene.

Note: Harry (of Harry's Market) lost a son in Vietnam.

(TOM *looks the joint over. With one finger he tips the lamp that kept falling over last year.* KAYLENE *reappears in the door frame with a paper bag; she startles* TOM.)

TOM: Jesus Christ! (*She comes in, sets bag down on coffee table.*)

KAYLENE: This is from Janis.

TOM: Who's that? (*She pushes the bag down, revealing a bottle of Southern Comfort, hands it to* TOM.)

KAYLENE: Joplin. It's her brand. It was my dad's for the fishing, but it's been reappropriated.

TOM: (*Gratefully.*) My sister Cheryl was going to get me some, but this'll come in.

KAYLENE: Yeah, I turned twenty-one in April. I like to buy booze, it's fun. Showing them my driver's license. They look at *it*, they look at *me*, they look at *it*. But I win. I buy all Neal's whiskey, all his beer, he throws a fit.

TOM: Is Neal waiting on you?

KAYLENE: Well . . . no.

TOM: Maybe I can find a couple of glasses.

KAYLENE: Uh, I don't drink it, are you kidding? (*Then.*) You know, I never come out here. I love the sun and the fish, but I never use this dump.

TOM: Say you love to fish?

KAYLENE: No, I love *the* fish. I hate *to* fish. It's cruel.

TOM: Yeah, I don't fish.

KAYLENE: It's cruel. Let's take that theory that as large as you can go, you can go that small.

TOM: (*Thinking about it.*) As large as you can go . . .

KAYLENE: You can go that small. We could be anywhere on the scale. Assume for a second we are not "earth." I mean, we are, but in the "grand plan," let's say, we're on the head of a pin—the whole world. No, this whole universe, we could go through the eye of a needle. Being so microscopic we've escaped annihilation from the outside, from outside forces, like other life, because the odds have been with us. We're too small. But at any instant some big shoe could come smashing down on the entire planet, on all of us. It would just be some guy walking to work. Get it? Some very large man.

TOM: What does this have to do with why you don't fish?

KAYLENE: So assume we're a little bigger, Tom, now don't be thick . . . (*She smiles and nudges him.*) We're not quite as teensy-tiny as I just said, we're a little further along the scale?

We're sitting around . . . all of a sudden a giant fish hook
comes down out of some gargantuan vastness and . . . (*Finger
in her mouth, acts it out.*) Ugh———! (*Then.*) It could happen to us like it happens to fish everyday. There they are
swimming along in their own world, literally, and bam!

TOM: I got news for you, Kaylene, it does happen to us.

KAYLENE: No, Tom, I mean metaphysically. (*Then.*) I'll take
that cigarette now. (*Then.*) Fishing, no, fishing is a loser.

TOM: (*He lights one, then hands it to her.*) Uh . . . I don't
know what you're doing here.

KAYLENE: I wanted to stay. Was it all right? (TOM *shrugs; she
smokes, moving around the room, righting the lamp.*) Your
daddy's a real charmer, I guess you know. We were picking
out my car and he goes on and on about you. Said you were
getting home, uh—

TOM: Last night.

KAYLENE: Or something like that. Then Daddy was coming
out here today. I thought to myself, who knows?

TOM: Who knows what?

KAYLENE: Who knows? (*Then.*) You had a girlfriend when you
were out here last year, where's she these days?

TOM: I couldn't tell you.

KAYLENE: Well who was it?

TOM: Casey Nichols.

KAYLENE: Oh, her . . . ! She got married. Married an asshole,
but nevertheless.

TOM: That makes me feel better.

KAYLENE: I knew your good friend. I mean just marginally.
(TOM *looks at her, no change.*) We used to say hey in the
halls back in high school.

TOM: He had a crush on you.

KAYLENE: No . . . ! Yeah?

TOM: I think so, yeah, maybe.

KAYLENE: I went to see his family. I said, I never really knew
your son but we went to high school together, and I just
wanted to . . . (*Then.*) Tom, I don't know how anybody stands
it. If one of my sisters was to die, I'd die too. I just would.

TOM: The thing is, Kaylene, you wouldn't. You can't.

KAYLENE: (*She crosses to him.*) Now. What do you say we go into The Texas Steer and have a peanut butter milkshake?

TOM: That makes me sick to think about.

KAYLENE: So bring your bottle, I'll buy you a Coke. Or, hey, Tom, you know what's fun at night?

TOM: I guess we've established it's not fishing.

KAYLENE: A swim. And I make a very mean hamburger on the barbecue.

TOM: (*Walking away from her.*) We'd have to go down to Harry's Market, I don't wanna do that.

KAYLENE: No, no, at *my* house. I wouldn't cook in this dive, I'm talking about at home. (TOM *goes to chest of drawers, his back to* KAYLENE, *pulls top drawer out, slides it in and out.*)

TOM: What, at Neal's place?

KAYLENE: It's my house, too. We take a dip in the pool, we slap on some hamburgers.

TOM: You guys got a pool?

KAYLENE: I know, it's disgusting, we got everything, I'm sorry. What do you say? (*Pause.*)

TOM: (*Slams drawer shut, turns on her.*) How come you're here?

KAYLENE: I thought I told you. Neal was coming fishing and—

TOM: No, shit, no: I mean this year. I stayed out there awhile last year, ya know, you never came around.

KAYLENE: I did know you were out here last year, but the time Dad mentioned it he said there were a couple of girls out here with you'all.

TOM: So what if there was?

KAYLENE: Was it "Casey"?

TOM: Hey. Yeah. It wasn't *you*. Where were *you*?

KAYLENE: I was going to bust in?

TOM: It wouldn't have hurt to have somebody bust in back then, even *some* people. You knew we were out here and leaving and you didn't even come out? That's beautiful, I love that.

KAYLENE: Tom . . .

TOM: What attention we got was appreciated, that's all.

KAYLENE: Tom, I told you!

TOM: So your old man saw Casey out here a night or two, so what? Maybe she just stopped by, brought a basket of fruit. You could have called, you could have come out.

KAYLENE: (*Quietly.*) I'm sorry.

TOM: Yeah, you oughta be. You should have risked it. Young people take chances, don't they? That's why there's so many young people over where I was, Kaylene.

KAYLENE: I don't understand . . .

TOM: Young people take chances. But you wouldn't even risk coming out here last year and saying hello cause you thought there might be another girl here, that's disappointing.

KAYLENE: My fault.

TOM: Tell me to fuck off, will ya? You don't owe me nothin'.

KAYLENE: No, don't on my account.

TOM: *Now* you want to know me, why is that?

KAYLENE: Oh, fuck off. (*Pause.*) I'll sit down if you will. (*She sits.* TOM *sits at a distance.* KAYLENE, *holding up two fingers for a cigarette.*) Please?

TOM: (*Setting the pack and matches down between them.*) Anybody ever call you "Kay"?

KAYLENE: It happens.

TOM: Seems like, be simpler. (*Then.*) I'm not a hero. I was a Saigon Warrior, that's how lucky I got. Some went North, I got Saigon because I could type. I didn't have to fight the war, hell, I didn't even have to fight the heat. I had it made. I had it made in the shade. Then I come back and everybody says "oooh, wow!" Well, shit.

KAYLENE: You feel guilty because you didn't die?

TOM: Hey, what are you—stupid?

KAYLENE: No, I'm not stupid.

TOM: Well that was a stupid thing to say.

KAYLENE: You were over there. I imagine you woulda gone the extra bit, like, to combat or whatever it was, long as you were there anyway.

TOM: Thanks, you're trying to make me a movie star.

KAYLENE: I don't think you're a movie star or a glory hog or any-thing else! And if you were or aren't, that's not why I'm here.

TOM: Did Neal make you come out here, Kay?

KAYLENE: I wouldn't be here if it was his idea, I'm at a re-bellious age. I'm here because I think you're cute.

TOM: Oh. Why didn't you just say that? After you say that, you can get away with anything.

KAYLENE: Tom . . . what are you going to do?

TOM: Uh-oh. You mean along the lines of with the rest of my life? I don't know . . . school, I guess. Did you go to college?

KAYLENE: I graduated early. I'm probably a genius.

TOM: I think I could do okay in school now, if I can get over this feeling everybody owes me something.

KAYLENE: *Owes* you something? You just got through saying you feel like a rat because you weren't actually in the combat.

TOM: Forget that. Forget I even said it. I take it all back, I'm Audie Murphy, baby. I *went*. That's all you need to know.

KAYLENE: You didn't get out of it where others got completely out of it, so—

TOM: So, yeah, you betcha! (*Then.*) Genius, I don't know, but you *are* bright, I like that, it's a plus for you.

KAYLENE: (*Playfully nods her approval. Then.*) Where do you go from here?

TOM: I thought we went to your house.

KAYLENE: I mean where do you have to report?

TOM: Savannah. First I'm going down to Miami to visit a friend of mine.

KAYLENE: Miami?

TOM: Come on, a guy like me, you gotta figure, I got friends all over the world.

KAYLENE: What if you spent your leave, I'm just making this up, around here somewhere?

TOM: Can't do it. I've got to go, I can't sit still yet.

KAYLENE: You don't have to explain, it was just an offer. We seem to be able to talk, that's all.

TOM: I hate talking.

KAYLENE: Fine.

TOM: I shoulda told you.

KAYLENE: Okay. Good-bye forever. (*But she just stands there.*)

TOM: See ya. (*Pause.*) I'll go cause that's a good friend down there, but I could come back.

KAYLENE: Don't put yourself out.

TOM: No real sweat, I could return, you never know. But if I were to come back early to see you, let's don't have any talking.

KAYLENE: I can't say a word?

TOM: Absolutely not.

KAYLENE: I guess I'll just have to think.

TOM: Think, yeah. We'll both . . . uh . . . I don't know, we'll both think. (*She hugs him.*) Get in my car, I'll be there in a minute. (*She kisses him, exits.* TOM *alone.*) Yeah, okay, Neal, way to come through. (*He picks up the whiskey bottle and follows* KAYLENE *Off.*)

Betrayal

Harold Pinter

Characters: Emma (36), Jerry (38)
Setting: England and Venice, Italy, 1968–77
Premiere: National Theatre, London, 1978
Publisher: Grove Press

Jerry and Emma have been having an affair for seven years. Both are married with families. Jerry is an old friend of Emma's husband, Robert. In fact, he was best man at Emma and Robert's wedding. In this scene, the two lovers break off their affair.

Note: The play starts in 1977 and moves backward in time. This scene takes place in a flat in the winter of 1975.

(*Silence.*)

JERRY: What do you want to do then?

(*Pause.*)

EMMA: I don't quite know what we're doing, any more, that's all.

JERRY: Mmnn.

(*Pause.*)

EMMA: I mean, this flat . . .

JERRY: Yes.

EMMA: Can you actually remember when we were last here?

JERRY: In the summer, was it?

EMMA: Well, was it?

JERRY: I know it seems—

EMMA: It was the beginning of September.

JERRY: Well, that's summer, isn't it?

EMMA: It was actually extremely cold. It was early autumn.

JERRY: It's pretty cold now.

EMMA: We were going to get another electric fire.

JERRY: Yes, I never got that.

EMMA: Not much point in getting it if we're never here.

JERRY: We're here now.

EMMA: Not really.

(*Silence.*)

JERRY: Well, things have changed. You've been so busy, your job, and everything.

EMMA: Well, I know. But I mean, I like it. I want to do it.

JERRY: No, it's great. It's marvelous for you. But you're not—

EMMA: If you're running a gallery you've got to run it, you've got to be there.

JERRY: But you're not free in the afternoons. Are you?

EMMA: No.

JERRY: So how can we meet?

EMMA: But look at the times you're out of the country. You're never here.

JERRY: But when I am here you're not free in the afternoons. So we can never meet.

EMMA: We can meet for lunch.

JERRY: We can meet for lunch but we can't come all the way out here for a quick lunch. I'm too old for that.

EMMA: I didn't suggest that.

(*Pause.*)

You see, in the past . . . we were inventive, we were determined, it was . . . it seemed impossible to meet . . . impossible . . . and yet we did. We met here, we took this flat and we met in this flat because we wanted to.

JERRY: It would not matter how much we wanted to if you're not free in the afternoons and I'm in America.

(*Silence.*)

Nights have always been out of the question and you know it. I have a family.

EMMA: I have a family too.

JERRY: I know that perfectly well. I might remind you that your husband is my oldest friend.

EMMA: What do you mean by that?

JERRY: I don't *mean* anything by it.

EMMA: But what are you trying to say by saying that?

JERRY: Jesus. I'm not *trying* to say anything. I've said precisely what I wanted to say.

EMMA: I see.

(*Pause.*)

The fact is that in the old days we used our imagination and we'd take a night and make an arrangement and go to a hotel.

JERRY: Yes. We did.

(*Pause.*)

But that was . . . in the main . . . before we got this flat.

EMMA: We haven't spent many nights . . . in this flat.

JERRY: No.

(*Pause.*)

Not many nights anywhere, really.

(*Silence.*)

EMMA: Can you afford . . . to keep it going, month after month?

JERRY: Oh . . .

EMMA: It's a waste. Nobody comes here. I just can't bear to think about it, actually. Just . . . empty. All day and night. Day after day and night after night. I mean the crockery and the curtains and the bedspread and everything. And the tablecloth I brought from Venice. (*Laughs.*) It's ridiculous.

(*Pause.*)

It's just . . . an empty home.

JERRY: It's not a home.

(*Pause.*)

I know—I know what you wanted . . . but it could never
. . . actually be a home. You have a home. I have a home.
With curtains, etcetera. And children. Two children in two
homes. There are no children here, so it's not the same kind
of home.

EMMA: It was never intended to be the same kind of home.
Was it?

(*Pause.*)

You didn't ever see it as a home, in any sense, did you?

JERRY: No, I saw it as a flat . . . you know.

EMMA: For fucking.

JERRY: No, for loving.

EMMA: Well, there's not much of that left, is there?

(*Silence.*)

JERRY: I don't think we don't love each other.

(*Pause.*)

EMMA: Ah well.

(*Pause.*)

What will you do about all the . . . furniture?

JERRY: What?

EMMA: The contents.

(*Silence.*)

JERRY: You know we can do something very simple, if we want
to do it.

EMMA: You mean sell it to Mrs. Banks for a small sum
and . . . and she can let it as a furnished flat?

JERRY: That's right. Wasn't the bed here?

EMMA: What?

JERRY: Wasn't it?

EMMA: We bought the bed. We bought everything. We bought
the bed together.

JERRY: Ah. Yes.

(EMMA *stands.*)

EMMA: You'll make all the arrangements, then? With Mrs.
Banks?

(*Pause.*)

I don't want anything. Nowhere I can put it, you see. I have a home, with tablecloths and all the rest of it.

JERRY: I'll go into it, with Mrs. Banks. There'll be a few quid, you know, so . . .

EMMA: No, I don't want any *cash*, thank you very much.

(*Silence. She puts coat on.*)

I'm going now.

(*He turns, looks at her.*)

Oh here's my key.

(*Takes out keyring, tries to take key from ring.*)

Oh Christ.

(*Struggles to take key from ring. Throws him the ring.*)

You take it off.

(*He catches it, looks at her.*)

Can you just do it please? I'm picking up Charlotte from school. I'm taking her shopping.

(*He takes key off.*)

Do you realize this is an afternoon? It's the gallery's afternoon off. That's why I'm here. We close every Thursday afternoon. Can I have my keyring?

(*He gives it to her.*)

Thanks. Listen. I think we've made absolutely the right decision.

(*She goes.*)

(*He stands.*)

Beyond Therapy

Christopher Durang

Characters: Bruce (30–34), Prudence (29–32)
Setting: New York City
Premiere: Phoenix Theatre, New York City, 1981
Publisher: Samuel French, Inc.

Bruce and Prudence are both in therapy. Bruce's therapist uses a stuffed Snoopy Dog to bark encouragement. Prudence and her therapist once had an affair, and he is constantly coming on to her. Prudence and Bruce meet through a personals ad. This scene takes place in a restaurant and opens the play.

(BRUCE *is seated, looking at his watch.* HE *is 30–34, fairly pleasant looking, probably wearing a blazer with an open shirt. Enter* PRUDENCE, *29–32, attractive, semi-dressed up in a dress or nice skirt and blouse. After hesitating a moment,* SHE *crosses to* BRUCE.)

PRUDENCE: Hello.

BRUCE: Hello.

PRUDENCE: (*Perhaps referring to a newspaper in her hand—* The New York Review of Books?) Are you the white male, 30 to 35, 6'2", blue eyes, who's into rock music, movies, jogging and quiet evenings at home?

BRUCE: Yes, I am. (*Stands.*)

PRUDENCE: Hi, I'm Prudence.

BRUCE: I'm Bruce.

PRUDENCE: Nice to meet you.

BRUCE: Won't you sit down?

PRUDENCE: Thank you. (*Sits.*) As I said in my letter, I've never answered one of these ads before.

BRUCE: Me neither. I mean, I haven't put one in before.

PRUDENCE: But this time I figured, why not?

BRUCE: Right. Me too. (*Pause.*) I hope I'm not too macho for you.

PRUDENCE: No. So far you seem wonderful.

BRUCE: You have lovely breasts. That's the first thing I notice in a woman.

PRUDENCE: Thank you.

BRUCE: You have beautiful contact lenses.

PRUDENCE: Thank you. I like the timbre of your voice. Soft but firm.

BRUCE: Thanks. I like *your* voice.

PRUDENCE: Thank you. I love the smell of Brut you're wearing.

BRUCE: Thank you. My male lover Bob gave it to me.

PRUDENCE: What?

BRUCE: You remind me of him in a certain light.

PRUDENCE: What?

BRUCE: I swing both ways actually. Do you?

PRUDENCE: (*Rattled, serious.*) I don't know. I always insist on the lights being out.

(*Pause.*)

BRUCE: I'm afraid I've upset you now.

PRUDENCE: No, it's nothing really. It's just that I hate gay people.

BRUCE: I'm not gay. I'm bisexual. There's a difference.

PRUDENCE: I don't really know any bisexuals.

BRUCE: Children are all innately bisexual, you know. If you took a child to Plato's Retreat, he'd be attracted to both sexes.

PRUDENCE: I should imagine he'd be terrified.

BRUCE: Well, he might be, of course. I've never taken a child to Plato's Retreat.

PRUDENCE: I don't think they let you.

BRUCE: I don't really know any children. (*Pause.*) You have wonderful eyes. They're so deep.

PRUDENCE: Thank you.

BRUCE: I feel like I want to take care of you.

PRUDENCE: (*Liking this tack better.*) I would like that. My favorite song is "Someone to Watch Over Me."

BRUCE: (*Sings softly.*) "There a somebody I'm longing duh duh . . ."

PRUDENCE: Yes. Thank you.

BRUCE: In some ways you're like a little girl. And in some ways you're like a woman.

PRUDENCE: How am I like a woman?

BRUCE: (*Searching, romantically.*) You . . . dress like a woman. You wear eye shadow like a woman.

PRUDENCE: You're like a man. You're tall, you have to shave. I feel you could protect me.

BRUCE: I'm deeply emotional, I like to cry.

PRUDENCE: Oh, I wouldn't like that.

BRUCE: But I *like* to cry.

PRUDENCE: I don't think men should cry unless something falls on them.

BRUCE: That's a kind of sexism. Men have been programmed not to show feeling.

PRUDENCE: Don't talk to me about sexism. You're the one who talked about my breasts the minute I sat down.

BRUCE: I feel like I'm going to cry now.

PRUDENCE: Why do you want to cry?

BRUCE: I feel you don't like me enough. I think you're making eyes at the waiter.

PRUDENCE: I haven't even seen the waiter.

   (BRUCE *cries.*)

PRUDENCE: (*Continued.*) *Please*, don't cry, please.

BRUCE: (*Stops crying after a bit.*) I feel better after that. You have a lovely mouth.

PRUDENCE: Thank you.

BRUCE: I can tell you're very sensitive. I want you to have my children.

PRUDENCE: Thank you.

BRUCE: Do you feel ready to make a commitment?

PRUDENCE: I feel I need to get to know you better.

BRUCE: I feel we agree on all the issues. I feel that you like rock music, movies, jogging, and quiet evenings at home. I think you hate shallowness. I bet you never read *People* magazine.

PRUDENCE: I do read it. I write for it.

BRUCE: I write for it too. Freelance actually. I send in letters. They printed one of them.

PRUDENCE: Oh, what was it about?

BRUCE: I wanted to see Gary Gilmore executed on television.

PRUDENCE: Oh, yes, I remember that one.

BRUCE: Did you identify with Jill Clayburgh in *An Unmarried Woman*?

PRUDENCE: Uh, yes, I did.

BRUCE: Me too! We agree on everything. I want to cry again.

PRUDENCE: I don't like men to cry. I want them to be strong.

BRUCE: You'd quite like Bob then.

PRUDENCE: Who?

BRUCE: You know.

PRUDENCE: Oh.

BRUCE: I feel I'm irritating you.

PRUDENCE: No. It's just that it's hard to get to know someone. And the waiter never comes, and I'd like to order.

BRUCE: Let's start all over again. Hello. My name is Bruce.

PRUDENCE: Hello.

BRUCE: Prudence. That's a lovely name.

PRUDENCE: Thank you.

BRUCE: That's a lovely dress.

PRUDENCE: Thank you. I like your necklace. It goes nicely with your chest hair.

BRUCE: Thank you. I like your nail polish.

PRUDENCE: I have it on my toes too.

BRUCE: Let me see.

(SHE *takes shoe off, puts foot on the table.*)

BRUCE: (*Continued.*) I think it's wonderful you feel free enough with me to put your feet on the table.

PRUDENCE: I didn't put my feet on the table. I put one foot. I was hoping it might get the waiter's attention.

BRUCE: We agree on everything. It's amazing. I'm going to cry again. (*Weeps.*)

PRUDENCE: *Please,* you're annoying me.

(HE *continues to cry.*)

PRUDENCE: (*Continued.*) What is the matter?

BRUCE: I feel you're too dependent. I feel you want me to put up the storm windows. I feel you should do that.

PRUDENCE: I didn't say anything about storm windows.

BRUCE: You're right. I'm wrong. We agree.

PRUDENCE: What kind of childhood did you have?

BRUCE: Nuns. I was taught by nuns. They really ruined me. I don't believe in God anymore. I believe in bran cereal. It helps prevent rectal cancer.

PRUDENCE: Yes, I like bran cereal.

BRUCE: I want to marry you. I feel ready in my life to make a long-term commitment. We'll live in Connecticut. We'll have two cars. Bob will live over the garage. Everything will be wonderful.

PRUDENCE: I don't feel ready to make a long-term commitment to you. I think you're insane. I'm going to go now. (*Stands.*)

BRUCE: Please don't go.

PRUDENCE: I don't think I should stay.

BRUCE: Don't go. They have a salad bar here.

PRUDENCE: Well, maybe for a little longer. (SHE *sits down again.*)

BRUCE: You're afraid of life, aren't you?

PRUDENCE: Well . . .

BRUCE: Your instinct is to run away. You're afraid of feeling, of emotion. That's wrong, Prudence, because then you have no passion. Did you see *Equus*? That doctor felt it was better to blind eight horses in a stable with a metal spike than to have no passion. (*Holds his fork.*) In my life I'm not going to be afraid to blind horses, Prudence.

PRUDENCE: You ought to become a veterinarian.

BRUCE: (*Very offended.*) You've missed the metaphor.

PRUDENCE: I haven't missed the metaphor. I made a joke.

BRUCE: You just totally missed the metaphor. I could never love someone who missed the metaphor.

PRUDENCE: Someone should have you committed.

BRUCE: I'm not the one afraid of commitment. You are.

PRUDENCE: Oh, dry up.

BRUCE: I was going to give you a fine dinner and then take you to see *The Tree of Wooden Clogs* and then home to my place for sexual intercourse, but now I think you should leave.

PRUDENCE: You're not rejecting me, buddy. I'm rejecting you. You're a real first-class idiot.

BRUCE: And you're a castrating, frigid-bitch!

(SHE *throws a glass of water in his face;* HE *throws water back in her face.* THEY *sit there for a moment, spent of anger, wet.*)

PRUDENCE: Absolutely nothing seems to get that waiter's attention, does it?

(BRUCE *shakes his head "no."* THEY *sit there, sadly.*)

(*Lights fade.*)

Danny and the Deep Blue Sea

John Patrick Shanley

Characters: Roberta (31), Danny (29)
Setting: The Bronx
Premiere: Circle in the Square, New York City, 1984
Publisher: Dramatists Play Service, Inc.

John Patrick Shanley describes his play as an Apache Dance, "a violent dance for two people, originated by the Parisian apaches. Parisian apaches are gangsters or ruffians."

Both characters are "violent and battered, inarticulate and yearning to speak, dangerous and vulnerable." Danny's hands are badly bruised and one of his cheeks is cut. He is dark, powerful, and finds it difficult to meet Roberta's gaze. Roberta is "physically depleted, with nervous, bright eyes." They meet in a bar and begin to talk. They are sitting at separate tables.

DANNY: You from here?

ROBERTA: Yeah.

DANNY: Where?

ROBERTA: Right up the block.

DANNY: What, you married?

ROBERTA: Divorced.

DANNY: Gotta kid?

ROBERTA: Yeah.

DANNY: Who's takin care of the kid?

ROBERTA: My mother. My mother always takes care of the kid.

DANNY: That's a good deal.

ROBERTA: Yeah. You gotta friend, you know, a girlfriend?

DANNY: No.

ROBERTA: No?

DANNY: We broke up.

ROBERTA: What was her name?

DANNY: Cecilia.

ROBERTA: Italian?

DANNY: Yeah.

ROBERTA: I'm Italian.

DANNY: She gave me a pain in my ass! She was very fine, but she'd make me go to her house. Sit around with her fuckin parents. And she'd talk in this totally fuckin phoney-ass way when her parents were around. Would you like a glass of soda, Danny? Oh, please be careful with your cigarette, Danny. Like she wasn't the same one I humped inna pay toilet! I'm sorry. I gotta bad mouth.

ROBERTA: Maybe she had to play phoney cause her parents were drivin her crazy?

DANNY: I don't think so.

ROBERTA: I hate my father. If I thought I wouldn't get in bad trouble I'd take a big knife and stab him in the face about fifty times.

DANNY: I hate my father, too.

ROBERTA: Yeah?

DANNY: He's dead, but I hate him anyway. He was a meat-packer. He used to get real mad all the time. One time he got so mad cause somebody did something, that he just fuckin died.

ROBERTA: I wish my father would die. He was the one who made me get married. This guy I knew got me pregnant. I was like eighteen. And my father made me get married to him. He wasn't a bad guy. We moved into this apartment. I was scared. But it was nice, too. I started, you know, to decorate. And then my parents started comin over all the time. This is how you put up curtains. This is how you wash the floor. My fuckin mother started cookin the fuckin meals!

And this guy, my husband, he was like, What the fuck is goin on? His parents were cool. Just like called once in a while on the phone. I felt so bad. Sick in the morning. Mother knockin on the door by twelve o'clock. My father comin in after work. And the guy, my husband, when he got there. It was like, Who the fuck are you?

DANNY: What's your name?

ROBERTA: Roberta.

DANNY: Mine's Danny.

ROBERTA: Sometimes I just start screaming, you know? For no reason at all. My mother thinks I'm crazy. Maybe you're right. Maybe I shoulda shot myself in the head when I turned thirty.

DANNY: You want some beer?

ROBERTA: Sure. (DANNY *brings over pitcher, pours some beer, and then goes back to his table.*)

ROBERTA: You waitin for somebody?

DANNY: No.

ROBERTA: Me neither.

DANNY: I don't know anybody anymore.

ROBERTA: I got a girlfriend. Shirley. She lives next door to me. Always has. Never got married. We used to have good times when we were kids. We both had long hair and we'd go bicycle riding. I have a picture home. We looked great. She's a pig now. She goes to these bars up in the two hundreds. They got live bands. Guys pick her up. She goes in cars with 'em. She'll get in any guy's car. We used to sniff glue in my bedroom and get fucked up. She uses a lotta dope now. I use some, but she uses a lot.

DANNY: I think I killed a guy last night.

ROBERTA: How?

DANNY: I beat him up.

ROBERTA: Well, that's not killing a guy.

DANNY: I don't know.

ROBERTA: What happened?

DANNY: I was at this party. A guy named Skull. Everybody was getting fucked up. Somebody said there was some guys outside. I went out. There were these two guys from another neighborhood out there. I asked 'em what they were doing there. They knew somebody. One of 'em was a big guy. Real drunk. He said they wanted to go, but something about twenty dollars. I told him to give me the twenty dollars, but he didn't have it. I started hitting him. But when I hit him, it never seemed to be hard, you know? I hit him a lot in the chest and face but it didn't seem to do nothing. I had him over a car hood. His friend wanted to take him away. I said okay. They started to go down the block. And they started to fight. So I ran after them. I hit on the little guy a minute, and then I started working on the big guy again. Everybody just watched. I hit him as hard as I could for about ten minutes. It never seemed like enough. Then I looked at his face . . . His teeth were all broken. He fell down. I stomped on his fuckin chest and I heard something break. I grabbed him under the arms and pushed him over a little fence. Into somebody's driveway. Somebody pointed to some guy and said he had the twenty dollars. I kicked him in the nuts. He went right off the ground. Then I left.

ROBERTA: You probably didn't kill him.

DANNY: I don't know.

ROBERTA: I seen a lotta people get beat up. They looked real bad, but they were all right.

DANNY: It don't matter.

ROBERTA: You ever been in jail?

DANNY: No.

ROBERTA: I wonder what it's like. Maybe it's crazy, but sometimes I think I'd like it.

DANNY: Why?

ROBERTA: I don't know. Just a change of scenery to keep me from going off my nut.

DANNY: I don't get it.

ROBERTA: What?

DANNY: You don't make me mad.

ROBERTA: So?

DANNY: Everybody makes me mad. That's why I don't ever

talk to nobody. That's why I'm sittin in this fuckin bar. I don't feel like walkin home. I feel like I'm gonna have to fight everybody in the whole fuckin Bronx to get home. And I'm too tired to fight everybody.

ROBERTA: You live with your mother?

DANNY: Yeah.

ROBERTA: Think she's worried?

DANNY: My mother's a fuckin dishrag. Dishrags don't worry.

ROBERTA: Is she stupid?

DANNY: I don't know.

ROBERTA: Well, what's she like?

DANNY: She works in a bakery. She gotta get up real early. When she comes home, she throws up.

ROBERTA: Why?

DANNY: From the sweetness. The smell of the sweetness is too much, and it makes her puke.

ROBERTA: My mother's nervous. There's something wrong with her thyroid.

DANNY: Why don't you rip her fuckin thyroid out?

ROBERTA: I don't know. (ROBERTA *comes over and joins* DAN-NY *at his table.*)

DANNY: What are you doin?

ROBERTA: I'm lonely.

DANNY: I think you're makin me mad.

ROBERTA: Cause I'm sittin here?

DANNY: Cause you want something, and I am definitely not up to fuckin nothin! You don't understand! I'm jumpin out of my fuckin skin! Everything hurts! I could bite your fuckin head! Leave me alone! Everything hurts! (*She grabs him by the shirt.*)

ROBERTA: You're crazy, you know that?

DANNY: Yeah, I know.

ROBERTA: You're lucky you don't stutter. You're lucky you don't bite your fuckin tongue! You're a lucky guy!

DANNY: What the fuck you sayin?

ROBERTA: Nothing you could understand, all right?

DANNY: You calling me stupid?

ROBERTA: I'm calling you crazy, Crazy! But what you don't know is I'm crazy, too! Yeah. You don't know me! I could do anything. I did something so awful. I ain't even gonna tell you what. If I told you, you wouldn't even look at me. (*She lets go of his shirt.*)

DANNY: There ain't nothing you coulda done would seem like anything to me. What'd you do?

ROBERTA: I'm not gonna tell you.

DANNY: Look, I think I killed a guy. What could be worse than that?

ROBERTA: Suckin off your father.

DANNY: What?

ROBERTA: A daughter suckin off her father. That'd be worse than killin somebody, wouldn't it?

DANNY: Did you do that?

ROBERTA: Answer me!

DANNY: I don't know. No. Did you do that?

ROBERTA: Yeah.

DANNY: I thought you hated the guy?

ROBERTA: Yeah, I always did. I always hated him and wanted to run away. But then, after, I hated him different. So I wanted to stick a butcher knife in his nose. Ja! Right in the middle of his nose. And then pull down slow till I got to his mouth.

DANNY: That wouldn't kill him. I don't think it would.

ROBERTA: It'd be good. People'd ask him why I did it, and he'd say, I don't know. But he'd know.

DANNY: I'm havin trouble breathin.

ROBERTA: Why? What's wrong?

DANNY: I start thinkin about it. Whenever I start thinkin about breathin, I can't breathe right.

ROBERTA: So forget it.

DANNY: A guy told me, if you think you're gonna have a heart attack, if you keep thinkin about it, even if your heart was all right to begin with, in the end, you'll have one. You can make your heart go bad.

ROBERTA: That's bullshit.

DANNY: It's true!

ROBERTA: How do you know?

DANNY: I can feel it happening! I don't wanna die like that. I don't wanna die from my own mind. I gotta think about something else. Davy Crockett. (*Sings.*) Davy! Davy Crockett . . . !

ROBERTA: He came into my room. He was drunk. It was real real dark. He was mad cause I'd gone out partyin and my mother was away and nobody'd been watching the kid. He was yellin at me and I was thinkin, He yells and I do nothin. So I started cryin and sayin I was sorry. He put his hand on my face. I put my hand out and I touched him. There. He got quiet. That's what did it. I made him get quiet. I could never make him do anything. That's why I did it. So I could make him do things. That was the only time. There was one other time after that when he wanted me to, but I wouldn't. And that was good, too. Right then.

DANNY: I was supposed to marry this girl Cecilia. I called her Sissy. She liked that, but she wouldn't let me call her that in front of her parents. I don't know what was with her and her parents.

ROBERTA: Did you hear what I told you about me and my father?

DANNY: Yeah, I heard.

ROBERTA: Would you be able to kiss a girl who'd done that?

DANNY: It don't mean nothin to me.

ROBERTA: Really?

DANNY: Sure really.

ROBERTA: Would you kiss me?

DANNY: What, you don't get kissed?

ROBERTA: Nobody knows but you.

DANNY: What'd you tell me for?

ROBERTA: I don't know.

DANNY: Well, I won't tell nobody.

ROBERTA: That don't help.

DANNY: What d'you want?

ROBERTA: How am I gonna get rid of this!

DANNY: What?

ROBERTA: What I done!

DANNY: I don't know.

ROBERTA: I can't stay like I am! I can't stay in this fuckin head anymore! If I don't get outta this fuckin head I'm gonna go crazy! I could eat glass! I could put my hand inna fire an watch the fuckin thing burn and I still wouldn't be outta this fuckin head! What am I gonna do? What? I can't close my eyes, man. I can't close my eyes and see the things I see. I'm still in that house! I wouldn't a believed it but I'm still in that house! He's there and I'm there. And my kid. Who's nuts already. It's like what could happen now? You know? What else could happen? But somethin's gotta. I feel like the day's gonna come when I could just put out my arm and fire and lightning will come outta my hand burn up everything for a thousand miles! It ain't right to feel as much as I feel.

DANNY: What you tellin me for?

ROBERTA: No reason, all right?

DANNY: You want something.

ROBERTA: So what. Don't you?

DANNY: No.

ROBERTA: Liar.

DANNY: Hey, you wanna smack? I don't lie!

ROBERTA: So what if you did, it ain't so terrible.

DANNY: I don't lie!

ROBERTA: All right.

DANNY: I'm tellin you the truth. I don't want nothin from you.

ROBERTA: I got a good deal in my house. I got somethin it's almost like my own apartment. When you get to the top of the stairs, there's a separate door to the room I sleep in. Don't have to deal with my parents at all if I go right in that room. I'd never deal with 'em if it weren't for the kid.

DANNY: I'm not goin anywhere with you.

ROBERTA: Who asked you to? So what are you goin to do?

DANNY: Stay here, drink my beer.

ROBERTA: All night?

DANNY: That's right.

ROBERTA: The place closes.

DANNY: So when it closes, I'll go someplace else!

ROBERTA: All the places close.

DANNY: I'll go someplace else!

ROBERTA: And get in a fight, right?

DANNY: Maybe. If people fuck with me!

ROBERTA: Ain't no maybe. You're gonna haveta fight. Because you were right. You're gonna haveta fight every motherfuckin body in the Bronx. And even it probably won't get you home.

DANNY: You don't know.

ROBERTA: I know.

DANNY: Get off my case, bitch!

ROBERTA: Come home with me.

DANNY: What for?

ROBERTA: Cause you're the one I told.

DANNY: That ain't no reason.

ROBERTA: Oh, yes it is! It is to me.

DANNY: No.

ROBERTA: Let me ask you something.

DANNY: I ain't tellin you shit.

ROBERTA: Tell me why your hands are all ripped up.

DANNY: I got in a fight!

ROBERTA: And that mark on your face.

DANNY: I got in a fight, I told ya!

ROBERTA: Yeah, you told me.

DANNY: That's right.

ROBERTA: And you think you killed somebody.

DANNY: That's right, too.

ROBERTA: Why?

DANNY: Shut up!

ROBERTA: I wanna know.

DANNY: What are you, a fuckin social worker! Shut up I said!

ROBERTA: Why don't you tell me before somethin happens and you can't tell me no more?

DANNY: You're tryin ta cross my fuckin line, man!

ROBERTA: That's right! I am. I've been sittin here starin at a spot on the wall for about a thousand years, and if I don't talk to somebody about somethin, somethin that means somethin, I'm gonna snap out! You understand? I'm gonna snap the fuck out!

DANNY: Don't you work no shit on my head or I'll kill ya, understand?

ROBERTA: I understand, okay? I just don't give a flyin fuck.

DANNY: You can do what you want out there, but don't you cross my line or you'll be dead!

ROBERTA: Then I'll be dead. That scares me about as much as Halloween.

DANNY: Don't push me.

ROBERTA: Why not? What else I got to do to pass the fuckin time!

DANNY: Don't, I'm tellin ya!

ROBERTA: I know, I know. You're a cold killer with a hair trigger and I better tiptoe outta your way before I get wasted. Pardon me if I don't faint.

DANNY: Please!

ROBERTA: You don't scare me, asshole. I see worse than you crawlin around in my sink. You're about as bad as a faggot in his Sunday dress! Your mama probably still gives you her tit when you get shook up! (*She starts slapping him.*) What's the matter, badass? Somebody get your matches wet? This is your time of the month? Huh? Huh? You don't remember how to pop your fuckin cork? Huh? Or do you get off on pigs rubbin their shoes on your ugly dick-lick face, you lowlife beefcake faggot! (*Snapping out, he roars and chokes her. She doesn't struggle.*)

DANNY: I told you! I told you!

ROBERTA: I . . . got . . .

DANNY: You can't push me!

ROBERTA: Harder.

DANNY: (*Lets her go in horror.*) Jesus!

ROBERTA: Why'd you stop?

DANNY: Don't talk to me.

ROBERTA: Who am I gonna talk to if I don't talk to you?

DANNY: (*Starts to cry.*) Leave me alone.

ROBERTA: No.

DANNY: Everybody leave me alone.

ROBERTA: Why you so quick with your hands?

DANNY: I don't know.

ROBERTA: You know.

DANNY: I'm too full.

ROBERTA: What?

DANNY: I'm too full . . . for anything . . . to move right. I can't . . . Watch out.

ROBERTA: Talk.

DANNY: Watch out. Listen. I can't stop myself if I hit you.

ROBERTA: That's all right. I don't care and I'm not scared.

DANNY: People can't talk to me anymore.

ROBERTA: I hear you.

DANNY: I can't work anymore. They don't want me on the truck.

ROBERTA: I hear you.

DANNY: It's like they don't listen to what they say to each other. If they was listenin, they'd have to start swingin. They'd have to.

ROBERTA: But you listen.

DANNY: I don't want to.

ROBERTA: But it ain't a question a want.

DANNY: No.

ROBERTA: It's how you are.

DANNY: They talk to each other. Nobody talks to me. I'm alone wherever I am.

ROBERTA: Me too.

DANNY: I start to think, I'm breathin, I'm breathin, and then that gets hard to do cause I'm thinkin about it, and I start to think about gettin a heart attack, and I feel pain, O NO, everything hurts! Everything hurts! Why does it keep on when I can't do anything. Somebody help me!

ROBERTA: I'll help you.

DANNY: Somebody help me.

ROBERTA: I'll help you, baby.

DANNY: Everything hurts all the time.

ROBERTA: I know, I know.

DANNY: The only thing that stops it is when I hit on somebody. Then I'm nobody and it's just the other guy I see. I can just jump on him and outta me. Make it go out, out!

ROBERTA: I'm gonna take you home, baby.

DANNY: I don't wanna.

ROBERTA: Yes, you do.

DANNY: What for?

ROBERTA: For love.

DANNY: Love?

ROBERTA: We're gonna love each other.

DANNY: I can't do that.

ROBERTA: We're gonna love each other. I hear the birds in the morning at my window. It always hurts me. We'll hear the birds in the morning.

DANNY: I gotta go home.

ROBERTA: You got no home.

DANNY: Yes, I do.

ROBERTA: You got no home. Just like me.

DANNY: I gotta go home.

ROBERTA: My poor sweetheart. He's gotta go home but he's got no home.

DANNY: No. You're right. I don't.

ROBERTA: Me neither. I got no home neither. But I'm gonna take you home, baby, and it's gonna be there.

DANNY: The guys I work with. The guys on the truck. They call me the Beast.

ROBERTA: No.

DANNY: They call me the Beast.

ROBERTA: Come on. Let's get outta here. Let's go home.

(*They exit, slowly and quietly. The lights go down.*)

A Different Moon

Ara Watson

Characters: Tyler Biars (mid-20s), Sarah Johnson (mid-30s)
Setting: Wraparound porch of the Biarses' house, Masefield,
 Arkansas, summer 1951
Premiere: WPA Theatre, New York City, 1983
Publisher: Dramatists Play Service, Inc.

Tyler Biars is home on leave from the army. In two weeks
he is going to head out to Korea. Dressed in fatigues, he is
"handsome, with an easy charm and an ever-ready, infectious
smile." Unexpectedly, Sarah Johnson shows up. She is from
Georgia and has been on the bus for the past four days. She
is tired and scared. Her brother and Tyler are army buddies.
She and Tyler barely know each other, but she is pregnant,
and he is the father.

Tyler is out when Sarah arrives. His sister calls him back
to the house, but instead of going to meet Sarah, he spends
four hours hiding out at the graveyard. This is the first time
they are alone.

———————

(TYLER *turns and walks downstage and lights a cigarette.*
 SARAH *slowly follows.*)
SARAH: It's a beautiful night.
TYLER: Sure is.
SARAH: Not too hot like at home. At home it's . . . it's . . . hot.
 I didn't know what else to do, Tyler. I was scared. (TYLER
 moves another step or two away—listening.) I don't want
 you to be mad—
TYLER: Sh-h-h. (*Gestures at her as he listens and looks out
 over the audience. Silence for a moment, then, in the dis-
 tance, the sound of a train whistle.*)
SARAH: Train.
TYLER: Sh-h-h.

SARAH: I rode on a train at night once. (TYLER *moves a step farther away from her. We hear two long calls, getting closer.*)

TYLER: (*Looking out.*) God, what a sound. Makes you want to just go. Not even care where. Just go. (*Realizes what he's said and glances at her.* SARAH *looks back at him.* TYLER *looks back out. Slight pause.*)

SARAH: (*Looking out.*) Look. There. You can see the smoke. Like little parachutes. Only going up instead of coming down. (*One long whistle.*) I didn't know what else to do after you ran off like that.

TYLER: I didn't "run off." I came home on furlough.

SARAH: But I didn't know when you were going.

TYLER: You should've. Same as your brother's.

SARAH: But I thought you'd come see me or . . . (*Two long whistles at their peak sound about a half mile away.*)

TYLER: My family was expecting me home.

SARAH: But I thought after we talked—after I told you—

TYLER: Sarah. (*Slight pause.*) You only said you might be.

SARAH: No. I told you I was sure.

TYLER: You hadn't even been to a doctor. How could you be sure?

SARAH: Well, I am. I've been to a doctor now and I am. (*Three long receding whistles. They both look after the train.*)

TYLER: You shouldn't have come here without letting me know first. You shouldn't've done that. You've got my mother all upset . . .

SARAH: I didn't tell her anything.

TYLER: Your being here, your presence told her, Sarah. You can't stay here.

SARAH: Where am I going to go?

TYLER: Home.

SARAH: I can't . . . (*Begins to cry.*) I can't go home. I . . . don't have . . . any money . . . (*And she covers her face with her hands.*)

TYLER: Don't cry. Crying isn't going to . . . (*Slightly irritated.*) Just don't.

SARAH: (*Wiping her face, but the tears still come for a moment longer.*) I don't mean to. I don't want to. I've cried so much these last few weeks . . . I mostly feel dry inside. Then it just starts . . . and I can't stop it.

TYLER: Your folks, they know?

SARAH: But they're not mad at you. They're mostly just mad at me.

TYLER: Jeez . . . I thought you said you'd been married before.

SARAH: I was.

TYLER: Well . . . you should've known not to let something like this happen.

SARAH: I was only sixteen and it only lasted a few days 'til my daddy found me and—

TYLER: Well, you're not sixteen now. You're thirty—(*Can't remember.*)—thirty some-odd . . .

SARAH: Thirty-four.

TYLER: Thirty-four? That's even too old to have a . . . that's too old.

SARAH: My mother had me when she was thirty-six.

TYLER: And look at her now.

SARAH: There's nothing wrong with my mother.

TYLER: That isn't even the point, Sarah. That's not the point.

SARAH: What is?

TYLER: The point is that you . . . *you* . . . (*At a loss for a brief moment—then.*) It . . . it might be . . . dangerous for you. (SARAH *looks at him.*) It might be.

SARAH: It's too late now.

TYLER: Maybe it isn't.

SARAH: (*Realizing.*) Oh, no, Tyler. No. I could never . . . Not ever. Never.

TYLER: All right. (TYLER *turns from her and goes back to the porch and sits. After a short moment, he sings.*)
"If I had the wings on an angel,
Over these prison walls I would fly.
Right in to the arms of my loved one
And there would I willingly die."
(TYLER *stops singing and lights a cigarette.*)

SARAH: (*Moving slowly, shyly toward him.*) I . . . I didn't know you could sing. You've got a real nice voice.

TYLER: Yeah.

SARAH: I mean it. You really do.

TYLER: I mean it, too. I really know I do.

SARAH: (*Smiles.*) Oh, you do?

TYLER: (*Smiles also.*) Yeah, I do. (SARAH *sits on the porch—some distance from him.*)

SARAH: Maybe that's what you should be.

TYLER: A singer?

SARAH: Yes.

TYLER: I am a singer. Didn't you hear me just now?

SARAH: No-o-o, a real one.

TYLER: Didn't that sound real?

SARAH: You know what I mean.

TYLER: Well . . . maybe I will be. Maybe I'll go to Hollywood and be a big singing movie star. (*He sings a few words of "I Dream of Jeannie."*)

SARAH: She doesn't like me being here, does she?

TYLER: I don't know.

SARAH: Who's Vicky?

TYLER: Vicky?

SARAH: Jean said Vicky'd sit with you in church tomorrow.

TYLER: Friend of hers.

SARAH: Not of yours?

TYLER: (*Defiant.*) Yeah. Mine, too.

SARAH: (*Looking down.*) Oh.

TYLER: (*Relents.*) No. Not of mine.

SARAH: (*Smiles.*) I like your mother.

TYLER: She's a real special lady.

SARAH: Did you grow up here in this house?

TYLER: No.

SARAH: I thought you did. Where did you?

TYLER: In a house on the other side of town mostly. Then we traveled around. Lived in Chicago. All over.

SARAH: Why? (TYLER *answers with a shrug.*) Why'd you come back here?

TYLER: My dad died.

SARAH: We lived out on that farm since I was ten. The only

other place I lived since then was when I got married that time but I never got too far away . . . This is the fartherest I've ever been. You like moving around?

TYLER: Yeah.

SARAH: Me, too. I mean, I think I'd like doing that, too.

TYLER: (*Stands.*) My uncle owns this house. He lets them live here for free. Don't tell her I told you that. Pride. She liked living here . . . in this house . . . in this town . . . It's where she grew up—her whole family, her mother, her father, her whole history is here. It's her home. She never liked moving around I don't think. Women just don't.

SARAH: Are you going to stay in the army?

TYLER: Probably. I probably will. I don't know.

SARAH: I think the army's a good career opportunity.

TYLER: Whatever happened to . . . to that guy you used to see? The one your mother was always talking about?

SARAH: She was just trying to—

TYLER: What was his name?

SARAH: George.

TYLER: George.

SARAH: I quit seeing him after I met you.

TYLER: You shouldn't've done that. I told you not to. I think—

SARAH: Tyler, I know what I didn't tell you. Daddy's bird-dog—Rosie?—had her pups.

TYLER: (*Disinterested.*) Good.

SARAH: You could have one.

TYLER: Sarah, what am I going to do with a birddog in Korea?

SARAH: (*Gets up and moves conquettishly, awkwardly toward him.*) Maybe . . . it they'd let you take it . . . maybe it could . . . keep you warm at night. I go out . . . to where they are in the barn sometimes and . . . and let them crawl over my legs . . . They're real warm and their bodies are real soft . . .

TYLER: Don't do that.

SARAH: What? I'm . . . not doing anything.

TYLER: Stop acting like that.

SARAH: I was only . . . I only want to talk to you, Tyler. That's all. It's hard to talk when . . . (*She looks over her shoulder at the door.*) Maybe . . . (*Looks at him.*) Maybe we could . . . go for a walk . . . Would you like to?

TYLER: Sarah . . .

SARAH: (*Moves slightly closer.*) I . . . wouldn't mind. I'd like to.

TYLER: No.

SARAH: It can't hurt anything now. It can't.

TYLER: No.

SARAH: I miss you, Tyler. (SARAH *is standing very close to him. They look at each other a long moment, then he roughly takes her in his arms and roughly kisses her two or three times. Finally, he pushes her away from him. She stands there a brief bewildered moment, then takes him by the hand and starts to try to pull him upstage left. He lets her hold his hand a brief moment, then pulls forcefully away and walks downstage leaving her crushed. She turns upstage.*)

TYLER: (*Angry.*) How do I even know it's mine? How do I know it isn't this George's?

SARAH: (*Turning.*) You know. You know.

TYLER: No, I don't. (*Accusingly.*) I'd only met you once. Once. And you'd been seeing that guy for . . . for years.

SARAH: I . . . never . . . (*Starts to cry.*)

TYLER: Stop it. Stop it right now.

SARAH: It's you. It's yours. I swear.

TYLER: You're trying to hang it on me because you think I'm your way out. Well, I'm not.

SARAH: I'm not trying to . . . I like you, Tyler. That's why. Nobody else has ever touched me . . . (*Quiet little voice.*) It *is* yours. It is . . . (*Her legs simply will no longer hold her up and she sinks to her knees.*) Oh, my lord . . . My lord, what am I going to do? Somebody . . . oh, please—please, oh, please help me . . . Help me . . . (TYLER *has watched this and only now relents and goes to her.*)

TYLER: Hey . . . Sarah . . . Come on, now . . . (*He tries to help her up.*) Sarah. (*Her legs are unsteady and he picks her up and carries her to the porch where he sets her down. She*

*immediately pulls her knees into her body, encircling them
with her arms. She buries her head in her arms.* TYLER
watches her, lights a cigarette and sits down beside her.)
Hello? Hey, in there. How can I talk to you if I can't see
you? (*He puts his hand on her arm.*)

SARAH: (*Lifting her head slightly.*) How can you say that to
me?

TYLER: (*Gently teasing.*) 'Cause you've got your head buried.

SARAH: About it's not being yours? How could you? (*Buries
her head again.*)

TYLER: (*After a brief pause.*) I shouldn't have . . . I was out
of line. O.k.? I'm sorry. (*He lifts her chin up.*) I am.

SARAH: My daddy called me a . . . a—

TYLER: He had no business calling you anything. I know you're
not. You're a very nice, very sweet girl.

SARAH: Am I?

TYLER: Yes.

SARAH: What are we going to do, Tyler?

TYLER: (*A deep sigh—he moves away.*) What do you want to
do?

SARAH: I don't know. I guess . . . you know . . .

TYLER: I'm leaving here in two weeks. I'll be gone a
year . . . almost a year. I couldn't be any help to you . . .

SARAH: Lots of husbands go off.

TYLER: You don't want to marry someone like me. I'm not
anywhere near being ready to settle down. Not near. I'm too
young for you. I'm not—

SARAH: I'm thinking about the baby.

TYLER: (*Sitting next to her.*) I'm thinking about that, too. What
kind of a father would I make? Just think about that—

SARAH: You'd be better than no father. I . . . I know you don't
love me. I know you don't, even though you said it that time.

TYLER: Oh, Sarah . . . (*Up and away.*) . . . don't make it sound
like I said it just to . . . I do . . . love you . . . but not . . . not
the kind of love you get married on.

SARAH: You could go wherever you wanted to. I wouldn't
mind if we moved around. I'd take real good care of you.

People don't have to love each other to be married, Tyler.
If we loved our little baby . . .

TYLER: I don't know . . . God . . . A baby . . . (*Stares hard
at her.*) It is mine?

SARAH: Yes.

TYLER: Mine.

SARAH: I had a dream about it. It was all wrapped up in a
blue blanket.

TYLER: (*Smiles.*) Yeah? (*With some pride.*) I always wanted
a . . . (*Stops himself.*) You know, you grow up and you want
to have kids . . . I don't know. I don't know what to say or
how I feel. I don't know how I feel, Sarah. My mind just
keeps skipping around. It doesn't seem to want to stop on
any one thing long enough to make any sense of it. Time. I
just need some time. We'll work it out.

SARAH: We will?

TYLER: Yes. We'll work it out.

SARAH: (*Looks at him a moment.*) Do you think you could . . .

TYLER: What?

SARAH: Nothing.

TYLER: Tell me.

SARAH: (*Shyly.*) Could you maybe put your arms around me
and . . . and say that to me? You don't have to . . . do anything else. Could you?

TYLER: (*Gently pulling her to him.*) We'll work it all out, Sarah.
(*Holds her a moment longer, then pushes her gently back
and smiles at her.*) So wipe that worried look off your face.

SARAH: (*Smiles.*) When?

TYLER: I thought that's all you wanted me to say. Look, you've
had all this time to think this through and I need to do that,
too. And we need to talk some more—

SARAH: I could talk all night.

TYLER: Not to me you couldn't. I'm beat. Besides, aren't you
supposed to be getting a lot of rest and stuff? You are, aren't
you? (SARAH *smiles and nods.*) Well, let's get to it, then.

SARAH: But I want—

TYLER: Nope. Tomorrow. Tomorrow we'll get up and have a
nice big breakfast and—

SARAH: I can only eat crackers in the morning.

TYLER: Well, maybe in the afternoon we'll go on a picnic. You can eat in the afternoon o.k.?

SARAH: (*Nods.*) All of us?

TYLER: Whatever. (SARAH *smiles lovingly at him.*) Just don't . . . push anything, Sarah. It'll be all right. I promise. Now, go on. (SARAH *walks to the door, opens it and turns.*)

SARAH: I don't feel scared now, Tyler.

TYLER: Good.

SARAH: Goodnight.

TYLER: See you tomorrow.

> (SARAH *exits.* TYLER *watches her go, then reaches in his pocket and pulls out his cigarettes. He finds the package empty and wads it up as he walks slowly downstage. He plays with the wadded-up pack by batting it around almost unconsciously. He stops, looks up at the moon and the sky as the lights fade down and night sounds increase. The lights go out.*)

Domino Courts

William Hauptman

Characters: Roy (30s), Ronnie (30s)
Setting: A tourist cabin in the Oklahoma Dust Bowl, 1939
Premiere: American Place Theatre, New York City, 1975
Publisher: Samuel French, Inc.

Floyd and Roy were Oklahoma bank robbers who called themselves "the Hot Grease Boys" and pulled their holdups disguised as Clark Gable and Fred Astaire. Four years before the play opens, Floyd retired and Roy moved north to open a nightclub. On the day the play takes place, the handsome, taut Roy comes back home for the first time—along with his mousy wife, Flo. He introduces himself to Floyd's wife, Ronnie ("Floyd wrote me lots about you. I don't know how he got such a good-looking woman"). Then Floyd and Flo go out for a swim, and the two are left facing each other.

———————————

ROY: How low you sunk. I don't believe it. Does he know?

RONNIE: No.

ROY: Four years . . . I wouldn't have thought he was your type.

RONNIE: (*Smoothing tablecloth nervously.*) He's not the man he was.

ROY: So I noticed.

RONNIE: He's got some kind of problem. I think he drinks.

ROY: He didn't drink before.

RONNIE: Well, something's wrong with him.

ROY: That's obvious.

RONNIE: Maybe you could help him out. I'd think so much of you, if you could light a fire under him.

ROY: (*Draws back suddenly.*) Please! Don't say that.

RONNIE: Why not?

ROY: Just don't. (*Smugly.*) You should have come with me. You wanted me, but you were afraid of me. So I guess you settled for Floyd out of disappointment.

RONNIE: I never wanted you.

ROY: What do you do now?

RONNIE: Play dominos.

ROY: What a waste. (*As he speaks,* RONNIE *picks up the plates and puts them in the kitchen. Then she crosses to the vanity, picks up a flit gun and walks around the room slowly, spraying.*) I remember the first time I saw you. I walked in the Comanche Cafe and there you were, looking great in your white uniform. It was thin as paper so I could almost see through it and you had a pencil stuck behind your ear. And you said, "May I take your order?" (*Grabbing her down left.*) You don't fool me. You're Floyd's wife now, but you'd still like to take orders from me, wouldn't you?

RONNIE: Do you really have a nightclub?

ROY: Hell, yes. (*He lets her go, walks upstage center.*) You should see it. A real night spot.

RONNIE: It sounds magic. I wish I could. Before, when I knew you, I always thought something magic was going to happen to me. I had premonitions, thought I could foretell the future. Sometimes I still think I can. I believed in ghosts.

ROY: Yeah.

RONNIE: I thought there was more to the world than just what you can see. I believed someday a ghost story would happen to me. But I never saw one. And I married Floyd, and now I play dominos. (*She walks around the room spraying again.*)

ROY: Did you have a premonition I was coming?

RONNIE: Yes.

ROY: You know why I left Oklahoma, doll?

RONNIE: You were running from the law.

ROY: They could never have caught me. No, I'd gotten too smart for this place. Didn't I tell you ghost stories were a lot of baloney? Nobody believes in ghosts—not if they're smart. And I was the brains of the Hot Grease Boys. (*She walks away, spraying.*) Come back here!

RONNIE: I'm nervous.

ROY: Stand still when I'm talking to you! (RONNIE *freezes.*) You've still got a good figure. Still dream of being in the movies? (*She smiles, drops Flit gun on bed. She removes her robe, straightens her shoulders so her breasts rise, and walks across the room stage right, almost in a trance, the robe flung over her shoulder. Then she catches herself and stops.*) Miss! (*She freezes.* ROY *sits at the cardtable like a customer. She approaches him like a waitress.*)

RONNIE: Could I take your order?

ROY: That's more like it. (*Leaning back in chair.*) I know a lot of things you don't. I'm smart. (*Pulling her down on his lap.*) You see those flies on the ceiling? How do you think they do it?

RONNIE: What?

ROY: Walk on the ceiling. Wouldn't you like to know how?

RONNIE: (*Uncomfortably; trying to get up.*) I shouldn't have left the windows open.

ROY: But wouldn't you like to know? Why do you think they can do it and we can't?

RONNIE: Because they're smart?

ROY: (*Grabbing her angrily now, trying to kiss her.*) Forget
Floyd. Come back up North with me—

RONNIE: What about your wife?

ROY: Forget Flo. Look at me—

RONNIE: No! (*She slaps him. He throws her roughly to the
floor.*)

ROY: (*Dramatically.*) Hell, you don't know what you're missing. I could show you sights you never dreamed of. Picture
it: you and me headed North, driving through the night.
There's a star hanging over the end of the road, and I point
the car at it. I'm driving faster and faster, the closer we get,
and I'm telling you things that make your mouth water. Just
us and the billboards going past in the dark, and the stars . . . I
could show you a star that's shining so hard it sweats . . . (ROY
has found the snaps on his suitcase. It springs open.)

RONNIE: What's that? (*He pulls out a black tuxedo.*)

ROY: That's my soup and fish—for the Panama Club.

RONNIE: You must look handsome in it. Let me see you wearing it.

ROY: (*Crossing to her.*) I might do it, doll—if you'll be nice
to me. (*Their faces are almost touching.*) You have on bright
red lipstick . . .

  (*They kiss.*)

---

the dreamer examines his pillow
John Patrick Shanley

Characters: Donna (20s), Dad (middle-aged)

Setting: Two New York apartments: Lower Broadway, Brooklyn Heights

Premiere: Double Image Theatre, New York City, 1986

Publisher: Dramatists Play Service, Inc.

A young man named Tommy sits in "a rough dirty white-washed concrete basement room" staring at his refrigerator. His ex-girlfriend Donna comes in and chews him out for trying to make her sixteen-year-old sister Mona. Over the course of a long, heated scene it becomes clear that Tommy and Donna can't stay away from each other. Finally, Donna leaves, vowing to go to the Heights and talk to her father. ("There's some questions I wanna ask him . . . I may want him to beat you up.")

———————————

(DONNA *is heard calling for her father through primal drums.*)

DONNA: DADDY. DADDY. DADDY. Daddy? Daddy? I've gotta talk to you. Daddy? (*The lights come up on Dad's Place. The drums cease. Dad's Place is at a physically higher level than Tommy's place.* DAD, *a powerful, handsome guy, is sitting in a chair. The only chair. He's wrapped in a huge, very soft, old red chamois robe. He's got a big drink in his hand and a bottle of liquor near his slippered foot. Hanging on a redwood wall behind him is a painting of a voluptuous nude woman. It's a good painting with a neo-expressionist feel.*)

DAD: (*To himself.*) Oh no no no no no no. It's my daughter come to make me a parent. (*To the offstage* DONNA.) I hear you. Come in. Come on. Come up. Jesus, I even recognize your voice. It's you. Your dead mother's little girl. Come on in and pull up a chair. Have a drink. How long's it been? Six months anyway. Not that I'm ribbin you to the purpose a bein more periodic. Nothin could be further from the truth. I'm thrilled I ain't seen you. I hate kids. Especially my own. At least other kids turn into adults. Eventually. If they live. But your own kids are always your kids. At least that's the common wisdom. And the other thing about your own kids, of course, is when they show up, you know, you know that they want something. And also, that they're probably angry. About something. Something you did and forgot fifteen years ago. But not them. Cause they're your kids. (*Enter* DONNA.)

DONNA: Hi, Dad.

DAD: Hi, Donna. Long time no daughter.

DONNA: Yeah, it's been a long time.

DAD: You look like shit.

DONNA: And you look like a big piece of red lint. So fucking what?

DAD: So. You're mad at me.

DONNA: Maybe I am. I don't really know. It ain't central, anyway. To what brings me up from lower Broadway. Where's all the paintings?

DAD: I sold some. Some are in storage.

DONNA: Getta lotta money for 'em?

DAD: Yeah.

DONNA: How much?

DAD: A lot.

DONNA: There were so many. Just the one now, huh?

DAD: Yeah, it's the last holdout. It's an old one, too. I did it what, maybe fifteen years ago. Funny the thing that pops outta the water when the ship goes down. I wouldn'a picked this one, but there we are. Here it is. Cheers.

DONNA: What ship went down?

DAD: Mine.

DONNA: I need to talk to you.

DAD: Oh no you don't.

DONNA: Yeah, I do too.

DAD: You're wrong.

DONNA: What's that on your finger?

DAD: A ring.

DONNA: Whose?

DAD: Mine.

DONNA: You never wore one.

DAD: It was your mother's. I stuck it on and I can't get it off. I may have to chop off this finger.

DONNA: Mona ain't here, is she?

DAD: No.

DONNA: Where is she?

DAD: I don't think she lives here anymore.

DONNA: Don't ya know for sure?

DAD: No.

DONNA: She's only sixteen, Dad.

DAD: So? When I was sixteen, I was eatin outta garbage cans in Philadelphia.

DONNA: That was you. You probably loved it. You get off on squalor. Mona's different. If she ate out of a garbage can, she'd die.

DAD: And a hellava way to go, too. Adios, mi Mona. Shit-canned at sweet sixteen.

DONNA: I'm glad to see you.

DAD: I can't think a why.

DONNA: Don't be a jerk. You're my father.

DAD: So?

DONNA: So? So don't be so freakin smug or I'll jam that drink up your nose.

DAD: You lay a finger on me, I'll break your back. You know I could and you know I would. So just forget the threats, all right?

DONNA: Is that the booze talkin?

DAD: Yeah, it's the booze. An several of my primitive ancestors that are jumpin around in my jungle brain.

DONNA: Well, just remember. Your ancestors are my ancestors.

DAD: Shh. Drums.

DONNA: Oh, you hear drums? It's probably high blood pressure.

DAD: The drums say, Fuck off.

DONNA: Why do you hate me?

DAD: I don't hate you.

DONNA: Why are you shutting me out?

DAD: Look, I ain't seen you in a very long time, Donna, which is great. It's put me inna great mood. But don't push it.

DONNA: I've got questions for you.

DAD: I don't answer questions.

DONNA: You'll damn well answer mine.

DAD: Or what?

DONNA: Or . . . I'll move back in. It could happen, Pops. The prodigal could return. Me an Mona could start up our old catfights.

DAD: ALL RIGHT. I grant you three questions.

DONNA: You grant me three? What is this, a friggin fairytale?

DAD: Call it whatever you want.

DONNA: I got more than three questions.

DAD: So take some away with you an work on em yourself. It ain't my job ta unravel every little thing for you.

DONNA: It ain't a matter a every little thing. There's hard stuff that I . . .

DAD: THREE QUESTIONS. THAT'S MY ONLY FUCKIN OFFER. TAKE IT OR LEAVE IT.

DONNA: All right. It'll take it. I agree. My first question is How do you see women?

DAD: You want an answer to this?

DONNA: I want your answer.

DAD: All right. I see all women bald. It started a long time ago. I found I was bein deceived by hair. I was all the time gettin the wrong impression a this woman or that woman cause their hair created a certain mystique. So I made a resolution one New Year's that whenever I looked atta potential woman, I'd shave her clean as a hardball, in my mind, and then I'd look at her and I'd see what I saw.

DONNA: Did it make a difference?

DAD: Shit yeah. In fact, the first woman that I shaved in this way was your mother. And the result was so . . . simple, that I got swept away and married her. The terrible thing was, on the honeymoon, in the morning, when I woke up, she had all this awful hair. What a shock that was. But, this is how we learn. Women who are not bald have hair. I still do though, see all women bald. I guess it's a weakness a mine now, a dream.

DONNA: I never saw paintings you did a bald women.

DAD: This is not what I did in my art, this is what I did in my life. I've never managed to be as dumb as an artist as I've been as a man. Close sometimes. Perilously close. But

I always managed to keep the bald woman out of the picture.

DONNA: Then why don't ya paint no more?

DAD: Oh, I dried up, I got the horrors, I drank myself out of it, I lost interest. I got obsessed with the fact a my own mortality, and every time I looked atta canvas all I saw was my own grave. And then there was the guilt and my nerves and I never got over the death of your mother. And the sight a you and Mona discouraged me, along with the heat an cold. And a tired feelin I got from time to time. And monsters from Jimjam Land. And illness. And fear of failure. And success. And heights. These are some a the reasons I don't paint anymore. Would you like me to go on?

DONNA: Shut up. I have two more questions.

DAD: You count funny, but okay. Would you like a drink?

DONNA: No.

DAD: You didn't learn ta say no from me. That's a good sign. Shows how much good my neglect a you is doin.

DONNA: Second question. What is sex for?

DAD: All right. Sex is for makin babies. I'll never forget when I figured that one out, I experienced fuckin vertigo. I was thirty years old. Before that I made like I knew, but I was really like one a those primitive tribesmen who thinks sex is a gift from the gods and babies come from bugbites. It's when your mother and my girlfriend got pregnant the same week . . . Somethin about all that news hittin me at once gave me the . . . Well, it was like the apple for Newton. What a moment that was. The zipper on my pants became like this major responsibility. I felt like I had the space shuttle in there. That's the first time sex went dead for me. When I found out what it was for. Has sex gone dead for you yet?

DONNA: No.

DAD: Don't worry, it will. It's a cycle thing. Somethin happens in your brain, or between you an somebody else, an it just goes dead. It's all shellfish. I got this deveined shrimp, and she's gotta shucked oyster.

DONNA: Don't tell me the story a your life an try ta make it pass for wisdom.

DAD: But there's a kicker, see? Cause after it's been dead for a while, an you're sure it's dead, deader than dead, it comes back. Yeah. Like a ghost but flesh an blood. Usually it comes about outta a moment a madness. You go nuts. You figure you can, your sex is dead, what'sit matter you wig out? Maybe you drink too much or you laugh too much. You do somethin ta stoke yourself up. And there's a woman there, usually the wrong woman, just some wrong woman, an suddenly you've got her. In the wrong place. The closet atta party, a bathroom, the storage room where you work at some shitty office job you don't care about an it's the Christmas party. It was dead. It was gone an buried in the cold cold ground, an suddenly you're high an your nailin some teenager like gangbusters against a buncha filing cabinets. Do you know what I'm talkin about? I'm talkin about sex, man. I don't know where it goes when it goes away, but it's a long ways off. But when it comes back, you don't remember what sex is for, you don't remember a goddamn thing except if you don't get it if you don't get to it, your eyeballs 'ill pop out, they'll pop right out the window, an you'll lose your mind. Then after maybe, you remember what it's for. When you're sittin like a bag a shit in some chair with rollers on it, an notice that your heart every once inna while is hittin your ribs like some youngblood boxer sparrin from the inside. An maybe you think, I coulda knocked her up. That coulda been a knockup I just did. But you just don't care. Cause you just found out that you ain't dead. You're just too glad, too glad too glad, to feel bad about anything. So when sex goes dead for you, and it will. That I promise you. Just remember. It comes back. It resurrects.

DONNA: Dad. Somethin's happened to me. It's made me have a lotta ideas. And I'm very upset. About it. And it's got to do with you.

DAD: How?

DONNA: Well, inna couple a ways. There's this guy. His name is Tommy. I'm in love with him.

DAD: So go kiss him or somethin.

DONNA: He's hurtin me. A lot.

DAD: So then go talk to him.

DONNA: I just did that. Listen. He . . . Well, he's been foolin with Mona, too.

DAD: He's seein you an Mona?

DONNA: Yeah.

DAD: My, my, my.

DONNA: He's all fucked up. He's stealin now. He looks like shit. But all that I can deal with. Even the Mona thing, I think. But this is the thing. In the whole way that this has come down, I thought I knew what I was doin. The me part of it. Till today. Another like level came into it. I always heard that girls went after guys who reminded em of their fathers. An I guess I kinda believed that idea or was spooked by it at least, so . . . I've always made double goddamn sure never to go near any guy I thought was like you, because then I'd like turn into my mother, right? A thought that makes me think a the phrase, Fate Worse Than Death. Anyways, I always steered clear of this certain kinda guy for that reason. Like this guy Tommy. I'm like absolutely sure he's totally different than you. And then today, I go to him, inta this pit where he's livin, and up on the wall is a painting a drawing he did.

DAD: This guy your seein?

DONNA: An Mona. A really lousy picture, self-portrait. But it scared me. I think more than anything that's ever happened ta me. I heard the fuckin "Twilight Zone" music. Cause here I am, goin along, thinkin things are one way, that I'm choosin an goin my own way, an maybe doin a terrible fuckin botch a that, but doin it. An then I see this picture. And I think, Do I really know what's goin on in my life? Or am I just a complete molecule or some shit. If this guy Tommy is turnin into you, then I'm in some kinda car I don't even know I'm in, and some guy inna scary mask is drivin, an he's had the route the map since the doctor smacked my ass. Where am I? I'm in love with this guy Tommy. He's drivin me crazy, yeah. He's tearin my heart out an steppin on it, yes. The whole thing I'm doin looks to be a total fuckup, but I can deal with that I can live with that. But what I wanna know gotta know is IS THIS MY LIFE OR WHAT? Is this my pain? My love? Or is what's goin on here just like history? You treated my mother like shit. You cheated on her. You lied to her. You humiliated her in public. When you had money, you wouldn't give her any. When she had money, you took it. You walked on her face with muddy shoes. When she was in the hospital, you didn't visit her. And then finally she just fuckin died. Now I hate your fuckin guts for that, but I decided a long time since that I wasn't gonna spend my whole life wishin you dead or different, cause I didn't want my life bossed by your life. I even thought, Maybe she deserved it. I knew I didn't know the whole story and never would an what was it my business anyway? But that was before. Today, I saw that picture on Tommy's wall, an it was writin on the wall to me, an the writin said, Watch Out. You could be in the middle of somebody else's life. So that' why I'm here. Because before I thought I didn't have to know about you to do my life, and now I see I better find out a few things. It's like medical history.

DAD: What bullshit.

DONNA: That's what you say when I pour out my heart to you?

DAD: I'm sorry. What you're afraid of just cracks me up, that's all.

DONNA: I don't understand.

DAD: All right, you want your father's smarts, I'll give you your father's smarts. What you have are women fears.

DONNA: Women fears.

DAD: That's right.

DONNA: I hate what I'm hearin.

DAD: Well, tough shit. You got women fears. That's what I know and I'm tellin you. When I talk to a woman, I feel like I'm yellin across the Indian Ocean. That's cause I'm a man. Do you wanna hear this or not?

DONNA: Yes.

DAD: Women are very concerned about bein trapped. All

women, or virtually, anyway. They worry about it, that's been my experience. So what they do, a lot of em, to feel strong, they trap a man. They trap some guy in their dream. And then they feel trapped cause they gotta guard what they caught. At least let me say, this is what happened with me an your mother. But there's a certain universal here.

DONNA: And men don't feel that?

DAD: What happens with men is a little different. I think that men recognize or make up that they are trapped, already, an what they do is, the man feeling is, they long to be free. Of mother, wife, job, art, whatever.

DONNA: Do you hear yourself? You sound like a total jerk. This stuff you're sayin can be knocked down by a three-year-old with a feather.

DAD: So what? I'm tryin to tell you somethin to get somewhere, somewhere maybe you'd like to get to. Don't think you can get everywhere by algebra, honey. Things ain't that straight. Life ain't at all like the psychological section in *The New York Times* three-warning-signs-to-look-for bullshit. Things ain't like that at all. If somebody's willin to talk to you an tell you shit they think is true, don't be so quick to knock it. People don't usually part with the weird shit they personally know because they know how easy it will be to punch holes in. Now I'm tellin you somethin. It's for you to poke through the soup an find the meat. So listen up. There's a level where you fear an want that's a woman level. This shit you just told me about bein afraid you're turning inta your mother, that's on the woman level, that's a women fear. So my suggestion about that is, you go talk to a woman about that. But there's another place under that place, where men an women can meet an talk, if you know what I mean. It's way down. An it's dark. An it's old as the motherfuckin stars. If you want something from me, or if you wanna tell me something, that's where we're gonna haveta be. (*A long pause.*)

DONNA: All right. (*A long pause.*) Tommy an me . . . When he loves me. In bed. When he puts his arms around me, and I can feel his skin, his heart beating, his breath, and I smell him, it's like Africa. It's like, I get scared because all of my guts shake . . . Sometimes I press my hands against myself because I think things are coming loose inside. He just touches me, starts to barely touch me, and I'm so frightened because it's so much, it's so hot, it's so close to losing my mind. It's beyond pleasure. It's . . . He takes me over. Like there's a storm, I get caught in this storm with electricity and rain and noise and I'm blind I'm blind. I'm seeing things, but just wild, wild shapes flying by like white flyin rain and black shapes. I feel I feel this this rising thing like a yell a flame. My hair I can feel my hair like slowly going up on its toes on my skull my skull. Everything goes up through me from my belly and legs and feet to my head and all these tears come out but it can't get out that way, so it goes down against my throat swells an through down to where it can get out GET OUT GET OUT. But it doesn't go out, so I, I EXPAND. Like to an ocean. To hold the size of it. An then it's maybe something you could speak of as pleasure, since then somehow I can hold it. I'm this ocean with a thousand moons and comets reflecting in me. And then I come back. Slowly. Slowly. From such a long way. And such a different size. And I'm wet. My body my hair. The bed is just soaked, torn up and soaked. There ain't a muscle left in me. I'm all eyes. My eyes are the size of like two black pools of water in the middle of an endless night. And Tommy's there. And he did it to me. He took me completely. I wasn't me anymore. I was just a blast a light out in the stars. What could be better than that? What could be better? It's like gettin to die, an get past death, to get to the universe, an then come back. In the world where we talk and fight and he fucks me over, it all just seems so unimportant after that. I don't understand how he can do that for me an then turn around an be such a, well, smaller. It is a small world this world, in comparison to where we go in bed. And I guess we gotta be smaller in it.

DAD: What are you tryin to tell me, Donna?

DONNA: I'm afraid.

DAD: Of what?

DONNA: I'm afraid to leave him or that he'll leave me. I'm

afraid to be without the sex we get to. Everything else seems like nothin next to it. But I can't give up who I am to be his love slave. That's what I'm afraid of. That I'll lose myself if I stay with him, and that I'll lose the sex if I get away.

DAD: I've felt that.

DONNA: You have?

DAD: Yeah.

DONNA: But that seems like a woman thing to me.

DAD: Nope. Men have that too. It's a very down thing. It's very near the bottom.

DONNA: In one way, he don't know a thing about me, not really. And in another way, what he knows is the key that lets me outta my life. It's like what he don't know about me is exactly what I don't care about anyway.

DAD: Yeah.

DONNA: You've really had this?

DAD: Oh yeah. I had this with your mother. It's why I always kept a girlfriend on the side. I hadda keep somethin away from her, so I didn't lose everything when we went nuts in bed. And too, because I wanted to protect what we had in bed by having something else goin that was not that intense. Sort've a comparison, a reminder. Somethin common to underline the extraordinary. Your mother was the love of my life.

DONNA: But if that's true, how the fuck could you treat her like you did?

DAD: That bed was what we had. When I got outta that bed, I didn't walk, I ran. When I got outta that bed the most important thing was that my feet hit the ground, found the fuckin ground. Do you understand? If there was gonna be anything else a me outside a that bed, it hadda be without her. Otherwise, she woulda taken me over all the way. I hadda create a second place in me and outta me where I could work. Do my painting. I got the studio. I got the girlfriend. WHY DO YOU REMIND ME OF THESE THINGS? It's so fuckin painful. Your mother's dead. My baby's dead.

DONNA: I can't believe this. You mean, you really loved her?

DAD: Shut up shut up. Can't you understand? All I have now is that little bit I kept from her. That little room. I can't even paint anymore. Why would I want to? What do I care what I see, why would I describe it? I hid part a me from her to save somethin cause I was scared. I'm so sorry. I'm so sorry. I shoulda given her that, too. If I'd given her everything, then when she died, I woulda died, too, and that woulda been the merciful end of it. Why did I save something? What for? It wasn't worth it. What I saved wasn't worth a goddamn thing. If I only known.

DONNA: I'm here.

DAD: I can't stand the sight a you. You remind me just enough ta make it unbearable. At least Mona don't look like her. You. Sometimes, the way you . . . Sometimes you could be her. But you're not. Sure I treated her like shit. I was so angry cause she had so much a me. I thought it was too much to let somebody have. And when she was dyin in the hospital, sure I didn't go an see her. I couldn't bear it. Don't you get it? I just couldn't bear to watch her leave me. You come here to tell me things you think I don't understand. So maybe you were right. Maybe you are turnin inta your mother. And maybe this guy Tommy is turnin inta me. I don't know. But the big news is you don't know who those people are. I promise you.

DONNA: You never told me.

DAD: It just woulda sounded like an apology for abuse.

DONNA: All my memories seem wrong now.

DAD: Good. Maybe now then you can remember a few things.

DONNA: Who am I?

DAD: Don't worry about it. I think you worry too much.

DONNA: I love this guy.

DAD: Come here, baby. I hate the sight a you, but let me hold you in my arms. (*He holds her.*)

DONNA: I don't see any future for me.

DAD: Good.

DONNA: It's not good.

DAD: You can't see the future anyway. It's a very realistic feelin you're havin.

DONNA: Can I move back home?

DAD: No.

DONNA: I want to.

DAD: You probably feel like suckin your thumb, too. But there's a time an place, an that time an place called home is gone now.

DONNA: What am I gonna do?

DAD: Well, that's a question. You could run away to the circus.

DONNA: This is the fuckin circus.

DAD: You wanna grapple an go inna single direction and stick with it, ride it out inna straight line right to heaven, the grave or whatever?

DONNA: Yes.

DAD: There's only one thing that goes straight, my baby, and it's not love. It is not love. You can chase that one forever, it won't come to you. It won't bow, it won't serve, it won't do what you want, what it should, it won't be how you thought, or was taught how it was meant ta be. You can't lead it cause it'll be draggin you wherever it wants. If you wanna go inna straight line, give up people. People are what zigzag. I'd rather predict the weather three months in advance, my sweet girl, then try to tell you one thing about the future of the dullest heart.

DONNA: I got one more question.

Edmond

David Mamet

Characters: Edmond (37), Glenna (28)
Setting: New York City
Premiere: Goodman Theatre, Chicago, 1982
Publisher: Samuel French, Inc.

An ordinary man named Edmond tells his wife, "I can't live this life," and leaves his home. In a series of brief scenes, he moves deeper and deeper into New York City's lowlife: bars, peep shows, whorehouses. Mugged by cardsharks, he pawns his wedding ring and buys a survival knife. Edmond is starting to lose his grip. He terrorizes a stranger on the subway. Then, when a black pimp tries to mug him, Edmond turns on him, beating him viciously. Right afterward, in a coffeehouse, he meets a waitress named Glenna. They go to her apartment.

(EDMUND *and* GLENNA *are lounging around semi-clothed.* EDMOND *shows* GLENNA *the survival knife.*)

EDMOND: You see this?

GLENNA: Yes.

EDMOND: That fucking nigger comes up to me, what am I fitted to do. He comes up, "Give me all your money." Thirty-seven years fits me to sweat and say he's underpaid, and he can't get a *job*, he's *bigger* than me . . . he's a killer, he don't care about his *life*, you understand, so he'd do anything. Eh? That's what I'm fitted to do. In a mess of intellectuality to wet my *pants* while this *coon* cuts my *dick* off . . . eh? Because I'm taught to *hate*. I want to tell you something. Something *spoke* to me, I got a *shock* (I don't know, I got mad . . .), I got a *shock,* and I spoke *back* to him, that motherfucker, I came out there with my *knife,* and stuck it in his *neck,* eh? "Up your ass, you coon . . . you want to fight, *I'll* fight you, I'll cut out your fuckin' *heart,* eh, *I* don't give a fuck."

GLENNA: Yes.

EDMOND: Eh? I'm saying, *I* don't give a fuck, *I* got some warlike blood in *my* veins, too, you fucking spade, you coon. "The *blood* ran down his neck."

GLENNA: (*Looking at knife.*) With that?

EDMOND: You bet your ass.

GLENNA: Did you kill him?

EDMOND: Did I kill him?

GLENNA: Yes.

EDMOND: I don't care.

GLENNA: That's wonderful.

EDMOND: And in that moment . . . when I *spoke*, you understand, 'cause that was more important than the *knife*, when I spoke back to him, I DIDN'T FUCKING WANT TO UNDERSTAND . . . let *him* understand *me* . . . I wanted to KILL him. (*Pause.*) In that *moment* thirty years of prejudice came out of me. (*Pause.*) Thirty *years*. Of all those um um um of all those cleaning ladies . . .

GLENNA: Uh-huh . . .

EDMOND: . . . uh? . . . who *might* have broke the lamp. SO WHAT? You understand? For the first *time*, I swear to god, for the first *time* I saw: THEY'RE PEOPLE, TOO.

GLENNA: (*Pause.*) Do you know who I hate?

EDMOND: Who is that?

GLENNA: Faggots.

EDMOND: Yes. I hate them, too. And you know why?

GLENNA: Why?

EDMOND: They suck cock. (*Pause.*) And that's the truest thing you'll ever hear.

GLENNA: I hate them cause they don't like women.

EDMOND: They *hate* women.

GLENNA: I know that they do.

EDMOND: It makes you feel good to *say* it? Doesn't it?

GLENNA: Yes.

EDMOND: Then *say* it. *Say* it. If it makes you feel whole. *Always* say it. *Always* for your*self* . . .

GLENNA: It's hard.

EDMOND: *Yes*.

GLENNA: Sometimes it's hard.

EDMOND: You're goddam right it's hard. And there's a *reason* why it's hard?

GLENNA: Why?

EDMOND: So that we will stand up. So that we'll be our*selves*. Glenna: (*Pause.*) . . . THERE IS NO *LAW* . . . there is no *history* . . . there is just *now* . . . and if there is a *God* he may love the weak, Glenna. (*Pause.*) But he respects the strong. (*Pause.*) And if you are a *man* you should be feared. (*Pause.*) You should be *feared* . . . (*Pause.*) You must know you command respect.

GLENNA: That's why I love the Theatre . . .

EDMOND: Yes.

GLENNA: Because what you must ask respect for is your-*self* . . .

EDMOND: What do you mean?

GLENNA: When you're on stage.

EDMOND: Yes.

GLENNA: For *your* feelings.

EDMOND: Absolutely. Absolutely, yes . . .

GLENNA: And, and *not* be someone else.

EDMOND: Why should you . . .

GLENNA: . . . that's why, and I'm so proud to *be* in this profession . . .

EDMOND: . . . I don't blame you . . .

GLENNA: . . . because your aspirations . . .

EDMOND: . . . and I'll bet that you're good at it . . .

GLENNA: . . . they . . .

EDMOND: . . . they have no bounds.

GLENNA: There's nothing . . .

EDMOND: . . . Yes. I understand . . .

GLENNA: To *bound* you but your soul.

EDMOND: (*Pause.*) Do something for me.

GLENNA: . . . uh . . .

EDMOND: *Act* something for me. Would you act something for me . . . ?

GLENNA: *Now?*

EDMOND: Yes.

GLENNA: Sitting right here . . . ?

EDMOND: Yes. (*Pause.*)

GLENNA: Would you really like me to?

EDMOND: You know I would. You see me sitting here, and you know that I would. I'd *love* it. Just because we both *want* to. I'd *love* you to. (*Pause.*)

GLENNA: What would you like me to do?

EDMOND: Whatever you'd like. What plays have you done?

GLENNA: Well, we've only done scenes.

EDMOND: You've only done scenes.

GLENNA: I shouldn't say "only." They contain the kernel of the play.

EDMOND: Uh-huh. (*Pause.*) What *plays* have you done?

GLENNA: In college I played Juliet.

EDMOND: In Shakespeare?

GLENNA: Yes. In Shakespeare. What do you think?

EDMOND: Well, I meant, there's *plays* named Juliet.

GLENNA: There are?

EDMOND: Yes.

GLENNA: I don't think so.

EDMOND: Well, there are.—Don't. Don't. Don't. Don't be so *limited*. And don't assume I'm dumb because I wear a suit and tie.

GLENNA: I don't assume that.

EDMOND: Because what we've *done* tonight. Since you met me, it didn't make a difference then. Forget it. All I meant, you say you are an actress . . .

GLENNA: I am an actress.

EDMOND: Yes. I say that's what you *say*. So *I* say what *plays* have you done. That's all.

GLENNA: The work I've done I have done for my peers.

EDMOND: What does that mean?

GLENNA: In class.

EDMOND: In class.

GLENNA: In class or workshop.

EDMOND: Not, not for a paying group.

GLENNA: No. Absolutely not.

EDMOND: Then you are not an actress. Face it. Let's start right. The two of us. I'm not lying to *you*, don't lie to *me*. And don't lie to yourself. *Face* it. You're a beautiful woman. You have *worlds* before you. I do, too. *Things* to do. Things you can *discover*. What I'm saying, start *now*, start *tonight*. With *me*. *Be* with me. Be what you *are*.

GLENNA: I am what I am.

EDMOND: That's absolutely right. And that's what I loved when I saw you tonight. What I *loved*. I use that word. (*Pause.*) I used that word. I loved a *woman*. Standing there. A working woman. Who brought life to what she did. Who took a moment to *joke* with me. That's . . . that's . . . that's . . . God *bless* you what you are. Say it: I am a waitress. (*Pause.*) Say it.

GLENNA: What does it mean if I say something?

EDMOND: Say it with me. (*Pause.*)

GLENNA: What?

EDMOND: "I am a waitress."

GLENNA: I think that you better go.

EDMOND: If you want me to go I'll go. Say it with me. Say what you are. And I'll say what *I* am.

GLENNA: . . . what *you* are . . .

EDMOND: I've *made* that discovery. Now: I want you to change your life with me. Right now: for what*ever* that we can be. *I* don't know what this is, *you* don't know. Speak with me. Right now. Say it.

GLENNA: I don't know what you're talking about.

EDMOND: Oh, by the Lord, yes you do. Say it with me. (*She takes out a vial of pills.*) What are those?

GLENNA: Pills.

EDMOND: For what? Don't take them.

GLENNA: I have this tendency to get anxious.

EDMOND: (*He knocks them from her hand.*) Don't take them. Go *through* it. Go *through* with me.

GLENNA: You're scaring me.

EDMOND: I am not. I know when I'm scaring you. *Believe* me. (*Pause.*)

GLENNA: Get out. (*Pause.*)

EDMOND: Glenna. (*Pause.*)

GLENNA: Get out! GET OUT GET OUT! LEAVE ME THE FUCK ALONE!!! WHAT DID I DO, PLEDGE MY LIFE TO YOU? I LET YOU FUCK ME. GO AWAY.

EDMOND: Listen to me: you know what madness is?

GLENNA: I told you go away.

EDMOND: I'm lonely, too. I know what it is, too. Believe me. Do you know what madness is?

GLENNA: (*Goes to phone, dials.*) Susie . . . ?

EDMOND: It's self-indulgence.

GLENNA: Susie, can you come over here . . . ?

EDMOND: Will you please put that *down*? You know how *rare* this is . . . ? (*He knocks the phone out of her hands.* GLENNA *cowers.*)

GLENNA: Oh fuck . . .

EDMOND: Don't be ridiculous. I'm *talking* to you.

GLENNA: Don't hurt me. No. No. I can't deal with this.

EDMOND: Don't be ridic . . .

GLENNA: I . . . No. Help! Help.

EDMOND: . . . you're being . . .

GLENNA: . . . HELP!

EDMOND: . . . are you *insane*? What the fuck are you trying to *do,* for godsake?

GLENNA: Help!

EDMOND: You want to wake the *neighbors*?

GLENNA: WILL SOMEBODY HELP ME . . . ?

EDMOND: Shut up shut up!

GLENNA: Will somebody help you are the get *away* from me! You are the *devil*. I know who you are. I know what you want me to do. Get *away* from me. I curse *you,* you can't kill me, get away from me I'm good.

EDMOND: WILL YOU SHUT THE FUCK UP? You fucking *bitch*. You're *nuts* . . . (*He strikes her with the knife.*) Are you *insane*? Are you *insane* you fucking *idiot* . . . You stupid fucking *bitch* . . . You stupid fucking . . . *now* look what you've done. (*Pause.*) Now look what you've bloody fucking done.

Entertaining Mr. Sloane

Joe Orton

Characters: Sloane (young), Kath (41)
Setting: A room
Premiere: New Arts Theatre, London, 1964

Publisher: Grove Press (from *The Complete Plays of Joe Orton*)

Kath, a middle-aged landlady, is looking to let a room. One evening, an exceptionally well-built young man named Sloane shows up. Kath shows him the house. This scene opens the play.

———————————

(*A room. Evening.* KATH *enters, followed by* SLOANE.)

KATH: This is my lounge.

SLOANE: Would I be able to use this room? Is it included?

KATH: Oh, yes. (*Pause.*) You mustn't imagine it's always like this. You ought to have rung up or something. And then I'd've been prepared.

SLOANE: The bedroom was perfect.

KATH: I never showed you the toilet.

SLOANE: I'm sure it will be satisfactory.

(*He walks round the room examining the furniture. Stops by the window.*)

KATH: I should change them curtains. Those are our winter ones. The summer ones are more of a chintz. (*Laughs.*) The walls need re-doing. The Dadda has trouble with his eyes. I can't ask him to do any work involving ladders. It stands to reason.

(*Pause.*)

SLOANE: I can't give you a decision right away.

KATH: I don't want you to. (*Pause.*) What do you think? I'd be happy to have you.

(*Silence.*)

SLOANE: Are you married?

KATH: (*Pause.*) I was. I had a boy . . . killed in very sad circumstances. It broke my heart at the time. I got over it though. You do, don't you?

(*Pause.*)

SLOANE: A son?

KATH: Yes.

SLOANE: You don't look old enough.

(*Pause.*)

KATH: I don't let myself go like some of them you may have noticed. I'm just over . . . As a matter of fact I'm forty-one. (*Pause.*)

SLOANE: (*Briskly.*) I'll take the room.

KATH: Will you?

SLOANE: I'll bring my things over tonight. It'll be a change from my previous.

KATH: Was it bad?

SLOANE: Bad?

KATH: As bad as that?

SLOANE: You've no idea.

KATH: I don't suppose I have. I've led a sheltered life.

SLOANE: Have you been a widow long?

KATH: Yes, a long time. My husband was a mere boy. (*With a half-laugh.*) That sounds awful, doesn't it?

SLOANE: Not at all.

KATH: I married out of school. I surprised everyone by the suddenness of it. (*Pause.*) Does that sound as if I had to get married?

SLOANE: I'm broadminded.

KATH: I should've known better. You won't breathe a word?

SLOANE: You can trust me.

KATH: My brother would be upset if he knew I told you. (*Pause.*) Nobody knows around here. The people in the nursing home imagined I *was* somebody. I didn't disillusion them.

SLOANE: You were never married then?

KATH: No.

SLOANE: What about—I hope you don't think I'm prying?

KATH: I wouldn't for a minute. What about—?

SLOANE: . . . the father?

KATH: (*Pause.*) We always planned to marry. But there were difficulties. I was very young and he was even younger. I don't believe we would have been allowed.

SLOANE: What happened to the baby?

KATH: Adopted.

SLOANE: By whom?

KATH: That I could not say. My brother arranged it.

SLOANE: What about the kid's father?

KATH: He couldn't do anything.

SLOANE: Why not?

KATH: His family objected. They were very nice but he had a duty you see. (*Pause.*) As I say, if it'd been left to him I'd be his widow today. (*Pause.*) I had a last letter. I'll show you some time. (*Silence.*) D'you like flock or foam rubber in your pillow?

SLOANE: Foam rubber.

KATH: You need a bit of luxury, don't you? I bought the Dadda one but he can't stand them.

SLOANE: I can.

KATH: You'll live with us then as one of the family?

SLOANE: I never had no family of my own.

KATH: Didn't you?

SLOANE: No, I was brought up in an orphanage.

KATH: You have the air of lost wealth.

SLOANE: That's remarkable. My parents, I believe, *were* extremely wealthy people.

KATH: Did Dr. Barnardo give you a bad time?

SLOANE: No. It was the lack of privacy I found most trying. (*Pause.*) And the lack of real love.

KATH: Did you never know your mamma?

SLOANE: Yes.

KATH: When did they die?

SLOANE: I was eight. (*Pause.*) They passed away together.

KATH: How shocking.

SLOANE: I've an idea that they had a suicide pact. Couldn't prove it of course.

KATH: Of course not. (*Pause.*) With a nice lad like you to take care of you'd think they'd've postponed it. (*Pause.*) Criminals, were they?

SLOANE: From what I remember they were respected. You know, H.P. debts. Bridge. A little light gardening. The usual activities of a cultured community. (*Silence.*) I respect their memory.

KATH: Do you? How nice.

SLOANE: Every year I pay a visit to their grave. I take sandwiches. Make a day of it. (*Pause.*) The graveyard is situated in pleasant surroundings so it's no hardship. (*Pause.*) Tomb an' all.

KATH: Marble? (*Pause.*) Is there an inscription?

SLOANE: Perhaps you'd come with me this trip?

KATH: We'll see.

SLOANE: I go in the autumn. I clean the leaves off the monument. As a tribute.

KATH: Any relations?

SLOANE: None.

KATH: Poor boy. Alone in the world. Like me.

SLOANE: You're not alone.

KATH: I am. (*Pause.*) Almost alone. (*Pause.*) If I'd been allowed to keep my boy I'd not be. (*Pause.*) You're almost the same age as he would be. You've got the same refinement.

SLOANE: (*Slowly.*) I need . . . understanding.

KATH: You do don't you. Here let me take your coat.
  (*She helps him off with his coat.*)
You've got a delicate skin.
  (*She touches his neck. His cheek. He shudders a little. Pause. She kisses his cheek.*)
Just a motherly kiss. A real mother's kiss.
  (*Silence. She lifts his arms and folds them about her.*)
You'll find me very sentimental. I upset easy.
  (*His arms are holding her.*)
When I hear of . . . tragedies happening to perfect strangers. There are so many ruined lives.
  (*She puts her head on his shoulder.*)
You must treat me gently when I'm in one of my moods.
  (*Silence.*)

SLOANE: (*Clearing his throat.*) How much are you charging? I mean—I've got to know.
  (*He drops his arms. She moves away.*)

KATH: We'll come to some arrangement. A cup of tea?

SLOANE: Yes I don't mind.

KATH: I'll get you one.

SLOANE: Can I have a bath?
KATH: Now?
SLOANE: Later would do.
KATH: You must do as you think fit.

FOB

David Henry Hwang

Characters: Grace (20), Steve (20)
Setting: Back room of a small Chinese restaurant in Torrance, California
Premiere: Stanford Asian American Theatre Project, Stanford, California, 1979
Publisher: Bard/Avon (from *Broken Promises*)

The play opens as a Chinese-American preppie describes the contempt of the ABC (American-Born Chinese) for the FOB (Fresh Off the Boat): "Clumsy, ugly, greasy FOB."

Grace is a journalism student at UCLA. An assimilated Chinese-American, she works part-time in her family's Chinese restaurant. A Chinese-speaking customer enters, wishing to buy *chong you bing*. When Grace gives him the cold shoulder, he tells her that he is "Gwan Gung, god of warriors, writers, and prostitutes!" This is Steve, a UCLA friend of Grace's, and Fresh Off the Boat. They pretend they have never met.

(*The back room of a small Chinese restaurant in Torrance, California. Single table, with tablecloth; various chairs, supplies. One door leads outside, a back exit, another leads to the kitchen. Lights up on* GRACE, *at the table. The music is coming from a small radio. On the table is a small, partially wrapped box, and a huge blob of discarded Scotch tape. As* GRACE *tries to wrap the box, we see what has been happening: The tape she's using is stuck; so, in order to pull it out, she must tug so hard that an unusable quantity of tape is dispensed. Enter* STEVE, *from the back door, unnoticed by* GRACE. *He stands, waiting to catch her eye, tries to speak, but his voice is drowned out by the music. He is dressed in a stylish summer outfit.*)

GRACE: Aaaai-ya!

STEVE: Hey!

(*No response; he turns off the music.*)

GRACE: Huh? Look. Out of tape.

STEVE: (*In Chinese.*) Yeah.

GRACE: One whole roll. You know how much of it got on here? Look. That much. That's all.

STEVE: (*In Chinese.*) Yeah. Do you serve *chong you bing* today?

GRACE: (*Picking up box.*) Could've skipped the wrapping paper, just covered it with tape.

STEVE: (*In Chinese.*) Excuse me!

GRACE: Yeah? (*Pause.*) You wouldn't have any on you, would ya?

STEVE: (*English from now onward.*) Sorry? No. I don't have *bing*. I want to buy *bing*.

GRACE: Not *bing*! Tape. Have you got any tape?

STEVE: Tape? Of course I don't have tape.

GRACE: Just checking.

STEVE: Do you have any *bing*?

(*Pause.*)

GRACE: Look, we're closed till five . . .

STEVE: Idiot girl.

GRACE: Why don't you take a menu?

STEVE: I want you to tell me!

(*Pause.*)

GRACE: (*Ignoring* STEVE.) Working in a Chinese restaurant, you learn to deal with obnoxious customers.

STEVE: Hey! You!

GRACE: If the customer's Chinese, you insult them by giving forks.

STEVE: I said I want you to tell me!

GRACE: If the customer's Anglo, you starve them by not giving forks.

STEVE: You serve *bing* or not?

GRACE: But it's always easy just to dump whatever happens to be in your hands at the moment.

(*She sticks the tape blob on* STEVE's *face.*)

STEVE: I suggest you answer my question at once!

GRACE: And I suggest you grab a menu and start doing things for yourself. Look, I'll get you one, even. How's that?

STEVE: I want it from your mouth!

GRACE: Sorry. We don't keep 'em there.

STEVE: If I say they are there, they are there.

(*He grabs her box.*)

GRACE: What—What're you doing? Give that back to me!

(*They parry around the table.*)

STEVE: Aaaah! Now it's different, isn't it? Now you're listening to me.

GRACE: 'Scuse me, but you really are an asshole, you know that? Who do you think you are?

STEVE: What are you asking me? Who I am?

GRACE: Yes. You take it easy with that, hear?

STEVE: You ask who *I* am?

GRACE: One more second and I'm gonna call the cops.

STEVE: Very well, I will tell you.

(*She picks up the phone. He slams it down.*)

STEVE: I said, I'll tell you.

GRACE: If this is how you go around meeting people, I think it's pretty screwed.

STEVE: Silence! I am Gwan Gung! God of warriors, writers, and prostitutes!

(*Pause.*)

GRACE: Bullshit!

STEVE: What?

GRACE: Bullshit! Bull-shit! You are not Gwan Gung. And gimme back my box.

STEVE: I am Gwan Gung. Perhaps we should see what you have in here.

GRACE: Don't open that! (*Beat.*) You don't look like Gwan Gung. Gwan Gung is a warrior.

STEVE: I am a warrior!

GRACE: Yeah? Why are you so scrawny, then? You wouldn't last a day in battle.

STEVE: My credit! Many a larger man has been humiliated by the strength in one of my size.

GRACE: Tell me, then. Tell me, if you are Gwan Gung. Tell me of your battles. Of one battle. Of Gwan Gung's favorite battle.

STEVE: Very well. Here is a living memory: One day, Gwan Gung woke up and saw the ring of fire around the sun and decided, "This is a good day to slay villagers." So he got up washed himself, and looked over a map of the Three Kingdoms to decide where first to go. For those were days of rebellion and falling empires, so opportunity to slay was abundant. But planned slaughter required an order and restraint which soon became tedious. So Gwan Gung decided a change was in order. He called for his tailor, who he asked to make a beautiful blindfold of layered silk, fine enough to be weightless, yet thick enough to blind the wearer completely. The tailor complied, and soon produced a perfect piece of red silk, exactly suited to Gwan Gung's demands. In gratitude, Gwan Gung stayed the tailor's execution sentence. He then put on his blindfold, pulled out his sword, and began passing over the land, swiping at whatever got in his path. You see, Gwan Gung figured there was so much revenge and so much evil in those days that he could slay at random and still stand a good chance of fulfilling justice. This worked very well, until his sword, in its blind fury, hit upon an old and irritable atom bomb.

(GRACE *catches* STEVE, *takes back the box.*)

GRACE: Ha! Some Gwan Gung you are! Some warrior you are! You can't even protect a tiny box from the grasp of a woman! How could you have shielded your big head in battle?

STEVE: Shield! Shield! I still go to battle!

GRACE: Only your head goes to battle, 'cause only your head is Gwan Gung.

(*Pause.*)

STEVE: You made me think of you as a quiet listener. A good trick. What is your name?

GRACE: You can call me "The Woman Who Has Defeated Gwan Gung," if that's really who you are.

STEVE: Very well. But that name will change before long.

GRACE: That story you told—that wasn't a Gwan Gung story.

STEVE: What—you think you know all of my adventures through stories? All the books in the world couldn't record the life of one man, let alone a god. Now—do you serve *bing*?

GRACE: I won the battle; you go look yourself. There.

STEVE: You working here?

GRACE: Part-time. It's my father's place. I'm also in school.

STEVE: School? University?

GRACE: Yeah. UCLA.

STEVE: Excellent. I have also come to America for school.

GRACE: Well, what use would Gwan Gung have for school?

STEVE: Wisdom. Wisdom makes a warrior stronger.

GRACE: Pretty good. If you are Gwan Gung, you're not the dumb jock I was expecting. Got a lot to learn about school, though.

STEVE: Expecting? You were expecting me?

GRACE: (*Quickly.*) No, no. I meant, what I expected from the stories.

STEVE: Tell me, how do people think of Gwan Gung in America? Do they shout my name while rushing into battle, or is it too sacred to be used in such ostentatious display?

GRACE: Uh—no.

STEVE: No—what? I didn't ask a "no" question.

GRACE: What I mean is, neither. They don't do either of those.

STEVE: Not good. The name of Gwan Gung has been restricted for the use of leaders only?

GRACE: Uh—no. I think you better sit down.

STEVE: This is very scandalous. How are the people to take my strength? Gwan Gung might as well not exist, for all they know.

GRACE: You got it.

STEVE: I got what? You seem to be having trouble making your answers fit my questions.

GRACE: No, I think you're having trouble making your questions fit my answers.

STEVE: What is this nonsense? Speak clearly, or don't speak at all.

GRACE: Speak clearly?

STEVE: Yes. Like a warrior.

GRACE: Well, you see, Gwan Gung, god of warriors, writers, and prostitutes, no one gives a wipe about you 'round here. You're dead.

(*Pause.*)

STEVE: You . . . you make me laugh.

GRACE: You died way back . . . hell, no one even noticed when you died—that's how bad off your PR was. You died and no one even missed a burp.

STEVE: You lie! The name of Gwan Gung must be feared around the world—you jeopardize your health with such remarks. (*Pause.*) You—you have heard of me, I see. How can you say—?

GRACE: Oh, I just study it a lot—Chinese American history, I mean.

STEVE: Ah. In the schools, in the universities, where new leaders are born, they study my ways.

GRACE: Well, fifteen of us do.

STEVE: Fifteen. Fifteen of the brightest, of the most promising?

GRACE: One wants to be a dental technician.

STEVE: A man studies Gwan Gung in order to clean teeth?

GRACE: There's also a middle-aged woman that's kinda bored with her kids.

STEVE: I refuse—I don't believe you—your stories. You're just angry at me for treating you like a servant. You're trying to sap my faith. The people—the people outside—they know me—they know the deeds of Gwan Gung.

GRACE: Check it out yourself.

STEVE: Very well. You will learn—learn not to test the spirit of Gwan Gung.

(STEVE *exits*.)

Getting Out

Marsha Norman

Characters: Arlene Holsclaw (late 20s), Bennie (50s)
Setting: A dingy apartment in Louisville; Pine Ridge State Prison in Alabama
Premiere: Actors Theatre of Louisville/Theatre de Lys, New York City, 1979
Publisher: Dramatists Play Service, Inc.

Arlene Holsclaw has just been released from an eight-year stretch in prison. Her parole statement lists her crime as "the second-degree murder of a cab driver in conjunction with a filling station robbery involving attempted kidnapping of attendant. Crime occurred during escape from Lakewood State Prison where subject Holsclaw was serving three years for forgery and prostitution."

In spite of her record, Arlene is determined to make a fresh start. But everyone from her past—her former pimp, her neighbors, her cab-driving mother—continues to deal with her as a criminal. Arlene finds herself haunted by Arlie, her former self. (The two roles are played by different actresses.)

Bennie also confuses Arlene with Arlie. A prison guard, he has quit his job and driven Arlene to her hometown. He is a widower and has known Arlene throughout her prison sentence. He has his own plans of establishing himself in her life on the outside.

(BENNIE *and* ARLENE *have finished their dinner.* BENNIE *puts one carton of slaw in the refrigerator, then picks up all the paper, making a garbage bag out of one of the sacks.*)

BENNIE: Ain't got a can, I guess. Jus use this ol sack for now.

ARLENE: I ain't never emptyin another garbage can.

BENNIE: Yeah, I reckon you know how by now. (*Yawns.*) You bout ready for bed?

ARLENE: (*Stand up.*) I spose.

BENNIE: (*Stretches.*) Little tired myself.

ARLENE: Thanks for the chicken. (*Dusting the crumbs off the bed.*)

BENNIE: You're right welcome. You look beat. How bout I rub your back. (*Grabs her shoulders.*)

ARLENE: (*Pulling away.*) No. (*Walking to the sink.*) You go on now.

BENNIE: Oh come on. (*Wiping his hands on his pants.*) I ain't all that tired.

ARLENE: I'm tired.

BENNIE: Well, see then, a back rub is just what the doctor ordered.

ARLENE: No. I don't . . . (*Pulling away.*)

BENNIE: (*Grabs her shoulders and turns her around, sits her down hard on the trunk, starts rubbing her back and neck.*) Muscles git real tight like, right in here.

ARLENE: You hurtin me.

BENNIE: Has to hurt a little or it won't do no good.

ARLENE: (*Jumps, he has hurt her.*) Oh, stop it! (*Slips away from him and out into the room. She is frightened.*)

BENNIE: (*Smiling, coming after her, toward the bed.*) Be lot nicer if you was layin down. Wouldn't hurt as much.

ARLENE: Now, I ain't gonna start yellin. I'm jus tellin you to go.

BENNIE: (*Straightens up as though he's going to cooperate.*) O.K. then. I'll jus git my hat. (*He reaches for the hat, then turns quickly, grabs her and throws her down on the bed. He starts rubbing again.*) Now, you just relax. Dont' you go bein scared of me.

ARLENE: You ain't gettin nuthin from me.

BENNIE: I don't want nuthin, honey. Jus tryin to help you sleep.

ARLENE: (*Struggling.*) Don't you call me honey.

BENNIE: (*Stops rubbing, but keeps one hand on her back. Rubs her hair with his free hand.*) See? Don't that feel better?

ARLENE: Let me up.

BENNIE: Why, I ain't holdin you down. (*So innocent.*)

ARLENE: Then let me up.

BENNIE: (*Takes hands off.*) O.K. Git up.

ARLENE: (*Turns over slowly, begins to lift herself up on her elbows. Bennie puts one hand on her leg.*) Move your hand.

BENNIE: (ARLENE *gets up, moves across the room.*) I'd be happy to stay here with you tonight. Make sure you'll be all right. You ain't spent a night by yourself for a long time.

ARLENE: I remember how.

BENNIE: Well how you gonna git up? You got a alarm?

ARLENE: It ain't all that hard.

BENNIE: (*Puts one hand in his pocket, leers a little.*) Oh yeah it is. (*Walks toward her again.*) Gimme a kiss. Then I'll go.

ARLENE: You stay away from me. (*Edging along the counter, seeing she's trapped.*)

BENNIE: (*Reaches for her, clamping her hands behind her, pressing up against her.*) Now what's it going to hurt you to give me a little ol kiss?

ARLENE: Git out! I said git out! (*Struggling.*)

BENNIE: You don't want me to go. You're jus beginning to git interested. Your ol girlie temper's flarin up. I like that in a woman.

ARLENE: Yeah, you'd love it if I'd swat you one. (*Gettin away from him.*)

BENNIE: I been hit by you before. I kin take anything you got.

ARLENE: I could mess you up good.

BENNIE: Now, Arlie. You ain't had a man in a long time. And the ones you had been no count.

ARLENE: Git out! (*Slaps him. He returns the slap.*)

BENNIE: (*Moving in.*) Ain't natural goin without it too long. Young thing like you. Git all shriveled up.

ARLENE: (ARLIE *turning on, now.*) All right, you sunuvabitch, you asked for it! (*Goes into a violent rage, hitting and kicking him.*)

BENNIE: (*Overpowering her capably, prison guard style.*) Little outta practice, ain't you? (*Amused.*)

ARLENE: (*Screaming.*) I'll kill you, you creep!

BENNIE: (*Struggle continues,* BENNIE *pinning her arms under his leg as he kneels over her on the bed.* ARLENE *is terrified and in pain.*) You will? You'll kill ol Bennie . . . kill ol Bennie like you done that cab driver? (*A cruel reminder he employs to stun and mock her.* ARLENE *looks as though she has been hit.* BENNIE *is still fired up, he unzips his pants.*)

ARLENE: (*Passive, cold and bitter.*) This how you got your Dorrie, rapin?

BENNIE: (*Unbuttoning his shirt.*) That what you think this is, rape?

ARLENE: I oughta know.

BENNIE: Uh-huh.

ARLENE: First they unzip their pants. (BENNIE *pulls his shirt out.*) Sometimes they take off their shirt.

BENNIE: They do huh?

ARLENE: But mostly, they just pull it out and stick it in. (BENNIE *stops, one hand goes to his fly, finally hearing what she has been saying. He straightens up, obviously shocked. He puts his arms back in his shirt.*)

BENNIE: Don't you call me no rapist. (*Pause, then insistent.*) No, I ain't no rapist, Arlie. (*Gets up, begins to tuck his shirt back in and zip up his pants.*)

ARLENE: And I ain't Arlie.

BENNIE: (ARLENE *remains on the bed as he continues dressing.*) No, I guess you ain't.

ARLENE: (*Quietly and painfully.*) Arlie coulda killed you.

Hello and Goodbye

Athol Fugard

Characters: Johnnie Smit (30s), Hester Smit (30s)
Setting: A railroad worker's shack in South Africa
Premiere: Library Theatre, Johannesburg, South Africa, 1965
Publisher: Oxford Press (in *Boesman and Lena & Other Plays*)

For years, Johnnie has lived in a shack with his father, a bad-tempered railroad man who retired when he lost his leg in an accident. Now the father has died, and Johnnie, disoriented by grief and loneliness, talks to himself in order to test his own sanity. Then Hester walks through the door. Johnnie does not recognize her.

(JOHNNIE *sits and reads a comic. A woman appears up stage and walks slowly into the light. She is wearing a coat and carrying a large and battered suitcase. This is* HESTER. JOHNNIE *looks up from his comic and watches her.*)

HESTER: (*Putting down the suitcase.*) Hello.

JOHNNIE: Hello.

HESTER: Didn't you hear me calling?

JOHNNIE: No.

HESTER: Well I did!

JOHNNIE: I'm not arguing.

HESTER: I thought nobody was home.

JOHNNIE: No. I've been sitting here, minding my own business. . . .

HESTER: Well then listen next time, for God's sake. First the taxi hooted. But he was in a hurry so I told him to drop me. I could see the light was on.

JOHNNIE: I've been reading. . . .

HESTER: I even started to wonder if it was the right place.

JOHNNIE: Fifty-seven A Valley Road. Smit's the name.

HESTER: You being funny? Anyway the door wasn't locked. So what you got to say for yourself?

JOHNNIE: Surprised of course. I mean, put yourself in my shoes. I'm sitting here, reading a comic, passing the time, and then you! Suddenly you're here too.

HESTER: Not even a word of welcome.

(*Pause.*)

JOHNNIE: Welcome.

HESTER: Don't kill youself!

JOHNNIE: Make yourself at home!

HESTER: I will.

JOHNNIE: What else? HospitaliTEA! How about a nice cup of. . . . No. Milk's finished. Can I offer you a refreshing glass of lemon squash? It's preserved with benzoic acid.

HESTER: Later. ·

(*She moves right and stares off in that direction.*)

Sleeping?

JOHNNIE: Who?

HESTER: Who? Him! Is he sleeping? Hell, you just woken up or something?

JOHNNIE: Me? No. I've been sitting here, reading. . . .

HESTER: Okay, okay. How's things otherwise?

JOHNNIE: Just a comic, mind you. Not a book. I've run out of reading-matter.

HESTER: I didn't come a thousand miles to talk about comics.

JOHNNIE: So?

HESTER: So change the subject.

JOHNNIE: There's no law against reading a comic in my own home.

HESTER: All right.

JOHNNIE: I admitted it wasn't a book.

HESTER: All right I said.

JOHNNIE: But I'm not harming anyone.

HESTER: For God's sake, all right. Read your bloody comic. All I wanted was a word of welcome. Is that asking so much? Look, let's start again. Have a cigarette.

(*They light cigarettes.*)

I'm leaving it to you.

JOHNNIE: What?

HESTER: The questions.

JOHNNIE: What questions?

HESTER: Or news.

JOHNNIE: No news, good news.

HESTER: Who cares? Let's hear it.

JOHNNIE: What?

HESTER: Anything. Just talk!

JOHNNIE: Okay.

HESTER: Good.

JOHNNIE: Can I be frank?

HESTER: Go ahead.

JOHNNIE: What do you want?

HESTER: How the hell do you like that!

JOHNNIE: I'm not telling you to go. Stay as long as you like. I admire your—what's the word?—pluck. I always admire people who pluck up courage and barge in. But still—you and your suitcase, out of the blue, the dark, on my doorstep and before I could blink an eye in my house! You follow? What's all this in aid of?

HESTER: Listen to him!

JOHNNIE: Look, I said you could stay. I'm just interested. . . .

HESTER: Are you mad?

JOHNNIE: See what I mean. Straight to the point. Anyway, me mad. I worked it out. I don't think I am, therefore. . . . No . . . those that think they are . . . to cut a long story short I'm not.

HESTER: Johnnie?

JOHNNIE: You even know my name.

HESTER: Am I hearing you right? Of course I know your name.
(*Pause.*)
I don't believe it.

JOHNNIE: Truth is stranger than fiction.

HESTER: You don't know who I am.

JOHNNIE: You got me guessing.

HESTER: Don't you recognize me at all?

JOHNNIE: I admit I haven't had a really good look yet. I start with the feet and work up.

HESTER: Shut up! So why did you just sit there? Why didn't you ask?

JOHNNIE: But I did. I asked you. . . .

HESTER: All right!

(*Pause.*)

I'm Hester. Your sister, Hester Smit.

(*Pause.*)

Didn't you get my letter?

JOHNNIE: What letter?

HESTER: I wrote. Fifty-seven A Valley Road, Port Elizabeth. Saying I was coming. I waited and waited for a reply. Didn't you get it?

JOHNNIE: No.

HESTER: Well, I'm Hester, and I come back to visit you, Johnnie, my brother. So what you waiting for? Don't you believe me?

JOHNNIE: Give me time.

HESTER: I'm Hester, I tell you!

JOHNNIE: Prove it.

HESTER: You got a sister called Hester, haven't you?

JOHNNIE: Yes.

HESTER: And she's been gone a long time.

JOHNNIE: Yes.

HESTER: Well, that's me.

JOHNNIE: So prove it.

HESTER: You got a birthmark there . . .

(*Pointing.*)

. . . what looks like the map of Africa upside down; and on your leg, your left leg I think—yes it is!—there's an operation from that time you were playing with the Boer War bullet and it went off. Are you satisfied?

JOHNNIE: But all of that's me. I know I'm Johnnie. It's *you*. You say you're Hester. Prove it.

HESTER: I'll hit you.

JOHNNIE: No you won't.

HESTER: How the hell would I know all about you if I wasn't me? If I wasn't Hester? I came *here*, didn't I? I know the address, your name, about him. . . .

(*Pointing off-right. Pointing off-left.*)

That was our room; this was a lounge-cum-kitchen but af-

ter Mommie died I went on growing which isn't good for
little boys to see so you moved in here and then it was
kitchen-cum-bedroom, which also didn't matter because mostly
there was a row on the go and nobody was talking to anybody else. Right or wrong? And when you got big and Daddy
got worse it was you used to look after him because I was
working at the Astoria Café, and that's his room and his lying there with only one leg left because of the explosion;
and all our life it was groaning and moaning and what the
Bible says and what God's going to do and I hated it! Right
or wrong? Right! And it was hell. I wanted to scream. I got
so sick of it I went away. What more do you want? Must I
vomit?

(*Pause.*)

Well, don't just stand there. Take a good look and see it's me.

(HESTER *moves close to* JOHNNIE—*she sees him properly
for the first time. When she speaks again it is with the pain
of recognition—what is and what was.*)

Johnnie! It's been a long time, *boetie.*

(*A small impulsive gesture of tenderness—hand to his
cheek?—which she breaks off abruptly. She moves away.*)

(*Flat, matter-of-fact voice.*)

Well, is it me?

JOHNNIE: (*Quiet certainty.*) Yes, it's you.

HESTER: You sure?

JOHNNIE: I'm certain.

HESTER: Hester Smit.

JOHNNIE: I remember. . . .

HESTER: My face hasn't changed?

JOHNNIE: . . . your hate! It hasn't changed. The sound of it.
Always so sudden, so loud, so late at night. Nobody else
could hate it the way you did.

HESTER: (*Weary scorn.*) This? Four walls that rattled and a
roof that leaked! What's there to hate?

JOHNNIE: Us.

HESTER: I've got better things to do with my hate.

JOHNNIE: You hated something. You said so yourself.

HESTER: All right, something. The way it was! All those years, and all of us, in here.

JOHNNIE: Then why have you come back?

HESTER: That was fifteen years ago.

JOHNNIE: You don't hate it now?

HESTER: Now. What's now? I've just arrived.

JOHNNIE: Tonight.

HESTER: I'll tell you tomorrow. Let me look at it in the light.

JOHNNIE: How long will you be staying?

HESTER: (*Ignoring the question.*) *Ja.* Fifteen years ago next month. I worked it out in the train. I was twenty-two. Best thing I ever did getting out of here.

JOHNNIE: Then why have you come back?

HESTER: You got lots of questions all of a sudden!

JOHNNIE: You said. . . .

HESTER: To hell with what I said. I'm here.

Hurlyburly

David Rabe

Characters: Eddie (30s), Darlene (30s)
Setting: Eddie and Mickey's house in the Hollywood Hills
Premiere: Goodman Theatre, Chicago, 1984
Publisher: Samuel French, Inc.

Eddie and Mickey are Hollywood casting directors who keep themselves pasted together with cocaine and liquor. Their married friend Phil, an actor, stays with them when he has marital problems. Another friend, Artie, drops by this male enclave to deliver a blond teenage runaway he found in an elevator, describing her as "a CARE package . . . just to stay in practice. In case you run into a woman."

Darlene is an L.A. photojournalist, beautiful and fashionable. First she was involved with Eddie, then she started seeing Mickey, and now she returns to an uneasy balance with Eddie. The following scene takes place in Act Three. Phil has been acting more and more unstable, and Eddie is worried about him.

EDDIE: Let's just hang around a little in case he calls.

DARLENE: I'm tired anyway.

EDDIE: It's the kid thing, you know, that's the thing. He could walk in a second it wasn't for the kid.

DARLENE: He should have then.

EDDIE: Exactly. But he couldn't. (*Heading for the stairs, beginning to take off his jacket.*) So what am I talking about? It's just a guy like Phil, for all his appearances, this is what can make him nuts. You don't ever forget about 'em if you're a guy like Phil. I mean, my little girl is a factor in every calculation I make—big or small—she's a constant. You can imagine, right?

DARLENE: Sure. I had a, you know—and that was—well, rough, so I have some sense of it, really, in a very funny way.

EDDIE: (*As he goes into his bedroom.*) What?

DARLENE: My abortion. I got pregnant. I wasn't sure exactly which guy—I wasn't going crazy or anything with a different guy every night or anything, and I knew them both very well, but I was just not emotionally involved with either one of them, seriously. (*Emerging from the bedroom, he freezes, staring down at her, his shirt half off.*) Though I liked them both. A lot. Which in a way made the whole thing even more confusing on a personal level, and you know, in terms of trying to figure out the morality of the whole thing, so I finally had this abortion completely on my own without telling anybody, not even my girlfriends. I kept thinking in my mind that it wasn't a complete baby, which it wasn't, not a fully developed person, but a fetus which it was, and that I would have what I would term a real child later, but nevertheless, I had these nightmares and totally unexpected feelings in which in my dreams I imagined the baby as this teenager, a handsome boy of real spiritual consequences, which now the world would have to do without, and he was always like a refugee, full of regret, like this treasure that had been lost in some uncalled-for way, like when a person of great potential is hit by a car. I felt I had no one to blame but myself, and I went sort of out of my mind for a while, so my parents sent me to Puerto Rico for a vacation, and I got myself back together there enough to come home with my head on my shoulders at least semi-straight. I was functional, anyway. Semi-functional, anyway. But then I told everybody what had happened. I went from telling nobody to everybody.

EDDIE: This was . . .

DARLENE: What?

EDDIE: When?

DARLENE: Seven and a half years ago.

EDDIE: That's what I mean, though; those feelings.

DARLENE: I know. I understood, see, that was what you meant, which was my reason for trying to make the effort to bring it up, because I don't talk about it all that much at all anymore, but I wanted you to know that when you said that about your daughter, I, in fact, in a visceral sense, knew what you were talking about.

EDDIE: (*Moving down the stairs toward her, as it seems they agree on everything.*) I mean, everybody has this baggage, and you can't ignore it or what are you doing?

DARLENE: You're just ignoring it.

EDDIE: You're just ignoring the person then, that's all. But at the same time your own feelings are—it's overwhelming or at least it can be. You can't take it all on.

DARLENE: No.

EDDIE: (*Holding her hand, he pats her in consolation.*) There's nothing I can do about all that, you know, that happened to you.

DARLENE: No.

EDDIE: It really messed you up, though.

DARLENE: For a while. But I learned certain things from it, too, you know.

EDDIE: (*Still holding her hand.*) Sure.

DARLENE: It was painful, but I learned these things that have been a help ever since, so something came out of it good.

EDDIE: So . . . these two guys. . . . Where are they?

DARLENE: Oh, I have no idea. This was in Cincinnati.

EDDIE: Right. (*Now he rises and begins mixing drinks for them both.*)

DARLENE: I don't know what happened to them. I think one got married and I have this vague sense that—I don't know what EXACTLY—but . . . no. I can't remember. But I have this sense that SOMETHING happened to him. I don't know what. Anyway, I rarely think about it anymore. I'm a very different person.

EDDIE: Did . . . they know each other?

DARLENE: The two guys?

EDDIE: Yeah.

DARLENE: No. I mean, not that I know of. Why?

EDDIE: Just wondering.

DARLENE: What?

EDDIE: Nothing. Just . . . you know.

DARLENE: You must have been wondering something. People don't just wonder nothing.

EDDIE: No, no. I was just wondering, you know, was it a pattern? That's all.

DARLENE: No.

EDDIE: I mean, don't get irritated. You asked me.

DARLENE: You asked me. I mean, I was trying to tell you something else entirely.

EDDIE: I know that.

DARLENE: So what's the point?

EDDIE: I'm aware absolutely of what you were trying to tell me. And I heard it. But am I just supposed to totally narrow down my whole set of perceptions, just filter out everything, just censor everything that doesn't support your intention? I made an association. And it was not an unreasonable association.

DARLENE: It was totally off the wall, and hostile.

EDDIE: Hostile?

DARLENE: And you know it.

EDDIE: Give me a break! What? I'm supposed to sit still for the most arcane association I ever hear in my life, that levitation leads to dogs? But should I come up with an equally— I mean, equally, shit—when I come up with a hundred percent more logical association, I'm supposed to accept your opinion that it isn't?

DARLENE: No, no, no.

EDDIE: Well, that's all it was. An association. That's all it was.

DARLENE: Okay.

EDDIE: I mean, for everybody's good, it appeared to me a thought worth some exploration, and if I was wrong, and I misjudged, then I'm sorry.

DARLENE: It's just something I'm very, sometimes, sensitive about.

EDDIE: Sure. What? The abortion.

DARLENE: Yeah.

EDDIE: (*Handing her the drink, he pats her hand.*) Sure. Okay, though? You okay now? You feel okay?

DARLENE: I'm hungry. You hungry?

EDDIE: I mean, if we don't talk these things out, we'll just end up with all this, you know, unspoken shit, following us around. You wanna go out and eat? Let's go out. What are you hungry for? How about Chinese?

DARLENE: Sure.

EDDIE: (*Grabbing up the phone and starting to dial.*) We could go to Mr. Chou's. Treat ourselves right.

DARLENE: That's great. I love the seaweed.

EDDIE: I mean, you want Chinese?

DARLENE: I love Mr. Chou's.

EDDIE: We could go some other place. How about Ma Maison?

DARLENE: Sure.

EDDIE: (*Hanging up the phone.*) You like that better than Mr. Chou's?

DARLENE: I don't like it better, but it's great. Which one is your preference?

EDDIE: Well, I want—you know—this should be—I'd like this to be your choice.

DARLENE: It doesn't matter to me.

EDDIE: Which one should I call?

DARLENE: Surprise me.

EDDIE: I don't want to surprise you. I want to, you know, do whatever you say.

DARLENE: Then just pick one. Call one. Either.

EDDIE: I mean, why should I have to guess? I don't want to guess. Just tell me. I mean, what if I pick the wrong one?

DARLENE: You can't pick the wrong one. Honestly, Eddie, I like them both the same. I like them both exactly the same.

EDDIE: Exactly?

DARLENE: Yes. I like them both.

EDDIE: I mean, how can you possibly think you like them both the same? One is French and one is Chinese. They're different. They're as different as—I mean, what is the world, one big blur to you out there in which everything that bears some resemblance to something else is just automatically put at the same level in your hierarchy, for chrissake, Darlene, the only thing they have in common is that they're both restaurants!

DARLENE: Are you aware that you're yelling?

EDDIE: My voice is raised for emphasis, which is a perfectly legitimate use of volume. Particularly when, in addition, I evidently have to break through this goddamn cloud in which you are obviously enveloped in which everything is just this blur totally void of the most rudimentary sort of distinction.

DARLENE: Just call the restaurant, why don't you?

EDDIE: Why are you doing this?

DARLENE: I'm hungry. I'm just trying to get something to eat before I faint.

EDDIE: The fuck you are. You're up to something.

DARLENE: What do you mean, what am I up to? You're telling me I don't know if I'm hungry or not? I'm hungry!

EDDIE: Bullshit!

DARLENE: (*Leaning up from her chair, she strides across the room.*) "Up to?" Paranoia, Eddie. Para-fucking-noia. Be alert. Your tendencies are coming out all over the place.

EDDIE: I'm fine.

DARLENE: (*Pacing near the base of the stairs.*) I mean, to stand there screeching at me about what-am-I-up-to is paranoid.

EDDIE: Not if you're up to something, it's not.

DARLENE: I'm not. Take my word for it, you're acting a little nuts.

EDDIE: I'm supposed to trust your judgment of my mental stability? I'm supposed to trust your evaluation of the nuances of my sanity? You can't even tell the difference between a French and a Chinese restaurant!

DARLENE: I like them both.

EDDIE: But they're different. One is French, and the other is Chinese. They are totally fucking different.

DARLENE: Not in my inner, subjective, emotional experience of them.

EDDIE: The tastes, the decors, the waiters, the accents. The fucking accents. The little phrases the waiters say. And they yell at each other in these whole totally different languages, does none of this make an impression on you?

DARLENE: It impresses me that I like them both.

EDDIE: Your total inner emotional subjective experience must be THIS EPIC FUCKING FOG! I mean, what are you on, some sort of dualistic trip and everything is in twos and you just can't tell which is which so you're just pulled taut between them on this goddamn high wire between people who might like to have some kind of definitive reaction from you in order to know!

DARLENE: Fuck you!

EDDIE: What's wrong with that?

DARLENE: Those two guys. I happened to mention two guys!

EDDIE: I just want to know if this is a pattern. Chinese restaurants and you can't tell the difference between people. (*They stand, staring at each other.*)

DARLENE: Oh, Eddie. Oh, Eddie, Eddie.

EDDIE: What?

DARLENE: Oh, Eddie, Eddie. (*Moving to the couch, she slumps down, sits there.*)

EDDIE: What?

DARLENE: I just really feel awful. This is really depressing. I really like you. I really do.

EDDIE: I mean . . .

DARLENE: What?

EDDIE: Well, don't feel too bad, okay?

DARLENE: I do, I feel bad. I feel bad.

EDDIE: (*Moving now, he sits down on the edge of the armchair, and leans toward her.*) But, I mean, just—we have to talk about these things, right? That's all. This is okay.

DARLENE: No, no.

EDDIE: Just don't—you know, on the basis of this, make any sort of grand, kind of overwhelming, comprehensive, kind of, you know, totally conclusive assessment here. That would be absurd, you know. I mean, this is an isolated, individual thing here, and—

DARLENE: No.

EDDIE: (*Moving to the couch, he tries to get close to her, settles on his knees on the floor beside the couch.*) Sure. I mean, sometimes what is it? It's stuff, other stuff; stuff under stuff, you're doing one thing you think it's something else. I mean, it's always there, the family thing, the childhood thing, it's—sometimes it comes up. I go off. I'm not even where I seem anymore. I'm not there.

DARLENE: Eddie, I think I should go.

EDDIE: I'm trying to explain.

DARLENE: (*Sliding away from him.*) I know all about it.

EDDIE: Whata you know all about?

DARLENE: Your fucking childhood, Eddie. You tol' me.

EDDIE: Whata you know?

DARLENE: I know all I—what is this, a test? I mean, I know: Your parents were these religious lunatics, these pious frauds, who periodically beat the shit out of you.

EDDIE: They weren't just religious, and they didn't just—

DARLENE: You father was a minister, I know.

EDDIE: What denomination?

DARLENE: Fuck you. (*She bolts away, starts gathering up her things: she's going to leave.*)

EDDIE: You said you knew.

DARLENE: I don't think there's a lot more we ought to, with any, you know, honesty, allow ourselves in the way of bullshit about our backgrounds to exonerate what is our just plain mean behavior to one another.

EDDIE: That's not what I'm doing.

DARLENE: So, what are you doing?

EDDIE: (*Following her.*) They took me in the woods; they prayed and then they beat the shit out of me; they prayed and beat me with sticks. He talked in tongues.

DARLENE: She broke your nose and blacked your eyes, I know.

EDDIE: Because I wanted to watch *Range Rider* on TV, and she considered it a violent program. (*Phone rings.*) So she broke my nose. That's insane.

DARLENE: But I don't care, Eddie. I don't care. (*She's really ready to go now.*)

EDDIE: Whata you mean?

DARLENE: I mean, it doesn't matter. (*She steps for the door.*)

EDDIE: It doesn't matter? What are you talking about? (*Grabbing her by the arm to detain her.*)

DARLENE: It doesn't.

EDDIE: No, no, no. (*As he grabs up the phone and yells into it.*) Hold on. (*Clutching* DARLENE *in one hand and the phone in the other, he turns to her.*) No, no; it matters, and you care. What you mean is, it doesn't make any difference. (*Releasing her, he speaks into the phone.*) Hello.

DARLENE: I can't stand this goddamn semantic insanity anymore, Eddie—I can't be that specific about my feelings—I can't. Will you get off the phone!

EDDIE: (*Into the phone.*) What? Oh, no. No, no. Oh, no.

DARLENE: What?

EDDIE: (*Into phone.*) Wait there. There. I'll come over. (*He hangs up and stands.*)

DARLENE: Eddie, what? You look terrible. What? (*He starts toward the front door.*) Eddie, who was that? What happened? Eddie!

EDDIE: Phil's dead.

DARLENE: What?

EDDIE: Car. Car.

DARLENE: Oh, Eddie, Eddie.

EDDIE: What?

DARLENE: I'm so sorry.

   (EDDIE *gives her a look and goes.*)

Joe Turner's Come and Gone

August Wilson

Characters: Zonia Loomis (11), Reuben (around 11)
Setting: A boardinghouse in Pittsburgh, August, 1911
Premiere: Yale Repertory Theatre, New Haven, 1986
Publisher: *Theatre* (Vol. XVII, No. 3)

Joe Turner takes place as children of the newly freed African slaves head to the northern cities. Foreigners in a strange land, they try to "give clear and luminous meaning to their song which is both a wail and a whelp of joy."

Zonia and her father, Herald Loomis, are searching for Zonia's mother. Asked why her mother ran away, she responds, "I don't know. My daddy say some man named Joe Turner did something bad to him once that made her run away." Zonia lived with her grandmother for seven years, and has spent the last four years with her father.

Reuben lives near the boardinghouse where Zonia is staying. He tells her that few kids live in the area. His best friend, Eugene, has died. "I still got his pigeons. He told me to let them go when he died. He say, 'Reuben, promise me when I die you'll let my pigeons go.' But I keep them to remember him by. I ain't ever gonna let them go." He sells pigeons to Mr. Bynum, a "conjure man," just as Eugene did.

———————————

(*It is early in the morning. The lights come up on* ZONIA *and* REUBEN *in the yard.*)

REUBEN: Something spooky going on around here. Last night Mr. Bynum was out in the yard singing and talking to the wind . . . and the wind it just be talking back to him. Did you hear it?

ZONIA: I heard it. I was scared to get up and look. I thought it was a storm.

REUBEN: That wasn't no storm. That was Mr. Bynum. First he say something . . . and the wind say it back to him.

ZONIA: I heard it. Was you scared? I was scared.

REUBEN: And then this morning . . . I seen Miss Mabel!

ZONIA: Who Miss Mabel?

REUBEN: Mr. Seth's mother. He got her picture hanging up in the house. She been dead.

ZONIA: How you seen her if she been dead?

REUBEN: Zonia . . . if I tell you something you promise you won't tell anybody?

ZONIA: I promise.

REUBEN: It was early this morning . . . I went out to the coop to feed the pigeons. I was down on the ground like this to open up the door to the coop . . . when all of a sudden I seen some feets in front of me. I looked up . . . and there was Miss Mabel standing there.

ZONIA: Reuben, you better stop telling that! You ain't seen nobody!

REUBEN: Naw, it's the truth. I swear! I seen her just like I see you. Look . . . you can see where she hit me with her cane.

ZONIA: Hit you? What she hit you for?

REUBEN: She say, "Didn't you promise Eugene something?" Then she hit me with her cane. She say, "Let them pigeons go." Then she hit me again. That's what made them marks.

ZONIA: Jeez man . . . get away from me. You done seen a haunt!

REUBEN: Shhhh. You promised, Zonia!

ZONIA: You sure it wasn't Miss Bertha come over there and hit you with her hoe?

REUBEN: It wasn't no Miss Bertha. I told you it was Miss Mabel. She was standing right there by the coop. She had this light coming out of her and then she just melted away.

ZONIA: What she had on?

REUBEN: A white dress. Ain't even had no shoes or nothing. Just had on that white dress and them big hands . . . and that cane she hit me with.

ZONIA: How you reckon she knew about the pigeons? You reckon Eugene told her?

REUBEN: I don't know. I sure ain't asked her none. She say Eugene was waiting on them pigeons. Say he couldn't go back home till I let them go. I couldn't get the door to the coop open fast enough.

ZONIA: Maybe she an angel? From the way you say she look with that white dress. Maybe she an angel.

REUBEN: Mean as she was . . . how she gonna be an angel? She used to chase us out her yard and frown up and look evil all the time.

ZONIA: That don't mean she can't be no angel cause of how she looked and cause she wouldn't let no kids play in her yard. It go by if you got any spots on your heart and if you pray and go to church.

REUBEN: What about she hit me with her cane? An angel wouldn't hit me with her cane.

ZONIA: I don't know. She might. I still say she was an angel.

REUBEN: You reckon Eugene the one who sent Old Miss Mabel?

ZONIA: Why he send her. Why he don't come himself?

REUBEN: Figured if he send her maybe that'll make me listen. Cause she old.

ZONIA: What you think it feel like?

REUBEN: What?

ZONIA: Being dead.

REUBEN: Like being sleep only you don't know nothin' and can't move no more.

ZONIA: If Miss Mabel can come back . . . then maybe Eugene can come back too.

REUBEN: We can go down to the hideout like we used to! He could come back everyday! It be just like he ain't dead.

ZONIA: Maybe that ain't right for him to come back. Feel kinda funny to be playing games with a haunt.

REUBEN: Yeah . . . what if everybody came back. What if Miss Mabel came back just like she ain't dead. Where you and your daddy gonna sleep then?

ZONIA: Maybe they go back at night and don't need no place to sleep.

REUBEN: It still don't seem right. I'm sure gonna miss Eugene. He's the bestest friend anybody ever had.

ZONIA: My daddy say if you miss somebody too much it can kill you. Say he missed me till it liked to killed him.

REUBEN: What if your mama's already dead and all the time you looking for her?

ZONIA: Naw, she ain't dead. My daddy say he can smell her.

REUBEN: You can't smell nobody that ain't here. Maybe he smelling old Miss Bertha. Maybe Miss Bertha your mama?

ZONIA: Naw she ain't. My mama got long pretty hair and she five feet from the ground!

REUBEN: Your daddy say when you leaving? (ZONIA *doesn't respond.*) Maybe you gonna stay in Mr. Seth's house and don't go looking for your mama no more.

ZONIA: He say we got to leave on Saturday.

REUBEN: Dag! You just only been here for a little while. Don't seem like nothing ever stay the same.

ZONIA: He say he got to find her. Find him a place in the world.

REUBEN: He could find him a place at Mr. Seth's house.

ZONIA: It don't look like we never gonna find her.

REUBEN: Maybe he find her by Saturday then you don't have to go.

ZONIA: I don't know.

REUBEN: You look like a spider.

ZONIA: I ain't no spider!

REUBEN: Got them long skinny arms and legs. You look like one of them Black Widows.

ZONIA: I ain't no Black Widow nothing! My name is Zonia!

REUBEN: That's what I'm gonna call you . . . Spider.

ZONIA: You can call me that, but I don't have to answer.

REUBEN: You know what? I think maybe I be your husband when I grow up.

ZONIA: How you know?

REUBEN: I ask my grandpap how you know and he say when the moon falls into a girl's eyes that how you know.

ZONIA: Did it fall into my eyes?

REUBEN: Not that I can tell. Maybe I ain't old enough. Maybe you ain't old enough.

ZONIA: So there! I don't know why you telling me that lie!

REUBEN: That don't mean nothing cause I can't see it. I know it's there. Just the way you look at me sometimes look like the moon might have been in your eyes.

ZONIA: That don't mean nothing if you can't see it. You supposed to see it.

REUBEN: Shucks, I see it good enough for me. You ever let anybody kiss you?

ZONIA: Just my daddy. He kiss me on the cheek.

REUBEN: It's better on the lips. Can I kiss you on the lips?

ZONIA: I don't know.

REUBEN: It don't hurt or nothing. It feels good.

ZONIA: You ever kiss anybody before?

REUBEN: I had a cousin let me kiss her on the lips one time. Can I kiss you?

ZONIA: Okay. (REUBEN *kisses her and lays his head against her chest.*) What you doing?

REUBEN: Listening. Your heart singing!

ZONIA: It is not.

REUBEN: Just beating like a drum. Let's kiss again. (*They kiss again.*) Now you mine, Spider. You my girl, okay?

ZONIA: Okay.

REUBEN: When I get grown, I come looking for you.
ZONIA: Okay.
 (*The lights fade.*)

A Kind of Alaska

(from *Other Places*)

Harold Pinter

Characters: Deborah (mid-40s), Hornby (early 60s)
Setting: An institution
Premiere: National Theatre, London, 1984
Publisher: Dramatists Play Service, Inc.

Other Places is a triple bill of short plays. *A Kind of Alaska* concerns the "re-awakening" of Deborah, a victim of *encephalitis lethargica,* or sleeping sickness.

In the winter of 1916–17, an epidemic of sleeping sickness spread across Europe. Many died; others fell into deep states of "sleep"—conscious of their surroundings but motionless and speechless. Deborah fell into this sleep when she was 16 years old. Hornby, a doctor, cares for her for twenty-nine years. He injects her with a newly developed drug (L-Dopa), which "re-awakens" her. In describing her condition to Deborah, Hornby tells her, "Your mind has not been damaged. It was merely suspended, it took up a temporary habitation . . . in a kind of Alaska."

This scene opens the play.

Note: Immediately following this scene, Pauline, Deborah's sister, sees that Hornby is trembling.

 (*A woman in a white bed. Mid-forties. She sits up against high-banked pillows, stares ahead.*
 A table and two chairs. A window.

A man in a dark suit sits at the table. Early sixties.
The woman's eyes move. She slowly looks about her.
Her gaze passes over the man and on.
He watches her.
She stares ahead, still.
She whispers.)

DEBORAH: Something is happening. (*Silence.*)

HORNBY: Do you know me? (*Silence.*) Do you recognise me? (*Silence.*) Can you hear me? (*She does not look at him.*)

DEBORAH: Are you speaking?

HORNBY: Yes. (*Pause.*) Do you know who I am? (*Pause.*) Who am I?

DEBORAH: No-one hears what I say. No-one is listening to me. (Pause.)

HORNBY: Do you know who I am? (*Pause.*) Who am I?

DEBORAH: You are no-one. (*Pause.*) Who is it? It is miles away. The rain is falling. I will get wet. (*Pause.*) I can't get to sleep. The dog keeps turning about. I think he's dreaming. He wakes me up, but not himself up. He's my best dog though. I talk French. (*Pause.*)

HORNBY: I would like you to listen to me. (*Pause.*) You have been asleep for a very long time. You have now woken up. We are here to care for you. (*Pause.*) You have been asleep for a very long time. You are older, although you do not know that. You are still young, but older. (*Pause.*)

DEBORAH: Something is happening.

HORNBY: You have been asleep. You have awoken. Can you hear me? Do you understand me? (*She looks at him for the first time.*)

DEBORAH: Asleep? (*Pause.*) I do not remember that. (*Pause.*) People have been looking at me. They have been touching me. I spoke, but I don't think they heard what I said. (*Pause.*) What language am I speaking? I speak French, I know that. Is this French? (*Pause.*) I've not seen Daddy today. He's funny. He makes me laugh. He runs with me. We play with balloons. (*Pause.*) Where is he? (*Pause.*) I think it's my birthday soon. (*Pause.*) No, no. No, no. I sleep like other people.

No more no less. Why should I? If I sleep late my mother wakes me up. There are things to do. (*Pause.*) If I have been asleep, why hasn't Mummy woken me up?

HORNBY: I have woken you up.

DEBORAH: But I don't know you. (*Pause.*) Where is everyone? Where is my dog? Where are my sisters? Last night Estelle was wearing my dress. But I said she could. (*Pause.*) I am cold.

HORNBY: How old are you?

DEBORAH: I am twelve. No. I am sixteen. I am seven. (*Pause.*) I don't know. Yes. I know. I am fourteen. I am fifteen. I'm lovely fifteen. (*Pause.*) You shouldn't have brought me here. My mother will ask me where I've been. (*Pause.*) You shouldn't have touched me like that. I shan't tell my mother. I shouldn't have touched you like that. (*Pause.*) Oh Jack. (*Pause.*) It's time I was up and about. All those dogs are making such a racket. I suppose Daddy's feeding them. Is Estelle going to marry that boy from Townley Street? The ginger boy? Pauline says he's got nothing between his ears. Thick as two planks. I've given it a good deal of rather more mature thought and I've decided she should not marry him. Tell her not to marry him. She'll listen to you. (*Pause.*) Daddy?

HORNBY: She didn't marry him.

DEBORAH: Didn't? (*Pause.*) It would be a great mistake. It would ruin her life.

HORNBY: She didn't marry him. (*Silence.*)

DEBORAH: I've seen this room before. What room is this? It's not my bedroom. My bedroom has blue lilac on the walls. The sheets are soft, pretty. Mummy kisses me. (*Pause.*) This is not my bedroom.

HORNBY: You have been in this room for a long time. You have been asleep. You have now woken up.

DEBORAH: You shouldn't have brought me here. What are you saying? Did I ask you to bring me here? Did I make eyes at you? Did I show desire for you? Did I let you peep up my skirt? Did I flash my teeth? Was I as bold as brass? Perhaps I've forgotten.

HORNBY: I didn't bring you here. Your mother and father brought you here.

DEBORAH: My father? My mother? (*Pause.*) Did they bring me to you as a sacrifice? Did they sacrifice me to you? (*Pause.*) No, no. You stole me . . . in the night. (*Pause.*) Have you had your way with me?

HORNBY: I am here to take care of you.

DEBORAH: They all say that. (*Pause.*) You've had your way with me. You made me touch you. You stripped me. I cried . . . but . . . but it was my lust made me cry. You are a devil. My lust was my own. I kept it by me. You took it from me. Once open never closed. Never closed again. Never closed always open. For eternity. Terrible. You have ruined me. (*Pause.*) I sound childish. Out of . . . tune. (*Pause.*) How old am I? (*Pause.*) Eighteen?

HORNBY: No.

DEBORAH: Well then, I've no idea how old I am. Do you know?

HORNBY: Not exactly.

DEBORAH: Why not? (*Pause.*) My sisters would know. We're very close. We love each other. We're known as the three bluebells. (*Pause.*) Why is everything so quiet? So still? I'm in a sandbag. The sea. Is that what I hear? A long way away. Gulls. Haven't heard a gull for ages. God what a racket. Where's Pauline? She's such a mischief. I have to keep telling her not to be so witty. That's what I say. You're too witty for your own good. You're so sharp you'll cut yourself. You're too witty for your own tongue. You'll bite your own tongue off one of these days and I'll keep your tongue in a closed jar and you'll never ever ever ever be witty again. (*Pause.*) She's all right, really. She just talks too much. Whereas Estelle is as deep as a pond. She's marvellous at crossing her legs. Sen-su-al. (*Pause.*) This is a hotel. A hotel near the sea. Hastings? Torquay? There's more to this than meets the eye. I'm coming to that conclusion. There's something very shady about you. Pauline always says I'll end up as part of the White Slave Traffic. (*Pause.*) Yes. This is a white tent. When I open the flap I'll step out into the Sahara Desert.

HORNBY: You've been asleep.

DEBORAH: Oh, you keep saying that! What's wrong with that? Why shouldn't I have a long sleep for a change? I need it. My body demands it. It's quite natural. I may have overslept but I didn't do it deliberately. If I had any choice in the matter I'd much prefer to be up and about. I love the morning. Why do you blame me? I was simply obeying the law of the body.

HORNBY: I know that. I'm not blaming you.

DEBORAH: Well, how long have I been asleep? (*Pause.*)

HORNBY: You have been asleep for twenty-nine years. (*Silence.*)

DEBORAH: You mean I'm dead?

HORNBY: No.

DEBORAH: I don't feel dead.

HORNBY: You're not.

DEBORAH: But you mean I've been dead?

HORNBY: If you had been dead you wouldn't be alive now.

DEBORAH: Are you sure?

HORNBY: No-one wakes from the dead.

DEBORAH: No, I shouldn't think so. (*Pause.*) Well, what was I doing if I wasn't dead?

HORNBY: We don't know . . . what you were doing.

DEBORAH: We? (*Pause.*) Where's my mother? My father? Estelle? Pauline?

HORNBY: Pauline is here. She's waiting to see you.

DEBORAH: She shouldn't be out at this time of night. I'm always telling her. She needs her beauty sleep. Like I do, by the way. But of course I'm her elder sister so she doesn't listen to me. And Estelle doesn't listen to me because she's my elder sister. That's family life. And Jack? Where's Jack? Where's my boyfriend? He's my boyfriend. He loves me. He loves me. I once saw him cry. For love. Don't make him cry again. What have you done to him? What have you done with him? What? What? What?

HORNBY: Be calm. Don't agitate yourself.

DEBORAH: Agitate myself?

HORNBY: There's no hurry about any of this.

DEBORAH: Any of what?

HORNBY: Be calm.

DEBORAH: I am calm. (*Pause.*) I've obviously committed a criminal offence and am now in prison. I'm quite prepared to face up to the facts. But what offence? I can't imagine what offence it could be. I mean one that would bring . . . such a terrible sentence.

HORNBY: This is not a prison. You have committed no offence.

DEBORAH: But what have I done? What have I been doing? Where have I been?

HORNBY: Do you remember nothing of where you've been? Do you remember nothing . . . of all that has happened to you?

DEBORAH: Nothing has happened to me. I've been nowhere. (*Silence.*)

HORNBY: I think we should—

DEBORAH: I certainly don't want to see Pauline. People don't want to see their sisters. They're only their sisters. They're so witty. All I hear is chump chump. The side teeth. Eating everything in sight. Gold chocolate. So greedy eat it with the paper on. Munch all the ratshit on the sideboard. Someone has to polish it off. Been there for years. Statues of excrement. Wrapped in gold. I've never got used to it. Sisters are diabolical. Brothers are worse. One day I prayed I would see no-one ever again, none of them ever again. All that eating, all that wit. (*Pause.*)

HORNBY: I didn't know you had any brothers.

DEBORAH: What? (*Pause.*)

HORNBY: Come. Rest. Tomorrow . . . is another day.

DEBORAH: No it isn't. No it isn't. It is not! (*She smiles.*) Yes, of course it is. Of course it is. Tomorrow is another day. I'd love to ask you a question.

HORNBY: Are you not tired?

DEBORAH: Tired? Not at all. I'm wide awake. Don't you think so?

HORNBY: What is the question?

DEBORAH: How did you wake me up? (*Pause.*) Or did you not

wake me up? Did I just wake up myself? All by myself? Or
did you wake me with a magic wand?

HORNBY: I woke you with an injection.

DEBORAH: Lovely injection. Oh how I love it. And am I beautiful?

HORNBY: Certainly.

DEBORAH: And you are my Prince Charming. Aren't you?
(*Pause.*) Oh speak up. (*Pause.*) Silly shit. All men are alike.
(*Pause.*) I think I love you.

HORNBY: No, you don't.

DEBORAH: Well, I'm not spoilt for choice here, am I? There's
not another man in sight. What have you done with all the
others? There's a boy called Peter. We play with his trains,
we play. . . . Cowboys and Indians. . . . I'm a tomboy. I knock
him about. But that was. . . . (*Pause.*) But now I've got all
the world before me. All life before me. All my life before
me. (*Pause.*) I've had enough of this. Find Jack. I'll say yes.
We'll have kids. I'll bake apples. I'm ready for it. No point
in hanging about. Best foot forward. Mummy's motto. Bit of
a cheek, I think, Mummy not coming in to say hullo, to say
goodnight, to tuck me up, to sing me a song, to warn me
about going too far with boys. Daddy I love but he is a bit
absent-minded. Thinking of other things. That's what Pauline
says. She says he has a mistress in Fulham. The bitch. I mean
Pauline. And she's only . . . thirteen. I keep telling her I'm
not prepared to tolerate her risible, her tendentious, her
eclectic, her ornate, her rococo insinuations and garbled in-
ventions. I tell her that every day of the week. (*Pause.*) Daddy
is kind and so is Mummy. We all have breakfast together
every morning in the kitchen. What's happening? (*Pause.*)

HORNBY: One day suddenly you stopped.

DEBORAH: Stopped?

HORNBY: Yes. (*Pause.*) You fell asleep and no-one could wake
you. But although I use the word sleep, it was not strictly
sleep.

DEBORAH: Oh, make up your mind! (*Pause.*) You mean you
thought I was asleep but I was actually awake?

HORNBY: Neither asleep nor awake.

DEBORAH: Was I dreaming?

HORNBY: Were you?

DEBORAH: Well was I? I don't know. (*Pause.*) I'm not terribly pleased about all this. I'm going to ask a few questions in a few minutes. One of them might be: What did I look like while I was asleep, or while I was awake, or whatever it was I was? Bet you can't tell me.

HORNBY: You were quite still. Fixed. Most of the time.

DEBORAH: Show me. (*Pause.*) Show me what I looked like. (*He demonstrates a still, fixed position. She studies him. She laughs, stops abruptly.*) Most of the time? What about the rest of the time?

HORNBY: You were taken for walks twice a week. We encouraged your legs to move. (*Pause.*) At other times you would suddenly move of your own volition very quickly, very quickly indeed, spasmodically, for short periods, and as suddenly as you began you would stop. (*Pause.*)

DEBORAH: Did you ever see . . . tears . . . well in my eyes?

HORNBY: No.

DEBORAH: And when I laughed . . . did you laugh with me?

HORNBY: You never laughed.

DEBORAH: Of course I laughed. I have a laughing nature. (*Pause.*) Right. I'll get up now. (*He moves to her.*) No! Don't! Don't be ridiculous. (*She eases herself out of the bed, stands, falls. He moves to her.*) No! Don't! Don't! Don't! Don't touch me. (*She stands, very slowly. He retreats, watching. She stands still, begins to walk, in slow motion, towards him.*) Let us dance. (*She dances, by herself, in slow motion.*) I dance. (*She dances.*) I've kept in practice, you know. I've been dancing in very narrow spaces. Kept stubbing my toes and bumping my head. Like Alice. Shall I sit here? I shall sit here. (*She sits at the table. He joins her. She touches the arms of her chair, touches the table, examines the table.*) I like tables, don't you? This is a rather beautiful table. Any chance of a dry sherry?

HORNBY: Not yet. Soon we'll have a party for you.

DEBORAH: A party? For me? How nice. Lots of cakes and lots of booze?

HORNBY: That's right.

DEBORAH: How nice. (*Pause.*) Well, it's nice at this table. What's the news? I suppose the war's still over?

HORNBY: It's over, yes.

DEBORAH: Oh good. They haven't started another one?

HORNBY: No.

DEBORAH: Oh good. (*Pause.*)

HORNBY: You danced in narrow spaces?

DEBORAH: Oh yes. The most crushing spaces. The most punishing spaces. That was tough going. Very difficult. Like dancing with someone dancing on your foot all the time, I mean *all* the time, on the same spot, just slam, slam, a big boot on your foot, not the most ideal kind of dancing, not by a long chalk. But sometimes the space opened and became light, sometimes it opened and I was so light, and when you feel so light you can dance till dawn and I danced till dawn night after night, night after night . . . for a time.

Landscape of the Body

John Guare

Characters: Betty Yearn (mid-30s to 40s), Marvin Holahan (40s)

Setting: A ferry to Nantucket; Greenwich Village

Premiere: Academy Festival Theatre, Lake Forest, Illinois, 1977

Publisher: Dramatists Play Service, Inc.

The play opens on the deck of a ferry boat sailing to Nantucket. A woman writes notes which she inserts into bottles and throws overboard. A man in disguise sits beside her. Betty recognizes him—Captain Marvin Holahan of New York's Sixth Precinct, Homicide Division.

The play then flashes back to five months earlier. Holahan interrogates Betty. Her son's body was found the previous afternoon, floating off an abandoned pier in Greenwich Village. His head was floating close by. Holahan suspects that Betty murdered him. She cannot believe it.

BETTY: I don't see how you can ask me these questions.

HOLAHAN: Easy.

BETTY: At this point in my life in history you could ask me these questions.

HOLAHAN: The kid is dead.

BETTY: I cannot cannot cannot—draw underlines under the cannot—cannot cannot cannot—six negatives make a positive—cannot understand—

HOLAHAN: How I can ask you these questions?

BETTY: How you can ask me these questions—

HOLAHAN: Lady, I'm not talking simple child-battering.

BETTY: The kid is dead. The kid is dead. You leave out the fact it's my kid.

HOLAHAN: Decapitation, Betty.

BETTY: My son is dead. My boy is dead. My kid killed. Not *the* kid. My kid.

HOLAHAN: The head chopped off, Betty. That's not Family Court. Chopped-off heads are not referrals to Family Counseling. That goes beyond child battering.

BETTY: Not *the* kid. *My* kid. *My* kid.

HOLAHAN: You and your boy friend didn't say my kid when you got out the hack saw. You must've said, oh, let me guess: you little bastard.

BETTY: I'm not going to throw up.

HOLAHAN: What did your kid see, Betty, that you had to chop his head off?

BETTY: If I throw up, it's like you win. You're not going to win.

HOLAHAN: Where's the boy's father?

BETTY: I haven't seen him in years.

HOLAHAN: Maybe the boy's father did it in revenge against you?

BETTY: Strangers don't do revenge. The father didn't even know where we live. I feel like I'm standing in that corner over there watching me, and if I try hard enough I can switch the dial and I'll see me on another channel. I'd like a laugh track around my life. I'd like a funny theme introducing my life. I'm standing right over there in that corner watching me.

HOLAHAN: Was your boy homosexual?

BETTY: He's fourteen, for God's sake.

HOLAHAN: Lady, we got bodies coming in here don't even live to be fourteen. Their ages never get off the fingers of two hands.

BETTY: There's a whole series of homosexual murders going on down there at Christopher Street. Maybe the kid was into something. I don't think so. Don't those murders involve decap—the heads off . . .

HOLAHAN: How do you know about that?

BETTY: Is that the clue that gives myself away? I read the papers. I hear on the street. Did you follow up that clue? Why did you drag me in here? I'm supposed to be out there, mourning, weeping—

HOLAHAN: Betty, I'm trying to be kind. If you're embarrassed confessing to such a heinous crime, you want me to get Sergeant Lorraine Dean down here? There ain't nothing Lorraine hasn't heard. She's a good woman, a good listener, heavy in the ankles, platinum blonde, a nice soft bosom that I swear has got seconal and libriums in. She'd hold you and rock you in the cradle of the deep and she'll sing "I'm confessing that I love you . . ." She'll sing that and make it easy for you to talk about what you did and get you help. She's got a nice voice Lorraine does. She could've made it big in the show biz department were it not for her tragedy in the ankle department. Should I get Lorraine down here and you can tell her all? You want Lorraine? "I just found joy. I'm as happy as a baby boy. With another brand new choo choo toy when I marry my Lorraine!" Betty? You could tell me too? There's nothing hadn't been poured into these ears. I'm taking courses at NYU nights in psychology. Things like you did happen all the time. We even had a spot quiz last week on a woman, went into a deep depression, drowned her two kids. Two! You just did one. Imagine how she feels. But they were infants. And she drowned them. I can't wait to ask my teacher about decapitation. You might help me get an honors. I might do a paper on you. Most infanticides are drownings or smotherings or an occasional throwing off a bridge . . .

BETTY: I remember when I was a little kid at the end of the McCarthy hearings when Joe McCarthy was destroying human lives, this great lawyer—

HOLAHAN: Welch. Joseph Welch.

BETTY: Stood up and said to McCarthy, Is there no such thing as human decency? And that question shocked everybody and destroyed Joe McCarthy.

HOLAHAN: I'll tell you that great lawyer Welch after that made a film for Otto Preminger called *Anatomy of a Murder* starring James Stewart and Lee Remick. Is there no such thing as human decency left?

BETTY: Is there no such thing as human decency left?

HOLAHAN: A damn good little question.

BETTY: Will I get off to go to my son's funeral?

HOLAHAN: Is Otto Preminger filming it?

BETTY: Am I booked? What's up? Do I go to my son's funeral?

HOLAHAN: Did you kill him?

BETTY: Do I get off for the funeral?

HOLAHAN: Say yes, beautiful Betty, and there's no place you can't go.

BETTY: I want my boy buried in Bangor, Maine, with his grandparents and his aunts and his uncles. I want him buried in Bangor with my father, with my sister Rosalie. Where I'll be buried when I die. I want him there. I want him out of New York.

HOLAHAN: You think it's fair to be at the funeral when you caused the funeral?

BETTY: I'm sorry, Your Honor, Mr. Kangaroo Court. I missed his death.

HOLAHAN: I keep thinking you were there.

BETTY: What is my motive? I cannot believe I am a suspect in my own son's death. I am supposed to be comforted. I am supposed to be held and allowed to cry and not made to feel . . . there's no insurance. I am no beneficiary. I cannot believe. I don't kill my own flesh and blood. I don't kill me. If I wanted to kill him, I would've killed me along with him. I don't kill me. I am here. Am I a car? A car you have to pull over to the side of the road and give a ticket to? You have to torture a certain number of people a day? Is this torture a routine formality? My boy is dead. I would like to grieve.

Life and Limb

Keith Reddin

Characters: Effie (20s), Franklin (20s)
Setting: Korea, New Jersey, Hell; 1952–56
Premiere: Playwrights Horizons, New York City, 1985
Publisher: Dramatists Play Service, Inc.

Franklin Clagg of Morristown, New Jersey, gets his wife Effie's name tattooed on his arm before he heads off to Korea, so "the other guys would see how much we're in love." The play's next scene finds him in an army hospital, recovering from the amputation of that arm. While hospitalized, he meets Tod, a sadistic teenage profiteer who will eventually claim Franklin's life. In this black-comic vision of selling one's soul to the devil, Hell is either a potholder factory, a Laundromat,

or a suburban supermarket. Here, Franklin is met by his wife
as he gets off the plane from Korea.

––––––––––––––––––––

(*Fort Dix Military Airfield. Fall 1953. A section of chain
wire fence and a sign indicating a military airfield. In the
darkness we hear the sound of a propellor transport plane.
It is very loud. The lights fade up on* FRANKLIN *in uniform,
his sleeve pinned to his jacket.* EFFIE *stands holding a box
of candy. She wears a stylish dress.*)

EFFIE: Hi Franklin!

FRANKLIN: Hi Effie!

EFFIE: You look good, Franklin.

FRANKLIN: Thanks. (*Pause.*)

EFFIE: Hey, I brought you some salt water taffy.

FRANKLIN: From Atlantic City?

EFFIE: You bet.

FRANKLIN: Nice. (*Pause.*)

EFFIE: They feed you enough in the hospital?

FRANKLIN: Why do you ask?

EFFIE: You look a little thin.

FRANKLIN: I lost some weight. The arm.

EFFIE: Stop.

FRANKLIN: That's probably why I look different.

EFFIE: I'm used to it already.

FRANKLIN: Hey, it's okay. (*Pause.*) They tell you it takes time.
To adjust. You lose a limb, this takes time to adjust. I talked
to some people.

EFFIE: Were they nice people?

FRANKLIN: They were okay. Mostly other guys who were
missing things, arms, legs, fingers. Some guys got it much
worse than me, you know.

EFFIE: Uh huh.

FRANKLIN: Some guys they're missing their . . . you know
what.

EFFIE: I'm sorry.

FRANKLIN: You step on a mine, blammo, it's gone.

EFFIE: I . . .

FRANKLIN: You can't ever get it back. (*Pause.*) Yeah, I talked to a lot of people.

EFFIE: You started combing your hair different.

FRANKLIN: I read in a magazine this is the new style.

EFFIE: I ain't seen that style yet.

FRANKLIN: Oh.

EFFIE: But I don't read magazines about combing hair.

FRANKLIN: Yeah, well this is how they do it now.

EFFIE: It's different.

FRANKLIN: You look the same.

EFFIE: You look older, Franklin.

FRANKLIN: I'm . . . you know my gums are acting up.

EFFIE: Your gums.

FRANKLIN: Something got . . . uh . . . messed up with, something you know happened to my gums over in Korea, and my teeth are loose and they hurt once in a while.

EFFIE: Doina and me, we seen this picture last week.

FRANKLIN: Really.

EFFIE: You're not gonna believe this, Franklin, this is something maybe you have not heard about, but this picture, it's exciting . . .

FRANKLIN: What?

EFFIE: This movie, it was in 3-D.

FRANKLIN: Huh?

EFFIE: This picture, it was like specially designed for three dimensional projection.

FRANKLIN: So?

EFFIE: So? So, well you watch this movie, see, and things they pop out at you, right out of the screen, they sorta come out at you, like real life, but it's a movie.

FRANKLIN: You and Doina seen this?

EFFIE: It was very wonderful and exciting, and we went twice in one week, over at the Plaza Theatre.

FRANKLIN: Twice.

EFFIE: This picture was called "Bwana Devil" and it starred Robert Stack and there was also Barbara Britton and Nigel

Bruce. You had to wear these special glasses. I brought one back for you. Here. (*She gives the glasses to* FRANKLIN. *He tries them on.*)

FRANKLIN: You look kinda green, Effie.

EFFIE: Oh, Franklin, jeez, this was something special. We're in deepest Africa, see, and these lions are killing all these guys working on the railroad. 'Til Robert Stack, see, he goes after them, and hunts them down, they had lions jumping out at you and everything.

FRANKLIN: Maybe we should go now. (*Pause.*)

EFFIE: Sure—

FRANKLIN: I feel like lying down for a while.

EFFIE: Okay. I'm sorry.

FRANKLIN: No.

EFFIE: You turn around and hundreds of people are wearing these cardboard glasses like you were on another planet, only it was the plain old Plaza Theatre.

FRANKLIN: Shut up.

EFFIE: I thought you'd want to know.

FRANKLIN: Stop talking.

EFFIE: I'm sorry, what did I do now?

FRANKLIN: Stop talking so stupid all the time, you truly embarrass me.

EFFIE: Franklin. . . .

FRANKLIN: Just got off the fucking plane and you're talking about some pissant movie and why am I still wearing these stupid glasses? (*He tears them off.*) What am I supposed to do now?

EFFIE: About what?

FRANKLIN: About working, getting a job, supporting us, making a goddam living.

EFFIE: You still okay, Franklin.

FRANKLIN: I'm not okay, I'm not, shit my mouth hurts. You make me mad. . . . (*He starts to cry.*) and I yell at you and my mouth hurts. I don't want to loose my teeth too, please Effie, don't let them pull my teeth. I've had these teeth since I was a kid. I need them, and my gums messed. . . .

EFFIE: It's okay, sssh. . . .

FRANKLIN: But.

EFFIE: Sssssssssh.

FRANKLIN: I can't eat the salt water taffy, don't you understand?

EFFIE: It's fine, Franklin, it's real good to have you back.

FRANKLIN: I'm fucking falling apart here.

EFFIE: You look good Franklin. You still got all your good parts. You're not missing any of that. (*Pause.*)

FRANKLIN: No.

EFFIE: Then it's okay. A lotta guys, hey, they're missing everything, many guys, they're dead, they have nothing.

FRANKLIN: That's right.

EFFIE: We're going home now, okay?

FRANKLIN: (*Wiping his eyes.*) Yeah.

EFFIE: Some people are over at the apartment want to say hello to you. Will you do that?

FRANKLIN: I don't want to see anybody.

EFFIE: They've been waiting all day to see you, why don't you say hello, you have a beer, you feel better.

FRANKLIN: Okay. A few beers.

EFFIE: Good.

FRANKLIN: We have a few beers, and they go. Then we can be alone. (*They start to walk off.*)

EFFIE: Sure.

(*Lights fade.*)

Mojo

Alice Childress

Characters: Teddy (40), Irene (mid-40s)

Setting: Teddy's apartment, New York City, fall 1969

Premiere: New Heritage Theatre, Harlem, New York City, 1970

Publisher: Dramatists Play Service, Inc.

Teddy, black and roughly good looking, is in the numbers business. He has a white girlfriend and says civil rights "don't make me no damn difference." He is about to head out of his apartment when his ex-wife shows up unexpectedly.

Irene is a lighter-skinned black woman, a little older than Teddy. Aside from her mink coat, her clothes are ordinary. She is neat but looks a bit thrown together. She and Teddy have not seen each other for a few months. Before Irene goes into the hospital, she has come to see her "buddy-boy."

———————————

TEDDY: (*Picks up the mink coat and strokes it. He is uneasy about her attitude.*) Mink . . . mink . . . alla this pretty mink. Go girl.

IRENE: Aw . . . ain't nothin but a animal's backside. They knock them in the head and slit their throat and sew em together. . . . Who the hell cares.

TEDDY: You the one bought it.

IRENE: I bought it off a junky. He was shiverin and shakin from head to toe . . . like at the North Pole . . . I gave him three hundred and fifty dollars. I ain't never enjoyed that coat . . . keep seein him shiverin and shakin . . . needin a fix.

TEDDY: Reenie, you didn't sell him the junk, you didn't make him take it.

IRENE: But I know he had to lift that to buy junk . . . had to boost it and sell it to me to keep his habit goin.

TEDDY: Well, damn, look what they did to the mink . . . knocked him in the head and slit his throat . . . and all like you say. That's life.

IRENE: You make me feel better. Don't go out.

TEDDY: You unreasonable, baby. I'd do anything in the world for you . . . you my buddy-girl, you know that. Ain't you my buddy-girl?

IRENE: No, I'm your wife. Well, anyway . . . your divorced wife. I'm the only wife you ever had.

TEDDY: (*Gets a dark trench coat from closet, examines it for*

*any stray piece of lint which might be found, of course it is
lintless.*) Why you wanta throw that in my face? I'm surprised
at you washin my face. You say . . . "I wanta be married . . . marry me." I married you . . . didn't see you no
more for a year and a half . . . then you pop up with some
paper . . . you want a divorce. I sign the paper. There's
somethin about a colored woman that makes her a self-willed,
non-understandable; but I been your buddy-boy through it
all. Now I'm gonna cut my little run down to a hour or forty-
five minutes . . . then I be right back. . . . (*He has one arm
in the coat.*)

IRENE: When I first met you . . . you wasn't nothin but a dinin
car waiter.

TEDDY: (*Pauses.*) Right.

IRENE: I taught you just about everything you know.

TEDDY: Just about, almost.

IRENE: I set you up in business . . . bought you a number
wheel . . . showed you where it was at . . . and I never asked
much in return. (*He now has the coat on.*) I say don't go
out . . . don't go out, dammit . . . I say that . . . don't go
out!

TEDDY: (*Sits down but still wears coat.*) I'm still here. Now
tell me what you was doin when I met you.

IRENE: I got a good memory. I was attendant in the ofay ladies
lounge . . . washin toilets, handin out toilet paper . . . A little saucer of change on the dressin table . . . a sign pasted
on the mirror . . . "*Ladies, your tips are my liveli-
hood.*" . . . "Towel, honey?" Pinnin up torn dress hems, wipin
up the floor behind sick drunks . . . laughin at their "Jew"
and "darky" jokes, wipin away their tears. Each one of em
tellin me how much they loved the colored woman who raised
em or cook the meals or whatever, tellin me how I must or
must not feel about the race problem . . . and how I must
not hate. . . . The same jokes, the same advice from one
damn rest room to another. Rest-room attendant!

TEDDY: Yeah, well . . . I'm not soundin on you . . . even though
you was the one soundin first. We been through some hard

days together. Reenie, all that you ever did for me . . . I tried to thank you. (*Looks at her suitcase.*)

IRENE: I'm gonna camp here for a couple of days.

TEDDY: Crazy. How is Philadelphia?

IRENE: That's one sad-ass city . . . bout to sink into the ground . . . but a little money is changin hands now and then. You don't come to see me like you used to.

TEDDY: Aw, you know, first one thing then another. (*Leans over the back of her chair and presses his cheek to hers.*) What you know? Sweet thing.

IRENE: Don't know. What you know, daddy? You good-lookin, two-timin, black, sweet-lovin-man, you.

TEDDY: Welcome home, it's been a long time.

IRENE: So good to hear the sounda your voice.

TEDDY: I've broken three dates with Berniece.

IRENE: What I care? Make it four . . . she'll forgive you. Call her and say somethin came up. If I ain't somethin', what is? I'm bein bad about it.

TEDDY: (*Unbuttons coat.*) I'm still here. You in some kinda trouble?

IRENE: Those damn doctors, what the hell they know. I gotta go in the hospital next Monday. . . . God knows what all they plannin, but I said to myself . . . I'm goin to see my buddy-boy first, no matter what.

TEDDY: Somethin serious? They say it's serious?

IRENE: Yes, serious, and don't make me name it . . . gives me the creeps.

TEDDY: Oh . . . well, you can't really know bout these things till you take alla the tests.

IRENE: I took the tests and they gave me the results . . . and it's serious. That's bout all I got to say on that.

TEDDY: Sweetheart, you know . . . they got all kindsa things goin on now with these operations and what you call . . . er, you call . . .

IRENE: Radiation.

TEDDY: That's right. Radiation.

IRENE: Radiation therapy. I know that. I'm not plannin to curl up and die. Much as I been through in life . . . live or die . . . this ain nothin.

TEDDY: There you go . . . everything's gonna end up happy . . . just like a Sidney Potenay movie.

IRENE: Makes you think . . . you get to summin up your whole life . . . that is, after your first feelings. I was shook . . . it shook me. I put up a good front . . . brave, strong and cool . . . but on the inside I was shook . . . it shook me. I recall goin in the bathroom . . . a place full of echoes . . . there I was feelin light-headed in the middle of nowhere . . . high up . . . lookin down on myself. That must be how it feels to be a mountain-climber, I'll bet. I leaned my head against the cold, tile wall . . . it was yellow tile . . . big, square, yellow tiles . . . and I cried out the fullness of my feeling . . . never cried like that before . . . never in this life. I got scared that I'd never stop . . . chokin and sobbin . . . and wonderin if I was chicken-hearted. Well, it seemed forever . . . but I stopped. They set the day for me to face the music . . . next Monday. I kept thinkin bout you and me and any unfinished business we might have. So I got on the highway and here I am.

TEDDY: (*Removing his coat.*) Thank you. I'm sure glad you thought about me. Glad you got here, too. This where you belong. We gonna see this through together . . . and everything's gonna end up a Sidney Potenay movie. To what hospital you goin?

IRENE: Back down in Philly. I'll write everything down for you.

TEDDY: Philly . . . that where you wanta be?

IRENE: Yes. It's all one anyway . . . no matter where. Stay with me.

TEDDY: (*Hanging up his things and hers.*) You couldn't chase me out. I wanta be here with you . . . I'm the one . . . it's you and me.

IRENE: You've always been good to me . . . most of the time . . . except for once or twice . . .

TEDDY: Reenie, why bring up the once or twice?

IRENE: You knocked me down once . . . and my eye was swole . . . I remember how you sapped me up somethin awful.

TEDDY: But why? Why would I do somethin like that? Think. What had you done?

IRENE: Not a thing . . . that I can recall. I shoulda hollered for the law and had you hauled off to jail . . . that's what.

TEDDY: You whipped on my girlfriend. You almost kill Sadie.

IRENE: Aw . . . she was just puttin on.

TEDDY: Aw, no she wasn't. You hit her with a chair leg. And for what? You didn't have no right to mess with that poor girl.

IRENE: She got on my nerves.

TEDDY: You and me wasn't together. You busted that up . . . yet you was always runnin down my women to pick a quarrel.

IRENE: Not all of em . . . just the ones I didn't like.

TEDDY: But who did you ever like? Name one.

IRENE: Mmmmmmmmmm, lemmie see. . . . You remember Sugar? I liked Sugar very much.

TEDDY: (*Looking in her empty glass.*) You liked Sugar cause she was homely.

IRENE: Maybe you right. . . . Now tell me why *you* liked her. Maybe her beauty was not to be seen.

TEDDY: (*With a proud, self-conscious grin.*) Aw, come on . . . cut it out. . . . S'matter with you! How bout the time you hit me in the head with the apple-juice bottle? . . . The blood runnin down and had to have stitches . . . look, look-a-there. (*Kneels and leans his head in her lap.*)

IRENE: Oh, the hair don't even grow there no more. (*She laughs.*) I almost knocked you into the next world.

TEDDY: You a mean, old bitch . . . just lookin at it gives you the jollies.

IRENE: You musta done somethin turble to aggravate me like that.

TEDDY: You done me awful.

IRENE: And you me.

TEDDY: You don't want another drink . . . do you?

IRENE: Yes, I do. Mix one and hand it to me.

TEDDY: Okay, whatcha want?

IRENE: Don't make me no difference. Drink is a drink.

TEDDY: (*As he makes a fresh drink.*) Reenie, why did you make me marry you?

IRENE: How could I make you? You was a full-grown man.

TEDDY: That was the craziest thing. Why?

IRENE: I had my reasons.

TEDDY: Was about seventeen years ago.

IRENE: Eighteen.

TEDDY: "Teddy," you said . . . "I want you to marry me cause every woman oughta be married one time." Two . . . three weeks of cuttin up, lovin and laughin, . . . then bam! You cut out on me. Looka here . . . still in the frame . . . damn postcard from Atlanta-damn-Georgia. . . . (*He looks at framed card over the bar.*)

IRENE: (*Reciting the message from memory.*) "Hey there, Teddy. Life is too short for you to be tied down . . . or me either. Forget it. . . . Love . . . Reenie."

TEDDY: One year later you come walkin in on me with a double order of barbecued ribs. I made you welcome . . . glad to see you. There we was sitting in the kitchen eatin our ribs, havin one ha-ha after another . . . and you say . . . "Teddy, I gotta take you to court and charge you with adultery cause it's proper for the man to be the guilty one."

IRENE: *That's* why I liked Sugar so much! She was so gracious bout helpin us out. Lord, yall looked funny when me and the witnesses knocked on the door. You had on a red-satin robe and she was in my black lace nightie . . . and the camera goin off . . . yall was too funny. I still got one-a them pictures somewhere. Look just like a Forty-second Street movie.

TEDDY: (*Hands her the drink.*) When last you been to a movie, baby?

IRENE: I really don't remember.

TEDDY: They don't wear clothes in Forty-second Street movies. And people no longer got to bust into bedrooms to get a divorce.

IRENE: The world turns . . . don't it?

TEDDY: "Let's get married, let's divorce." Why you do like that? Why?

IRENE: Teddy, did you ever love me?

TEDDY: You know it.

IRENE: Not that buddy-love. . . . (*Phone rings.* TEDDY *picks it up.*)

TEDDY: Uh-huh, yeah, you right. I certainly do apologize. Listen . . . I say *listen* . . . this is a *bad* time. The wrong day. Well, I got a fella here and we goin over some Philadelphia business, tryin to get somethin set up. No need to holler. Let's leave it that I'll call tomorrow and we make it definite. Aww, now, course I do. You know I do. Sure I do. Yeah, I know you do too. (*Smacks his lips to send a kiss.*)

IRENE: Mmmmmm . . . nothin makes him sick. (*Smacks her lips in imitation.*)

TEDDY: (*Hangs phone up.*) Aw, why you wanta act ugly? Now . . . what was we talkin about?

IRENE: Why did you marry me? You coulda said no.

TEDDY: I did it cause I thought that much of you. (*He opens drawers of a chest.*) Your things can go in here . . . plenty space. (*Opens the suitcase on a bench.*) If marryin meant somethin to you I was glad to oblige. That's the same way I felt bout that damn fool divorce business. It was somethin you wanted and I could give it to you. Woman, I think a whole lotta you.

IRENE: (*Suddenly solemn.*) Teddy, I want you to stay over there and keep unpackin that bag for me so I don't haveta look you in the face . . . and I want you to listen good . . . listen hard and let me say it all.

TEDDY: Right.

IRENE: The reason I asked you to be my husband was . . . I wanted to have a baby . . . and I wanted you for the father. . . . I didn't want the child to be outta wedlock . . . I didn't think it was too much any of your business . . . because you didn't seem to love me like I loved you. . . . I went on off and had the baby. . . . (*Dead silence for a few seconds.*)

TEDDY: I don't believe you.

IRENE: It's true. We got a daughter. Her name used to be Teddi . . . T-e-d-d-i. It was that for a few weeks.

TEDDY: What's her name now?

IRENE: I don't know.

TEDDY: Where is she?

IRENE: I . . . I don't know . . . truly I don't.

TEDDY: Why don't you know, Reenie?

IRENE: I got scared bout leavin her around here and there . . . I got to bein sorry that I brought a child here who might be like us . . . knocked about. The doctor saw how it was with my mind. . . .

TEDDY: Your mind?

IRENE: Felt like I was goin stone-crazy . . . no sleep . . . pacin the floor . . . up and down, down and up. Such a pretty baby. . . . I was afraid I might hurt her. . . . Rest-broken and pacin the floor and no way to turn. . . . I didn't want to hurt her.

TEDDY: You couldn't turn to me?

IRENE: No, somehow I couldn't. The doctor told me bout some folks who were well off . . . "Professional," he said. Maybe a lawyer or another doctor . . . or a teacher. I got to seein her in my mind's eye . . . livin nicely and havin a pretty home and a mama and a papa . . . and bein proud of em. . . . Out of it, Teddy! free as black can be, free to get in some school, and live right. So I signed the papers and turned her over.

TEDDY: To who?

IRENE: They don't like you to know cause you might turn up and make trouble. They don't tell.

TEDDY: I'm sorry. We got a very sad story. Everytime I see you . . . you be laughin and pokin fun at yourself . . . always makin fun of yourself . . .

IRENE: Just trying to beat the next fella to it. If you laugh at yourself. . . . Well, that's how it was.

TEDDY: Is this her picture: (*Takes a framed picture out of case.*)

IRENE: No. That's a baby picture of one of Martin Luther King's children. I cut it outta the *Ebony* magazine . . . and framed it. . . . Just cause it's cute.

TEDDY: Sorry . . . sorry to my heart. I'm sorry.

IRENE: I had to come and tell you, Teddy. . . . As hurtful as it is . . . it's your business . . . ain't nobody got the right to keep your business from you . . . even if it's painful.

TEDDY: You right. At least it put your mind . . . at rest.

IRENE: Oh, dear heart . . . it ain't that easy. Instead of one child . . . I had thousands. When she was two . . . I looked at every two-year-old I passed. . . . "Is that her . . . this one . . . that one?" When she was five . . . "There's one look just like Teddy." Years of lookin at strange, raggedy-ass children runnin round the streets . . . "That her?" Gets worse as the years pass. . . . Now I look at some baby-face hooker standin on the corner with her mouth fulla that tough talk . . . "Come on home with me, baby." I stand there wonderin . . . "Is that my daugher?" The hooker see me starin and say . . . "What you lookin at, bitch?"

TEDDY: (*Trying to believe.*) That wasn't her. She's with some lawyer or school teacher. That's what . . . a civil rights lawyer and his wife.

IRENE: (*Unpacking as he fixes drink for himself.*) I loved you so much, Teddy. I came here to let you know that much. I'm sorry I wasn't able to say it before. When we were around each other . . . it was all fightin and pokin fun . . . mockin ourselves. I believe niggers think it's disgraceful to love one another . . . fightin like hell to cover up what's in the heart. My daddy once said to mama . . . "Sheeeeet . . . what's love, what's that? Better git yourself some money." Sayin them things right in fronta me. I'm tryin to eat the little bitta grits and bacon and make out that I don't hear what I'm hearin. She say . . . "Nigger, get the hell out." He slam the door and gone. She sit down and cry . . . then look at me and say . . . "Gal, you a mill-stone round my neck." Ain't like no Teevee story with us. . . . Love is hard to live round when a woman is washin out her last raggy pair-a drawers . . . and her man ain't got a quarter to put in her hand. When it's like that it's embarrassin to love each other. . . . If you stop laughin at yourself for too long a time . . . they'll have to put you way in a strait-jacket. I passed through this world . . . and for what? I don't even know who I am.

Open Admissions

Shirley Lauro

Characters: Calvin Jefferson (18), Professor Alice Miller (late 30s)

Setting: A cubicle speech office at a city college in New York, late fall, 6:00 P.M.

Premiere: Ensemble Studio Theatre, New York City, 1981

Publisher: Samuel French, Inc. (one-act version)

Calvin is a freshman in the open admissions program at the college. He is black, powerfully built, handsome. He uses "street speech" jargon. He knows this program is supposed to be his big chance, but finds "nothing is happenin to me in my head except I am gettin more and more confused about what I knows and what I don't know." He refuses to accept his "B" grade and insists Alice sit down and teach him.

Alice is a speech communications professor. She intended to be a Shakespearean scholar, but has landed at a city college where she has been teaching for twelve years. She is overloaded with work, exhausted, and right now wants to go home.

In describing *Open Admissions*, Shirley Lauro writes, "The play begins on a very high level of tension and intensity and builds from there. . . . The high level of tension is set by both Alice and Calvin and occurs from the moment Calvin enters. . . . Alice does not want the scene to take place. The audience's experience from the start should be as if they had suddenly tuned in on the critical round of a boxing match."

Note: Open Admissions was originally produced Off Broadway as a one-act. It was later expanded into a full-length play for Broadway. This scene is from the one-act version.

ALICE: It's "last," not "lass"; "first," not "firss." That's your friend, that good old "Final T"! Here *it* when I talk?

CALVIN: Sometimes. When you say *it*, hitti*n* i*t* like tha*t*!

ALICE: Well, you should be going over the exercises on it in the speech book all the time, and recording yourself on your tape recorder. (*She pats book sack.*)

CALVIN: I don't got no tape recorder.

ALICE: Well, borrow one! (*She turns away.*)

CALVIN: (*Crosses in back of* ALICE *to her right.*) On that Shakespeare scene I jiss did? Thass why I got a "B"? Because of the "Final T's"?

ALICE: (*Backs downstage a step.*) Well, you haven't improved your syndrome, have you?

CALVIN: How come you keep on answerin me by axin me somethin else?

ALICE: And that's the other one.

CALVIN: What "other one?"

ALICE: Other most prevalent deviation. You said: "axing" me something else.

CALVIN: Thass right. How come you keep axin me somethin else?

ALICE: "Asking me" Calvin, "asking me"!

CALVIN: I jiss did!

ALICE: No, no. Look. That's classic Substandard Black! Textbook case. (*She puts purse and booksack down and crosses to diagram on blackboard.*) See, the jaw and teeth are in two different positions for the two sounds, and they make two completely different words! (*She writes "ass-king," and "axing" on the blackboard, pronouncing them in an exaggerated way for him to see.*) "Ass-king" and "ax-ing." I am "ass-king" you the question. But, the woodcutter is "ax-ing" down the tree. Can't you hear the difference? (*She picks up his speech book from desk.*) Here.

(CALVIN *follows her to desk.*)

ALICE: Go over to page 105. It's called a "Sharp S" problem with a medial position "sk" substitution. See? "skin, screw, scream"—those are "sk" sounds in the Primary Position. "Asking, risking, frisking—that's medial position. And "flask, task, mask"—that's final position. Now you should be working on those, Calvin. Reading those exercises over and over again. I mean the way you did the Othello scene was just ludicrous: "Good gentlemen, I *ax* thee—" (*She crosses to the board and points to "ax-ing." She chuckles.*) That meant Othello was chopping the gentlemen down!

CALVIN: How come I had to do the Othello scene anyhow? Didn git any choice. An Franklin Perkins an Sam Brown an Lester Washington they had to too.

ALICE: What do you mean?

CALVIN: An Claudette Jackson an Doreen Simpson an Melba Jones got themselves assigned to Cleopatra on the Nile?

ALICE: Everyone was assigned!

CALVIN: Uh-huh. But everybody else had a choice, you know what I mean? That Judy Horowitz, she said you told her she could pick outa five, six different characters. And that boy did his yesterday? That Nick Rizoli? Did the Gravedigger? He said he got three, four to choose off of too.

ALICE: (*Crosses to* CALVIN.) Well some of the students were "right" for several characters. And you know, Calvin, how we talked in class about Stanislavsky and the importance of "identifying" and "feeling" the part?

CALVIN: Well how Doreen Simpson "identify" herself some Queen sittin on a barge? How I supposed to "identify" some Othello? I don't!

ALICE: (*Crosses to blackboard, picks up fallen chalk.*) Oh, Calvin, don't be silly.

CALVIN: (*Crosses center.*) Well, I don'! I'm not no kind a jealous husband. I haven' got no wife. I don' even got no girlfriend, hardly! And thass what it's all about ain't it? So what's it I'm supposed to "identify" with anyhow?

ALICE: (*Turns to* CALVIN.) Oh, Calvin, what are you arguing about? You did a good job!

CALVIN: "B" job, right?

ALICE: Yes.

CALVIN: (*Crosses to* ALICE.) Well, what's that "B" standin for? Cause I'll tell you somethin you wanna know the truth: I stood up there didn' hardly know the sense a anythin I read, couldn't hardly even read it at all. Only you didn't notice. Wasn't even listenin, sittin there back a the room jiss thumbin through your book.

　(ALICE *crosses to desk.*)

CALVIN: So you know what I done? Skip one whole paragraph, tess you out—you jiss kep thumbin through your book! An then you give me a "B"! (*He has followed* ALICE *to desk.*)

ALICE: (*Puts papers in box and throws out old coffee cup.*) Well that just shows how well you did the part!

CALVIN: You wanna give me somethin I could "identify" with, how come you ain' let me do that other dude in the play . . .

ALICE: Iago?

CALVIN: Yeah. What is it they calls him? Othello's . . .

ALICE: Subordinate.

CALVIN: Go right along there with my speech syndrome, wouldn' it now? See, Iago has to work for the Man. I identifies with him! He gits jealous man. Know what I mean? Or that Gravedigger? Shovelin dirt for his day's work! How come you wouldn't let me do him? Thass the question I wanna ax you!

ALICE: (*Turns to* CALVIN.) "Ask me," Calvin. "Ask me!"

CALVIN: (*Steps stage right*) "Ax you?" Okay, man. (*Turns to* ALICE.) Miss Shakespeare, Speech Communications 1! (*Crosses upstage of* ALICE.) Know what I'll "ax" you right here in this room, this day, at this here desk right now? I'll "ax" you how come I have been in this here college three months on this here Open Admissions an I don't know nothin more than when I came in here? You know what I mean? This supposed to be some big break for me. This here is where all them smart Jewish boys has gone from the Bronx Science and went an become some Big Time Doctors at Bellevue. An some Big Time Judges in the Family Court an like that there. And now it's supposed to be my turn.

(ALICE *looks away and* CALVIN *crosses right of* ALICE.)

CALVIN: You know what I mean? (*He crosses up right.*) An my sister Jonelle took me out of foster care where I been in six homes and five schools to give me my chance. (*He crosses down right.*) Livin with her an she workin three shifts in some "Ladies Restroom" give me my opportunity. An she say she gonna buss her ass git me this education I don't end up on the streets! (*Crosses on a diagonal to* ALICE.) Cause I have got *brains*!

(ALICE *sits in student chair.* CALVIN *crosses in back, to her left.*)

CALVIN: You understand what I am communicatin to you? My high school has tole me I got brains an can make somethin outta my life if I gits me the chance! And now this here's supposed to be my chance! High school says you folks gonna bring me up to date on my education and git me even. Only nothin is happenin to me in my head except I am getting more and more confused about what I knows and what I don't know! (*He sits in swivel chair.*) So what I wanna "ax" you is: How come you don't sit down with me and teach me which way to git my ideas down instead of givin me a "B."

(ALICE *rises and crosses up right.*)

CALVIN: I don't even turn no outline in? Jiss give me a "B." (*He rises and crosses right of* ALICE.) An Lester a "B"! An Melba a "B"! An Sam a "B"! What's that "B" standin for anyhow? Cause it surely ain't standin for no piece of work!

ALICE: Calvin, don't blame me!

(CALVIN *crosses down right.*)

ALICE: I'm trying! God knows I'm trying! The times are rough for everyone. I'm a Shakespearean scholar, and they have me teaching beginning Speech. I was supposed to have twelve graduate students a class, nine classes a week, and they gave me thirty-five freshmen a class, twenty classes a week. I hear 157 speeches a week! You know what that's like? And I go home late on the subway scared to death! In graduate school they told me I'd have a first-rate career. Then I started here and they said: "Hang on! Things will improve!" But they only got worse . . . and worse! Now I've been here for twelve years and I haven't written one word in my field! I haven't read five research books! I'm exhausted . . . and I'm finished! We all have to bend. I'm just hanging on now . . . supporting my little girl . . . earning a living . . . and that's all . . . (*She crosses to desk.*)

CALVIN: (*Faces* ALICE.) What I'm supposed to do, feel sorry for you? Least you can *earn* a livin! Clean office, private phone, name on the door with all them B.A.'s, M.A.'s, Ph.D.'s.

ALICE: You can have those too. (*She crosses down right to* CALVIN.) Look, last year we got ten black students into Ivy League graduate programs. And they were no better than you. They were just *perceived* (*Points to blackboard.*) as better. Now that's the whole key for you . . . to be perceived as better! So you can get good recommendations and do well on interviews. You're good looking and ambitious and you have a fine native intelligence. You can make it, Calvin. All we have to do is work on improving your Positive Communicator's Image . . . by getting rid of that Street Speech. Don't you see?

CALVIN: See what? What you axin *me* to see?

ALICE: "*Asking*" me to see, Calvin. "*Asking*" me to see!

CALVIN: (*Starts out of control at this, enraged, crosses U.S. and bangs on file cabinet.*) Ooooeee! Ooooeee! You wanna *see*? You wanna *see*? Ooooeee!

ALICE: Calvin stop it! STOP IT!

CALVIN: "Calvin stop it"? "Stop it"? (*Picks up school books from desk.*) There any black professors here?

ALICE: (*Crosses up right.*) No! They got cut . . . the budget's low . . . they got . . .

CALVIN: (*Interrupting.*) Cut? They got CUT? (*Crosses to* ALICE *and backs her to the downstage edge of desk.*) Gonna *cut you*, lady! Gonna cut you, throw you out the fuckin window, throw the fuckin books out the fuckin window, burn it all mother fuckin down. FUCKIN DOWN!!!

ALICE: Calvin! Stop it! STOP IT! YOU HEAR ME?

CALVIN: (*Turns away, center stage.*) I CAN'T!! *YOU* HEAR *ME*? I CAN'T! *YOU* HEAR *ME*! I CAN'T! YOU GOTTA

GIVE ME MY EDUCATION! GOTTA TEACH ME! GIVE
ME SOMETHING NOW! GIVE ME NOW! NOW! NOW!
NOW! NOW! NOW!

(CALVIN *tears up text book. He starts to pick up torn pages
and drops them. He bursts into a wailing, bellowing cry in
his anguish and despair, doubled over in pain and grief.
It is a while before his sobs subside. Finally,* ALICE *speaks.*)

ALICE: Calvin . . . from the bottom of my heart . . . I want
to help you . . .

CALVIN: (*Barely able to speak.*) By changin my words? Thass
nothin . . . nothin! I got to know them big ideas . . . and
which way to git em down . . .

ALICE: But how can I teach you that? You can't write a paragraph, Calvin . . . or a sentence . . . you can't spell past
fourth grade . . . the essay you wrote showed that . . .

CALVIN: (*Rises.*) What essay?

ALICE: (*Crosses to up left files, gets essay and hands it to
CALVIN.*) The autobiographical one . . . you did it the first
day . . .

CALVIN: You said that was for *your* reference . . . didn't
count . . .

ALICE: Here . . .

CALVIN: (*Opens it up. Stunned.*) "F"? Why didn't you tell me
I failed?

ALICE: (*Crosses to desk, puts essay down.*) For what?

CALVIN: (*Still stunned.*) So you could teach me how to write.

ALICE: (*Crosses down left.*) In sixteen weeks?

CALVIN: (*Still can't believe this.*) You my teacher!

ALICE: That would take years! And speech is my job. You need
a tutor.

CALVIN: I'm your job. They outa tutors!

ALICE: (*Turns to him.*) I can't do it, Calvin. And that's the
real truth. I'm one person, in one job. And I can't. Do you
understand? And even if I could, it wouldn't matter. All that
matters is the budget . . . and the curriculum . . . and the
grades . . . and how you look . . . and how you talk!

CALVIN: (*Pause. Absorbing this.*) Then I'm finished, man.

(*There is a long pause. Finally:*)

ALICE: (*Gets essay from desk, refiles it and returns to desk.*) No, you're not. If you'll bend and take what I can give you, things will work out for you . . . Trust me . . . Let me help you, Calvin . . . Please . . . I can teach you speech . . .

CALVIN: (*Crosses to up center file cabinet. Long pause.*) Okay . . . all right, man . . . (*Crosses to student chair and sits.*)

ALICE: (*Crosses to desk, takes off raincoat and sits in swivel chair.*) Now, then, we'll go through the exercise once, then you do it at home . . . please, repeat after me, slowly . . . "asking" . . . "asking" . . . "asking"

CALVIN: (*Long pause.*) Ax-ing . . .

ALICE: Ass-king . . .

CALVIN: (*During the following, he now turns from* ALICE, *faces front, and gazes out beyond the audience; on his fourth word, lights begin to fade to black.*) Ax-ing . . . Aks-ing . . . ass-king . . . asking . . . asking . . . asking . . .

Out of Gas on Lovers Leap

Mark St. Germain

Characters: Myst (17), Grouper (17)

Setting: A yellow convertible parked on a promontory overlooking the New England town of Grosset Bay

Premiere: WPA Theatre, New York City, 1985

Publisher: Dramatists Play Service, Inc.

Mystery Angeleeds and Chauncey "Grouper" Morris have just graduated from White Oaks Academy, an exclusive boarding school for students with behavioral disorders. Myst is the illegitimate daughter of rock star Snow Angeleeds. Grouper is the son of Senator Clifford Morris. Instead of attending their classmates' graduation party, they have driven out to a clifftop lookout. They are best friends, and Myst has the hots for the virginal Grouper, who claims he is waiting for it to be "historic." Later tonight, they will sleep together for the first time. And they will jump off the cliff.

MYST: You think we should go to Whorrie Laurie's party tonight?

GROUPER: You want to?

MYST: I don't know. It is our graduation.

GROUPER: That's right. Now we start real life.

MYST: You sound so nasty when you say that.

GROUPER: When do we leave for Seaside?

MYST: We don't necessarily have to go to Seaside just to live by the ocean, you know.

GROUPER: What do you mean?

MYST: I'm sure my mother would give us her house at Malibu—

GROUPER: Bite your tongue!

MYST: Why?

GROUPER: First of all, it's not even the same ocean. The Pacific Ocean's for pussies.

MYST: You're crazy.

GROUPER: It is *far* more mellow than the Atlantic.

MYST: Ocean is ocean.

GROUPER: Can you imagine *rides* on the beach at Malibu? Can you picture roller coasters and whips and haunted houses—

MYST: Whips and haunted houses, maybe—

GROUPER: Does the Polar Bear club come out in sub-zero temperature in bathing suits to swim every New Year's Day at Malibu? Shit, if it ever got really cold out there they'd close the state. How can you even mention Seaside Heights and Malibu in the same breath? Seaside Heights is *real*. It's for real people, regular working people. The only thing you work for in Malibu is a tan—

MYST: (*Cutting him off.*) I was at the Malibu house this Christmas.

GROUPER: (*Stopped.*) So?

MYST: My mom, old Leather Stocking, had a Christmas party and invited everybody from the record company, and got stoned to oblivion because a couple of the biggies didn't show. She's not imaginative enough to think they might have families or people they actually liked who they'd rather see that day. Christ, I felt sorry for anybody who had to spend Christmas with us. She sat around petting my hair whenever I got close enough, saying to all these guys, "This is my little girl, would you believe it? This is Mystery." And meanwhile, these guys are eyeing the both of us trying to decide whose bones to jump—

GROUPER: I know whose I would—

MYST: Then jump.

GROUPER: I will.

MYST: I'm waiting.

GROUPER: Have you ever done it in a Ferris wheel? The largest Ferris wheel on the East Coast, on a pier right in the middle of the ocean? They'd stop the thing and look up and see the seat on the top rocking back and forth. That would be a first, even for you.

MYST: My mom bought me a doll for Christmas. One of these antique dolls that cost half a Porsche—

GROUPER: Why do I get the impression I'm talking to myself?

MYST: She watched me unwrap it; she was jumping up and down like she was ten years old and I said, "Snow"—because God knows I can't call the woman "Mother" in front of company, "Snow, I think you need this more than I do."

GROUPER: (*Imitating radio transmission.*) This is Earth calling Angeleeds—Earth calling Angeleeds—come in please—

MYST: Funny—

GROUPER: (*Excited.*) I'm getting contact—a transmission from somewhere past Saturn—

MYST: Grouper!

GROUPER: (*Looking at her.*) Success! You *can* hear, you *can* listen. (*He grabs her.*) Then listen harder. (*Pause.*) I love you. More than I ever loved anybody. More than anybody's ever loved anybody. Because I'm totally sure we can be happy together 'till we both die. (*Pause.*) That's it, then. We live together, get married, or I jump off this cliff tonight. Your choice.

MYST: Don't your parents expect you home for the summer.

GROUPER: Probably. They always expect the worst. So?

MYST: (*Pause.*) My mom was talking about maybe going to France for a while.

GROUPER: (*Pause.*) France?

MYST: Yeah; you know—the Eiffel Tower and drinking on the street?

GROUPER: She's taking you?

MYST: I didn't say I'd go . . .

GROUPER: You'd rather spend the summer with her.

MYST: Of course not! (*Pause.*) But even you have to admit there's a difference between Paris and Seaside Heights.

GROUPER: (*Ice cold.*) Get in the car.

MYST: Where are we going?

GROUPER: *We* are going nowhere, that's where we're going.

MYST: Grouper—are you driving over the edge?

GROUPER: You'll wish. I'm dropping you at Whorrie Laurie's party. (*Tries to start car, it won't turn over.*) Maybe you'll get lucky if somebody's looking for seconds.

MYST: Oh come on. Stop. This is our night.

GROUPER: Call your mother. Tell her to fly over early *if* you can reach her.

MYST: Did I say I'd go? I never said that.

GROUPER: You thought about it.

MYST: What if I did? What's wrong with that?

GROUPER: If you don't know there's nothing I can tell you. (*Tries car again; only a click is heard.*) Goddamn it!

MYST: You want me to look under the hood?

GROUPER: Watch it, Myst—

MYST: Watch what?

GROUPER: DON'T START YOUR MECHANICAL SUPE-RIORITY SHIT AGAIN!!

MYST: Grouper, my mother lived with a race car driver! I had to pick up something.

GROUPER: I bet you did.

MYST: Funny.

GROUPER: Your mom lived with everybody. And if she didn't like 'em enough to live with, she just fucked them.

MYST: Hey—beef up those memoirs, right?

GROUPER: I'm not kidding around, Myst. (*Car is not turning over.*) SHIT!

MYST: *You* always want to hear who her latest is. You *subscribe* to *People*, for Godsake. (*Begins to get out of car.*) Let me take a look—

GROUPER: Stay in the car!

MYST: But you don't know anything about motors!

GROUPER: STAY IN THE CAR! (*Gets out, tries to open hood and can't. Myst reaches down in car, releases hood lock. Hood pops open. He looks at her, then away, leaning over the engine.*) Goddamn piece of Italian shit. (*Screams over cliff's edge.*) This is it! I'm going Jap next time!

MYST: (*Watches him.*) You want me to try to turn it over? (*He looks at her.*) The motor. You watch down there, I'll crank it up here.

GROUPER: (*Grudging.*) All right. (MYST *tries again. Nothing.* GROUPER *kicks the bumper a few more times, looks back in.*) Try again. (*She does; nothing.* GROUPER *screams into the engine.*) WHAT'S WRONG WITH YOU?

MYST: (*Looking at dashboard.*) Ah, Grouper—

GROUPER: I'm concentrating! (*He hits spark plugs with beer can.*) Why do I bother wasting good money on gas?

MYST: If you took that car your father wanted to give you—

GROUPER: Did I ask your opinion about anything?

MYST: I thought guys were supposed to like cars.

GROUPER: Sexist bullshit. Guys with metal between their ears like cars. I *hate* this car.

MYST: You hate every car.

GROUPER: True. I wish I were born two hundred years ago. I swear. How many times did you read about horses having heart attacks on people.

MYST: (*Looking back at dashboard.*) Grouper—

GROUPER: I'm trying to fix it! Would you turn it goddamn over, please?

MYST: Were any of these indicators broken?

GROUPER: No! Of course not! (*Pause.*) What do you mean, "Indicators"?

MYST: The gauges—the dials on the dashboard.

GROUPER: They work fine. Would you turn the key now—

MYST: Group—

GROUPER: MYST! JUST GIVE THE FUCKER GAS, WILL YOU?

MYST: I can't.

GROUPER: WHY NOT?

MYST: You're out of gas.

GROUPER: Huh?

MYST: THERE'S NO FUCKING GAS!

GROUPER: (*Slams hood, wipes off hands.*) Fixed. (*Gets in car.*) Now what is all this shit about France?

MYST: My mom wants me to go. But I said . . .

GROUPER: (*Cutting in.*) Let's get this straight, Myst. Right now, okay? Real straight. . . .

MYST: (*Turns away.*) I'll walk back to town for gas—

GROUPER: Didn't you hear what I said before? What's the matter with you?

MYST: Nothing's the matter with me. Why don't you get real? Have a beer or a joint—get control of yourself.

GROUPER: I just asked you to marry me! That was a proposal!

MYST: I don't want to hear it. So I didn't listen.

GROUPER: I knew it!

MYST: I don't want to deal with it right now, okay? Can't I just enjoy my fucking graduation night?

GROUPER: I'm talking the rest of our lives and you're worried about your fucking graduation night?

MYST: (*Angry.*) Couldn't you have just bought me a corsage or something? You kill me, Grouper.

GROUPER: Don't you love me?

MYST: Grouper; we're young. We are. I mean, how can you

want to get so serious when neither of us ever even had a *job* yet?

GROUPER: I love you, Myst. More than anyone in the whole world. More than anyone in the whole school. (GROUPER *climbs over windshield to hood.*)

MYST: Grouper—what are you doing?

GROUPER: (*Walks slowly down hood towards guardrail.*) Remember me, okay? (*Turns, bounces on hood as if diving board, readying himself.*)

MYST: (*Terrorized.*) Don't—Grouper—GROUPER! (GROUPER *leaps, jumping off sideways so that he lands safely on the ground.*) Grouper—You asshole! How dare you do that to me! You stupid bastard!

GROUPER: I'm sorry, Myst. I'm sorry—

MYST: (*Punches him.*) YOU SON OF A BITCH! YOU SHITTY SON OF A BITCH SCUM!!

GROUPER: (*Holding her arms.*) I know—I know—but how did it feel?

MYST: Let go of me!

GROUPER: How did it feel when you thought I was jumping?

MYST: I was scared! I hated you. I missed you. (*She pulls free.*) This is to get back at me for Christmas, isn't it?

GROUPER: No—not at all—

MYST: Damn right it is. For me going away and leaving you here—

GROUPER: That has nothing to do with it—

MYST: (*Getting more and more upset.*) I tried to call! Every day I did! I called your house, and they never told me a thing—I never knew 'till I got back here . . .

GROUPER: I know that.

MYST: Grouper, you cannot do this to me. You can't love me this much! I can't handle it!

GROUPER: I can't help it, Myst. I swear to God.

MYST: Oh Grouper. You don't believe in God. (*Hugs him.*)

GROUPER: That's not my fault.

MYST: You are the worst thing that ever happened to me.

GROUPER: I wish I didn't care about you, Myst. I really do. I wish I could spit in your face and never see you again.

MYST: Get in the car. (*They do, arms around each other.*) Kiss me. (*He does.*)

GROUPER: To me it's all simple. I see my parents and they're fucked up. I see your mother and she's fucked up. Everybody I know who's gone after things like money and magazine covers all get fucked up. You don't *need* that. All I want is one little thing, Myst. I want to be happy.

MYST: That's not a little thing, Grouper.

GROUPER: You know what my father told me six thousand, seven hundred and fifty-two times? The only intelligent thing the guy ever said, so he said it a lot. He'd say, "Chauncey—"

MYST: (*Cutting in.*) "Chauncey." Christ!

GROUPER: "There's only one way to get what you want in this world. Go after it with your life. Live for it. Be ready to die for it." And he's right. Even though *he's* so dumb he's wasting *his* life as a third-rate handshaker who's not even sneaky enough to make it to Vice-President.

MYST: Grouper, everybody wants to be happy. Everybody tries to be—

GROUPER: But they don't work at it, Myst. They get sidetracked. I'm working on it; I'm planning for it. We work for just enough money to live on, right, and if one of us works in a restaurant we can even cut down on food costs. We'll lay on the beach all summer and relax—no pressures, no problems. We'll take long walks, there's miles of beach, and if we walk south there's a park, Island Beach State Park, and there's a bird sanctuary. We can go there if we feel like getting away—just the two of us.

MYST: And if *we* have any kind of problem, one of the two of us, what then? Go down to the beach and bitch to the birds?

GROUPER: We talk to each other.

MYST: Talk. Just like that, right? Work it out calmly and rationally. Like you did at Christmas—

GROUPER: I thought you didn't love me and nothing was worth it anymore—

MYST: So you'd stick it to me *and* your father, one shot, right?

GROUPER: My father?

MYST: Ripping up your state flag and tying pieces of it together to hang yourself with—

GROUPER: You know I don't wear belts—

MYST: You walked all the way 'cross campus to the gym! You could have borrowed a belt from somebody—

GROUPER: There was nobody on campus! Everybody was on vacation. I had to break into the gym. Let's not start in on it, okay?

MYST: No; it's not okay. I should listen to a guided tour for happiness from a guy who strung himself up from a basketball hoop? Why would you hang yourself from a baseketball hoop?

GROUPER: Myst—

MYST: You could have swallowed pills or sat in the car with the motor running—

GROUPER: This is a convertible!

MYST: Then why the gym? Why not your room or a tree or something? Why pick the gym to hang yourself in?

GROUPER: I don't know. (*Pause.*) It seemed kind of . . . athletic.

MYST: Bullshit. Tell me why. If you love me, Grouper, tell me why.

GROUPER: (*Pause.*) I wanted to get the scoreboard lit up, you know how they do it at the games? But I couldn't get the power on. I wanted it to say "Visitors 1, Home Team, Zip."

MYST: (*Laughs; he laughs with her.*) What did your parents say when Percy called them?

GROUPER: They didn't know much at first. Percy called them Christmas Eve. Told my dad, "Chauncey had a bit of an accident on the basketball court today . . ."

MYST: (*Laughing.*) He said that?

GROUPER: (*Continuing as Percy.*) "I'm afraid the boy missed the basket, Senator. Landed on his head, he did. Is there anyone you could send up to keep an eye on him?"

MYST: Who came?

GROUPER: Nobody. I told them to stay away. And they did.

MYST: It must have been horrible being in the infirmary on Christmas.

GROUPER: Better than being home.

Progress

Doug Lucie

Characters: Ange (20), Lenny (21)
Setting: Ronee and Will's apartment in London
Premiere: Bush Theatre, London, 1984
Publisher: Methuen, Inc.

Ange, a young working-class woman, leaves her husband after he beats her. She is shy, somewhat reserved, though she also has a tough streak. Ange's husband, Lenny, is an inarticulate car mechanic with "animal cunning and an evil sense of humor." Unannounced, he shows up where she is staying, at the home of an upper-class social worker.

ANGE: Dunno.

LENNY: What d'you mean? Dunno?

ANGE: I mean, I dunno.

LENNY: Don't be stupid. Either you like it or you don't.

ANGE: I like it.

LENNY: Good. (*Pause.*) How come I don't get a cup of tea?

ANGE: 'Cause you ain't staying.

LENNY: Says who?

ANGE: I do.

(*He takes a packet of sandwiches out of his overalls pocket.*)

LENNY: I've got to have something to wash me dinner down.

ANGE: What d'you think you're doing?

LENNY: It's me dinner. This is me dinner hour so I'm gonna have me dinner.

ANGE: Not here you ain't.

(*He stuffs a sandwich in his mouth.*)

LENNY: Bleedin' well am.

ANGE: You horrible pig. (*Beat.*) Who made them, then?

LENNY: Me mum. (*Beat.*) Egg and cress. Lovely.

ANGE: You don't like egg.

LENNY: I do the way me mum does it.

ANGE: You can't do nothing with egg, 'cept boil it.

LENNY: She mashes it up. With salad cream. Tasty.

ANGE: Get food poisoning if your mum made it.

LENNY: Dead tasty.

> (*He eats. She goes to the kitchen. He looks round the room. He picks up the* Spare Rib *and reads it. She comes back in with a cup of tea.*)

What the fucking hell d'you call this?

> (*She snatches it off him.*)

ANGE: I call it a magazine. What d'you call it?

LENNY: Pile o'crap, I call it.

ANGE: It's nothing to do with you.

LENNY: Load o' bollocks. (*Pause.*) Here, Dink and Wobbler had a scrap last night. Down the Duke. Dink bust his finger. (*Beat.*) Pretty good scrap, they reckon.

> (*Pause.*)

ANGE: Kids.

LENNY: Eh?

ANGE: Nothing.

LENNY: What?!

ANGE: Kids! You are. Bloody scraps. Bloody stupid nicknames. You're supposed to grow outa that sorta thing when you leave school, y'know.

> (*Pause.*)

LENNY: They're *my* mates.

ANGE: You can have them.

> (*Pause.*)

LENNY: Right. When you coming back?

ANGE: You what?

LENNY: I got the motor outside. You can dump your gear in it now if you like. Don't matter if I'm a bit late back. (*Pause.*) You ain't making a lot of noise here, doll. (*Pause.*) C'mon. You've usually got enough rabbit for both of us.

ANGE: 'S not true. I can't say nothing, case you don't like it.

LENNY: Only when you're talking crap.

ANGE: Yeah. Which is most of the time, according to you.

LENNY: Well, you ain't exactly Mastermind, are you?

ANGE: Which university did you go to, then?

(*Beat.*)

LENNY: I asked you a question. When you coming back?

ANGE: Dunno.

LENNY: Don't know fuck all, you. (*Pause.*) Listen, I ain't got time to muck about. Get your stuff. (*Beat.*) C'mon.

ANGE: I ain't going nowhere. Not yet.

(*Beat.*)

LENNY: Ange. 'Case you've forgotten, you're my wife.

ANGE: 'Case you've forgotten, I ain't a punch-bag.

LENNY: You're my wife.

ANGE: Makes it all right, does it?

LENNY: You ain't s'posed to piss off every time we have a bit of a barney.

ANGE: What *am* I s'posed to do?

(*Beat.*)

LENNY: What other women do.

ANGE: What, like Rose?

LENNY: Like Rose what?

ANGE: Your rotten brother breaks her nose and won't even let her go to the hospital, 'case the Old Bill do him for it. I ain't standing for nothing like that.

LENNY: When'd I ever break your nose?

ANGE: Had a bloody good try.

LENNY: 'S just a little tap. Anyway, you hit me.

ANGE: You hit me first.

(*Pause.*)

LENNY: Look . . . I won't. All right? I won't hit you again.

ANGE: Pigs might fly.

LENNY: I won't. (*Beat.*) I never knew you was gonna leave, did I? Wouldn't have hit you if I did.

ANGE: What do you expect me to do? (*Pause.*) Eh?

LENNY: I dunno. (*Pause.*) Me mum never left me dad when he hit her.

ANGE: I ain't your mum. And I ain't gonna end up like her, neither.

LENNY: What do you mean?

ANGE: You know what I mean. You can end up like your dad if you want, but I ain't ending up like your mum.

LENNY: I dunno what you're on about.

ANGE: Don't you?

LENNY: No.

(*Beat.*)

ANGE: Comin' home from work, and if your dinner ain't on the table shouting your head off and kicking the poor bloody dog's what I'm on about. Not letting my mates in the house is what I'm on about. And if they do manage to get past the front bloody door, telling us to shut up 'cause you're watching "Crossroads" is what I'm bloody on about.

LENNY: Well, you sat there jabbering on. Drives me fucking mad.

ANGE: And you sat there, like bloody God in front of the bloody telly. Drives me mad.

LENNY: What's wrong with watching the telly all of a sudden? I work bloody hard all day, I wanna come home and relax.

ANGE: With your flies undone.

LENNY: You what?

ANGE: You always undo your trousers, soon as you get in that chair.

(*Beat.*)

LENNY: What's that got to do with anything?

ANGE: I hate it.

LENNY: What? Me undoing me trousers?

ANGE: Yeah. It's gross. (*He looks puzzled.*) D'you know what I'm talking about?

LENNY: I ain't got a fucking clue.

ANGE: That's it, innit? You ain't. You don't understand nothing I say 'cause you never listen. (*The door slams.*) Oh Christ. Now I'm in for it.

Quartermaine's Terms

Simon Gray

Characters: Melanie Garth (40s), Henry Windscape (40s)
Setting: Staff room of the Cull-Loomis School of English for
   Foreigners, Cambridge
Premiere: Queen's Theatre, London, 1981
Publisher: Samuel French, Inc.

Melanie and Windscape are teachers at the Cull-Loomis
School of English for Foreigners. Outside school, Windscape's
life revolves around his wife, Fanny, and their three children.
Melanie cares for her mother, a stroke victim, whom she
resents. She regrets letting her mother talk her out of marrying
Windscape years ago and secretly still loves him.

WINDSCAPE: (*Enters middle french doors; to top steps, stops,
   seeing* MELANIE.) Hello, Melanie, (*crosses to up right end
   of center table, puts papers down, pipe on papers, puts on
   jacket.*) my dear, I thought everyone had gone.
MELANIE: How are they taking to the croquet?
WINDSCAPE: At the moment they find it a bit sedate, I think,
   but another time or two around and they'll discover just how
   much—how much incivility is possible on our tranquil English lawns. (*Crosses to locker #3.*) Now, I really ought to be
   sorting myself out—I promised Fanny I'd be home by six—
   now where's my briefcase (*Picks it up.*)—ah, yes—and a pile
   of papers (*picks them up top shelf*) I seem to remember
   (*Crosses upstage around table to up right end of center table,
   puts briefcase on table, then paper on top of other papers,
   straightens tie, buttons jacket.*)—to be marked by Monday—
MELANIE: How is Fanny?
WINDSCAPE: Oh, very well thanks, very well—a bit tired in
   the evenings, what with the children on the one hand and

her two hours voluntary with the Old Age Pensioners—but she's enjoying every minute of her day—

MELANIE: Good!—And the children—all well?

WINDSCAPE: Oh Yes—they're fine! (*Opens briefcase, takes out clips.*) Susan's a little tense at the moment, actually, with her entrance exams—a pity she's taking them so early, I think, but she insists she's in with a particularly bright lot and deosn't want to fall behind or let herself down so she works away until all hours. (*Pulls out right chair at center table, puts leg up, puts clip on.*) Quite often after Fanny and I have gone to bed. But she's developing quite an interest in—in—well, philosophical speculation, I suppose it is, really—the other evening—(*Bending during this to put on his clips.*)—she suddenly insisted in the middle of supper—she'd been very quiet until then—she suddenly insisted that we couldn't prove that other people existed—and that perhaps when we thought about them or remembered them or saw and heard them even—we were actually just making them up—and of course I took her up on this and attempted to explain how it is we do know that other people exist, including people we don't even know exist, (*Puts on second clip.*) if you fol-low—(*Laughing.*) and she kept saying "But you can't prove it, Daddy, you can't actually prove it!" And she was right. (*Picks up books and papers.*) I found myself getting quite tangled in my own arguments.

MELANIE: I've always thought she was the one who takes most after you.

WINDSCAPE: Yes, yes—perhaps she does, perhaps she does—I'm afraid I rather like to think so anyway—but you haven't seen them for ages have you, you really must come over sometime soon—Fanny would love to see you again. We all would.

MELANIE: That would be lovely.

WINDSCAPE: I'll get Fanny to give you a ring over the weekend or—

MELANIE: Good.

WINDSCAPE: Right—well, oh, by the way, I've been meaning

to ask—how is your mother's day-nurse working out, the one with the name out of Dickens?

MELANIE: Nurse Grimes. Well enough so far—she seems a very efficient, cheerful little soul—a little too cheerful for my taste perhaps, as apparently she belongs to one of those peculiar revivalist sects that seem to be springing up all over the place now—you know, meeting in each other's homes and chanting prayers and dancing about in their love of God. At least that's how she describes it—but Mother seems to like her.

WINDSCAPE: Well, that's the main thing, isn't it?

MELANIE: Yes. Yes it is.

WINDSCAPE: (*Crosses downstage of center table, exits up left thru hallway.*) Well do give her my—my very best—see you Monday, Melanie, my dear.

MELANIE: See you Monday, Henry.

(WINDSCAPE, *carrying papers, books, etc., goes off left. Sound of door closing.* MELANIE *sits. Lets out a sudden wail, and then in a sort of frenzy, tears at the page of the book from which she's been copying, sobbing. She rises and crosses up center, checks herself as door opens.*)

WINDSCAPE: (*Laughing, he enters down left thru hallway downstage of center tale to downright end, picks up briefcase.* MELANIE, *hearing* HENRY'S *laugh, crosses downstage to table, picks up purse and crosses upstage right with back to room, takes handkerchief out of purse.*) What on earth can I be thinking of—going off with all these in my arms and leaving my briefcase behind—I do that sort of thing more and more now—perhaps it's premature senility—(*Crossing left to left center as if to go upleft, turns downstage thinking.*) or did I get switched on to the wrong track and think I was going off to teach a class—I must have as I went out that way—(*Turns to look at* MELANIE, *sees torn page of book; little pause.*) Melanie—Melanie—(*Hesitates, then crosses to left of table, puts briefcase on left end table, still holding papers.*) Is something the matter?

MELANIE: She hates me, you see.

WINDSCAPE: Who?

MELANIE: Mother.

WINDSCAPE: Oh, Melanie, I'm sure that's not—not—why do think she does?

MELANIE: (*Turns to face* HENRY.) She says I've abandoned her. Betrayed her. When I come back in the evenings she won't speak to me. She sits silent for hours, while I prepare supper and chatter to her, and then when I've got her to the table she refuses to eat. Since that second attack she can only work one side of her mouth, but she can eat perfectly well. She says Nurse Grimes feeds her and so I should too, but when I try she lets the food fall out of her mouth, and—stares at me with such malevolence, until suddenly she'll say something—something utterly—last night she said "It's not my fault you've spent your life in my home. I've never wanted you here, but as you're too stupid to make an intelligent career, and too unattractive to make any reasonable man a wife, I was prepared to accept the responsibility for you. And now you refuse to pay your debt . . ." And coming out of the side of her mouth, in a hoarse whisper, like a—like a gangster in one of those films you used to take me to. (*Crosses to right of up right chair at center table.*) And she wets herself, too. She wets herself all the time.

WINDSCAPE: Oh, Melanie, I'm so sorry. Of course I realized that last attack must have left her more—more incapacitated—and—possibly even a little incontinent—

MELANIE: She's not incontinent, Henry. She does it on purpose. Out of spite. She never does it with Nurse Grimes, of course. Only with me. She says that as I'm behaving like a neglectful parent, she'll behave like a neglected child. "The only child you'll ever have." (*Puts purse on up right chair at center table, stands behind chair.*) And she gives Nurse Grimes things—things that belong to me or she knows I love that we've had for years—the buttons from Daddy's uniform or the other day a silly lithograph of a donkey that's hung in my room since I was ten—of course Nurse Grimes gives them back but—but and the worst thing is I'm beginning to hate her, to hate going home or when I'm there have such dreadful feelings—because the thought of years—it could be years apparently—years of this—and so wishing she would have another attack and die now—too dreadful—too dreadful—almost imagining myself doing something—

WINDSCAPE: I'm so sorry I had no idea. What can one say. She must love you really, mustn't she, or she wouldn't—wouldn't resent your being away from her so much—

MELANIE: (*Crosses to between up right and up left chair at center table.*) But I can't give up my teaching, Henry, I can't. Your getting me this job was the best thing that ever happened to me—of course she always despised it. (*Sits up left chair.*) Even before she was ill she used to say teaching foreigners was a job for failures—but I love it and—and I've got to think of myself now. Haven't I?

WINDSCAPE: Yes. Yes, of course you have. Finally, one always must. I wish I could give you some comfort, my dear.

MELANIE: You do, Henry. Your just being here and my knowing that—that you care about me makes all the difference. All the difference. It always has. (*She begins to cry.*) Oh what a fool I was not to—not to marry you when you gave me the chance—all those years ago—I keep thinking of it now—and what Mother said about your being too young and not knowing what you were doing—and—and blighting your career—of course I'm happy that you're so happy—I wouldn't have been able to make you as happy, but even then she was my enemy—my real enemy—I'm sorry, I'm sorry—(*Sobbing.*)

WINDSCAPE: (*Hesitates, then with reluctance puts paper on table, puts his hands on her shoulders, crosses to upstage and left of* MELANIE.) There there, my dear, there there mustn't think of the past—it's the—the future—the future—there there—(*The telephone rings. After a moment:*) Perhaps I'd better—perhaps I'd better—um—(*Releasing himself, and crosses down left to phone on table down left telephone.*) Hello. Oh hello, Nigel, yes it is! No, Anita's gone I'm afraid—at least I think she has—have you seen Anita in the last half hour—(MELANIE, *now handkerchiefing her tears, shakes her*

head.) Melanie hasn't seen her either so I'm fairly sure—
yes, of course I will. (*Listens.*) You're in London 'phoning
from the station so you'll be here before eight, right, got
that—but if Melanie or I do see her by any unlikely—yes,
right, goodbye—and oh, Nigel, good luck with your first
issue. We're all looking forward to it enormously—yes—
goodbye. (*Hangs up, crosses upstage to up left end of center
table.*) That was Nigel—for Anita—as you probably realized
and—and anyway she's certainly left, hasn't she—Look, Melanie, you must come around, and have a real talk with Fanny—
take you out of yourself—away from your problems—

MELANIE: (*Her back to* HENRY.) Thank you, Henry.

WINDSCAPE: No, we'd love to see you, I'll get her to ring you.
All right? And now I must—I really must (*Crossing up center
to top step middle french windows stopped by.*)

MELANIE: Yes, you must get back.

WINDSCAPE: (*Turns to look at her—she is not looking at him.*)
Yes. See you Monday, my dear. (*Exits up center as:*)

MELANIE: Monday, Henry.

(MELANIE *sits for a moment, then sees the briefcase, reg-
isters it, then the papers, rises, takes them to* WINDSCAPES's
*locker, puts them in, goes back to the table, puts her note-
book in her briefcase, pushes her chair in, then turns to
the book, looks down at it, tries futilely to sort it out,
pressing the page flat with her hand.*)

Reckless

Craig Lucas

Characters: Rachel (30s), Lloyd (30s)
Setting: Various Springfields in various states
Premiere: The Production Company, New York City, 1983
Publisher: Dramatists Play Service, Inc.

It is Christmas Eve. Tom and Rachel Fitzsimmons are in bed with the TV blinking silently and lovely deep snowdrifts outside. Suddenly, Tom bursts into tears and tells Rachel he's taken out a contract on her life. A hit man is coming to kill her; the whole thing has been staged to look like an accidental shooting during a burglary. At first Rachel doesn't believe him, but when she hears glass break downstairs, she takes Tom's advice and flees. She stands at a payphone in bathrobe and slippers, trying to explain this to her friend Jeanette. Then a man named Lloyd Bophtelophti offers to give her a lift.

RACHEL: Jeanette? Rachel. Merry Christmas . . . No, I can't, listen, you got a minute? No, everything's fine. Everything's fine, he's fine. Uh-huh. Would you—Would you and Eddie mind taking a little spin down here to the Arco station at Route 3 and Carl Bluestein Boulevard? . . . No, no—No, nothing like that, I just came outside . . . Uh-huh. Oh, isn't it, it's beautiful, uh-huh. Listen, Jeanette, Tom . . . Tom took a, uh . . . It's funny . . . Well, he took a contract out on my life . . . Contract. Uh-huh. Well, I mean, the man broke in downstairs—(*A man approaches in the darkness.*)— so I, uh, climbed out the window and jumped off the garage, but I didn't want to ring your bell, you know, I thought he might be following my tracks in the snow and you have all those pretty lights, so I thought maybe you'd zip down here, you and Eddie, we'd all have some egg nog or—The Arco station? Would you mind? . . . Jeanette—No, I know, I am, I know, I'm a kidder, no, but seriously, Jeanette—Merry Christmas to *you* to—Jeanette? JEANETTE??? (*Turns, sees the man.*) AAAAAGH! Oh god, my god, no! Please— . . . Oh, did you want to use the phone? I'm sorry, I, uh . . . I just— Please, go right ahead.

LLOYD: I'm just trying to find a gas station.

RACHEL: This is a gas station, right here, you found one. Merry Christmas.

LLOYD: Merry Christmas. You need a lift?

RACHEL: No. Yes. No.

LLOYD: It's no problem.

RACHEL: No, thank you. I mean, yes . . .

LLOYD: It's no trouble. Come on, hop in.

(The car.)

RACHEL: Thank you.

LLOYD: Better?

RACHEL: Yes.

LLOYD: Where you headed? . . . Some night.

RACHEL: Yes. Yes. Christmas. I love Christmas.

LLOYD: Yeah.

RACHEL: Snow . . . You have a family?

LLOYD: No. Well, sort of. Now I do. I mean—You?

RACHEL: No . . . No, no—Oh, this? This is just constume, I
just wear this, see? *(Tosses her wedding ring out the window.)*
Goodbye! . . . That felt wonderful. Maybe you should just
let me off up at the, uh . . . I could get off anywhere, you
know. Oh, you wanted to get gas. Where do you live?

LLOYD: Springfield.

RACHEL: Springfield . . . The field of spring . . .

LLOYD: You and your husband have a fight or something?

RACHEL: I'm not married. You married? You have a girlfriend?

LLOYD: Just Pooty.

RACHEL: Pooty . . . Pooty . . . Oh, my son does the cutest
thing. I was married before. He's four and a half. My son
has custody—My father—Oh god. My son is four and a half.
My husband has custody. My father is dead. And he does
this thing—There are two boys, but Jeremy's just three. But
Tom—Junior, not my husband, Tom Senior, but Tom Junior
is always firing everybody. You know, if he doesn't like what
you're doing, he fires you. He'll say to his babysitter who is
usually my friend Jeanette who can't have kids of her own
because of this thing in her—uterus—He'll say to Jeanette,
you know, uh, "You're fired, Jeanette!" Because she wants
to put him to bed or something. And just today he fired me.

I mean, on Christmas Eve! I said, "You're going to fire your own mother?" "That's right," he says, "You're fired" . . .

LLOYD: Now you're fired.

RACHEL: Now I'm fired. What does Pooty do? Is that her name?

LLOYD: Pooty.

RACHEL: What does she do?

LLOYD: She works.

RACHEL: That's good. Do you work?

LLOYD: Uh-huh.

RACHEL: How did I know that? I've never worked . . . You and Pooty . . . Did you tell me your name?

LLOYD: Lloyd.

RACHEL: Lloyd.

LLOYD: Bophtelophti.

RACHEL: Bophtelophti. Isn't that an interesting name. I'm— Mary Ellen. Sissle. Is my maiden name.

LLOYD: Nice to meet you.

RACHEL: Don't let go of the wheel! Nice to meet you too. My father always said, "Don't interfere with the driver while the vehicle is in motion." . . . You think I'm escaped from an institution, don't you?

LLOYD: Are you? . . . What's so funny?

RACHEL: Nothing. I'm sorry. I just suddenly saw everything from how . . . I mean, me in my house dress and my slippers.

LLOYD: It's cool.

RACHEL: Yes, it was! . . . I always wanted to do something reckless, you know?

LLOYD: Yeah?

RACHEL: Run away in the middle of the night in your slip and your slippers with some strange man who would ruin your reputation and disappoint your parents terribly and disappoint your friends and just make you really happy. Well, I think we get these ideas from rock and roll songs actually which is why I never did anything like that or really would except here I am. But no, I mean, this isn't really like that, I just meant I always thought about it, you know, running

away and becoming . . . I don't know what I thought I'd
become . . . But running away. And here I am.

LLOYD: Here you are.

RACHEL: On my way to . . .

LLOYD: Meet Pooty.

RACHEL: Meet Pooty . . . Lloyd?

LLOYD: Yeah?

RACHEL: Do you think we ever really know people? I mean,
I know we know people . . .

LLOYD: You mean really.

RACHEL: But really.

LLOYD: You mean *know* them.

RACHEL: Do you think?

LLOYD: Well . . . I really don't know.

RACHEL: I don't know either. I mean. I suppose I know lots
of people.

LLOYD: Sure you do.

RACHEL: And you know lots of people.

LLOYD: Pooty.

RACHEL: Yes. We live our lives and we know lots of people
and—I don't know what I'm saying. Did you get a Christmas
tree?

LLOYD: Yep.

RACHEL: That's good . . . "Oh, Christmas tree, Oh—" (*She
cries.*)

LLOYD: It's all right.

RACHEL: Of course it's all right . . . God I hate the holidays
sometimes.

LLOYD: I know . . . You see your parents?

RACHEL: Not since they died . . .

LLOYD: You'll spend Christmas with us.

The Red Coat

(from *Welcome to the Moon*)

John Patrick Shanley

Characters: John (17), Mary (16)
Setting: Nighttime on a side street, under a streetlight
Premiere: Ensemble Studio Theatre, New York City, 1982
Publisher: Dramatists Play Service, Inc.

   Welcome to the Moon is an evening of six short plays by John Patrick Shanley. *The Red Coat*, printed here in its entirety, is the first.

(*Nighttime on a side street. A street light shines down on some steps through a green tree. Moonlight mixes in the shadows. A seventeen-year-old boy sits on the steps in a white shirt with a loosened skinny tie, black dress pants, and black shoes. He is staring off. His eyes are shining. A sixteen-year-old girl enters, in neighborhood party clothes: short skirt, blouse, penny loafers.*)

JOHN: Hi, Mary.
MARY: Oh! I didn't see you there. You're hiding.
JOHN: Not from you, Mary.
MARY: Who from?
JOHN: Oh, nobody. I was up at Susan's party.
MARY: That's where I'm going.
JOHN: Oh.
MARY: Why did you leave?
JOHN: No reason.
MARY: You just gonna sit here?
JOHN: For a while.
MARY: Well, I'm going in.
JOHN: Oh. Okay . . . Oh! I'm not going in . . . I mean came out because . . . Oh, go in!

MARY: What's wrong with you, John?

JOHN: I left the party because you weren't there. That's why I left the party.

MARY: Why'd ya leave the party 'cause I wasn't there?

JOHN: I dunno.

MARY: I'm going in.

JOHN: I left the party 'cause I felt like everything I wanted was outside the party . . . out here. There's a breeze out here, and the moon . . . look at the way the moon is . . . and I knew you were outside somewhere, too! So I came out and sat on the steps here and I thought that maybe you'd come and I would be here . . . outside the party, on the steps, in the moonlight . . . and those other people . . . the ones at the party . . . wouldn't be here . . . but the night would be here . . . and you and me would be talking on the steps in the night in the moonlight and I could tell you . . .

MARY: Tell me what?

JOHN: How I feel!

MARY: How you feel about what?

JOHN: I don't know. I was looking out the window at the party . . . and I drank some wine . . . and I was looking out the window at the moon and I thought of you . . . and I could feel my heart . . . breaking.

MARY: Joh . . .

JOHN: I felt that wine and the moon and your face all pushing in my heart and I left the party and I came out here.

MARY: Your eyes are all shiny.

JOHN: I know. And I came out here looking for the moon and I saw that street light shining down through the leaves of that tree.

MARY: Hey yeah! It does look pretty.

JOHN: It's beautiful. I didn't know a street light could be beautiful. I've always thought of them as being cold and blue, you know? But this one's yellow . . . and it comes down through the leaves and the leaves are so green! Mary, I love you!

MARY: Oh!

JOHN: I shouldn't've said it. I shouldn't've said it.

MARY: No, no. That's all right.

JOHN: My heart's breaking. You must think I'm so stupid . . . but I can feel it breaking. I wish I could stop talking. I can't. I can't.

MARY: I never heard you talking like this before.

JOHN: That's 'cause this is outside the party and it's night and there's a moon up there . . . and a street light that's more beautiful than the sun! My God, the sidewalk's beautiful. Those bits of shiny stuff in the concrete . . . look how they're sparkling up the light!

MARY: You're crying! You're crying over the sidewalk!

JOHN: I love you, Mary!

MARY: That's all right. But don't cry over the sidewalk. You're usually so quiet.

JOHN: Okay. Okay. (*A pause. Then* JOHN *grabs* MARY *and kisses her.*)

MARY: Oh . . . you used your tongue. (*He kisses her again.*) You . . . should we go into the party?

JOHN: No.

MARY: I got all dressed . . . I tasted the wine on your . . . mouth. You were waiting for me out here? I wasn't even going to come. I don't like Susan so much. I was going to stay home and watch a movie. What would you have done?

JOHN: I don't know. (*Kisses her again. She kisses him back.*)

MARY: You go to St. Nicholas of Tolentine, don't you?

JOHN: Yeah.

MARY: I see you on the platform on a Hundred and Forty-ninth Street sometimes.

JOHN: I see you, too! Sometimes I just let the trains go by until the last minute, hoping to see you.

MARY: Really?

JOHN: Yeah.

MARY: I take a look around for you but I always get on my train. What would you have done if I hadn't come?

JOHN: I don't know. Walked around. I walk around a lot.

MARY: Walk around where?

JOHN: I walk around your block a lot. Sometimes I run into you.

MARY: You mean that was *planned*? Wow! I always thought you were coming from somewhere.

JOHN: I love you, Mary. I can't believe I'm saying it . . . to you . . . out loud. I love you.

MARY: Kiss me again. (*They kiss.*)

JOHN: I've loved you for a long time.

MARY: How long?

JOHN: Months. Remember that big snowball fight?

MARY: In the park?

JOHN: Yeah. That's when it was. That's when I fell in love with you. You were wearing a red coat.

MARY: Oh, that coat! I've had that for ages and ages. I've had it since the sixth grade.

JOHN: Really?

MARY: I have really special feelings for that coat. I feel like it's part of me . . . like it stands for something . . . my childhood . . . something like that.

JOHN: You look nice in that coat. I think I sensed something about it . . . the coat . . . it's special to me, too. It's so good to be able to talk to you like this.

MARY: Yeah, this is nice. That's funny how you felt that about my coat. The red one. No one knows how I feel about that coat.

JOHN: I think I do, Mary.

MARY: Do you? If you understood about my red coat . . . that red coat is like all the good things about when I was a kid . . . it's like I still have all the good kid things when I'm in that red coat . . . it's like being grown up and having your childhood, too. You know what it's like? It's like being in one of those movies where you're safe, even when you're in an adventure. Do you know what I mean? Sometimes, in a movie the hero's doin' all this stuff that's dangerous, but you know, becausa the kind of movie it is, that he's not gonna get hurt. Bein' in that red coat is like that . . . like bein' safe in an adventure.

JOHN: And that's the way you were in that snowball fight! It was like you knew that nothing could go wrong!

MARY: That's right! That's right! That's the way it feels! Oh, you do understand! It seems silly but I've always wanted someone to understand some things and that was one of them . . . the red coat.

JOHN: I do understand! I do!

MARY: I don't know. I don't know. I don't know about tomorrow, but . . . right this minute I . . . love you!

JOHN: Oh, Mary!

MARY: Oh, kiss me, John. Please!

JOHN: You're crying!

MARY: I didn't know. I didn't know two people could understand some things . . . share some things. (*They kiss.*)

JOHN: It must be terrible not to.

MARY: What?

JOHN: Be able to share things.

MARY: It is! It is! But don't you remember? Only a few minutes ago we were alone. I feel like I could tell you anything. Isn't that crazy?

JOHN: Do you want to go for a walk?

MARY: No, no. Let's stay right here. Between the streetlight and the moon. Under the tree. Tell me that you love me.

JOHN: I love you.

MARY: I love you, too. You're good-looking, did you know that? Does your mother tell you that?

JOHN: Yeah, she does.

MARY: Your eyes are shining.

JOHN: I know. I can feel them shining.

(*The lights go down slowly.*)

Stops Along the Way

Jeffrey Sweet

Characters: Donna (early 40s), Larry (30ish)
Setting: Various roadside locales between Ohio and Baltimore
Premiere: New York Public Theatre, New York City, 1981
Publisher: Dramatists Play Service, Inc.

Larry recently taught an Adult School course called "The Romantic Imagination" at a college in Baltimore. Donna was one of his students, and they became lovers. Then Larry left for a university job in Ohio. Five weeks prior to this scene, Donna left her husband and turned up without warning at his Ohio apartment. Now their affair has burned itself out, and Larry is driving Donna back to her husband in Baltimore. Here, car trouble has forced the ex-lovers to spend the night in a motel.

Note: The scene published here incorporates revisions made by the author in 1987, and varies somewhat from the published text.

(*A motel room. Two beds. Doors to john and outside. At rise,* DONNA *is alone, attending to something in her suitcase.* LARRY *enters from outside after a beat.*)

DONNA: You have any luck?

LARRY: The guy that drove the towtruck put me onto someone.

DONNA: And?

LARRY: It'll be ready in the morning.

DONNA: Did he say what was wrong?

LARRY: Near as I can make out, something isn't feeding right. I don't know. All I know is it's costing me extra to get it done overnight.

DONNA: How much extra?

LARRY: Hundred fifty.

DONNA: Talk about your highway robbery.

LARRY: It was either that or not have the car ready tomorrow.

DONNA: You want me to chip in?

LARRY: I can handle it.

DONNA: I can chip in a little if you want.

LARRY: Don't worry about it, OK? Anyway, it was about due to happen. It's an old car. I've had it since before grad school.

DONNA: If you're sure.

LARRY: It's only money. Easy come, easy blow.

(*He flops onto one of the beds.*)

DONNA: There's a pool out back. You want to frolic?

LARRY: Not really.

DONNA: What's the matter? Afraid you might enjoy it?

LARRY: I told Elliot we were going to be delayed till tomorrow.

DONNA: (*A little startled.*) You called him?

LARRY: Somebody had to.

DONNA: What did you say?

LARRY: That we were delayed and we'd probably hit Baltimore a little after noon.

DONNA: What did he say?

LARRY: Just yes, that he'd see us.

DONNA: Did he sound disappointed?

LARRY: He didn't say.

DONNA: But did he *sound* . . .

LARRY: I don't know what he sounded.

(*A beat.*)

DONNA: Did he ask about our sleeping arrangements?

LARRY: Of course. His first question.

DONNA: Did he?

LARRY: No.

DONNA: He's going to wonder.

LARRY: Want me to call him back and say, "Oh, by the way, I got a room with two beds? Not to worry."

DONNA: It may be two beds, but it's one room.

LARRY: That was strictly an economic decision.

DONNA: If you say so.

LARRY: Sleeping together at this point would be a real smart idea. Really appropriate.

DONNA: What if I have a bad dream in the middle of the night and want you to keep the bogeyman away?

LARRY: Don't.

DONNA: I can't control what I dream. A bad dream doesn't ask permission.

LARRY: What do you say we get some dinner?

DONNA: What would it matter, one last time for old times' sake?

LARRY: (*Overlapping.*) Maybe we can find one of those famous truck stops they always talk about.

DONNA: I think it would be nice, one last time.

LARRY: Look, you're going back to your husband. I am taking you back to your husband.

DONNA: So?

LARRY: There's a responsibility there.

DONNA: What is this? Some sort of gentlemen's code?

LARRY: You got it.

DONNA: When it is and isn't appropriate to sleep with someone else's wife.

LARRY: We've got a handbook, you know. Us guys. That's what it's called: the "Us Guys Handbook." It comes with a membership card and a secret handshake.

DONNA: I believe it.

LARRY: Good. Now let's get some dinner, OK?

(*A beat.* DONNA *smiles seductively, approaches him slowly till she is very close.*)

DONNA: Would you really kick me out? If you woke up in the middle of the night and there I was next to you, would you really just shove me out?

LARRY: Without pause for thought or breath.

(*A beat.*)

Now, are you going to join me or not? I'm hungry.

DONNA: You do have a kind of a deal, don't you? You and Elliot.

LARRY: Deal?

DONNA: You keep hands off, and he relieves you of me.

LARRY: There is no deal.

DONNA: No?

LARRY: For God's sake, I've talked to him twice in my life, and they were hardly what you'd call heavy discussions.

DONNA: OK, then understanding. Spoken, unspoken, whatever.

LARRY: Back to the "Us Guys Handbook"?

DONNA: Just because you joke about it doesn't make it not true. Well, I'm not bound by it—your code. Your fucking male, masculine code. I don't have to satisfy it just to make it easy for the two of you.

LARRY: I really don't know what you're talking about, you know that? What's more, I don't think you do either.

DONNA: I am not irrational. Don't you start with that bullshit.

LARRY: I guess I'm going to be eating alone, hunh?

DONNA: Well, what if I don't want to play along with you and Elliot? What if I don't want to go back to him?

(A beat.)

LARRY: Don't be silly.

DONNA: Why is that silly?

LARRY: It was settled.

DONNA: Maybe I want it unsettled.

LARRY: You're just trying to start something.

DONNA: Maybe it never occurred to you that I might want to do something else?

LARRY: Like what?

DONNA: There are lots of possibilities. It's not as if I just have a choice between you and Elliot.

LARRY: All right. I can see that.

DONNA: There's a whole world of other people out there. Other things.

LARRY: You're absolutely right.

DONNA: Other options.

LARRY: Millions of them.

DONNA: There *are*.

LARRY: I know. A wealth of opportunity.

DONNA: You laugh. You think it's funny.

LARRY: Is there something you want to do? Something specific you have in mind?

DONNA: What difference would it make to you?

LARRY: I want to see you happy.

DONNA: Tell me another one.

LARRY: If there's something you'd rather do, if you don't want to go back to Baltimore, just say the word.

DONNA: Yeah, and what would you do?

LARRY: I'll do what I can to help.

DONNA: A letter of recommendation, hunh?

LARRY: Whatever I can.

DONNA: I know what you think. You think there's nothing I could do that anybody'd want to pay me for. You think I'd starve or shoplift or go on welfare.

LARRY: I think you're so good at figuring out what I think, you should become a professional mind-reader. I'll be glad to find you a crystal ball.

DONNA: You're so damn clever.

LARRY: Then tell me. You've got something in mind, just tell me. You want to be a coal miner, I'll buy you a pick. You want to be a brain surgeon, I'll get you a scalpel. Only don't you put that on me. Don't you tell me that I'm forcing you to go back to Elliot, because it doesn't matter one damn to me if you go back to him or not.

DONNA: You should have put me on the plane. It would have been kinder.

LARRY: It wouldn't have been right.

DONNA: And this is?

LARRY: No.

(*A beat.*)

DONNA: How long did you wait? Before telling me it was over? You only said it that other night. But you must have *known* you were going to say it—what?—days ago. Maybe a week, maybe more. It must have been awful for you. All that time, knowing what you were going to have to say. And meanwhile, there I was, bouncing along. Piling on all this unwanted affection. Tell you what kind of a fool I am, I thought it was going pretty well.

(*A beat.*)

How well did you have it planned, Larry? How detailed?

Did you outline it like you do with your lectures? Five-by-seven notecards held together with a rubber band?

LARRY: It wasn't like that.

DONNA: You mean that little speech of yours was extemporaneous? Then you have my admiration, boy. You really do. Because it came out a model of . . . I mean, tight and logical and well-proportioned.

LARRY: Just what is this supposed to . . .

DONNA: (*Interrupting.*) I want to *understand.* I want to know why it didn't work out. Because we should have. Or at least we should have lasted longer. I mean, five weeks—Christ. Even a banana republic lasts longer than five weeks. I left my husband for you.

LARRY: Did I ask you to? You just showed up.

DONNA: You let me in. What, do you think this is something that I do? That this is a habit? Every few months I tell Elliot to fuck himself and descend on someone else?

LARRY: No.

DONNA: Well, it isn't. It was you. I wanted to be with you. I'm sorry if that was an imposition. Maybe I should have called you, but I thought it was OK. I mean, you did open the door. You didn't ask me anything. You held me. You made me welcome. And I thought we'd be able to just pick it up again. We had been so . . . easy together before.

LARRY: It was different. It was bound to be. Different places, different situations.

DONNA: Sure. In Baltimore, you could afford to be generous. A married lady. Talk about insurance. You could say anything—be sympathetic, reassuring. No risk of obligation. But I show up on your doorstep in Ohio and it gets scary, right?

(*A beat.*)

Tell me something: is there any feeling left, or is it now just a matter of responsibility?

(*A beat.*)

Does it touch you at all?

LARRY: Of course it does.

DONNA: And how would I know that?

LARRY: What would it take to convince you? Some demonstration? You want me to bleed?

DONNA: (*Ironically.*) I don't think you have any blood *to* bleed. Just motor oil or something.

LARRY: There's a pretty compliment.

DONNA: You know the real reason behind you breaking us up? You were beginning to *feel* something. For the first time in your life you were beginning to feel something, and it scared the shit out of you.

LARRY: Well, this is a relief. Here I thought you were going to say I'm a repressed homosexual.

DONNA: No such luck.

LARRY: But I'm just a zombie, hunh?

DONNA: OK, laugh. Make a joke out of it.

LARRY: What do you *expect* me to do?

DONNA: No, I *expect* you to laugh. It's like I said—nothing touches you.

LARRY: Right.

DONNA: I'm just sorry, that's all. I thought I saw real potential for a human being. I was wrong. You're just a clever facsimile.

LARRY: All this because I won't fuck you tonight?

(*A beat.*)

DONNA: You're a bastard.

LARRY: I know.

(*A beat.*)

DONNA: No, you aren't.

LARRY: Yes, I am.

DONNA: Yes, you are.

(*A beat. She exits. Lights fade.*)

Strange Snow
Steve Metcalfe

Characters: Martha Flanagan (30s), Joseph "Megs" Megessey
  (30s)
Setting: The Flanagans' house
Premiere: Manhattan Theatre Club, New York City, 1982
Publisher: Samuel French, Inc.

Martha Flanagan is a shy high school teacher who spends
her Friday nights at home correcting papers and her Saturday
mornings cleaning up the beer cans emptied by her brother,
David, a moody Vietnam vet who makes his living as a trucker.
Big-boned and formerly fat, Martha still sees herself as "a
battleship. With the face of an icebreaker." She has given up
on romance . . . or so she thinks.

Well before dawn, a boisterous stranger leaps onto Martha
and David's front porch hollering. Martha runs downstairs
brandishing a golf club and threatens to call the police. The
man on the porch is Joseph "Megs" Megessey, a fast-talking,
rowdy mechanic and Vietnam buddy of David's. It's opening
day of trout season, and Megs has come by to fetch David.
Infectiously cheerful, he grabs the contemptuous Martha and
dances her around the kitchen, crooning about trout. She's
half shocked and half charmed. When a hungover David staggers downstairs, she surprises them both by downing a beer
and agreeing to come on the fishing trip.

Nobody catches any fish. Martha gets soaked to the skin.
David, who's angry at his sister's attraction to "crazy" Megs,
gets so drunk that Megs has to carry him into the house.
Martha changes into warm clothes and heats up some soup.
She is attracted to Megs but also resistant.

MARTHA: (MARTHA *crosses to kitchen.*) *You* are having some
  soup.

MEGS: (MEGS *follows*.) *Soup* would be great.

MARTHA: (MEGS *sits chair stage right*. MARTHA *puts on apron*.) Come on. To the kitchen. Sit. Split pea with ham. Home made.

MEGS: You're kiddin. By god, if food doesn't come out of a can, I usually have a hard time recognizing it.

MARTHA: I'll have you know I'm a very good cook.

MEGS: Well, goddam, we're a team cause I like to eat.

MARTHA: (MARTHA *gets soup from fridge, gets spoon from drawer*.) Do your girlfriends cook for you?

MEGS: Tell you the truth, Martha, most a the girls I know don't know a waffle iron from a Frisbee. I been keepin a kinda low profile in the girlfriend department. Got kinda tired of mud wrestlers and hog callers. What about you, Martha? You must have to fight'm off with tomahawks.

MARTHA: (MARTHA *puts soup in pan*.) I'm sorry to inform you I've given up the fight.

MEGS: Come on, woman, you're built like a brick shithouse!

MARTHA: What?

MEGS: Oh, goddam. Me and my mouth again. (MEGS *crosses up right of* MARTHA.) Sorry, Martha, but you are. I noticed it straight off.

MARTHA: That's the most ridiculous thing I've ever heard.

MEGS: No.

MARTHA: I'm shapeless.

MEGS: Solid. You're sturdy. You're a battleship!

MARTHA: Agreed. With the face of an icebreaker.

MEGS: No—oh.

MARTHA: Yes.

MEGS: N—

MARTHA: (MARTHA *puts pan on stove*.) Stop contradicting me! I know what I am. Plain and unattractive.

MEGS: Martha, I saw the picture in there. You used to be.

MARTHA: (MARTHA *clears table dishes to sink. Wipes table with cloth. Crosses to stove, stirs soup*.) You're very nice to try and convince me otherwise but I look in the mirror every morning. I live with what I see. The soup will be ready in a moment.

MEGS: Y'know, Martha, some people, they get awful ugly the minute they open their mouths. And other people, like you, Martha, they grow on you. The more you get to know'm, the better lookin they get.

MARTHA: Very few share your opinion.

MEGS: Oh. You give'm a chance to? (MEGS *sits in chair.*)

MARTHA: Look, I'm not one of those pieces of fluff you see in men's magazines. Does that make me less a woman? It does not. (*Pause.*) And I'm a fool because for some stupid reason I think it does. And so I buy contact lenses and clothes I can't really afford. You think I'd of learned by now. You think I'd have learned at the start. (*Pause.*) The soup is almost hot. (*Pause.*) David had to even get me a date for my high school formal. I was on the decorations committee, the tickets committee. I put together the whole thing. Nobody asked me to go. David rounded up his friends and told them one of them had to invite me or he'd beat them all up. I think perhaps they drew straws. I didn't know. Suddenly I was invited, that's all that mattered. I was so happy. Well, it was something that couldn't be kept quiet. (MARTHA *crosses downstage stage right of table.*) David's blackmail. I heard rumors. I confronted David. He wouldn't admit what he'd done but I knew. (*Pause.*)

MEGS: You go? (*Pause.*)

MARTHA: I got very sick the night of the prom. A twenty-four-hour thing. David meant well.

MEGS: I crashed mine. Yeah, I did. Just walked in wearin a motorcycle jacket, steel-toed jack boots, and shades, stood there like a madman, grinnin at all those tuxedos, hopin somebody'd try to throw me out. I think perhaps I also was very sick on the night of the prom.

MARTHA: Wouldn't we have made a lovely couple. (*Crosses to stove, stirs soup.*)

MEGS: You'da gone with me?

MARTHA: What?

MEGS: If, y'know, I'da like, asked you, you'da gone with me?

MARTHA: Well . . . yes.

MEGS: Nah.

MARTHA: Yes.

MEGS: Nah.

MARTHA: (*Angrily.*) Why do you always contradict me? Yes, I would have gone with you.

MEGS: Well, goddam, woman! We'da had a great time!! I can see it! (*He jumps up, moves to the kitchen door.*) I come to pick you up. I knock on the door. (*He exits out the door. He knocks. Bam, Bam, Bam.*)

MARTHA: What are you doing? What are you doing!?

MEGS: (*Opening the door, stepping in.*) This ain't detention, Martha. It's the prom. Answer the door.

MARTHA: You're in. (*He realizes that he is. He grins. He shuts the door. He does a slow spin as if showing off something. Down right.*)

MEGS: Hah!? Hah!?

MARTHA: What?

MEGS: Your mom. She thinks I look very dashing in my tuxedo.

MARTHA: Oh, you do.

MEGS: (*Whipping off his hat.*) The corsage is as big as a goddam dogwood tree. (*He tosses his hat into the refrigerator.*) Your father comes over to shake hands. He smells my breath to see if I've been drinking. (*He exhales.*) I have!

MARTHA: He approves. And offers you an apéritif for the road.

MEGS: Too late! You make your entrance down the stairway! you look . . . terrific!

MARTHA: My gown is silk and gossamer. (MARTHA *crosses down right;* MEGS *counters.*)

MEGS: Yeah. And you look terrific. Your hair is just so. Hey! Know what it is?

MARTHA: (*Breaking the spell.*) Preposterous.

MEGS: No! It's beautiful.

MARTHA: My shoes?

MEGS: Listen, you could click your heels three times and they'd take you to Kansas.

MARTHA: Ridiculous.

MEGS: No! (*He retrieves his hat from the refrigerator.*) There

is a moment of embarrassment as I try to pin on your corsage.
I am timid.

MARTHA: Of the occasion?

MEGS: Of your gunboats!

MARTHA: (*Giggling, slapping at him.*) Stop! (*She takes the hat and puts it on her head, the bill facing backwards.*)

MARTHA: I smile reassuringly. (*She does.*)

MEGS: And the air is heavy with the portent of things to come! (*Offering his arm.*) Shall we go? (MEGS *offers his arm, leads* MARTHA *centerstage.*)

MARTHA: The chariot awaits?

MEGS: (*He mimes opening a car door for her.*) 57 Chevy, roars like a p.t. boat but smooth as glass. In accord with the occasion I have thrown all the empty beer cans in the backseat.

MARTHA: How thoughtful. We arrive?

MEGS: We knock'm dead. You're beautiful.

MARTHA: (*Softly.*) You're handsome.

MEGS: We dance! (*He does a ferocious dance: a combination of the jerk and the swim. He sings the instrumental lead to "In-A-Gadda-Da-Vida" by the Iron Butterfly as he dances. He stops, grinning. Then:*) They play a slow one. (*He begins to sing "Michelle" by the Beatles. He opens his arms to her. She comes to him. They sway.*) What a terrific dancer you are.

MARTHA: (*Shyly.*) And you.

MEGS: If I step on your feet you give me a shot to the kidneys, o.k.? (*He pulls her very close, his hands going down around her waist. She stiffens.*)

MARTHA: This is stupid.

MEGS: Just dancing. (*And he holds her tighter still.*)

MARTHA: (*With a growing terror at his embrace.*) Please. Stop it. Get your hands off me! (*She struggles free from him, rips the hat from her head, tosses it away from her, staggers to the stove. Pause.*)

MEGS: (MEGS *crosses stage left to* MARTHA.) That's the thing about shy people, Martha. They think everybody's looking.

Nobody is. Cept me. (*Unable to hide his anger, his frustration, his hurt.*) And I like what I see!

MARTHA: For god's sake, sit down. The soup is ready.

MEGS: That bad a dancer, huh! Yeah . . . (*He moves to exit out the kitchen door and suddenly, almost without thinking, he punches out one of the panes of glass in the door.*)

MARTHA: Joseph!   MEGS: Oh god, I'm
  Your hand—   sorry . . .

MEGS: (MEGS *crosses down left to table.* MARTHA *crosses stage right of* MEGS.) I'll pay for it, I promise, oh, I'm so sorry, I'll pay for it. (*And he is hiding his hands from her. She is trying to see if they're cut.*)

MARTHA: I don't care about the glass! Is your hand cut!?

MEGS: No, they're fine! (*And she sees the scars on his hands. Embarrassed, he tries to hide them. She won't let him.*) My hands . . . they ain't so pretty . . .

MARTHA: You've done it before . . .

MEGS: Yeah . . .

MARTHA: Why . . .

MEGS: (*He pulls hand back, takes hat from counter, crosses to living room.*) I dunno why, Martha. I'm real sorry. Listen, you tell Davey so long for me. (*He starts to leave, going into the living room, heading for the front door.*)

MARTHA: Joseph? (*He stops.*) I'd have wanted you to take me to the prom. (*Pause.*)

MEGS: Yeah?

MARTHA: (*Softly.*) Yes.

MEGS: Really?

MARTHA: (*Softly.*) Yes. (*Pause.*) Will you sit and have soup with me?

A Taste of Honey

Shelagh Delaney

Characters: Jo (nearly 18), Boy (22)
Setting: A comfortless flat in Manchester and the street outside
Premiere: Theatre Royal, Stratford, London, 1958
Publisher: Grove Press

Jo lives with her mother, Helen, "a semi-whore." They move from one ugly flat to another, always running from somebody. Jo is fed up. She looks forward to leaving Helen and starting her own life. This is the first time we see Jo with her boyfriend, a twenty-two-year-old black sailor.

(Jo *and her* Boy Friend *are walking in the street. They stop by the door.*)

Jo: I'd better go in now. Thanks for carrying my books.

Boy: Were you surprised to see me waiting outside school?

Jo: Not really.

Boy: Glad I came?

Jo: You know I am.

Boy: So am I.

Jo: Well, I'd better go in.

Boy: Not yet! Stay a bit longer.

Jo: All right! Doesn't it go dark early? I like winter. I like it better than all the other seasons.

Boy: I like it too. When it goes dark early it gives me more time for—(*He kisses her.*)

Jo: Don't do that. You're always doing it.

Boy: You like it.

Jo: I know, but I don't want to do it all the time.

Boy: Afraid someone'll see us?

Jo: I don't care.

Boy: Say that again.

Jo: I don't care.

BOY: You mean it too. You're the first girl I've met who really didn't care. Listen, I'm going to ask you something. I'm a man of few words. Will you marry me?

JO: Well, I'm a girl of few words. I won't marry you but you've talked me into it.

BOY: How old are you?

JO: Nearly eighteen.

BOY: And you really will marry me?

JO: I said so, didn't I? You shouldn't have asked me if you were only kidding me up. (*She starts to go.*)

BOY: Hey! I wasn't kidding. I thought you were. Do you really mean it? You will marry me?

JO: I love you.

BOY: How do you know?

JO: I don't know why I love you but I do.

BOY: I adore you. (*Swinging her through the air.*)

JO: So do I. I can't resist myself.

BOY: I've got something for you.

JO: What is it? A ring!

BOY: This morning in the shop I couldn't remember what sort of hands you had, long hands, small hands or what. I stood there like a damn fool trying to remember what they felt like. (*He puts the ring on and kisses her hand.*) What will your mother say?

JO: She'll probably laugh.

BOY: Doesn't she care who her daughter marries?

JO: She's not marrying you, I am. It's got nothing to do with her.

BOY: She hasn't seen me.

JO: And when she does?

BOY: She'll see a coloured boy.

JO: No, whatever else she might be, she isn't prejudiced against colour. You're not worried about it, are you?

BOY: So long as you like it.

JO: You know I do.

BOY: Well, that's all that matters.

JO: When shall we get married?

BOY: My next leave? It's a long time, six months.

Jo: It'll give us a chance to save a bit of money. Here, see . . . this ring . . . it's too big; look, it slides about . . . And I couldn't wear it for school anyway. I might lose it. Let's go all romantic. Have you got a bit of string?

BOY: What for?

Jo: I'm going to tie it round my neck. Come on, turn your pockets out. Three handkerchiefs, a safety pin, a screw! Did that drop out of your head? Elastic bands! Don't little boys carry some trash. And what's this?

BOY: Nothing.

Jo: A toy car! Does it go?

BOY: Hm hm!

Jo: Can I try it? (*She does.*)

BOY: She doesn't even know how it works. Look, not like that. (*He makes it go fast.*)

Jo: I like that. Can I keep it?

BOY: Yes, take it, my soul and all, everything.

Jo: Thanks. I know, I can use my hair ribbon for my ring. Do it up for me.

BOY: Pretty neck you've got.

Jo: Glad you like it. It's my schoolgirl complexion. I'd better tuck this out of sight. I don't want my mother to see it. She'd only laugh. Did I tell you, when I leave school this week I start a part-time job in a bar? Then as soon as I get a full-time job, I'm leaving Helen and starting up in a room somewhere.

BOY: I wish I wasn't in the Navy.

Jo: Why?

BOY: We won't have much time together.

Jo: Well, we can't be together all the time and all the time there is wouldn't be enough.

BOY: It's a sad story, Jo. Once, I was a happy young man, not a care in the world. Now! I'm trapped into a barbaric cult . . .

Jo: What's that? Mau-Mau?

BOY: Matrimony.

Jo: Trapped! I like that! You almost begged me to marry you.

BOY: You led me on. I'm a trusting soul. Who took me down to that deserted football pitch?

JO: Who found the football pitch? I didn't even know it existed. And it just shows how often you must have been there, too . . . you certainly know where all the best spots are. I'm not going there again . . . It's too quiet. Anything might happen to a girl.

BOY: It almost did. You shameless woman!

JO: That's you taking advantage of my innocence.

BOY: I didn't take advantage. I had scruples.

JO: You would have done. You'd have gone as far as I would have let you and no scruples would have stood in your way.

BOY: You enjoyed it as much as I did.

JO: Shut up! This is the sort of conversation that can colour a young girl's mind.

BOY: Women never have young minds. They are born three thousand years old.

JO: Sometimes you look three thousand years old. Did your ancestors come from Africa?

BOY: No. Cardiff. Disappointed? Were you hoping to marry a man whose father beat the tom-tom all night?

JO: I don't care where you were born. There's still a bit of jungle in you somewhere. (*A siren is heard.*) I'm going in now, I'm hungry. A young girl's got to eat, you know.

BOY: Honey, you've got to stop eating. No more food, no more make-up, no more fancy clothes; we're saving up to get married.

JO: I just need some new clothes too. I've only got this one coat. I have to use it for school and when I go out with you. I do feel a mess.

BOY: You look all right to me.

JO: Shall I see you tonight?

BOY: No, I got work to do.

JO: What sort of work?

BOY: Hard work, it involves a lot of walking.

JO: And a lot of walking makes you thirsty. I know, you're going drinking.

BOY: That's right. It's one of the lads' birthdays. I'll see you
tomorrow.

JO: All right. I'll tell you what, I won't bother going to school
and we can spend the whole day together. I'll meet you down
by that ladies' hairdressing place.

BOY: The place that smells of cooking hair?

JO: Yes, about ten o'clock.

BOY: Okay, you're the boss.

JO: Good night.

BOY: Aren't you going to kiss me good night?

JO: You know I am. (*Kisses him.*) I like kissing you. Good
night.

BOY: Good night.

JO: Dream of me.

BOY: I dreamt about you last night. Fell out of bed twice.

JO: You're in a bad way.

BOY: You bet I am. Be seeing you!

JO: (*As she goes.*) I love you.

BOY: Why?

JO: Because you're daft.

Vanishing Act

Richard Greenberg

Characters: Minna (young), Spence (young)
Setting: A summerhouse, a dock, an open space
Premiere: Ensemble Studio Theatre, New York City, 1986
Publisher: Dramatists Play Service, Inc.

Minna, a beautiful young woman, lives with her family. She
has always had money and been pursued by men. Currently,
two men are in love with her. The first is Sky, her fiancé. The
second, Spence, was first smitten with her years ago. He is now
standing on the dock, ready to drown himself. He claims Minna

has nothing to do with this, yet makes certain she knows of his plans in time to stop him from jumping. Sky believes Spence wants to get Minna alone so he can "flaunt his pain to his ultimate advantage." Minna says she knows what she has to do and goes off with Spence.

(*An open space.*)

MINNA: I don't do this for everyone.

SPENCE: I don't know why I've come.

MINNA: I'm a witch.

SPENCE: I think you're a witch.

MINNA: I am.

SPENCE: Do you want me to stir something? Curse my mother? Speak the Ineffable Name of the Lord?

MINNA: Sit down.

SPENCE: I have no desire to move.

MINNA: This may change our lives.

SPENCE: Do I whirl in place? Defy the Sabbath? Drink the blood of a virgin?

MINNA: You have to think.

SPENCE: I don't any more.

MINNA: Quiet. (*She stands behind him, puts her hands to his temples.*)

SPENCE: I—

MINNA: Quiet. (*He is quiet.*) This is what you have to remember: The best moment of your life.

SPENCE: I can't remember that.

MINNA: Yes you can.

SPENCE: There weren't any.

MINNA: Don't be trying. Shut your eyes. (*He does so.*)

SPENCE: This is what I was aiming for.

MINNA: The best moment.

SPENCE: Can you be in it?

MINNA: I knew it!

SPENCE: You don't understand.

MINNA: Go on.

SPENCE: Two years ago.

MINNA: Yes.

SPENCE: You were walking out of a room.

MINNA: Where was the room?

SPENCE: In the house. The—what do you call the living room?—the atelier? You people with your words.

MINNA: We used to call it the parlor.

SPENCE: I think you were calling it the drawing room.

MINNA: What precisely did you see in the room?

SPENCE: The lighting was artful. You had dressed for effect, trying to snare me. A filmy thing. A single light went out, decapitating you. Your spine became visible.

MINNA: My spine?

SPENCE: Each vertebra in utter articulation. Bone-blue. Pink skin. It became my organizing principle.

MINNA: My spine?

SPENCE: I took the memory everywhere. Boston. New York. San Francisco. Singapore.

MINNA: You've been to Singapore?

SPENCE: I would take it to Singapore.

MINNA: What happened when I left the room?

SPENCE: You didn't leave the room. The light snapped on. Your dress floated back onto your shoulders. It was yellow.

MINNA: This was your best moment?

SPENCE: I was stunned. I was happy! I had penetrated the nature of things. Take me onto your back. (*She bends, they interlock arms, she hoists him up, back to back, she spins him once, lowers him gently. Sadly.*) Yes. I knew that's how it would be.

MINNA: Open your eyes. What do you see?

SPENCE: Nothing.

MINNA: What happened next?

SPENCE: You vanished.

MINNA: How?

SPENCE: I never knew. The lights went out. I was in no particular place. You were gone.

MINNA: Were you still happy?

SPENCE: For weeks. For weeks.

MINNA: Stay very still. What do you hear? (*Music starts distantly.*)

SPENCE: Nothing.

MINNA: What's the next thing you remember?

SPENCE: Writing a letter. I wrote, "Don't laugh: I've seen a spine. I think it was erotic and mysterious and I understand things better. For this reason I must quit my job and go seeking after a different kind of life I know you'll believe me when I tell you that everything until now has been turmoil and confusion and this course I've found can be the only salvatory one for me." And then I vanished.

MINNA: You vanished. Were you happy?

SPENCE: Ecstatic.

MINNA: What do you hear?

SPENCE: Music.

MINNA: Loud music?

SPENCE: Faint, very faint music.

MINNA: Continue.

SPENCE: I travelled. I travelled out of people's lives. Out of corruptions. Entanglements. In some places I assumed other names.

MINNA: Did you think of me?

SPENCE: Your spine. The way it flowed out of your dress. A perfect reed. (*The music gets louder. The lights change. Stars dimly appear in the sky.*)

MINNA: Do you see anything?

SPENCE: Stars.

MINNA: Bright stars?

SPENCE: Dim stars. Where are they—? How—?

MINNA: Go on. You assumed other names!

SPENCE: (*Continuing; but awed.*) I did out of character things. Flamenco dancing. Political boostering. Short order cooking . . . This is utterly fantastic. (*The lights brighten, the stars grow more intense.*)

MINNA: Don't stop. What happened next?

SPENCE: It didn't last. Somebody died. My life came rushing

back to me. I went home. Took back my name. My clothes still smelled like me. I walked the routes I'd walked before. I tried to remember you leaving the room. I tried to picture it. All I could see was you—some girl. I remembered the conversation that had been going on. "Are you going out, Minna?" "Yes, I'm going out." "Would you buy me some pastels?" "The stores are closed, mother." Conversation that did me no good. I came back here and all I found was you. Some girl . . . (*The music grows louder. More stars.*)

MINNA: What do you see?

SPENCE: Stars! Everywhere stars. (*Another constellation lights up.*)

MINNA: Which stars?

SPENCE: The Big Dipper! Cassiopeia! (*The music swells:* SPENCE *grows more and more excited.*)

MINNA: Are you happy?

SPENCE: They're magnetising my hands, tugging at the crown of my head! Pulling me up!

MINNA: Are you happy?

SPENCE: They're drawing on my fingertips, yanking the heels of my hands! Constellations flashing—! (*The stars change colors.*) The Pleiades! Orion! Shooting, falling, singing into me!

MINNA: Are you happy? (*The music is now overwhelming; the stars thrilling.* SPENCE *is whirling around the stage, magnetised by some force outside himself. It gets crazy, out of control.*)

SPENCE: My God—I'm—

MINNA: Are you happy?

SPENCE: Yes! . . . It's too much—too beautiful—I'm dizzy—

MINNA: I have you! (*He nearly collapses into her arms. She props him up.*)

SPENCE: It was too much . . . too much . . . much . . .

MINNA: I know . . . (*They are in each other's arms. They sway back and forth. The lights and music subside to a tolerable level.*)

SPENCE: What did you do? I'm scared for you . . .

MINNA: Sshh—

SPENCE: But—

MINNA: Sshh. I know . . . (*Their swaying turns almost imperceptibly into a slow dance. After a moment,* MINNA's *body gives slightly, a swooning, an exhaustion.* SPENCE *holds her up.*)

SPENCE: Are you all right?

MINNA: You're the subject here.

(*The music crests just a little; they dance around and around.*)

A Weekend Near Madison

Kathleen Tolan

Characters: Nessa (early 30s), Jim (early 30s)

Setting: A hand-built home near Madison, Wisconsin, Autumn 1979

Premiere: Actors Theatre of Louisville, 1983

Publisher: Samuel French, Inc.

David, a psychiatrist, and his wife, Doe, a writer, are visited by their old friend Nessa. A lesbian feminist singer, she is coming through town with her band. David's younger brother, Jim, has hitchhiked up in the pouring rain to see her. He and Nessa were lovers a long time ago, before she "came out." Now Nessa and her lover, Samantha, want a baby. They would like Jim to father it.

NESSA: (*Voice lowered.*) Jimmy, how do they seem to you?

JIM: Who?

NESSA: Dody and David.

JIM: Oh. They seem okay.

NESSA: Do you think so?

JIM: Sure. Why?

NESSA: Well, I couldn't tell.

JIM: You've only been here one day.

NESSA: Well, that's true. That's true.

JIM: And us being here keeps it from being one of their typical days.

NESSA: Yeah. Yeah, that's true. So you think they're okay.

JIM: I don't know. I really don't know, Vanessa. David has been pretty involved with his patient.

NESSA: Oh, yeah. Yeah. (*Pause.*) And Dody seems okay to you?

JIM: What do you mean?

NESSA: She seemed so upset . . .

JIM: You've always managed to touch a nerve with Dody.

NESSA: Oh, yeah, well . . . but I mean even before that. I mean, I don't feel like we've really connected.

JIM: I don't know, Nessa. Dorothy isn't always completely here.

NESSA: Now that's true. That's really true. Dody. This morning she was standing at the counter with half an orange in one hand and one of those juicers—not the automatic kind—the glass—this. (*She has found juicer on counter.*)

JIM: Yeah.

NESSA: And she was just standing there, holding the orange in the air, and finally she said, "You know, sometimes I forget how to do this." And we laughed, and then she made the juice. But she was serious.

JIM: Yeah.

NESSA: I guess she's always been like that.

JIM: Yeah.

NESSA: But you think they're happy?

JIM: I don't know, Vanessa.

NESSA: (*Pause.*) It seems weird that they don't have kids.

JIM: Why is that?

NESSA: Well, they've been married five years, and were together a long time before that.

(*Silence.*)

NESSA: Well, Sammy and I want to have a baby.

JIM: Oh.

NESSA: She doesn't want to have it and I do. We talked about artificial insemination, but that seemed so—artificial, d'you know? Something didn't feel right about it. Not theoretically, but the actual experience. And we thought about just going out and picking up some guy, but you don't know anything about him, you know? He might be diseased, or a maniac, or something, and the point would be to not get to know him well enough to find any of that out. (*Beat.*) And we thought of asking a gay man, but the gay men we know would either love a child themselves and would want partial rights, which we decided we wouldn't want to do, or else they really don't like women, so that wouldn't work. (*Pause.*) So I thought of asking David.

JIM: You're kidding.

NESSA: It seemed like a really good idea before we got here. David and Dody and I have a past together. We've had a wonderful friendship that's meant a lot to all of us. And it seemed like it'd be better to conceive a child with a friend. And the fact that he and Doe have been so solid for so long and will probably have their own kids if they want kids, so he wouldn't feel possessive. And being a shrink would make it easier for him to see the whole situation objectively, to remove himself, I mean in a good way. . . . And since he and I were never lovers—

JIM: Since when?

NESSA: Oh, that. I forgot about that. That was just a couple of drunken nights. I mean we were never, you know, involved.

JIM: Right.

   (*Silence.*)

NESSA: I'm sorry . . . I'm sorry I brought this up.

JIM: Why?

NESSA: Well, you seem pissed off. (*Pause.*) Jimmy, this may sound really, you know, ridiculous to you—I mean, two women want to have a baby—now that's really funny. But it's not a joke—it's my life. I don't know how to do this. (*Pause.*) I—

deeply—deeply—want a child. We've looked into adopting one—politically, that seemed like a better choice, but being a gay couple is an enormous handicap—I mean, the agencies just don't want to consider that you could really have a happy, stable home—I mean, that's just too threatening—I mean, that you could be a good parent and everything. And—but—but also I feel . . . to have the capacity to grow a child, to be a part of that cycle, to continue it . . . to feel it grow inside me, and bear it and nurse it and . . . to care for another life . . . I know it sounds corny, but it's real . . .

JIM: (*Pause.*) Okay.

NESSA: Okay, what?

JIM: Okay, I accept what you're saying. I'm sorry I was defensive.

NESSA: Oh.

JIM: But I can't say that I think David is going to be open to this plan.

NESSA: Yeah. Both of us thought . . . we don't feel as sure as we did before about asking him.

JIM: Yeah.

NESSA: In fact, we both feel a lot better about asking you.

JIM: What? (*Pause.*) Asking me? But—you were saying—you were saying that one of the important things is that David's married. And that you and he hadn't—hadn't been involved.

NESSA: I know. I know, but now I don't think that's important, if it's okay with you.

JIM: You don't?

NESSA: No. Samantha and I talked it out and she agrees. She really likes you.

JIM: Oh. Well, I like her too.

NESSA: And we both feel we could trust you. (*Pause.*) Jimmy, I don't want to bulldoze you—I really don't. I know I always do that and I don't mean to—I don't want to do that . . . but if you did—if you felt okay about it . . .

JIM: Vanessa. (*Pause.*) I don't know. I don't think . . . I mean . . . I mean, I'd really like to help you out, but . . .

NESSA: It's okay. It's okay. I understand.

JIM: No, no—I mean, I'd like to be of help . . .

NESSA: Listen, Jimmy, I mean, it's okay. Don't feel bad.

JIM: (*Pause.*) I'll think about it, okay?

NESSA: Really?

JIM: I mean, I think it's a bad idea, but I'll think about it.

NESSA: Okay. Right. Well, here's the thing—I mean, just so you know, while you're thinking about it. We'll be leaving tomorrow for Beloit. You could come with us, or we could meet up in Milwaukee in three days if you—or even if you just want to hang out and talk about it some more—I mean, depending on your job in Philadelphia, but we could work that out. I'd like to get started right away if you decide yes, because I think I'll be ovulating sometime in the next week or so.

JIM: Uh-huh.

NESSA: (*Pause.*) But, Jimmy?

JIM: Huh?

NESSA: Well, I just want to say that you're a part of my life. I mean, that's just there, d'you know, whatever happens, that'll just always be there.

JIM: Uh-huh.

NESSA: But—. I'll just let you think about it. I know it's heavy. I mean, this wasn't one of the possibilities we were told about when we were kids. So . . . but I'll just go find Sammy. If you want to come down, Dody said there were a couple of extra rods in the front closet. . . . So I'll see you later, okay?

JIM: Okay.

NESSA: Or maybe I should just hang out here, in case things come up—d'you know? I mean if you have any thoughts.

JIM: No, why don't we talk about it more later.

NESSA: Yeah. Right. That seems good. Okay then. I'll just be down at the river.

What the Butler Saw

Joe Orton

Characters: Dr. Prentice (middle-aged), Geraldine Barclay (young)
Setting: Consulting room of an exclusive psychiatric clinic
U.S. Premiere: McAlpin Rooftop Theatre, New York City, 1970
Publisher: Samuel French, Inc.

What the Butler Saw is an outrageous high-style farce in which a doctor's attempt to hide a seduction from his wife leads to multiple cross-dressing (sometimes in straitjackets) and ever-wilder lies. This is the opening scene.

(*The consulting room of an exclusive, private psychiatric clinic. A spring day. Doors lead to main hall up right, the wards and dispensary down right. Double doors up left lead to a hall and the garden off stage. Open closet with hangers and hooks down left above proscenium and just off stage. Desk, chairs, consulting couch upstage with curtains.*

(Dr. PRENTICE *enters briskly from the hall.* GERALDINE BARCLAY *follows him.*)

PRENTICE: Take a seat. Is this your first job?

GERALDINE: Yes, Doctor.

PRENTICE: (*Puts on a pair of spectacles, stares at her. He opens a drawer in the desk, takes out a notebook. Picking up a pencil.*) I'm going to ask you a few questions. (*He hands her a notebook and pencil.*) Write them down. In English, please. (*He returns to his desk, sits, smiles.*) Who was your father? Put that at the head of the page. (GERALDINE *crosses her legs, rests the notebook upon her knee and makes a note.*) And now the reply immediately underneath for quick reference.

GERALDINE: I've no idea who my father was.

PRENTICE: (*Is perturbed by her reply although he gives no evidence of this. He gives her a kindly smile.*) I'd better be frank, Miss Barclay. I can't employ you if you're in any way miraculous. It would be contrary to established practice. You did have a father?

GERALDINE: Oh, I'm sure I did. My mother was frugal in her habits, but she'd never economize unwisely.

PRENTICE: If you had a father why can't you produce him?

GERALDINE: He deserted my mother. Many years ago. She was the victim of an unpleasant attack.

PRENTICE: (*Shrewdly.*) She was a nun?

GERALDINE: No. She was a chambermaid at the Station Hotel.

PRENTICE: (*Frowns, takes off his spectacles and pinches the bridge of his nose.*) Pass that large, leather-bound volume, will you? I must check your story. To safeguard my interests, you understand? (GERALDINE *lifts the book from the bookcase and takes it to* DR. PRENTICE. *Consulting the index.*) The Station Hotel? (*Opening the book, running his finger down the page.*) Ah, here we are! It's a building of small architectural merit built for some unknown purpose at the turn of the century. It was converted into a hotel by public subscription. (*Nods, wisely.*) I stayed there once myself as a young man. It has a reputation for luxury which baffles the most undemanding guest. (*Closes the book with a bang and pushes it to one side.*) Your story appears, in the main, to be correct. This admirable volume, of course, omits most of the details. But that is only to be expected in a publication of wide general usage. (*Puts on his spectacles.*) Make a note to the effect that your father is missing. Say nothing of the circumstances. It might influence my final decision. (GERALDINE *makes a jotting in her notebook.* DR. PRENTICE *takes the leather-bound volume to the bookcase.*) Is your mother alive? Or has she too unaccountably vanished? That is a trick question. Be careful—you could lose marks on your final scoring.

GERALDINE: I haven't seen my mother for many years. I was brought up by a Mrs. Barclay. She died recently.

PRENTICE: I'm so sorry. From what cause?

GERALDINE: An explosion, due to faulty gas-main, killed her outright and took the roof off the house.

PRENTICE: Have you applied for compensation?

GERALDINE: Just for the roof.

PRENTICE: Were there no other victims of the disaster?

GERALDINE: Yes. A recently erected statue of Sir Winston Churchill was so badly injured that the special medal has been talked of. Parts of the great man were actually found embedded in my stepmother.

PRENTICE: Which parts?

GERALDINE: I'm afraid I can't help you there. I was too upset to supervise the funeral arrangements. Or, indeed, to identify the body.

PRENTICE: Surely the Churchill family did that?

GERALDINE: Yes. They were most kind.

PRENTICE: You've had a unique experience. It's not everyone who has their stepmother assassinated by a public utility. (*Shakes his head, sharing the poor girl's sorrow.*) Can I get you an aspirin?

GERALDINE: No, thank you, sir. I don't want to start taking drugs.

PRENTICE: Your caution does you credit, my dear. (*Smiles in a kindly fashion.*) Now, I have to ask a question which may cause you embarrassment. Please remember that I'm a doctor. (*Pause.*) What is your shorthand speed?

GERALDINE: I can manage twenty words a minute with ease, sir.

PRENTICE: And your typing speed?

GERALDINE: I haven't mastered the keyboard. My money ran out, you see.

PRENTICE: (*Takes the notebook and puts it aside.*) Perhaps you have other qualities which aren't immediately apparent. (*Pulls aside the curtains on the couch.*) Kindly remove your stockings. I wish to see what effect your stepmother's death had upon your legs.

GERALDINE: Isn't this rather unusual, Doctor?

PRENTICE: Have no fear, Miss Barclay. What I see before me

isn't a lovely and desirable girl. It's a sick mind in need of psychiatric treatment. The body is of no interest to a medical man. A woman once threw herself at me. I needn't tell you that this is spoken in confidence. She was stark naked. She wished me to misbehave myself. And, d'you know, all I was conscious of was that she had a malformed navel? That's how much notice I take of women's bodies.

GERALDINE: Please forgive me, Doctor. I wasn't meaning to suggest that your attentions were in any way improper. (*Takes off her shoes and stockings.* DR. PRENTICE *runs a hand along her legs and nods, sagely.*)

PRENTICE: As I thought. You've a febrile condition of the calves. You're quite wise to have a check-up. (*Straightens and takes off his spectacles.*) Undress. (*Turns to the desk and takes off his coat.*)

GERALDINE: I've never undressed in front of a man before.

PRENTICE: I shall take account of your inexperience in these matters. (*Puts his spectacles on the desk and rolls back his cuffs.*)

GERALDINE: I couldn't allow a man to touch me while I was unclothed.

PRENTICE: I shall wear rubber gloves, Miss Barclay.

GERALDINE: (*Is worried and makes no attempt to conceal her growing doubts.*) How long would I have to remain undressed?

PRENTICE: If your reactions are normal you'll be back on your feet in next to no time.

GERALDINE: I'd like another woman present. Is your wife available?

PRENTICE: Mrs. Prentice is attending a more than usually lengthy meeting of her coven. She won't be back until this evening.

GERALDINE: I could wait until then.

PRENTICE: I haven't the patience, my dear. I've a natural tendency to rush things . . . something my wife has never understood. But I won't trouble you with the details of my private life till you're dressed. Put your clothes on this. Lie on the couch.

(GERALDINE *unzips and removes her dress and shoes.* DR.
PRENTICE *puts dress on hanger and hangs it in down left
closet. Puts shoes on closet floor.*)

GERALDINE: What is Mrs. Prentice like, Doctor? I've heard
so many stories about her. (*Stands in her panties and bra.*)

PRENTICE: My wife is a nymphomaniac. Consequently, like
the Holy Grail, she's ardently sought after by young men. I
married her for her money and, upon discovering her to be
penniless, I attempted to throttle her . . . a mental aberra-
tion for which I've never forgiven myself. Needless to say,
our relationship has been delicate ever since.

GERALDINE: (*With a sigh.*) Poor Dr. Prentice. How trying it
must be for you. (*Climbing on to the couch.*) I wish there
were something I could do to cheer you up. (*Closes the
curtains.*)

PRENTICE (*Puts on a white surgical coat.*) Well, my dear, if
it'll give you any pleasure you can test my new contraceptive
device.

GERALDINE: (*Looks through the curtain and smiles sweetly.*)
I'll be delighted to help you in any way I can, Doctor.

PRENTICE: (*With an indulgent, superior smile.*) Lie on the
couch with your hands behind your head and think of the
closing chapters of your favorite work of fiction. The rest may
be left to me.

The Wrong Man

Laura Harrington

Characters: Nadia, John (ages unspecified)
Setting: A balcony outside a party
Premiere: New Dramatists, New York City, 1985
Publisher: Broadway Play Publishing (in *Short Pieces from the
New Dramatists*)

The Wrong Man was part of an evening of five-minute plays

performed at New Dramatists. The play is printed here in its entirety.

———————————

(*A party.* NADIA *is alone on the balcony, dancing.* JOHN *enters, watches* NADIA *and begins dancing with her. She dances with him for a beat or two, then turns her back on him.*)

JOHN: Excuse me—

NADIA: (*Turning to face him.*) No . . . We're not going to do that.

JOHN: I just wanted to know—

NADIA: —My name.

JOHN: Right.

NADIA: I've done that before. You've done that before. Tonight we're going to do something new . . . Instead of the usual banalities we're going to lie to each other.

JOHN: Oh, sure.

NADIA: About the last time we met—

JOHN: What are you talking about?

NADIA: The last time we met. Which was the first time. That's where we start.

JOHN: The first time . . . ?

NADIA: Before anything happened.

JOHN: (*Sarcastic.*) Right. Before anything happened.

NADIA: You've got it now.

JOHN: You're serious about this.

NADIA: Very.

(*A beat.*)

JOHN: I'm not sure I know how to do this.

NADIA: It's easy. Believe me.

(*Pause*)

JOHN: Okay . . . Okay . . . It was a party . . .

NADIA: A dance.

JOHN: A party, a dance . . . You were dancing.

NADIA: I could feel you watching me.

JOHN: I had been watching you for a very long time.

NADIA: I was careful near you . . .

JOHN: A summer night.

NADIA: Late summer.

JOHN: You sat next to another girl who turned to you and said: "You're very beautiful" . . . and you laughed.

NADIA: I'd been drinking . . . it was a party . . .

JOHN: A dance.

NADIA: And I'd been dancing . . .

JOHN: You sat next to me. Very close. Your thigh lay pressed against mine . . . I felt that I could almost, not quite, touch your breast . . .

NADIA: I was heady with liquor, with the night, with the surprise of your heat, with this girl telling me I was beautiful . . . I looked up, you were reaching your arms out to pull me to my feet, and I thought . . . "He is going to pick me right up out of my skin."

JOHN: I'd never touched you.

NADIA: I'd never touched you and I thought that you would pull me straight out of my skin.

JOHN: Your dress was a fine fabric, almost as fine as your skin . . . your shoulders—I ran my hands across your shoulders. I lifted your hair and put my hand to the nape of your neck.

NADIA: This was the first time . . .

JOHN: Yes.

NADIA: I was facing you. I was cold. We were children.

JOHN: No. A hot summer night. By the ocean.

NADIA: Near enough to smell the sea.

JOHN: We were no longer children.

NADIA: We came inside to dance.

JOHN: We weren't touching. Just dancing close. You were laughing . . . I watched the pulse at the base of your throat . . .

NADIA: I wondered what you would do, how you would do it . . . whether you would promise me things.

JOHN: I talked to you. I was so terrified that I couldn't stop talking . . . all of the things that I told you about . . . from the first time I'd seen you and been afraid to speak.

NADIA: No. You didn't say a word. We were walking, along the beach, not saying anything. And you kissed me. Startled me.

JOHN: I told you I would love you always.

NADIA: We lay down. You put your head on my breast. I pushed you away. Not like that. Not like a child coming to his mother.

JOHN: No. I talked until I had no breath left. I promised you everything I could think of. We were by the road, walking in the roadside. I couldn't stop talking until you kissed me . . . you pushed me by a fence. You put your hands inside my shirt . . . I was afraid to touch you.

NADIA: It was a beach.

JOHN: Another man, another time.

NADIA: No. (*She moves toward him.*) You pulled me out of my skin. When I stood up I was a new person.

JOHN: (*Backing off.*) But I've never touched you.

NADIA: And I don't know your name.

   (*A beat.*)

JOHN: Right.

   (*A beat.*)

NADIA: It's just as well.

JOHN: Yes. Just as well.

   (JOHN: *exists.*)

SCENES FOR

TWO WOMEN

Between Daylight and Boonville

Matt Williams

Characters: Carla (mid-20s), Marlene (mid-30s)
Setting: A temporary trailer court in the strip-mining country of southern Indiana.
Premiere: Wonderhorse Theatre, New York City, 1980
Publisher: Samuel French, Inc.

Three miners' wives and their kids pass their time in the makeshift "recreation area" between two of the trailers. The oldest woman, Loretta, is a spry 60-year-old who still gets hot flashes every time she sees Cary Grant. She is always seen smoking a Camel cigarette. The youngest wife, Carla, feels she is wasting her life. She is packing to leave her husband for the third time this month. She is best friends with Marlene, who is about seven months pregnant. There is an air of tranquillity and calm about Marlene.

There has been an explosion at the mine. Two hours have passed and the women still have heard no news. The whistle blows, and they know it's serious. Then they hear sirens. They try to remain calm. Tensions run high as they wait for word about the men.

Note: Loretta is not feeling well and has gone inside to lie down.

(CARLA *and* MARLENE *are quiet for several moments, then* MARLENE *picks up a magazine and begins to read. Long pause . . .*)

MARLENE: You think the ghost of Elvis really talked to this woman? She swears Elvis sends her messages through her poodle. (*Beat.*) That Jeff Bridges is cute, ain't he? I think he's better lookin' than his brother. Don't you think? He was suppose to be seein' Farrah for a while. Lee didn't know it. Now she's seein' Ryan O'Neal. I kinda feel sorry for Lee.

(*Sirens are heard again.* MARLENE *stops reading for a moment, then, with some effort, continues.*) You know who I really feel sorry for? Dinah Shore. She's had a rough time. Burt left her for that flyin' nun. That Sally Fields. He still loves Dinah, but he's seein' Sally cause she's younger. Sally. You like that name? Sally.

CARLA: Would you lay off that name crap? I'm sick of hearin' it.

MARLENE: I thought you wanted to help me pick out a name.

CARLA: Well, I don't. And I'm tired of those stupid stories.

MARLENE: They're not stupid.

CARLA: Yes, they are.

MARLENE: No, they're not.

CARLA: I don't want to hurt your feelin's, but those magazines are junk, Marlene. Trash junk!

MARLENE: Are not! Lots of people read them.

CARLA: Ignorant people.

MARLENE: That's not true.

CARLA: Only stupid people read that kind of stuff.

MARLENE: Are you sayin' I'm stupid?

CARLA: No.

MARLENE: Yes, you are.

CARLA: No, I'm not. I'm just sayin' you read junky magazines.

MARLENE: You're sayin' I'm stupid.

CARLA: OK, Marlene. You're stupid! Stupid for readin' that junk. My god, you got a high school diploma. You graduated, I didn't.

MARLENE: So what!

CARLA: You're wastin' your time readin' that garbage. Worryin' about flyin' nuns and plucked eye brows. If I'd of graduated, I'd of done things by now. Been gone and got a job . . .

MARLENE: Excuses! That's all you got are excuses. You always got an excuse when you don't want to do somethin'. If you were really goin' to leave, you would of done it a long time ago.

CARLA: I will.

MARLENE: You don't really want to leave here. You always

got an excuse to stay, or you wait for me to give you one so you don't have to go. You'll never leave here. Never!

CARLA: I swear I will.

MARLENE: Then go. Don't wait around. Go. But you ain't goin' to find nothin' better than what you got right here.

CARLA: I got nothin'.

MARLENE: You're like a little kid. Always wantin' somethin' you ain't got, lookin' for somethin' . . .

CARLA: I am meant for more than this.

MARLENE: More than what? There can't be more than your family. That's the most important thing in the world.

CARLA: Crap! That is a bunch of crap.

MARLENE: It is not. Stacy and Larry love you and need you.

CARLA: No they don't. Stacy ain't needed me since she learned how to walk. And Larry sure as hell don't.

MARLENE: You don't want to face the fact you love Larry, do you? Because you're afraid if you do, it'll keep you from leavin' and findin' your destiny or whatever it is you're lookin' for. But I got news for you, you don't find happiness. You create it.

CARLA: Who the hell are you to tell me what to do?

MARLENE: I thought I was your friend.

CARLA: You're nothin' but an ol' breed dog for Big Jim.

MARLENE: Don't talk about Big Jim.

CARLA: You're not any better than Margaret in there.

MARLENE: I ain't goin' to listen to you.

CARLA: That's why you can stomach this place.

MARLENE: (*Picking up the magazines.*) I'm goin' inside with Lorette . . .

CARLA: You sit around all day readin' those magazines, waitin' for Big fuckin' Jim to come home.

MARLENE: He is my husband. I love him!

CARLA: No! You worship him.

MARLENE: Just cause you're unhappy, don't start in on . . .

CARLA: Marlene.

MARLENE: We got somethin' special no one can take away.

CARLA: Open your eyes!

MARLENE: We need each other. And that's special.

CARLA: (*Overlapping lines.*) You're blind.

MARLENE: He's special.

CARLA: You don't have any idea.

MARLENE: I am his wife . . .

CARLA: You don't know . . .

MARLENE: . . . and he is my husband!

CARLA: . . . about him and Wanda! (*Pause.*)

MARLENE: (*Harsh whisper.*) That is a lie.

CARLA: I didn't mean . . . It just came out.

MARLENE: It is a lie.

CARLA: I'm sorry, Marlene. But it is not a lie.

MARLENE: It is a lie.

CARLA: You ever wonder why he don't touch you no more? Why he ain't laid a hand on you in months?

MARLENE: I'm pregnant.

CARLA: That's an excuse.

MARLENE: He don't want nothin' to go wrong.

CARLA: An excuse. Cause he's seein' Wanda.

MARLENE: Lie.

CARLA: For months.

MARLENE: Liar.

CARLA: Marlene . . .

MARLENE: Lie!

CARLA: They're sleepin' together!

MARLENE: (*Breaks down.*) Lie! Lie! Lie! Lie . . . (*It is quiet for several moments.* CARLA *moves to* MARLENE.)

CARLA: It's the truth, Marlene. Why do you think I hate her so much? Especially when you're so nice to her. I wanted to tell you, but I didn't want you to be hurt. I didn't want it to come out like this. You were so happy . . . (*Pause.*) But you got to face the facts. He's a man. Just like Larry. Like Cyril. He's not some sort of God. You got to realize that. Even though I wanted you to know, I hoped you'd never find out. But you had to sooner or later. They been together for months, ever since her husband died.

MARLENE: Before that.

CARLA: What?

MARLENE: Jim was seein' her before her husband died.

CARLA: You knew? (MARLENE *nods "Yes."*) You knew about them?

MARLENE: From the start.

CARLA: All this time you knew.

MARLENE: Yes, Carla. I knew.

CARLA: Why? Why did you act like you didn't know?

MARLENE: Because I don't want to lose what I got. My husband. My children. My family. That's all I got. All I ever wanted. My whole life. I'd rather go on pretendin' and not think about it, than lose the only thing I've got.

CARLA: I didn't know.

MARLENE: Don't touch me!

CARLA: Oh, Marlene. I'm sorry.

MARLENE: Please stay away! Let me alone.

CARLA: I never worried about you, cause I didn't think you had any problems. That nothin' bothered you . . . Why didn't you tell me?

MARLENE: I want to go inside.

CARLA: Marlene, I love you. (*Beat.*) I never said that to you ever, I know. But I do. You know that don't you?

MARLENE: It's gettin' late. I need to start supper.

CARLA: I understand now. I do.

MARLENE: Just let me alone.

(MARLENE *picks up the magazines and starts inside.*)

Blue Christmas

Eric Lane

Characters: Susan Williams (mid-20s), Jane Hammill (late 50s/ early 60s)

Setting: Jane's home, suburban Ohio, 1984

Premiere: Staged reading, 92nd Street Y, New York City, 1987
Publisher: Orange thoughts

When Susan is 7 years old, her father runs away. Her family does not hear from him. He dies, and she—now in her mid-20s—and her younger brother, Mark, travel to Ohio to find out who their father really was. Watching Susan, you sense that she had to become an adult before she had a chance to be a child. She works very hard at maintaining control of her emotions.

Susan and Mark meet their father's new wife, Jane, a manicurist who at times may appear scattered, but is extremely strong-willed and entirely capable of defending herself. Jane shows Mark his father's photo equipment. This is the first time that she and Susan get to speak alone.

(SUSAN *sits, drinks some coffee. She reaches for a frank 'n' blanks. It's cold. She eats it anyway. She opens a bottle of nail polish, smells it, then puts it back. She takes her cup, pours more coffee, cream. Moves to the Christmas tree, looks at an ornament.*

(SUSAN *looks in the direction of* MARK *and* JANE *exited and does not see them. She crosses to the record player and turns on an Elvis song. As it plays, she seems to connect with it, somehow softening.* JANE *moves into the doorway.* SUSAN *realizes, and her immediate impulse is to cut off the song.*)

JANE: No. leave it.

(SUSAN *puts down the needle again.*)

This always was one of his favorites.

SUSAN: What happened to Mark?

JANE: Thought I'd let him look around by himself. Would you like some more coffee?

(SUSAN *indicates cup; she has just taken some.* JANE *pours herself some more.*)

SUSAN: The tree's nice.

JANE: Excuse me?

SUSAN: The tree.

JANE: You like it? I wasn't sure I was going to get one this year, what with— Well, I just wasn't sure.

SUSAN: It's nice.

JANE: Thanks.

　(*Re: hors d'oeuvres.*)

　Help yourself.

SUSAN: Maybe later.

JANE: If they're cold I can always . . .

　(*Feels one.*)

　Why don't I pop these in the microwave?

SUSAN: I don't think so.

JANE: It'll take, what—? A minute. Not even.

SUSAN: I'm really not that hungry. Thank you though.

JANE: (*Nods.*) Your aunt tells me you're a lawyer.

SUSAN: I work in an office, but I'm not a lawyer.

JANE: No?

SUSAN: Office manager.

JANE: That sounds impressive. What does it mean?

SUSAN: Pretty much what it sounds like. I manage the office.

JANE: I bet you like it—working there, I mean.

SUSAN: It pays the rent. God, there's another one. (*Off* JANE'*s look.*) Just something Mark and I were discussing before. Phrases you hear growing up then—It's nothing important.

JANE: You hear, then what?

SUSAN: Then find yourself saying them. Things your mother should be saying, not you. "It pays the rent," or I don't know—

JANE: "Cut off my legs and call me shorty."

SUSAN: I suppose that depends on your mother.

JANE: Sort of when somebody tells you to do something, then blames you for it.

SUSAN: Your mother would actually say that?

JANE: If it fit. Or if she wanted to stop the conversation. Either way it seemed to work.

SUSAN: I'd imagine it would.

(JANE *takes out a cigarette.*)

JANE: Do you mind if I—?

SUSAN: Go ahead.

(JANE *lights it.*)

JANE: What kind? Of cases, I mean. At the office. That you handle.

SUSAN: Mostly corporate. Someone finds a piece of metal in a box of cereal. They sue the company. We get to defend them.

JANE: The company?

SUSAN: Nothing particularly humanitarian but—

JANE: It pays the rent.

SUSAN: Exactly.

JANE: Was your mother interested in law?

SUSAN: My mother?

(*Laughs slightly.*)

What made you think that?

JANE: I don't know. Usually you—well, I don't mean you exactly, but people in general wind up becoming interested in what they grow up surrounded by.

SUSAN: Or in reaction against it.

JANE: I guess. But I like to think I became who I am because of the people I was around, not in spite of them.

SUSAN: Well, sometimes what you'd like to think isn't the way things are.

JANE: You're right. Sometimes they're better.

SUSAN: Or worse.

JANE: Sometimes.

SUSAN: Quite often.

JANE: That's a nice ring you're wearing. Looks like the kind someone might give a little girl. I haven't seen one of those since, well, it's been a long time. It must've been hard when Bill left.

SUSAN: George. Before my father abandoned us his name was George.

JANE: It must've been hard.

SUSAN: We managed. On weekends I worked as cashier in my grandparents' poultry market in Brooklyn.

JANE: Live poultry?

SUSAN: Cages lining the walls. You'd go in, select what you wanted, they'd weigh it, then slaughter it for you. Unless you wanted to take it home live.

JANE: You mean like a pet chicken.

SUSAN: Possibly. Or for voodoo rituals. Once it was sold, I didn't ask questions.

JANE: Must've been fresh.

SUSAN: It didn't matter. After working there I wasn't able to eat poultry. I still can't. I was the only woman—well, "woman"—I must've started when I was in fifth grade. The men in the slaughtering room would try to gross me out.

JANE: How'd they do that?

SUSAN: Let's just say it involved a live chicken and a lit cigarette and leave it at that.

(JANE *puts out her cigarette.*)

I didn't mean—

(SUSAN *starts to laugh.* JANE *realizes what she has done and laughs as well.*)

Yes, it was . . . Hard. You asked me before. I never let them see how much it bothered me.

JANE: So what if you did?

(SUSAN *shrugs.* "Blue Christmas" *begins to play.*)

JANE: You know this one?

SUSAN: "Blue Christmas."

JANE: Bill's favorite. It could be the middle of summer. 95°, and he's singing "Blue Christmas."

(JANE *hums along.*)

SUSAN: I remember seeing him.

JANE: Elvis?

SUSAN: My father. The week Elvis died. I walk out of a store, and there he is. I start to follow, and just as I'm almost up to him, he turns the corner. I see it isn't my father at all. Just the way he walked that reminded me. The shoulders hunched in. Or the way the nails were filed—straight across then rounded at the end. It's the middle of August and all over the city I'm following men carrying copies of "Blue Christmas."

JANE: That happens to me all the time. Why just the other day—Thursday—yeah, it must've been Thursday—I stopped in this card store—

SUSAN: It was only that one week. Almost as though, I don't know—I could feel his presence.

JANE: You must've felt the same way since.

SUSAN: Not like that.

JANE: I guess it just brought back memories—Elvis dying and all.

SUSAN: Must've been.

(*The record starts to skip.* JANE *picks up the needle, cleans record.*)

Played that so many times I guess it's starting to wear through.

SUSAN: Does that actually work?

JANE: Seems to. You have to be careful though. You don't want to put too much pressure. On the record, I mean. Or, well—

SUSAN: I wonder what's keeping him.

JANE: Mark? Last I saw he was trying out some of the equipment.

SUSAN: In the darkroom?

JANE: Why? Is there anything wrong?

SUSAN: He said he wanted to get settled in at the motel. By the time he mixes the chemicals then waits for them to cool—

JANE: Already mixed.

SUSAN: Still, if they've been sitting for the past few months— How could that be?

JANE: What's that?

SUSAN: You said he was trying the equipment.

JANE: Did I? What I figured, at least.

SUSAN: "Last I saw." That's what you said. Those chemicals would have gone bad by now.

(*A beat.*)

JANE: Not if I mixed them this morning.

SUSAN: Why was that?

JANE: Habit, I guess. Bill always had me mix the chemicals for him. I guess I just haven't gotten out of the habit.

SUSAN: But it's been months since—

(JANE *puts down the needle on "Blue Christmas," cutting* SUSAN *off.*)

JANE: Yeah, this always was his favorite. Whenever we'd go to the water, on vacation, I mean. There are lakes around here but—This one time, these blowfish started swimming around. Must've been, well, hundreds of them, out of nowhere, just swimming around us. Bill tried catching them, with his hands, I mean. But they'd fill up with air, then let it out and slip right through his fingers. Bill told me to just stand there, in the water, and they started nibbling at my heels. I guess they couldn't eat and fill up at the same time. How he knew that, I don't know. But he started catching them, one after the other, just picking them out of the water, then throwing them back in. I remember after, he buried me in the sand. Packed tight against my body. Bill standing there, the sun behind him, just this shadow across the sky.

(*The record skips again.* JANE *picks up the needle.*)

SUSAN: How long do you think you'll keep mixing those chemicals?

JANE: (*Shrugs.*) Maybe a week. Maybe ten years from now.

SUSAN: How long?

JANE: Give yourself some time.

SUSAN: Who said anything about me?

(JANE *starts the song again. She puts on her smock top, listens.* SUSAN *exits.*)

Elm Circle

Mick Casale

Characters: Janet Ann (15), Brenda (older)
Setting: Various places in the United States, 1977
Premiere: Playwrights Horizons, New York City, 1984

Publisher: Dramatists Play Service, Inc.

In Janet Ann Maxwell's loosening mind, she starred in *Annie Hall* and *The Godfather*, and is the author of *Roots*, *Even Cowgirls Get the Blues*, and *Changing*. She narrates the play from a motel in Memphis as Elvis Presley's funeral procession goes past. In a series of flashbacks, we see how she got there, and how her mind snapped.

Janet Ann is from Elm Circle, New York, a suburb of Troy whose elms died a long time ago from Dutch elm disease. Aching to make her mark in the world, she talks her brother Tommy into running away to Manhattan with her. They dream of being singers, but Tommy likes drugs more than practicing music. Janet Ann takes off on a cross-country trip with a dealer named Sky, whose dreams are as far-fetched as hers. Somewhere in Ohio, he ditches her. After waiting for him for two days, Janet Ann decides to continue to Hollywood. This scene takes place on the cross-country train.

———————

(BRENDA TUBBS *appears, on the train, carrying two cans of Coke in hand with plastic cups on top.*)

BRENDA: Ya know, my granpaw once tol me—he fished tuna fer two years in California—he'd say all we wuz wuz ocean water all propped up 'n sealed closed. 'N if we ever wanted to get ridda the blues, all we hadda do wuz put a lil salt inna lil cup 'o water 'n chug. (*She hands a can to* JANET ANN.) This is the closest I could git t' salt water on this here train.

JANET ANN: Are you telling me I look blue?

BRENDA: So just do what they say—have a Coke 'n' a smile.

JANET ANN: I'm happy.

BRENDA: Where ya headin'?

JANET ANN: I'm very happy.

BRENDA: The name's Tubbs, Brenda.

JANET ANN: Nice to meet you.

BRENDA: Likewise.

JANET ANN: I'm heading to the South Pacific. My father is

Marlon Brando. He has this island out there. He's starting a new society.

BRENDA: Ya know, Missy, yer like findin' one o' my ol' mirrors.

JANET ANN: I was outside Nashville on this farm that was really a recording studio. I was cutting this record with Kris Kristofferson. I hated to leave. Maybe that's why I look blue to you.

BRENDA: Aw, Missy, doncha recognize me? I'm that skinny lil thang in the white polky dot dress. Goin' up Deetroit t' build me some cars. I wuz gonna be the purtiest spot-welder on the line. I wuz gonna have my pitcher on the cover of *Life* magazine. Folks'd come fer miles around jist t' see me work.

JANET ANN: Did they?

BRENDA: Oh, they come t' see me work. But not in no auto plant.

JANET ANN: What did you do?

BRENDA: I danced. Sorta.

JANET ANN: I took dancing.

BRENDA: I didn't wear no clothes.

JANET ANN: When I was in *Hair* I did a nude scene.

BRENDA: This weren't no Broadway show.

JANET ANN: Well, I think if it's important to the storyline it's not bad to perform naked. I mean, if it's for art.

BRENDA: Oh, I did it fer Art all right. An' Bill. An' George. An' any other hy-yoop that'd stuff a few bucks down my panties.

JANET ANN: I wouldn't work in a place like that.

BRENDA: Ya think I wanted to?

JANET ANN: I mean, I don't have to. I've got a lot of other jobs all lined up.

BRENDA: So did I.

JANET ANN: I'm famous.

BRENDA: So wuz I. Shoot, there wasn't a conventioneer hit Deetroit who didn't know my name.

JANET ANN: But I make movies.

BRENDA: So did I.

JANET ANN: I mean real movies.

BRENDA: Ya caint git much realer'n movies I made.

JANET ANN: Thanks for the soda.

BRENDA: Slow down there, Missy. I know what you need. You need a lil operation. You need a lil transplant surgery. You lost yer funny-bone. We gotta replace it wi' one o' yer ribs.

JANET ANN: No. Don't. I'm ticklish. (BRENDA *digs her fingers into* JANET ANN's *ribs.*)

BRENDA: Callin' Dr. Tubbs! Callin' Dr. Tubbs!

JANET ANN: All right. All right. I give. (BRENDA *eases off.*) I give, lady, I give.

BRENDA: Go home. Missy.

JANET ANN: I can't.

BRENDA: Why not?

JANET ANN: I've got this movie. A remake of *Johnny Belinda*. My mother's favorite movie.

BRENDA: I thought you wuz a—goin' t' the South Pacific?

JANET ANN: I am, but I have to wait in L.A. for this friend of mine who knows the address for the boat to the island then this movie came up.

BRENDA: I thought Marlon Brando wuz yer daddy.

JANET ANN: He is.

BRENDA: Then why doncha jist ask him fer the address?

JANET ANN: Well, he's in his Winnebago someplace in Montana and—

BRENDA: Go home.

[CONDUCTOR: The next stop is Memphis. Memphis is next.]

JANET ANN: And anyway I have to stop in Memphis. I was talking to Elvis on the phone this morning. I promised I'd get off to cut an album.

BRENDA: Honey . . .

JANET ANN: What?

BRENDA: Elvis is dead.

JANET ANN: What?

BRENDA: He died yesterday.

JANET ANN: How do you know? You don't know Elvis.

BRENDA: It wuz in alla papers.

JANET ANN: Maybe you shouldn't always believe what you read. You should see some of the lies they've written about me—

BRENDA: Go home.

JANET ANN: But I live on this island.

BRENDA: Ya ain't who ya say ya are.

JANET ANN: You think I'm just a liar. You think I'm just a bullshit artist.

BRENDA: Stay on the train. Git off wi' me in Lil Rock. We can call yer parents. We can see some sights together. 'N you ken go back home.

JANET ANN: You can't bear the sight of me because you're packing it in and I'm not.

BRENDA: I know ya don't want no advice.

JANET ANN: Not from you. (*A conductor is heard calling "The stop is Memphis, Memphis, Tennessee!"*)

BRENDA: At least lemme know yer name so I can call yer parents an' tell 'em you're okay.

JANET ANN: But Elvis is waiting for me at the station.

BRENDA: Go ahead then. Wind up as stupid as I wuz.

JANET ANN: Just because you wound up some kind of stripper you think everybody else will. Well, that's just your tough luck being who you are. That's not going to happen to me.

BRENDA: Fine. Feel sorry for yerself. Thank ya gotta prove somethin' to the world before yer parents'll want ya. But ya know what? But ya know what? Ya know what it took me longer'n you been alive t' learn? The world don't care, Missy!

JANET ANN: Maybe not about you!

Final Placement

(from *Win/Lose/Draw*)

Ara Watson

Characters: Luellen (20s to early 30s), Mary (30s)
Setting: A large office
Premiere: Actors Theatre of Louisville, 1980
Publisher: Dramatists Play Service, Inc.

Mary Hanson is a social worker. *Final Placement* concerns one of her cases: Jimmy James, a four-year-old victim of child abuse.

A doctor detects physical abuse and Mary investigates. Jimmy is placed in foster care and his physical and emotional states improve. His parents enter group therapy. They are said to make progress—especially Jimmy's mother. He is returned to them. Soon after, Jimmy's mother holds his hands on a hot stove. He sustains first- and second-degree burns. His parents abandon him, and he is put up for adoption.

While Jimmy is in foster care, his parents never contact the social worker. Until today. Luellen, Jimmy's mother, walks ten miles in the hot sun to speak to Mary. She wants Jimmy back.

Note: Luellen's feet are blistered; her shoes are off.

MARY: Here's your . . . (LUELLEN *turns, takes the cup and drinks.*) You walked a very long way on a very hot day to see me . . . Luellen? . . . (LUELLEN *looks at her quickly and then away.*) and I *would* like to know why—what I can do to help you—but you are going to have to tell me. (*No response.*) Will you? (*No response.*) Well. I'm sorry, I wish I had more time, but I do have this appointment, so, if you'll let me get my things together, I'll take you—

LUELLEN: (*Quickly and with a new energy.*) No, but, see,

see, I got this real good idea. It's real good, too. See, I'm
fixin' to move out on ol' Ray. He just don't know it yet, but
I am. I'm goin' to get me a place to live and I'm goin' to get
me a job maybe with the phone company maybe. My girlfriend works for the phone company. Or a waitress. I could
do that.

MARY: Jobs are a little hard to find these days, but . . . but
that sounds . . . I think you'd enjoy working . . .

LUELLEN: (*Big smile.*) I think I would, too. And my girlfriend
lives in a duplex and her neighbors is goin' to move maybe
and I could move in there if they did. It's got a fenced-in
backyard and a big side yard and I wouldn't even let ol' Ray
even come visit only if he got over doin' them things.

MARY: (*Realizing.*) Wait a minute—

LUELLEN: (*Going on.*) I know he don't mean to. He just loses
his temper sometimes is all, but he's gettin' a whole lot better
'bout it since we went to that group. I sure do 'preciate you
makin' us go to them meetin's. See, we had a lot of pressure
on us and we was probably just takin' it out on—

MARY: Luellen. Wait a minute here.

LUELLEN: No, no. I still wouldn't let him come and stay. Not
no matter how much he yelled at me or how much he begged
me, he couldn't. A daddy don't need to be with his son like
a mama does. (*Slightly choked, but going on.*) A mama needs
to be with her child. You know that, don't you? I know you
do and I'm goin' to get a place for me and Jimmy to live and
you can—

MARY: You know that's—

LUELLEN: (*Going on.*) And you could come visit Jimmy ever'day.
You could take him out in your car and you could buy him
a Coke and ask him questions . . . I'd share him with you.
We could share him. (*She looks pleadingly at* MARY. *Pause.*)

MARY: Luellen, please don't do this to yourself.

LUELLEN: I ain't—

MARY: You're hurting yourself with this. You're building up
a fantasy that—

LUELLEN: It ain't a fantasy. I thought it all out.

MARY: Thinking it out doesn't mean it can happen that way.

LUELLEN: (*A protest.*) Yes!

MARY: No. I'm sorry.

LUELLEN: (*Looks at her a moment—quietly.*) You ain't sorry.

MARY: Yes, I am. I'm sorry for how you feel right now. I know how very—

LUELLEN: You know what? You know what it's like to have your kid stole by the Welfare? To sit in a room and remember that your little boy ain't bein' quiet 'cause he's sleepin' or into somethin', but that he's bein' quiet 'cause he ain't even there no more? And you don't know where he is or when he's comin' back? You don't know.

MARY: No, I guess . . . no one can . . . really . . . but you have to . . .

LUELLEN: (*Watching her coldly.*) What? I have to what? Forget about him? You ain't got no kids, do you?

MARY: No.

LUELLEN: No. You want one?

MARY: Someday.

LUELLEN: Like my Jimmy? (MARY *doesn't answer this.*) I know you like him a whole lot. You like him better than the other ones? He your favorite? You know what ol' Ray told me oncet after you'd come out to visit? He said, "You better watch out, Lu girl. That woman wants your baby for herself and she's a'gonna get him, too." That's what he said, but I didn't believe him. Sometimes, though, that Ray knows what he's talkin' 'bout. You got him?

MARY: What?

LUELLEN: You got him at your house, ain't you?

MARY: No. That's—

LUELLEN: You don't want me to know where you live 'cause—

MARY: This is a state agency. There are rules here, Luellen. Even if I wanted to do something like—

LUELLEN: Oh, you want to. You want to and you did. (*The two look at each other a long moment.*)

MARY: (*Reasonably.*) No matter how much I care about Jimmy— and I do, I care about him—that simply isn't the reason he

was taken out of your home. You know that. I did not "steal"
him. He is not at my house. OK? Now. I want you to tell
me precisely what it is you think I can do, so I can answer
you in as clear a way as possible . . . so we understand each
other.

LUELLEN: (*Trying to be "reasonable" in turn.*) I want to see
Jimmy.

MARY: I understand that, but what do you want *me* to do?

LUELLEN: I want you to go get him.

MARY: I can't do that. I don't have that authority. It's out of
my hands.

LUELLEN: You go get him and bring him here.

MARY: I can't—

LUELLEN: Go get him.

MARY: You were in the courtroom. You heard what the judge
said.

LUELLEN: Then call him.

MARY: Who?

LUELLEN: Call that judge. Right now. Tell him I can have my
baby back.

MARY: I'm not going to argue with you—

LUELLEN: Call him.

MARY: This interview is ended.

LUELLEN: Call him. (*She moves in on* MARY.)

MARY: I can't call the judge!

LUELLEN: Yes, you can! (*Continuing to move in on* MARY—
cold and menacing.) And you better.

MARY: (*Backing—fear showing.*) Luellen.

LUELLEN: You better do it. (*She is almost in* MARY'S *face.*)

MARY: Get out of my face.

LUELLEN: (*Fists clenched.*) I mean it!

MARY: Now . . . stop this!

LUELLEN: If you don't, I'll do something. I'll hurt you. I can.
I ain't kiddin' either. (LUELLEN *begins to raise her fists and
as she does,* MARY *starts to turn to run from her, but instead
knocks into the chair with everything still piled on it. The
chair overturns making a loud crashing sound. The crash*

causes both women to stop. MARY *is almost immediately shocked into fury and* LUELLEN *is cowed.*)

MARY: God-damnit! God-damn-it! (*Turns on* LUELLEN *who steps back.*) Just who the hell do you think you are? What do you think you're doing here? You can't ever—not ever in this life—see that child again. Not ever.

LUELLEN: (*More of a cry.*) Yes, I can.

MARY: Do you think the state or the judge would put that little boy back after what you did?

LUELLEN: I didn't . . . I never done—Ray. Ray done it.

MARY: You! You! Face that reality at least. You. You admitted it to me, to the judge—

LUELLEN: (*Shaking her head.*) Ray.

MARY: Ray may have done a lot of it, but not that last, Luellen.

LUELLEN: (*Childlike.*) Well . . . he made me.

MARY: He made you hold that child's hands on a hot stove 'til he had first and second degree burns? I'll tell you one thing, Ray couldn't have made me do that!

LUELLEN: (*Meekly.*) We was just teaching him—

MARY: (*Going on.*) And, then, you ran off and left him, just left him—*and* in all the months we've had him in foster care, you haven't contacted me once, not one time, to find out how he was doing. So why today? Why do you people suddenly turn up out of the blue and think—Christ. (*Takes a breath to calm herself.*) We explained everything to you six months ago. (*Brief pause.*) You could hold a gun to my head or a knife to my throat and it still wouldn't get him back for you. (*Pause.*)

LUELLEN: What am I gonna do?

MARY: I don't know. (*Pause.*) See someone. Let me make an appoint—

LUELLEN: Talkin' to a stranger ain't goin' to help.

MARY: It can.

LUELLEN: I was right 'bout you wantin' Jimmy, wasn't I? (*No answer.*) I know I was. That's how come me to come to see you. It gets so quiet sometimes, I thought you'd understand about it. Ray told me. He said, "The Welfare don't understand nothin' 'bout people's feelin's. They ain't never goin' to help you." (*Brief pause.*) My girlfriend's fixin' to have a little baby. I been givin' her all Jimmy's baby things.

MARY: I'm sure that's very hard for you.

LUELLEN: I'm givin' her a baby shower at my house. (*Pointing to the clothes.*) Could I have one of those to give to her? (MARY *gives her two boxes.*)

MARY: I wish you'd let me get you in to see someone. (LUELLEN *goes over and puts her shoes on.*)

LUELLEN: Don't hurt none.

MARY: At least, let me take you—

LUELLEN: I don't want you to.

MARY: (*Taking change from her billfold.*) Let me give you bus fare, then. (MARY *hands her the money and* LUELLEN *takes it without saying anything.*) I'm . . . I'm sorry I lost my . . . I shouldn't have . . . (LUELLEN *without ever looking at* MARY *turns and walks out, leaving* MARY *standing there watching her.*)

Footfalls
Samuel Beckett

Characters: May (40s), Woman's Voice (89/90)
Setting: Dimly lit stage
Premiere: Royal Court Theatre, London, 1976
Publisher: Grove Press (from *The Collected Shorter Plays of Samuel Beckett*)

Samuel Beckett is the author of *Waiting for Godot, Endgame,* and *Krapp's Last Tape,* among many other plays. The following is the complete text of *Footfalls.*

(MAY [M], *disheveled grey hair, worn grey wrap hiding feet, trailing.*
WOMAN'S VOICE [V] *from dark upstage.*

*Strip: downstage, parallel with front, length nine steps,
width one metre, a little off centre audience right.*

r l r l r l r l r←

L ———————————————————— R

→l r l r l r l r l

Pacing: starting with right foot [r], *from right* [R] *to left* [L],
with left foot [l], *from L to R.*
Turn: rightabout at L, leftabout at R.
Steps: clearly audible rhythmic tread.
*Lighting: dim, strongest at floor level, less on body, least on
head.*
Voices: both low and slow throughout.
Curtain. Stage in darkness.
Faint single chime. Pause as echoes die.
Fade up to dim on strip. Rest in darkness.
*M discovered pacing towards L. Turns at L, paces three more
lengths, halts, facing front at R.*
Pause.)

M: Mother. (*Pause. No louder.*) Mother.   (*Pause.*)
V: Yes, May.
M: Were you asleep?
V: Deep asleep. (*Pause.*) I heard you in my deep sleep. (*Pause.*)
There is no sleep so deep I would not hear you there. (*Pause.
M resumes pacing. Four lengths. After first length, synchron-
ous with steps.*) One two three four five six seven wheel one
two three four five six seven wheel. (*Free.*) Will you not try
to snatch a little sleep?
  (M *halts facing front at R. Pause.*)
M: Would you like me to inject you again?
V: Yes, but it is too soon.
  (*Pause.*)
M: Would you like me to change your position again?
V: Yes, but it is too soon.
  (*Pause.*)
M: Straighten your pillows? (*Pause.*) Change your drawsheet?
(*Pause.*) Pass you the bedpan? (*Pause.*) The warming-pan?

(*Pause.*) Dress your sores? (*Pause.*) Sponge you down?
(*Pause.*) Moisten your poor lips? (*Pause.*) Pray with you?
(*Pause.*) For you? (*Pause.*) Again.
  (*Pause.*)
V: Yes, but it is too soon.
  (*Pause.*)
M: What age am I now?
V: And I? (*Pause. No louder.*) And I?
M: Ninety.
V: So much?
M: Eighty-nine, ninety.
V: I had you late. (*Pause.*) In life. (*Pause.*) Forgive me again.
 (*Pause. No louder.*) Forgive me again.
  (M *resumes pacing. After one length halts facing front at*
  L.
  Pause.)
M: What age am I now?
V: In your forties.
M: So little?
V: I'm afraid so. (*Pause.* M *resumes pacing. After first turn*
 at L.) May. (*Pause. No louder.*) May.
M: (*Pacing.*) Yes, Mother.
V: Will you never have done? (*Pause.*) Will you never have
 done . . . revolving it all?
M: (*Halting.*) It?
V: It all. (*Pause.*) In your poor mind. (*Pause.*) It all. (*Pause.*)
 It all.
  (M *resumes pacing. Five seconds. Fade out on strip.*
   All in darkness. Steps cease.
   Pause.
   Chime a little fainter. Pause for echoes.
   Fade up to a little less on strip. Rest in darkness.
 M *discovered facing front at* R.
 Pause.)
V: I walk here now. (*Pause.*) Rather I come and stand. (*Pause.*)
 At nightfall. (*Pause.*) She fancies she is alone. (*Pause.*) See
 how still she stands, how stark, with her face to the wall.

(*Pause.*) How outwardly unmoved. (*Pause.*) She has not been out since girlhood. (*Pause.*) Not out since girlhood. (*Pause.*) Where is she, it may be asked. (*Pause.*) Why, in the old home, the same where she— (*Pause.*) The same where she began. (*Pause.*) Where it began. (*Pause.*) It all began. (*Pause.*) But this, this, when did this begin? (*Pause.*) When other girls of her age were out at . . . lacrosse she was already here. (*Pause.*) At this. (*Pause.*) The floor here, now bare, once was— (M *begins pacing. Steps a little slower.*) But let us watch her move, in silence. (M *paces. Towards end of second length.*) Watch how feat she wheels. (M *turns, paces. Synchronous with steps third length.*) Seven, eight, nine, wheel. (M *turns at L., paces one more length, halts facing front at R.*) I say the floor here, now bare, this strip of floor, once was carpeted, a deep pile. Till one night, while still little more than a child, she called her mother and said, Mother, this is not enough. The mother: Not enough? May—the child's given name—May: Not enough. The mother: What do you mean, May, not enough, what can you possibly mean, May, not enough? May: I mean, Mother, that I must hear the feet, however faint they fall. The mother: The motion alone is not enough? May: No, Mother, the motion alone is not enough, I must hear the feet, however faint they fall. (*Pause.* M *resumes pacing. With pacing.*) Does she still sleep, it may be asked? Yes, some nights she does, in snatches, bows her poor head against the wall and snatches a little sleep. (*Pause.*) Still speak? Yes, some nights she does, when she fancies none can hear. (*Pause.*) Tells how it was. (*Pause.*) Tries to tell how it was. (*Pause.*) It all. (*Pause.*) It all. (M *continues pacing. Five seconds. Fade out on strip. All in darkness. Steps cease. Pause. Chime a little fainter still. Pause for echoes. Fade up to a little less still on strip. Rest in darkness. M discovered facing front at R. Pause.*)

M: Sequel. (*Pause. Begins pacing. Steps a little slower still.*

After two lengths halts facing front at R. Pause.) Sequel. A little later, when she was quite forgotten, she began to— (*Pause.*) A little later, when as though she had never been, it never been, she began to walk. (*Pause.*) At nightfall. (*Pause.*) Slip out at nightfall and into the little church by the north door, always locked at that hour, and walk, up and down, up and down, his poor arm. (*Pause.*) Some nights she would halt, as one frozen by some shudder of the mind, and stand stark still till she could move again. But many also were the nights when she paced without pause, up and down, up and down, before vanishing the way she came. (*Pause.*) No sound. (*Pause.*) None at least to be heard. (*Pause.*) The semblance. (*Pause. Resumes pacing. After two lengths halts facing front at R. Pause.*) The semblance. Faint, though by no means invisible, in a certain light. (*Pause.*) Given the right light. (*Pause.*) Grey rather than white, a pale shade of grey. (*Pause.*) Tattered. (*Pause.*) A tangle of tatters. (*Pause.*) Watch it pass— (*Pause.*)—watch her pass before the candelabrum, how its flames, their light . . . like moon through passing rack. (*Pause.*) Soon then after she was gone, as though never there, began to walk, up and down, up and down, that poor arm. (*Pause.*) At nightfall. (*Pause.*) That is to say, at certain seasons of the year, during Vespers. (*Pause.*) Necessarily. (*Pause. Resumes pacing. After one length halts facing front at L. Pause.*) Old Mrs. Winter, whom the reader will remember, old Mrs. Winter, one late autumn Sunday evening, on sitting down to supper with her daughter after worship, after a few half-hearted mouthfuls laid down her knife and fork and bowed her head. What is it, Mother, said the daughter, a most strange girl, though scarcely a girl any more . . . (*Brokenly.*) . . . dreadfully un— . . . (*Pause. Normal voice.*) What is it, Mother, are you not feeling yourself? (*Pause.*) Mrs. W. did not at once reply. But finally, raising her head and fixing Amy—the daughter's given name, as the reader will remember—raising her head and fixing Amy full in the eyes she said—(*Pause.*)—she murmured, fixing Amy full in the eye she murmured, Amy did you observe anything . . . strange at Evensong? Amy: No, Mother, I did not. Mrs. W: Perhaps it was just my fancy. Amy: Just what exactly, Mother, did you perhaps fancy it was? (*Pause.*) Just what exactly, Mother, did you perhaps fancy this . . . strange thing was you observed? (*Pause.*) Mrs. W: You yourself observed nothing . . . strange? Amy: No, Mother, I myself did not, to put it mildly. Mrs. W: What do you mean, Amy, to put it mildly, what can you possibly mean, Amy, to put it mildly? Amy: I mean, Mother, that to say I observed nothing . . . strange is indeed to put it mildly. For I observed nothing of any kind, strange or otherwise. I saw nothing, heard nothing, of any kind. I was not there. Mrs. W: Not there? Amy: Not there. Mrs. W: But I heard you respond. (*Pause.*) I heard you say Amen. (*Pause.*) How could you have responded if you were not there? (*Pause.*) How could you possibly have said Amen if, as you claim, you were not there? (*Pause.*) The love of God, and the fellowship of the Holy Ghost, be with us all, now, and for evermore. Amen. (*Pause.*) I heard you distinctly. (*Pause. Resumes pacing. After three steps halts without facing front. Long pause. Resumes pacing, halts facing front at R. Long pause.*) Amy. (*Pause. No louder.*) Amy. (*Pause.*) Yes, Mother. (*Pause.*) Will you never have done? (*Pause.*) Will you never have done . . . revolving it all? (*Pause.*) It? (*Pause.*) It all. (*Pause.*) In your poor mind. (*Pause.*) It all. (*Pause.*) It all.

(*Pause. Fade out on strip. All in darkness.*
Pause.
Chime even a little fainter still. Pause for echoes.
Fade up to even a little less still on strip
No trace of MAY.
Hold ten seconds.
Fade out.)

Graceland

Ellen Byron

Characters: Bev Davies (42), Rootie Mallert (22)
Setting: Outside Graceland, June 4, 1982
Premiere: Philadelphia Festival Theatre for New Plays, 1983
Publisher: Dramatists Play Service, Inc.

It is three days before Elvis's home, Graceland, is to be opened to the public. Two women, Bev and Rootie, are camped outside. Each has her own reason for needing to be the first inside.

(BEV DAVIES *enters, humming snatches of an Elvis song. She is wearing a matching polyester set of pants and a vest, and a heavily curled wig. She carries a cooler, large bag, beach chair, and pop-up tent. She sets down everything but the tent, which she begins to assemble. It comes together rapidly. Absorbed in her efforts, she doesn't notice the entrance of* ROOTIE MALLERT, *whose gaze is held by the vision of the mansion, out front. She doesn't notice* BEV. ROOTIE *is wearing tattered shorts, a faded shell neck tee shirt and clunky sandals. She carries a pillow and a brown paper bag. As* ROOTIE *rests herself on the pillow,* BEV *notices* ROOTIE *and sets up her chair in an authoritative manner.* ROOTIE *takes a makeup purse out of her brown paper bag, and begins checking herself out intently. This is a nervous habit which she repeats several times during the play. She is suddenly aware of* BEV *through the compact mirror, and looks over. There is a moment of silence.*)

ROOTIE: Hey.
BEV: Hello. (*There is another awkward pause. Finally—*)
ROOTIE: Nice chair.
BEV: Thank you. I was here first.
ROOTIE: Pardon?

BEV: I said I was here first. *I* was here first.

ROOTIE: Oh. (*Pause*.) I think I was.

BEV: Excuse me?

ROOTIE: I'm sorry ma'am, I hope you don't mind, but I think I was here first, I really do.

BEV: (*Stares at* ROOTIE, *then turns and stares straight ahead. With finality*—) I was here first.

ROOTIE: I put my pillow down before you put your chair down.

BEV: What?!

ROOTIE: Well, I heard you put your chair down in the grass, and my pillow was already down by then.

BEV: That's crazy, that is just crazy. How the hell could you hear that? Grass doesn't make noise.

ROOTIE: A chair is louder than a pillow.

BEV: What the hell does that mean? A pin is louder than a feather but that doesn't mean you could hear it fall in the grass.

ROOTIE: I put my pillow down first.

BEV: But my tent was already up.

ROOTIE: But I sat down before you, that's what counts.

BEV: No it doesn't—

ROOTIE: Yes it does—

BEV: No it doesn't—

ROOTIE: Yes it does—

BEV: No it doesn't.

ROOTIE: Yes it *does*. (*A stalemate*.)

BEV: What are you doing here anyway? Why don't you just chase after one of those teenage idol types and leave this to the people who really care?

ROOTIE: I care.

BEV: You care?

ROOTIE: I care.

BEV: What could you possibly know? (ROOTIE *just looks at her for a moment, then faces front and begins speaking. As she speaks, her face develops a radiant, almost mystical glow*.)

ROOTIE: He was born on January 8, 1935, at 12:02 P.M. His identical twin, Jessie Garon, was stillborn, and buried the next day. He attended Lawlor Elementary School and got his first guitar on his eleventh birthday. It cost $12.75, and his mama bought it for him at the Tupelo Hardware Store. He made his first record on Monday, July 5th, at Sun Studio and his whole life changed when his mama died on August 14, 1958. (BEV *is silent for a moment. Then rapid-fire:*)

BEV: What she die of?

ROOTIE: (*Equally fast.*) Heart attack complicated by hepatitis.

BEV: What was the first song he ever recorded?

ROOTIE: "My Happiness," in 1953.

BEV: What's his father's name?

ROOTIE: Vernon.

BEV: When was his father born?

ROOTIE: April 4, 1916.

BEV: (*Pause.*) I was still here first. (*Pause, then—*)

ROOTIE: Who wrote "Heartbreak Hotel"?

BEV: Hoyt Axton's mother.

ROOTIE: Who was his favorite actress to work with?

BEV: Shelley Fabares.

ROOTIE: When did he make his first screen test?

BEV: April 15, 1956, and he read from some play called *The Rainmaker*.

ROOTIE: What's his favorite cigarette?

BEV: Lucky Strike.

ROOTIE: (*Pause.*) Elvis didn't smoke.

BEV: Of course he didn't smoke, Lord, I knew that, you just threw me off with all that other stuff. It's early. I don't think good early.

ROOTIE: *I* was here first.

BEV: Now one damn minute. I was the first person to enter the Meditation Garden and Gravesite when it opened and I was the first person to go into his museum when it opened and I was the first person to touch his statue when they unveiled it and now that in three days, when they are finally going to open his home, the most sacred place of all, I am goddamned well going to be the first person to set foot through those doors.

ROOTIE: I have to be. I'm sorry, ma'am, but I have to be.

BEV: What the hell do you mean, you *have* to be?

ROOTIE: I have to get to him.

BEV: Get to him? Are you crazy? He's dead.

ROOTIE: I know that. But I'm gonna make him come back. If you love somebody enough, you can. I was watching this movie yesterday and it was called *Brigadoon*, and Gene Kelly made a whole village come back just because he loved the girl so much.

BEV: What are you talking about?

ROOTIE: If I got in there first, and was just by myself for five minutes, I could talk to him—

BEV: Hold on one minute. First of all, you will never get in there alone, they got guards on the laundry shelves for chrissake, and second: *I was here first.*

ROOTIE: Yeah, but if you're first, don't they give you a prize or something? I could ask for my prize to be just five minutes alone in there. My cousin was the first customer when they opened a new K mart in her town and they gave her all sorts of stuff.

BEV: Oh come on, does this look like a K mart to you? (*She waves toward the house.* ROOTIE *is silent.*)

ROOTIE: I have to go in first.

BEV: Who the hell do you think you are? I have dedicated my life to this man, to preserving his memory, to showing the world there is only one true singer and that's Elvis. I turned my whole basement into a memorial room to him. Threw out my kids' Ping-Pong table and set up my whole collection. I got records, pictures, even a scarf he used to wipe the sweat from his face in Vegas, '72. I have got every liquor bottle that was ever made as an Elvis statue. Even TV shows have interviewed me. I have loved him with the purest and truest love possible since I was fifteen and if you think I'm just gonna hand that over to some stupid kid, all I have to say to you is no, repeat NO, goddamn, repeat GOD-DAMN, way.

ROOTIE: But I have to be in there first or it won't work.

BEV: What do you mean? What won't work? Are you talking about magic or some—oh my God, you're one of those crazy cult people. I'm getting the guards.

ROOTIE: Please, I don't know nothing about that stuff—

BEV: I am getting you thrown off these grounds.

ROOTIE: Okay, okay, fine. You go ahead and get 'em, but you can't prove nothing. Besides, then they'll probably chase both of us away. (BEV *hesitates for a moment.* ROOTIE *grabs her pillow and throws it directly in front of* BEV's *chair, then sits with resolute determination.* BEV *turns around, sees her, and grabs her chair, placing it squarely in front of* ROOTIE ROOTIE *grabs her pillow and throws it in front of* BEV's *chair,* BEV *grabs her chair and puts in in front of* ROOTIE, *who picks it up from the back and places it behind her. As she is doing this,* BEV *grabs* ROOTIE's *pillow, heaves it behind her chair, and throws herself into the seat.* ROOTIE *grabs the pillow and they face off for a moment. Then* ROOTIE *walks around her, heading toward the mansion.* BEV *scoots forward in her chair, and* ROOTIE *stops.* ROOTIE *goes to take another step, and* BEV *goes to scoot again. A standoff.* ROOTIE *decides to try another approach. She slowly lowers herself to the ground, on an even level with* BEV's *chair.*) That's a beautiful suit.

BEV: What?

ROOTIE: I always wanted a suit like that.

BEV: What the hell are you talking about?

ROOTIE: Well, they never come in my size.

BEV: Why not? What size do you wear?

ROOTIE: (*Very nonchalant as she adjusts her pillow so that it is slightly ahead of* BEV's *chair.*) Oh, I guess about a three. (BEV *stands up.*)

BEV: A three? Well, that just ain't healthy. How can you be a real woman and wear a scrawny size like a three? (*As she sits, she pulls her chair ahead.*)

ROOTIE: My Weebo always said that if a woman ain't got a shelf, then she should at least be as thin as a sideways door.

BEV: Your who-bo?

ROOTIE: Weebo. That's my husband. Since he was best friends with my brother Beau, Weebo was like little Beau. See?

BEV: Sure. Wee-bo. Well, I guess that's about the name I'd expect from a man who thinks women should look like sideways doors, what the Hell am I doing *talking* like this?! (*She pulls her chair forward.*)

ROOTIE: Ma'am? Excuse me, ma'am?

BEV: What?!

ROOTIE: I'll tell you why I got to go in there first.

BEV: Shoot.

ROOTIE: Well—the day it opens is Beau's birthday.

BEV: Weebo?

ROOTIE: No, Beau, my brother.

BEV: Oh, that explains everything. You want to get in there first so you can ask Elvis' ghost to wish your brother a Happy Birthday. Look, I'll make a deal with you. I'll give you a dollar and you can go buy him a card, ok? (*She gets her bag and begins searching through it.*)

ROOTIE: I can't, I can't send it to him.

BEV: What's the matter, can't spell his address?

ROOTIE: He's dead.

BEV: Oh. I—Oh. Well, my God, why the hell didn't you say so? That's a terrible thing to do, letting me go on like that.

ROOTIE: I'm sorry.

BEV: I accept your apology.

ROOTIE: He died in the war.

BEV: Korean?

ROOTIE: No, Viet Nam.

BEV: Oh.

ROOTIE: He was an Army man. They're the toughest.

BEV: I know it. My husband was Army, too.

ROOTIE: No, you're kidding. Ain't that something? Here we are, two total strangers, and we're both related to the army.

BEV: Small world.

ROOTIE: The funny thing is—I don't mean ha ha funny, I mean, funny, funny—well, there are people, you just can't see them going on past a certain point. It's like with Beau.

I could never think what he'd be doing later on. I don't think
he knew either, and that's why he joined up.

BEV: I know what you mean. I had this best friend in high
school, Francene. We were like sisters, just so close. But
Francie was wild, drove like a maniac, went all the way with
boys, drank like a truckdriver. Killed in a car crash senior
year. Guess I kind of expected it all along.

ROOTIE: I talk to him sometimes. Least I try to. Elvis was his
favorite person in the whole world. I bet they're probably
best friends by now.

BEV: Well if that's so, I bet Francie's friends with him, too.
We were crazy for him together.

ROOTIE: Maybe they're dating up there.

BEV: Who?

ROOTIE: Elvis and Francene.

BEV: That's the craziest thing I ever heard. Dating in Heaven?!
(*Half to herself.*) I'll kill her.

ROOTIE: Well, who knows? Ain't nobody I ever heard of who
could tell you first-hand what goes on up there. For all we
know, maybe they got Friday night beer blasts and drive-in
movies.

BEV: (*Laughing in spite of herself.*) Stop.

ROOTIE: No, I know that can't be. Because if Heaven is in
the clouds, all those cars would come crashing through.

BEV: I can't believe you. You're like one of those kids they
find in the woods after ten years. Haven't you ever heard of
gravity?

ROOTIE: What?

BEV: Gravity. That's what keeps things in the sky from falling
on your head, like planes and cars. Wait—now I still don't
see what all this has to do with you going in there first. (BEV
moves her chair again. ROOTIE *moves with her, eager to
explain.*)

ROOTIE: See, I got something I need Beau to help with. And
Elvis was the most important person in Beau's life, he walked
like him, dressed like him, he even tried to talk like him.
So since Beau's birthday is also the very first day Elvis' house

is open, I figured that if I were the first person inside, everything would all come together, and I'd get a sign from the
Heavens, and Weebo would see me on TV and be real sorry
about what he done, and everything would be all taken care
of.

BEV: Honey, I'm gonna tell you something, and I hope you'll
understand and not take it too personal. This is *nutty* talk.
Now why don't you just run along—

ROOTIE: I don't care, I gotta do something. Beau's the only
one who ever talked to me, and I know Elvis would help,
he's such a good person.

BEV: Honey, they are both dead, may they rest in peace.

ROOTIE: I know, but there are some things more powerful
than death even. Like *Brigadoon.*

BEV: Your mama ever tell you about fairy tales?

ROOTIE: I don't remember, she died when I was little. (*Want-
ing to change the subject.*) What's your name? Mine is Rootie.
Rootie Mallert. (*She sticks her hand out, and disconcerted,*
BEV *shakes it.*)

BEV: Huh? Oh, Bev. Bev Davies.

ROOTIE: Bev. That's a nice name.

BEV: I hate it. It's a fat name. Even feels fat. (*She puffs out
her cheeks as she says it.*) Bev. No wonder I got such a weight
problem. When you got a fat name, the deck's already stacked
against you. Now, Rootie. That's a skinny name. And look
at you—see what I mean.

ROOTIE: (*She says it experimentally.*) Rooo-tie. You're right.
It does feel skinny.

BEV: See?

ROOTIE: Bev, now do you believe me, about Beau and being
here, and all?

BEV: Well, I am just so confused I don't know what to think.
How do I know you're not just making all this up? You win
my sorry feelings and then when I get good and sappy, you
zip in right ahead of me. (ROOTIE *runs to get a frayed picture
out of her bag.*)

ROOTIE: Look—there's Beau, and that's Weebo right next to

him. They were best buddies. I never even figured he saw
me, but I guess after Beau, I was the next best thing.

BEV: Nice-looking boys. Who are all the others?

ROOTIE: That's Billy, Barney, Baxter, and Brad. And that's
my dad.

BEV: Where are they now?

ROOTIE: Well, Billy and Barney died in a car wreck right after
Beau, then Baxter—no wait, I'm sorry, that ain't right. First
Brad went off to California, then Baxter got thrown in jail
for stabbing that guy in a bar, then Billy and Barney got
killed, and Daddy died of a heart attack. I keep getting it all
mixed up. But look, doesn't Beau look just like Elvis? And
Weebo always dressed like Beau, so he looks like Elvis too.
A little.

BEV: You ain't seen nothing yet. (BEV *pulls out two pictures
from her bag.*) Take a look at these pictures. What can you
see?

ROOTIE: One's Elvis. Who's the other one?

BEV: What do you mean, who's the other one, they both look
exactly alike. That's my husband, Tyler.

ROOTIE: He's blonde.

BEV: I know. Elvis was blonde when he started.

ROOTIE: ELVIS?? Oh, Bev, Elvis wasn't blonde, he had real,
real dark hair.

BEV: Oh no he didn't, when Elvis first started he had light
hair, just like Ty's. The Colonel made him dye it. *That's* a
little known fact.

ROOTIE: Really?

BEV: Yes ma'am. So in a way, Ty looks more like Elvis than
Elvis did.

ROOTIE: But Ty's got two chins.

BEV: So? What does that matter? Look at those faces—they
could practically be identical twins.

ROOTIE: Even their eyes are different colors—

BEV: (*Highly insulted, she whips pictures out of* ROOTIE's
hand.) Well what the hell would you know anyway? (*She sits
down and pulls out a* Reader's Digest. ROOTIE *makes a move*

toward her, then moves her pillow sideways. Thinking that
BEV *is unaware, she sneaks her pillow ahead slightly. Without*
looking up from her magazine, BEV *snaps out at her—)*
Don't you move that rag another inch. Look honey, people
have tried to sneak ahead of me every goddamn time and no
one's made it yet. I didn't come all the way from Delaware
three days early just to get a tan, so watch it.

ROOTIE: I was just trying to get comfortable.

BEV: Hah.

Homesteaders

Nina Shengold

Characters: Jake (24), Laurel (14)

Setting: A home-built cabin in Shelter Cove, Alaska

Premiere: Capital Repertory Company, Albany, New York, 1983

Publisher: Samuel French, Inc.

An adventurous, troubled young woman named Jake (short
for Jacqueline) has taken a ferryboat up to Alaska, hoping to
change her life by changing her environment. A fisherman
named Neal Raftery invites her to his remote island cabin to
work as a summertime "deckhand." Attracted to Neal and
intrigued by his life, Jake leaps at the chance—only to learn
that Neal's life is a lot more complex than he has revealed.
The first major shock is the entrance of his fourteen-year-old
daughter, Laurel.

Laurel Sierra Millis's parents separated when she was eight.
Neal and his brother went north to Alaska, and Neal's ex-wife
Celia took Laurel to California. Laurel is smart, sarcastic, and
very deeply bruised. She has come up to spend a summer
with the father she barely knows, and she's angry and hurt to
find herself pre-empted by his new girlfriend.

This scene takes place on a "sauna night" (the primitive

cabin has no running water, but there's a wood-fired sauna out back). Jake has lived there for nearly a month. Moments earlier, Laurel came in from the sauna to find her father and Jake embracing on the couch . . . Laurel's bed. Jake tried to apologize, Laurel ran out, and Neal stormed out of the cabin to chop some more wood. Now Jake is determined to make up with Laurel.

——————————

(JAKE *sighs. Drains her drink. She goes to the cassette player and changes the tape to a '70s folk-rock song by a female vocalist.* LAUREL *comes quietly onto the porch. She looks around behind her, then peeks through the crack of the door.* JAKE *refills her glass. She realizes that* LAUREL *is watching and moves quickly to the door.*)

JAKE: Laurel? (LAUREL *pushes past her and gets out a blow dryer.*) Look, we might as well talk to each other. I understand how you—

LAUREL: Shut up. (*She turns on the dryer. The cabin lights dim.*)

JAKE: Oh come on. (*Pause, dryer buzz.*) I am sick of this, Laurel.

LAUREL: (*Shuts off the dryer.*) You're a whore. (*Turns it back on.* JAKE *pulls out the plug.*)

JAKE: Don't call me names. You don't even know me.

LAUREL: You're screwing my father.

JAKE: Yeah I am. You want to know why?

LAUREL: Because he pays you. You're a whore.

JAKE: (*Angry.*) Does it ever occur to you that you're not the only person on earth who's lonely? You don't know the first thing about me.

LAUREL: Yes I do. You're an only child and your parents are divorced.

JAKE: That's right. Exactly like you.

LAUREL: I am not like you. You fuck with men.

JAKE: I'm ten years older than you.

LAUREL: I don't care.

JAKE: I can fuck who I want!

LAUREL: He's my father! (*Pause.*)

JAKE: Look, this is awkward for me too.

LAUREL: Can I dry my hair now?

JAKE: It's not even wet. (LAUREL *rolls up the dryer cord angrily.*) And he doesn't pay me. (LAUREL *looks at her.*) I felt too weird about it.

LAUREL: What are you, rich or something?

JAKE: I've got eighty dollars in traveler's checks and a ferry ticket. I'm rolling in wealth. You want some bourbon?

LAUREL: I don't like it. It makes me puke.

JAKE: How about a joint?

LAUREL: You got dope? Can I roll it?

JAKE: Sure. Front pocket of my pack.

LAUREL: (*Starts up the loft ladder, stops and turns.*) This doesn't mean I like you.

JAKE: Who says I like you?

LAUREL: (*Climbs up, gets a zip-lock pouch, starts rolling a joint.*) Do we have to listen to this crud?

JAKE: Whatever you want.

LAUREL: Supertramp.

JAKE: All right. (*She changes the tape. A loud blast of pop-rock.* JAKE *turns it way down.*)

LAUREL: Cut me a break. I can't even hear it.

JAKE: Sure you can.

LAUREL: Louder.

JAKE: I'll meet you halfway. (*She turns it up a little, picks up her drink and climbs to the loft.*) So is it right in San Francisco, where you live?

LAUREL: Sausalito.

JAKE: That's supposed to be nice.

LAUREL: It's a pit.

JAKE: Really?

LAUREL: Ritsy-titsy tourist shit. It's gross.

JAKE: You roll a mean joint.

LAUREL: What else is there to do in junior high? (*She lights up. Does not pass the joint.*)

JAKE: Good point. What does your mother do? (LAUREL *gives her the eye.*) What is this, a family trait? I'm just trying to be friendly. (*Pause.*) Okay, fine. We'll get stoned and stare at the wall. (*She reaches for the joint.*)

LAUREL: What does your father do?

JAKE: (*Beat.*) Fixes teeth.

LAUREL: Gross me out, he's a dentist?

JAKE: *Please.* Orthodontist.

LAUREL: (*Taking the joint back.*) Celia's a therapist.

JAKE: What kind of therapy? Psychoanalysis?

LAUREL: Acupressure. Postural reintegration. She plays with people's bodies.

JAKE: Do you live alone, the two of you?

LAUREL: Huh. I wish.

JAKE: A boyfriend?

LAUREL Not any more. She married it. Rob. He wants me to call him dad. Fuck that.

JAKE: What does he do?

LAUREL: Screws her.

JAKE: (*Patient.*) Does he work?

LAUREL: He sells stuff. Swimming pools and stuff. He's a moron. (*She picks up a sweater and pulls it on.*)

JAKE: That's mine.

LAUREL: So? (*Pause.*) They just had a kid.

JAKE: Really?

LAUREL: Justin Avery. Is that a revolting name or what?

JAKE: So you're not an only child.

LAUREL: I'm Daddy's only child. (*Pause.*) Is he good in bed?

JAKE: Come on. I thought we were past all that.

LAUREL: Is he?

JAKE: Drop it.

LAUREL: He's got a big dick.

JAKE: Do you ask your mother that kind of question?

LAUREL: I don't have to. She leaves the door open.

JAKE: Oh god.

LAUREL: Is he good in bed?

JAKE: Cut it out.

LAUREL: "I'm just trying to be friendly." Oh, I can't ask you questions?

JAKE: Not like that.

LAUREL: Okay, like you asked me. About your growing up and stuff.

JAKE: All right.

LAUREL: When was the first time you got laid?

JAKE: I said no sex.

LAUREL: You said no Daddy. How old were you your first time?

JAKE: (*Beat pause.*) Seventeen.

LAUREL: That's old. Did it hurt?

JAKE: (*Laughing in spite of herself.*) Laurel!

LAUREL: Francine told me it kills the first time.

JAKE: Who's Francine?

LAUREL: Her parents run the Baker bar. You know. She's got this frizzy blond hair.

JAKE: I'm not sure I—

LAUREL: Double-D tits.

JAKE: Oh *her.* Sure I know her. How could you miss her? You guys are friends?

LAUREL: Sure. She's the only person anywhere near my age. When you and Daddy sell fish, do you spend much time in Baker?

JAKE: Not usually. Why?

LAUREL: I don't know, nothing. I was just wondering if you might know some people.

JAKE: Like who?

LAUREL: Just some people. (*She offers* JAKE *gum.* JAKE *shakes her head no.*) You know a guy called Mick Beale?

JAKE: Dick Beale.

LAUREL: Mick. Mick. *Mick* Beale. He's tall with a dirty blond beard? He's got a sailboat called the *Layla*? (JAKE *shakes her head.*)

JAKE: I don't know him. Mick Beale.

LAUREL: You know Ted Osterman? Him and Mick sailed up from Santa Cruz. You might have seen him with Francine.

JAKE: Oh, do they date?

LAUREL: *Date,* god. Nobody dates.

JAKE: Well what do you call it?

LAUREL: Fucking.

JAKE: You said Francine is your age?

LAUREL: She's sixteen.

JAKE: And how old is Ted?

LAUREL: I don't know. Younger than daddy.

JAKE: All right—

LAUREL: He's *fourteen* years older than you.

JAKE: I'm aware of that, Laurel.

LAUREL: Are you in love with him? (JAKE *does not answer*.) I said—

JAKE: I heard you.

LAUREL: Cause if you are you got a few surprises.

JAKE: What's that supposed to mean?

LAUREL: Oh, nothing.

Hothouse

Megan Terry

Characters: Jody (19), Roz (late 30s)

Setting: A small house in the fishing village of Edmonds (near Seattle), spring, c. 1955

Publisher: Samuel French, Inc.

Jody is a "pretty young woman. When she is funny she is cute; when she is sad, intensely beautiful." She and her boyfriend, David, have been dating for six weeks. She lives at home with her grandmother, Grandma's boyfriend Banty, and her mother, Roz.

Roz is "an extremely beautiful woman—earthy, charged with energy. She emanates sex; her eyes shine with life, but often cloud with confusion." Roz is still married to Jody's father, Jack. She has a boyfriend, Andy, whom Jody refers to as "that spider brain" and "mooch."

Roz's best friend from childhood, Doll, is having an affair

with her husband. Roz and her boyfriend go on a bender and bring Doll back to the house. Roz tells her their friendship is over and throws her out. Roz and Jack intend to get a divorce, which Jody vehemently opposes.

It is late. Grandma goes to sleep, leaving Roz and Jody alone.

Note: Ray was Jody's first love. He was killed in Korea.

———————————

ROZ: Want a night-cap, honey? (*Sings one line of:*) "Amapolla, my pretty little poppy . . ."

JODY: (*Walking backward.*) I'll finish this one. I need a clear head tomorrow. David is coming all the way from school for lunch.

ROZ: My God, is he still around? Isn't that a little long for you to be going with the same guy?

JODY: (*Offended.*) Is it?

ROZ: But I have a date with the lawyer tomorrow. I won't be here for lunch. Invite him for dinner instead.

JODY: I'm not sharing this one with you. I want to be alone with him.

ROZ: He's not our kind of people. That time you brought him down for a drink, he was so tight-assed, I don't know how he got the whiskey in his mouth. What's he do besides live off the G.I. Bill?

JODY: Plays piano in that new trio at the Lakewood.

ROZ: I don't drink at that horse piss place anymore. Why that cheap bastard even waters his bar whiskey. I watched him— it isn't even fresh water—he keeps it in an old douche bag . . .

JODY: David's really good . . . You've got to hear him. (*Starting for the phone.*) I'll phone him we're coming. Let's put on our coats and go down there right now.

ROZ: It's too late. Besides, they won't let me in the Lakewood for a few days. They need to buy some new chairs. I did 'em a favor busting those worm-eaten stools—some old barfly coulda got killed falling through the rotten wood. No, I just don't think that boy is our kind of people.

JODY: He has good manners. You haven't seen any before.

ROZ: (*Feeling more and more threatened by the thought of David.*) Ah, he's still wet behind the ears.

JODY: (*Snapping back.*) How can you say that about a man, who's fought in the war.

ROZ: There's more than one kind of war.

JODY: He's twenty-five years old.

ROZ: Baby balls!

JODY: Well, stay here then. I feel like seeing him, and right now!

ROZ: Don't go. Let's have another drink together.

JODY: I don't feel like it.

ROZ: I'll sing to you. Come on, get out the uke, and play for me.

JODY: Take the uke down to the boat and sing Dad back home?

ROZ: He can drop dead! Come on, I'll teach you. God knows you can't carry a tune . . . I can't understand it.

JODY: I can, too, carry a tune. David says he could make me into another Anita O'Day. He says I can understand complicated musical forms.

ROZ: Get her! Complicated musical forms my little white ass! You can't even sing the melody to "Flaming Mamie" against me.

JODY: If you'd stop brain-washing me, maybe I could.

ROZ: O.K., smart ass, match me. (*She gets set to do a song.*) They call me Flaming Mamie.

I'm a sure fire scorcher. (JODY *joins her.*)

I'm the hottest baby in town.

And when it comes to lovin'

I'm a human oven

I really burn men down.

(*She gestures to* JODY *to really give but* JODY *falters and stops singing.*)

JODY: O.K. You're the end. I give up. Goodbye.

ROZ: You're going to bed. (*Coming out of her entertainer role.*) You're not leaving this house.

JODY: Yes I am.

ROZ: You'll do nothing of the sort.

JODY: Don't pull that on me.

ROZ: You heard me.

JODY: You're drunk!

ROZ: Who's drunk?

JODY: We are.

ROZ: Don't you talk to your mother that way! Who are you—

JODY: I don't know, but I'm damn well going to find out. (*She makes for the door, but comes back grabbing* ROZ *by the shoulders.*) Listen, go and talk to Dad. Please. He's the one who's always come to you. You go to him for a change. See what happens?

ROZ: He'd puke in my face.

JODY: What'll happen to you two if you divorce?

ROZ: He started it, I didn't. Who cheated first?

JODY: It takes two.

ROZ: Yeah, let's dance. "Pardon me boy, is that the Chattanooga choo choo . . . track 29—" etc. . . . (*She dances.*)

JODY: (*Throwing herself back on the daybed.*) Screw it! . . . since Ray was killed, I tuned out on the world. Out! Out! Out! And I'm gonna stay out!

ROZ: You can't bring back the dead. Try not to think about it.

JODY: Momma . . . ?

ROZ: Your one and only . . . (*Still dancing.*)

JODY: (*Struggling to get out the words.*) Why? Is Andy better than Dad? Or were you just trying to make Dad jealous or what is it all about?

ROZ: (*She stops and looks at* JODY. *She feels uncertain.*) You know all about the birds and bees.

JODY: (*Definite.*) I'm talking about *you* . . .

ROZ: (*Shrugging.*) I don't get you.

JODY: Mother . . . is Andy better in bed?

ROZ: (*Refusing to comprehend.*) Better than what?

JODY: Better than Dad.

ROZ: (*Quietly.*) It isn't that. Jack . . . Jack . . . is . . . was . . .

JODY: (*Rushing—to cover the pain of asking.*) I know it couldn't always be like your honeymoon or something, but didn't anything last? Don't you ever . . . you know . . . get longing for him, ache for him?

ROZ: (*The cool charm back.*) Your dad's a good lover. That's why I married him.

JODY: Well, he didn't dissolve after the ceremony, did he?

ROZ: (*Seriously trying to reassure* JODY.) You were a love child. A real love child.

JODY: What happened then?

ROZ: (*Tries to pour a drink.*) Oh, you know. The damn fishing season. He'd be gone months at a time.

JODY: (*Aggressive.*) But you loved him, didn't you?

ROZ: (*Defiant.*) Sure, I loved him . . . what is this?

JODY: (*Struggling again.*) I need to know . . . I need to know for my own life.

ROZ: (*Justifying herself.*) Well, so many things got broken up. He was gone in the South Pacific four whole years. He left me alone four whole years, for God's sake.

JODY: Well, other women . . .

ROZ: Look, baby, you and I both know I'm no Mrs. Miniver.

JODY: (*Getting up from the bed.*) Please try to tell me, it's harder for me to ask than for you to answer. But I've got to know. I've been worried sick you'd leave each other, and if you really do, then I've got to know why. If it's stupid game-playing jealousy, and crud like that, I'll kill you.

ROZ: Hey there, simmer down. Sometimes I don't get you.

JODY: You don't have, because I get you. But David mixes me up. Or I mix him up. Oh God! (*Blurting.*) How do you keep it straight, who you're with.

ROZ: (*Slowly—trying to clue in.*) When you're having a love party?

JODY: Right.

ROZ: What's the problem?

JODY: Then there shouldn't be any effort?

ROZ: (*Drinking.*) You're in orbit, kid.

JODY: I get confused.

ROZ: The whole joint's confused.

JODY: When I'm with David, when I'm having the best time with him, when I forget who . . . what I am . . . is it because I'm pretending?

ROZ: (*In control again.*) Relax. David don't know the difference. When I'm with Andy I pretend he's Clark Gable, and he probably closes his eyes and thinks I'm Betty Grable. If he can think.

JODY: Which is doubtful. (*Slowly watching* ROZ.) How long has it been for you and Dad?

ROZ: (*Defiant.*) Well, hell, it isn't my fault. He moved back to his boat a whole month ago.

JODY: Well, when did you sleep with him before he moved out?

ROZ: (*Pours herself a drink.*) It was . . . it was . . . what difference does it make?

JODY: When?

ROZ: Oh, it must have been on my birthday or something. He always wanted to love me on my birthday, it was the nicest present he could think of to give me.

JODY: That's over a year ago then, because your birthday was three weeks ago, and he left a week before that!

ROZ: (*Puts her glass down.*) My God!

JODY: What's the matter with you? Why do you two stay away from each other so much?

ROZ: I never realized it was such a long time. (*She sits.*)

JODY: (*Trying to kid.*) You're a real danger to the boys. Eh? Well, you put up a great front!

ROZ: Jody, baby, do you think . . .

JODY: You're the only one who can really know.

ROZ: What do you mean?

JODY: Maybe it's his fault. Maybe he doesn't want you anymore.

ROZ: What do you mean he doesn't want me? All I have to do is touch the back of his neck and his hair stands up. What do you mean, he doesn't want me?

JODY: Prove it.

ROZ: All right. All right. You'll see!

JODY: When?

ROZ: I'll send him a telegram.

JODY I bet you're afraid to be alone with him.

ROZ: Are you kidding?

JODY: You hardly ever are. We always got a house full of people ninety four hours a day. You have to dump the beds over to find a place to sleep.

ROZ: (*Attacking.*) What have you been doing? Are you sleeping with that college punk?

JODY: (*Yelling.*) It's not because I haven't tried.

ROZ: Be sure you take care of yourself.

JODY: Don't worry.

ROZ: You don't know the trouble you can get into.

JODY: Oh, Mother, please. I'm not a moron.

ROZ: Miss know-it-all! Well, make your own mistakes.

JODY: Thanks. I don't mind if I do.

ROZ: Stop fighting with me!

JODY: Well, you stop fighting with me . . .

ROZ: I don't want to fight.

JODY: Neither do I. Why'd you come home so late?

ROZ: I couldn't let Jensen get away . . .

JODY: That's so dumb! What you want to grind Doll into the mud for? That's too easy. You should go get Dad to come home.

ROZ: I don't know how.

JODY: Just try, just go and say: Jack, come home. I want you.

ROZ: (*Quietly—by rote.*) Jack come home. I want you. I want you. Oh God, I do want you . . . I'll think about it. I will, I'll try to think about it.

JODY: You damn well better. Sometimes I could shake you 'til the booze curdles. (*Very tired and emotionally exhausted, she gets into her bed.*) Will you sing to me now? Not all those jazzy things, but something . . . what did you say your voice used to be called?

ROZ: Contralto? But now it's plain old whiskey tenor.

JODY: That's it, contralto. I wonder if mine would be contralto?

ROZ: It would be if you could carry a tune.

JODY: I'm going to learn.

ROZ: You can't learn it, you got to feel it.

JODY: Then I'll learn to feel it. (*A little desperate.*) Mother . . .
sing! Sing contralto.

ROZ: Go to sleep, baby. (*She covers her with blanket.*)
Close your eyes up tight my honey
Momma sing a song so funny
'Bout a little yellow hen
She had baby chicks and then . . .
  (*She brushes hair off* JODY's *forehead.*)
Turalooo-ra-loo-ra-loo
Turalooo-ra-loo-ra-loo
  (*She picks up glass of whiskey; sips, gazing at* JODY.)
I should have had lots like you. Why didn't I have lots and
lots of chicks. I have so much love to give. So much to give.
Oh Jack, damn your hide.

In the Boom Boom Room

David Rabe

Characters: Chrissy (young), Susan (young)
Setting: Philadelphia go-go bar
Premiere: Vivian Beaumont Theatre, New York City, 1973
Publisher: Samuel French, Inc.

Chrissy has just left her job at the A&P to become a go-go
dancer. A sweet-natured, inarticulate woman, she is struggling
to come to terms with the brutal facts of her life: a mother
who tried to abort her, a father and uncles who beat and
molested her as a child, and the mixed-up or violent men in
her love life. The hope in her life is the pure and genuine joy
that she feels while she dances. She loves and studies dancing;
she dreams about being the best. As hard as Chrissy's life has
been, she is fundamentally naïve, too innocent to realize that

the seamy world of go-go dancing will plunge her even deeper into the violence and degradation she is fighting to escape.

Susan is the emcee of the go-go club where Chrissy dances. She is a proud, fiercely confident woman who is putting herself through college with the money from her club work. Susan is bisexual and strongly attracted to Chrissy.

CHRISSY: How's the coffee?

SUSAN: Fine. (*Silence.*)

CHRISSY: You never been interested in astrology, huh?

SUSAN: No; why? (*As she crosses to the table and settles a little wearily down on a chair.*)

CHRISSY: It's got a long history. Greeks, even.

SUSAN: (*Who has been rotating her neck.*) My neck is killin' me.

CHRISSY: Want me to give you a rubdown? I will; I know how. (*Moving behind* SUSAN, *her hands beginning to work on* SUSAN's *neck.*) Boy, I just sat up the other night all night sittin' in a chair, I was waiting to yell "Fire!" I couldn't not think there was gonna be a fire and I was worried no one would warn us.

SUSAN: (*Laughing a little, as if* CHRISSY *has been telling a joke.*) That is probably true. But no reason to sit up all night.

CHRISSY: And I'm the one who spit in Melissa's shoe.

SUSAN: My God, Chrissy, did you really?

CHRISSY: Oh, she's so good. You know she is. I'll never be that good. It's 'cause she's ballin' that nigger.

SUSAN: Would you say that to their faces?

CHRISSY: I don't know. Maybe. Like I been doin' a number a funny things lately. See, I was in New York last week 'cause I just wanted to be and get outa stupid Philadelphia, so I got in this bar and was picked up by this funny little soldier in a soldier suit. He kept talkin' how he hadda go to the war and he was very afraid though he was actin' other. So when he got me back to the hotel, he kissed me. I put my tongue real deep into his mouth, till I felt him turn on. Then I left him standin' there and I felt real pleased how I was leavin' him. But now I'm ashamed. I mean, whatsamatter with me? We got no right to be bad to men. Nothin' ever works out for them. They just try and try. (CHRISSY *has taken off her sunglasses. She doesn't like them.*)

SUSAN: That's not true.

CHRISSY: Oh, it is. (*And she moves away from* SUSAN.)

SUSAN: You know what you're sayin' about men most of the time is a buncha crap. I mean, there's a lotta crazy mean people out there runnin' loose out there gonna cut your heart right outa you, you ain't on the alert. I saw this guy walk up to this other guy in this bar in New York, this topless bar we was in, and he pops a razor out of his pocket, and he cuts the guy across the stomach, and when he reaches for his stomach, he cuts him across the throat. He was like waving this magic wand. Wave-wave, you're dead.

CHRISSY: Wow.

SUSAN: I'm tellin' you.

CHRISSY You ever work in one of them places?

SUSAN: What?

CHRISSY: Topless.

SUSAN: Not on your life.

CHRISSY: Me neither. I wouldn't either, ever. (*She crosses back to* SUSAN, *sits down.*) There was this really beautiful girl I saw I couldn't believe the stuff she was doin'. I mean, rubbin' herself between her legs and pretendin' to lick her fingers then. That's disgustin'. And all the girls doin' different stuff; and not together or to the music even, the men all just lookin' at 'em. And she coulda been a great dancer, too— this one girl. I could see she coulda, but she was just doin' this shit. And she was so pretty. What was she doin'? Dancin's gotta have prettiness in it.

SUSAN: (*Sipping the coffee.*) You shoulda asked her what she was doin'.

CHRISSY: Yeh. You want more coffee?

SUSAN: No.

CHRISSY: See, I just gotta tell you somethin'. (*Rising abruptly, she begins again to pace.*) See, I just been more nervous than I think I oughta from the time Al left. So I been figurin' there's somethin' wrong with me in my mind maybe the way I always got no luck and I oughta get it straightened out so I can get on with my career in my dancin' and have some luck. See, and Eric was talkin' always about this underplace is in us from his therapy. So I been thinkin' maybe the way my uncles Billy and Michael beat me sometimes is down there—or my father with a belt, he says, but I don't remember it—but that's all just wounds of the body is my point, and they heal unlike those of the spirit which is where the underplace it, I would guess. You know about this?

SUSAN: Some.

CHRISSY: Ain't it somethin'? This stuff down there talkin' to us about what we should do, we think it's us, but it's it—we don't know what we're doin'. So I been thinkin' and thinkin' and maybe the bad stuff done to me is the way my momma made me nearly a abortion.

SUSAN: What?

CHRISSY: See, my momma didn't wanna have me as a baby.

SUSAN: Now that's not true. You know that's not true.

CHRISSY: She tole me. She had two others before I was even there, and then she tried one on me but it didn't work.

SUSAN: She told you she didn't wanna have you?

CHRISSY: One afternoon. We were very poor. We were very, very poor. So I'm thinkin' about mental therapy, Susan. You think I should or I shouldn't?

SUSAN: Might be good. You thinkin' about individual or group? It can be good sometimes, as long as you go to a woman's group of an individual woman therapist; but go to a woman.

CHRISSY: Oh, I couldn't do that.

SUSAN: It's best, believe me. I was with this woman's group for six months or so and I found out a lot. Or all I needed. After just a little I was able to say what I needed. You go to a man therapist, you'll get the meaning of the word—"ther-a-pist." The Rapist. (*And she laughs a little.*) Yeh, I was doin' this crossword puzzle—all of a sudden, I saw—that's what it was. The Rapist. Exactly what he'll do to your mind. I'm so much freer now, Chrissy, believe me.

CHRISSY: That's what I want. I'm very sensitive to everything. I mean, inside right now, I don't believe you really think my coffee I made is good, you're just sayin' it. I mean, whata you think a me, Susan? Like if you was to point me out on the street and describe me to somebody who don't know me at all, what would you say?

SUSAN: Well, I—

CHRISSY: (*Leaping to her feet.*) See! See! I could do it about you in a second. It would be so damn easy about you. You're so proud and capable. Leo's are exactly what you are. But I'm a Libra—my sign is scales and balance. I'm supposed to be dedicated to justice and harmony. I'm supposed to be a born mediator—I don't even know what's goin' on, for crissake. And on the other I'm whimsical an' moody an' sentimental. I got all the bad and none a the good, or maybe I got none a them. Would you say I got some? It's so depressin'.

SUSAN: You have a lovely gentleness about you, Chrissy.

CHRISSY: Think a what I did to that poor soldier and he was so scared.

SUSAN: If he's stupid, he's stupid.

CHRISSY: He just didn't know the rules. I'm speaking out for fairness like I gotta if I'm ever gonna be a Libra! (CHRISSY *flops down in the chair at the table beside* SUSAN. SUSAN *sits quietly, looking at* CHRISSY. *She then leans a little forward.*)

SUSAN: It's their pride, Chrissy; their goddamn pride. Each and every man in the world thinkin' he's got some special inner charm we all of us just been waitin' to have.

CHRISSY: They don't mean to hurt us.

SUSAN: Chrissy, is that what you believe?

CHRISSY: It's true. I know it is. They just don't know how not to. (*And there is a silence as* SUSAN *reaches across the table to put her hand on* CHRISSY's *arm.*)

SUSAN: I want to make love to you, Chrissy.

CHRISSY: Huh?

SUSAN: Didn't you hear me?

CHRISSY: Huh?

SUSAN: Have you ever made love with a woman?

CHRISSY: I'm gonna get a drink of water. (*She starts to rise, but* SUSAN *holds on, staring out from behind her sunglasses.*)

SUSAN: They prize themselves so highly, sitting out there when we're dancing, thinking it's them making us move so fancy—and the fancier we move, the better they think they are. So they give gifts for special dances and then think they're the ones making you move in that beautiful way they know they could never make you move in bed. I take no gifts. They like to think of themselves as weapons entering flesh—making life or death. I think of them as a straw going into the sea and the sea, scarcely noticing, takes them in. I turn on their feeble minds from as far away as the moon. (*Finished, she releases* CHRISSY's *hand and* CHRISSY *rises.*)

CHRISSY: Don't you like them? I thought you did.

SUSAN: I did. I do. I will again. But there are so many ways of making do.

CHRISSY: But I . . . want a relationship.

SUSAN: I could give you that.

CHRISSY: But you're not a man, see?

SUSAN: No.

CHRISSY: See?

SUSAN: I'm a person.

CHRISSY: But what would I be? I don't know.

SUSAN: You would be a person, too; we would be two people.

CHRISSY: But would I be a man person or a woman person?

SUSAN: You would be yourself.

CHRISSY: But that's what I don't know what it is! I don't! (SUSAN, *after a moment, looks away in weariness.*)

SUSAN: You make too much of it.

CHRISSY: I wanted you to help me, tell me, Susan!

SUSAN: You've got to stop being afraid of everything!

CHRISSY: I have! I stare down people on the subways all the time now. I don't care what they are or how big they are; I stare 'em down.

SUSAN: (*Gathering up her things, some books, her purse.*) I'm going. Got classes tomorrow. (*As she starts away,* CHRISSY *stands, watching.*)

CHRISSY: I didn't wanna make you feel bad. (SUSAN *stops.
Very gently, she looks back at* CHRISSY.)
SUSAN: Chrissy, it's really very nice. It's like you do it yourself,
only it's a surprise.
CHRISSY: Oh.
SUSAN: Yes.
CHRISSY: Thank you for asking. And don't be mad at me,
okay?
SUSAN: No. I'll see you at work. (*And turning, she leaves.*)

Laundry and Bourbon

James McLure

Characters: Hattie, Elizabeth (both mid- to late-30s)
Setting: Elizabeth's back porch
Premiere: McCarter Theatre Company, Princeton, New Jersey, 1980
Publisher: Dramatists Play Service
    Elizabeth is a "strong, sensuous woman, straightforward
and without self-pity. She is capable of handling most men
other than Roy, her husband. Therein lies the attraction." She
is out on her back porch when her best friend, Hattie, comes
over. Hattie is quite a talker. She enjoys watching "Let's Make
a Deal" reruns and is used to getting her own way. She blames
everything that has gone wrong in her life on her husband,
Vernon. After a disastrous morning chasing her kids around
J.C. Penney, she drops them off at her mother-in-law's. It is
a hot summer afternoon. The two women fold laundry and
drink bourbon on Elizabeth's back porch.

ELIZABETH: God I hate laundry.
HATTIE: Try doing it for three kids.

ELIZABETH: Week in. Week out. It's the same old clothes.

HATTIE: You can only look at so many pairs of Fruit of the Loom before you want to puke.

ELIZABETH: I'd like to burn everything in this basket and start all over. Everything except this shirt.

HATTIE: Why that shirt's all frayed.

ELIZABETH: It is now, but I remember the first time Roy wore this shirt.

HATTIE: When was that?

ELIZABETH: On our first date. He drove up in that pink Thunderbird in this shirt with all the pearl buttons. He looked just like Paul Newman in *Hud*. (HATTIE *holds up a pair of boxer shorts.*)

HATTIE: God these shorts are big.

ELIZABETH: What?

HATTIE: These Jockey shorts they're so big. They're not that wide. They're for a narrow body, but they're so long . . .

ELIZABETH: I suppose.

HATTIE: . . . Why're they so long.

ELIZABETH: Roy likes them big. Says he needs a lot of room.

(*Pause.*)

HATTIE: Whew it's hot out here. (Pause.) Lordy, how's a body supposed to keep cool?

ELIZABETH: Nothing to do but fix a bourbon and Coke and just sit and sweat.

HATTIE: I can't do that.

ELIZABETH: You can't sweat?

HATTIE: No. Fix a drink in the afternoon in front of the kids.

ELIZABETH: Why not?

HATTIE: Children learn by example.

ELIZABETH: So?

HATTIE: Well, all I need is to come home to a house full of kids sitting around drinking margaritas. You don't know what it's like raising a family.

ELIZABETH: No, I don't.

HATTIE: And lemme tell you, summertime is the worst.

ELIZABETH: What do you do?

HATTIE: I send them outside.

ELIZABETH: In this heat.

HATTIE: I give 'em a salt pill and say, play outside.

ELIZABETH: Don't they collapse from heat prostration?

HATTIE: Anything to slow them down.

ELIZABETH: I wish you'd let me take them sometimes.

HATTIE: Elizabeth, you're not used to kids. The strain would kill you. (ELIZABETH *moves downstage. Leans against porch post looking out over the land. Pause.*) Elizabeth, what are you staring out at the road for?

ELIZABETH: No reason. There's nothing to see.

HATTIE: That's the truth. Nothing green to look at. God, it's depressing living on the edge of a desert.

ELIZABETH: But just think millions of years ago all this land was under water.

HATTIE: Well . . . at least it would have been cool.

ELIZABETH: I like this land, but sometimes it gets too hot and burnt for people. It's still too wild and hard for anything to grow. (*Pause.*) Oh, look Hattie!

HATTIE: What is it?

ELIZABETH: Look at that cloud.

HATTIE: It's just a cloud.

ELIZABETH: Yeah, but look how it's throwing a shadow across the land. God, doesn't that shadow look peaceful gliding over the land. Doesn't it look cool? It reminds me of a cool dark hand stroking a hot surface. (*Pause.*) Lately I've felt so hot and hollow inside I've wanted something to come along and touch me like that.

HATTIE: Elizabeth, what's the matter with you?

ELIZABETH: Nothing, Hattie nothing.

HATTIE: (*Pause.*) You're doing it again, staring out at that hill. There ain't nothing out there but the highway and the road up to the house. Now, what're you expecting to see?

ELIZABETH: I was hoping to see a 1959 pink Thunderbird convertible come over that hill.

HATTIE: You've got tears in your eyes! Don't you tell me nothing's the matter! What is it? (*Pause.*)

ELIZABETH: Roy's been gone two days. (*Silence.*)

HATTIE: Why that son of a bitch! No wonder you've been so weird. Here, you sit yourself down here. I'm gonna fix you a drink and you're gonna tell me all about it.

ELIZABETH: I don't want another drink.

HATTIE: Hush up. Hattie's taking care of you now. The doctor is *in*. (ELIZABETH *sits.* HATTIE *exits to kitchen, talking.*) I knew there was something wrong the minute I laid eyes on you. First you don't answer the doorbell, and as soon as I saw you I could tell something was the matter. That son of a bitch. (HATTIE *returns, having mixed drinks in record time.*) Well, what brought it on this time?

ELIZABETH: I don't know. Things haven't been the same since he came back.

HATTIE: From Vietnam?

ELIZABETH: Yeah.

HATTIE: I know. I seen the change. But believe me you've been perfect about it.

ELIZABETH: I haven't been anything. I haven't done anything. He was the one that went off for two years. He was the one got shot up. He's the one that has nightmares.

HATTIE: Nightmares.

ELIZABETH: Yeah, almost every night. (*Pause.*) Anyway, now he's back and he can't seem to get nothing started. He made me quit the job at the pharmacy. He worked some out at his dad's place. He's done some rough-necking out in the oil fields. But then always gets in fights and gets himself fired.

HATTIE: Well . . . what's he got to say for himself.

ELIZABETH: He says he's looking for something.

HATTIE: Hmnnn. What?

ELIZABETH: He doesn't know what. He says everything has changed here in Maynard.

HATTIE: Nothing's changed in Maynard since the Civil War.

ELIZABETH: I want him back the way it used to be.

HATTIE: Elizabeth, he's always been wild and unmanageable.

ELIZABETH: (*Flaring.*) I don't want to manage him. I don't want to break his spirit. That's why I married him, his spirit. Roy Caulder wasn't going to take no crap from anyone or anything. He and Wayne Wilder were gonna shake up the world.

HATTIE: Need I remind you that Wayne Wilder is currently serving five to ten for car theft?

ELIZABETH: (*Quietly.*) Roy's different than Wayne.

HATTIE: I wouldn't be too sure.

ELIZABETH: I just wished I knew he was safe. He could be hurt.

HATTIE: Or he could be with another woman.

ELIZABETH: I hope that's all it is.

HATTIE: Elizabeth, how can you say that?

ELIZABETH: Any man worthwhile is gonna look at other women. That's natural. And sometimes they wander a bit.

HATTIE: A bit? That man's done more wandering than Lewis and Clark.

ELIZABETH: You're exaggerating.

HATTIE: Last year? Last year! He took off for five days.

ELIZABETH: (*In spite of herself, smiling.*) Yeah. He had himself quite a time.

HATTIE: You mean he told you what he did?

ELIZABETH: Oh, sure.

HATTIE: Well, you never told me.

ELIZABETH: No.

HATTIE: But I'm your best friend. You're supposed to tell me everything.

ELIZABETH: It was different then. We'd had a fight and he left in a huff. Drove off to El Paso. Picked up a girl hitchhiking.

HATTIE: What was her name?

ELIZABETH: Hattie, how should I know? She was a hitchhiker.

HATTIE: A little tramp probably! A little hippie road slut! What's she look like?

ELIZABETH: Blond.

HATTIE: A little blond hippie bitch that never washed or nothing I'll bet!

ELIZABETH: Oh yeah, and there was one other thing . . .

HATTIE: What?

ELIZABETH: She had a tattoo.

HATTIE: A *tattoo* on her arm?

ELIZABETH: Not exactly on her arm.

HATTIE: God . . . where?

ELIZABETH: On her behind.

HATTIE: No! On her behind! How disgusting! . . . What did it say?

ELIZABETH: "Born to be wild."

HATTIE: Oh Lord! Lord!

ELIZABETH: Then Roy went down to El Paso, got in a four-day poker game, won a hundred bucks and come on home.

HATTIE: Weren't you mad?!

ELIZABETH: Yes.

HATTIE: Didn't you want to shoot him?!

ELIZABETH: Yeah.

HATTIE: I would've.

ELIZABETH: I thought it was what he needed to get something out of his system. For a while it seemed to work. (*Pause.*)

HATTIE: Y'know half his trouble is that damn car of his.

ELIZABETH: What do you mean?

HATTIE: He gets behind the wheel of that car and he thinks he's the cock of the walk, the best-looking thing in these parts.

ELIZABETH: (*Proudly.*) He still is.

HATTIE: (*Grudgingly.*) Yeah.

ELIZABETH: Even the girls in high school today. I see them in town looking at him the way we did.

HATTIE: I never looked at him that way.

ELIZABETH: Hattie you still do.

HATTIE: I tell you it's that damn car. When he gets in it he thinks he's young and free again. (*Pause.*) Somebody ought to take that car away from him.

ELIZABETH: (*Warming to the memory.*) I remember the first day he drove into town in that car.

HATTIE: So do I.

ELIZABETH: He'd worked three years, summers and winters, for the down payment.

HATTIE: Only slightly used.

ELIZABETH: Roy and Wayne drove right through the center of town.

HATTIE: They looked like a couple of sultans.

ELIZABETH: It was bright pink.

HATTIE: It glistened like sin.

ELIZABETH: I remember I was coming out of the drug store with an ice cream cone.

HATTIE: What flavor.

ELIZABETH: Vanilla. And the sun off the hood was blinding. Couldn't even see the car. Then it passed into one shadow and I saw it. For the first time. It was beautiful, and Roy hardly knew me then but he waved at me, and I dropped my vanilla cone right there on the pavement. And I knew . . . he was the one.

HATTIE: Yeah. All through high school we double-dated.

ELIZABETH: Remember drive-ins, Hattie.

HATTIE: I sure do. More like wrestling matches.

ELIZABETH: One couple would get the car one night.

HATTIE: The other the next.

ELIZABETH: We'd drive around and drive around and then go make out.

HATTIE: Wayne and me didn't even drive around.

ELIZABETH: (*Rising.*) God, I want them back. I wished tonight was ten years ago. And Roy was coming to pick me up in that pink Thunderbird. I wished I could buy back some of the nights of summer I had in that car. When everything was cool and free and driving along the highway away from this stupid town. With the wind coming at you and the stars all the way to the horizon, like diamonds that went all the way to dawn. (*Pause.*) Then driving off the road somewhere. By a lake maybe. Anywhere. Being off from town with the boy you loved better than anything ever in your whole life. I remember us making love for the first time. Really slow and gentle. God. He was gentle then. He taught me my body. I'd never really felt with my body before Roy. Suddenly it was like every pore of my skin was being opened like in a rain storm, feeling and holding everything you possibly wanted right there in your arms. What I wouldn't give to have those nights again. Just one night when the back seat of that Thunderbird was sweeter than all the beds in the world. (*Slight pause.*)

HATTIE: They took a lot of girls out in that car.

ELIZABETH: We were different.

HATTIE: Were we? (*They stare at each other.*) Look how he's treating you now. (*Pause.*) Elizabeth you're getting all sentimental and romantic. That happened to me once. I let a man run all over me.

ELIZABETH: What'd you do?

HATTIE: I wrote a poem.

ELIZABETH: You?

HATTIE: Yep. Worst afternoon of my life. Never do it again. That's what happens when you get all sentimental and miserable. You write poems. Just like old Emily Dickens.

ELIZABETH: Emily Dickinson.

HATTIE: That's the one. Poor gal was a miserable godforsaken old maid all her life and when she died all that was left was just a drawerful of poems.

ELIZABETH: What was your poem about, Hattie?

HATTIE: I wrote a poem about Wayne Wilder. He was a mean person and it was a mean poem. It was right after high school graduation. Wayne told me he was jilting me. You and Roy was getting married and Wayne Wilder was jilting me. Hit me like a ton of bricks. I went out back of the girls' gym, cried and wrote a poem. I still remember it.

"Oh Wayne you don't know, I love you so well
 But you son of a bitch
 I hope you roast in hell."

(*Pause.*) Not much of a poem, I guess. But then I decided to get practical like Hattie's always had to be. I went back to where everybody was in their caps and gowns and I saw Vernon Dealing standing there. He'd just been fiddlin' under some car hood. Even in his cap and gown his hands were dirty. But he was a good man and I knew he liked me. I got him to take me out. I got him to propose. Within a month we were married. Poor Vern. Never knew what hit him. (*Pause.*)

ELIZABETH: What are you telling me this for?

HATTIE: Roy's just like Wayne. He ain't never gonna change.

ELIZABETH: Maybe not.

HATTIE: I've known you all my life. I know you need a marriage and you want a family. Am I right.

ELIZABETH: Yes.

HATTIE: Then wake up. You can't leave the important things in life like marriage and children up to the menfolk. If they had their way they'd just stick to their football and their fishing and their Thunderbirds and just be boys forever. (*Pause.*) Now, if Roy straightens up, that's one thing. If not . . . well, you got to make a decision.

ELIZABETH: (*Privately.*) Maybe it's already been made for me.

HATTIE: What do you mean?

ELIZABETH: Nothing, Hattie. Forget I said that.

HATTIE: Don't tell me it's nothing . . . you're pregnant aren't you? (*Silence.*)

ELIZABETH: Yeah.

HATTIE: I knew it! I knew it the minute I walked in here today. Oh Elizabeth! That's wonderful!

ELIZABETH: What's wonderful about it? It comes at the worst possible time.

HATTIE: Wrong. It comes at the best possible time. Well, don't you see? This might be just the thing to make Roy straighten up and fly right.

ELIZABETH: And if it doesn't?

HATTIE: Then . . . to hell with him.

ELIZABETH: (*With difficulty.*) I guess . . . you're right.

HATTIE: Oh honey! Let me give you a hug. That's the smartest thing you ever did.

ELIZABETH: (*Pulling away.*) What do you mean?

HATTIE: Getting pregnant, of course.

ELIZABETH: Hattie, I didn't get myself pregnant, on purpose. I didn't plan it this way. (*Pause.*)

HATTIE: Are you sure?

ELIZABETH: (*Slightest hesitation.*) Yes! Yes, I'm sure. I don't know if Roy can take this right now. He doesn't know what he's doing himself.

HATTIE: Well, that's not your problem.

ELIZABETH: (*Angry.*) It's every bit my problem. It couldn't be any more my problem.

HATTIE: (*Pause.*) I didn't mean to get you all upset. I just meant . . .

ELIZABETH: (*Calmer.*) I know, Hattie, I know. I just don't want to talk about it anymore. (*Awkward pause.*)

HATTIE: Oh, well sure. Sure. Uh, say mind if I use your phone?

ELIZABETH: (*Smiling.*) Of course.

HATTIE: Figure I better check on the kids. No telling what devilment they've gotten up to. (*Dialing.*) Everything gonna turn out fine you'll see.

Lydie Breeze

John Guare

Characters: Lydie Breeze (15), Beaty (early 30s)
Setting: A house in Nantucket, New York City, 1895
Premiere: American Place Theatre, New York City, 1982
Publisher: Dramatists Play Service, Inc.

Fifteen-year-old Lydie Breeze lives with her widowed father and their Irish serving girl, Beaty. Lydie has been temporarily blinded in an accident. This scene, which takes place at dawn, opens the play. *Lydie Breeze* is part of a cycle of plays about the history of a nineteenth-century Nantucket family.

(LYDIE HICKMAN *enters the parlor, carrying a lit candle. She places it on the table, kneels, her hands in prayer.*)

LYDIE: Beaty? I'm ready. (LYDIE *pounds her palm on the table in a steady rhythm.* BEATY *enters. She is an Irish serving girl in her early thirties.*)

BEATY: I came out of my room. I'd been asleep. I heard the shutters banging back and forth. No air. I woke up suffocating. And yet I heard the shutters banging in the breeze.

LYDIE: But there was no breeze.

BEATY: No air. The banging. Your mother's feet swinging against the banister.

LYDIE: My mother's feet swinging against the banister.

BEATY: Your father heard my scream. He came out of his room. He was drawn out of bed by my scream. He is naked. She is above him swinging. Her feet making that shutter-slamming sound. Your father sees the body. He climbs up to where your mother's neck is. He takes the rope in his mouth and bites it till it is freed. Your mother's body drops. Drops to the floor.

LYDIE: There. She falls there.

BEATY: Your sister runs out of her room. She sees the body. She sees her naked father. She sees you. Excuse me, she says, I'm having a horrible dream, and goes peacefully back to sleep.

LYDIE: My father—

BEATY: Your father takes your mother's face and pushes the tongue back in her mouth. He slaps her face. Breathe. Breathe. He slaps the dead woman's face.

LYDIE: Bring her back to life.

BEATY: And he wrapped his legs around your mother's body to hold her upright and he kept squeezing her to get the air in. Kept squeezing her.

LYDIE: To bring her back to life.

BEATY: But he failed. He failed. And he dropped your mother's body and went out the door, down naked to the beach. He swam for a long while. I thought he would die. To join her in death. It would have restored my faith in men.

LYDIE: Don't wish my father dead.

BEATY: Does he keep your mother alive? Early morning priests say Mass. Hoc est enim corpus. Hoc est enim. And the priest eats the flesh of Christ and Christ is alive for one more day. We must keep your mother alive.

LYDIE: Keep my mother alive.

BEATY: Say her name. Her name—her name.

LYDIE: Lydie Breeze.

BEATY: We must be very still. Et introibo ad altare Dei.

LYDIE: Mea culpa. Mea culpa. Mea maxima culpa.

BEATY: Lydie Breeze, what is it you want me to do?

LYDIE: What is it you want me to do?

BEATY: I feel this great task you want me to do.

LYDIE: I feel this great task you want me to do.

BEATY: When I die—

LYDIE: When I die—

BEATY: When I pass over to the other side you will meet me and you will ask, "Did you do my task?"

LYDIE: Mother—What is the It?

LYDIE & BEATY: What is the It?

BEATY: We must be very still.

LYDIE: Are you here?

BEATY: Hoc est enim corpus. Hoc est enim.

LYDIE: You're in this room. Near enough to see me?

BEATY: She's here.

LYDIE: Mother?

BEATY: Oh, yes! She's here. Sure as Christ is in that early morning Mass. Show your mother what I'm teaching you! Lydie Breeze! Listen!

LYDIE: Take two eggs and separate. Take four cups of sugar.

BEATY: No, dear. Six.

LYDIE: Six. Stir in currants and raisins.

BEATY: Yes. Add the flour.

LYDIE: Flour. Bake. I forgot the vanilla. I forgot the nutmeg. I forgot the salt! Mother, don't listen!

BEATY: Show your mother you know the alphabet.

LYDIE: A. B. C. D. E. F. G. H. I. J. K. L. M. N. O. P. Q. R. S. T. U. V. W. X. Y. Z.

BEATY: Lydie Breeze, I'm teaching her as you taught me. As well as I can.

LYDIE: Ma, can you heal my eye?

BEATY: Of course she can heal your eye. She can do every blessed thing. Lydie Breeze, I was a child. I was a servant. Hired to work. Hired to clean. But you made me special. You taught me as I teach her how to foretell weather from sunsets. How to circle a ring on a long strand of hair to predict an unborn baby's sex. How to tell time from sticks in sand. I used to sit and listen to you, Lydie Breeze. Instructing the men. Reading. Questioning. Aipotu. You called this place—

LYDIE: Aipotu! Utopia backwards.

BEATY: And those men betrayed you. Your father betrayed her.

LYDIE: Don't say this.

BEATY: Your father betrayed her! She only wanted greatness for them. And he's forgotten. He's forgotten her. Hoc est enim corpus. (*Pause.*) She is gone.

LYDIE: No!

BEATY: She is gone. Men forget. You'll see what men are.

LYDIE: I'll never see what men are.

BEATY: Oh, they'll come into you.

LYDIE: They'll never come into me.

BEATY: Have your periods started? Wait. Wait. (BEATY *leaves the room.*)

LYDIE: I'm never going to have periods.

BEATY: (*Off.*) You'll see. You'll see the blood. You'll hear your body saying, "Watch me. Watch my blood. I'm getting you ready for the blood between men and women."

LYDIE: I don't have periods. My friend Irene Durban and I don't have periods. We made a pact. If anything like that happened to her she would tell me. She would send me a code. She would send me a shredded bee. (BEATY *enters with a wash basin and cloth.*)

BEATY: Shredded bee?

LYDIE: She would send me a bee with its wings pulled off. I have received no mail all summer. It won't happen to Irene. It won't happen to me. I am safe. I am my mother. Losing my sight is a present from her. Dead to the world so she can come in me. (BEATY *bathes* LYDIE's *eye.*)

BEATY: You have not lost your sight. You had an accident.

LYDIE: I have been blinded!

BEATY: Temporary. Temporary. By the end of the week, your eye will be healed.

LYDIE: A week is a very long time.

BEATY: Do you want to be a little blind beggar? I'll get you a cane and a little tin cup. We can put you outside the front door. (*She puts dark glasses with smoked lenses over* LYDIE's *eyes.*)

LYDIE: You're a cruel person.

BEATY: A truthful person.

LYDIE: You haven't told me one thing that's true.

BEATY: I told you about men.

LYDIE: You and your men.

BEATY: One man. Only one man. And I told you about your mother. Why did you have to be born when it was all over? Why couldn't you have known your mother in all her glory?

LYDIE: We'll keep her alive. The two of us.

BEATY: If only your eye would never heal. I could be your eyes.

LYDIE: You are.

BEATY: I could always take care of you.

LYDIE: You will. Always.

BEATY: Why do you have to change?

LYDIE: I won't. I promise you that.

BEATY: Your body will change. You'll fall in love. You'll forget about your mother. (BEATY *leaves the room.*)

LYDIE: I won't. I won't change. Ma? Do you want me to join you before I change? Is that the It? Ma? Ma?! (*Pause.*) Beaty, don't leave me alone!

(LYDIE *runs out of the room after* BEATY.)

The Mound Builders

Lanford Wilson

Characters: D.K. (Delia) Eriksen (38), Dr. Jean Loggins (25)
Setting: A farmhouse near an archaeological dig in Blue Shoals, Illinois
Premiere: Circle Repertory Company, New York City, 1975
Publisher: A Mermaid Dramabook (Hill and Wang)

Archaeologist August Howe is in his office trying to organize what is left of the wreckage of last summer's expedition. As he searches through slides, he dictates his notes into a tape machine, and the play flashes back to the previous summer.

August, his partner Dan Loggins, and several students are excavating a Mississippian Indian mound site in southern Illinois. Their overstuffed household includes both of their wives, August's eleven-year-old daughter, and his sister D.K. (Delia) Eriksen, a brilliant but dissipated novelist. As August puts it, "My sister's dying again; she was scraped up off the streets in Cleveland; apparently the hospitals there haven't the facilities or the will." The hospital has flown her down, and D.K. has been carried, against her will, into the house. She says she refuses to die "in this godforsaken Grant Wood mausoleum." Yet she is too weak to go anyplace else. She likes Jean, and the two women become friends.

Jean, Dan's wife, is an intern gynecologist. She has read D.K.'s books. After two miscarriages, Jean is pregnant again. She says she now understands "the source of that smug glow pregnant women have. You really do feel the miracle of it all."

Note: In this scene, D.K. remains on the lounge. She is not walking around yet.

DELIA: Did they fight? (JEAN *looks around to her.*) The Temple Mound people?
JEAN: (*Not really thinking about it.*) Apparently. When they

came—I think everyone would like to agree that they were runaways from the Toltecs, but haven't found substantial correlation; the books are all very careful about sweeping pronouncements, but it's all looking like a mud version of the Toltecs—so when they came up they fought off whoever was here. And built the first fortifications and all that. Probably kept the first slaves.

DELIA: You feed it all into a computer—and the facts and fancies the doctors have printed or typed or brushed and the computer would print out NOTHING APPLIES. It doesn't scan. The truth is in dreams and nightmares, but you haven't succeeded in getting that down. Rank was the ultimate genius, sure, but he couldn't tell you how to keep from cutting your wrist while you're shaving your legs.

JEAN: So you stopped shaving your legs.

DELIA: Cause and—
  (*Coughs.*)

JEAN: (*Beat.*) Effect. I wouldn't think you'd have much faith in computers.

DELIA: Well—"faith" . . .

JEAN: Exactly.

DELIA: It's all going to be facts, Doctor. Art is part of a primitive culture, really. The future is photography. We won't have time for anything more subtle than lies.

JEAN: You have a way of conveying the impression you know all the answers.

DELIA: The answer to which is, Yes, but I don't know any of the questions.

JEAN: Neat.

DELIA: Isn't that neat? It's a lie, but it's neat. I know the questions by rote. I just don't stand up well under them.

JEAN: No, neither do I. I won the spelling bee when I was a kid. Did beautifully, then had a complete collapse.

DELIA: I'd think so.

JEAN: Learned a lot of words.

DELIA: That's usually enough for a good impression. Spelling bee? God.

JEAN: *The* spelling bee. When I was what? Twelve. National Champion.

DELIA: Dear God.

JEAN: No one in the neighborhood went to the dictionary, they all came to me. I was tutored by my grandmother so I was the only kid who used the old-fashioned English grammar school method of syllable spelling. Charmed the pants off them. It started out as a kind of phenomenon or trick—then when my teachers realized they had a certifiable freak on their hands, they made me study for it.

DELIA: We're all freaks—all us bright sisters.

JEAN: It wasn't so bad until the competitions started. I mean, it wasn't like the little girl practicing her violin with her nose against the windowpane, watching all the other little girls at play. But I managed to work it into a nervous breakdown. (*Pause.*) I couldn't stop. Every word that was said to me, I spelled in my head. (*In an easy, flowing, but mechanical rhythm.*) Mary, go to bed. Mary go to bed. Mary. M-A-R-Y. Mary. Go. G-O. Go. Mary go. To. T-O. To. Mary go to. Bed. B-E-D. Bed. Mary go to bed. Mary go to bed: M-A-R-Y-G-O-T-O-B-E-D. Mary, go to bed.

DELIA: Mary?

JEAN: Mary Jean. (*She wanders to the door to gaze out.*) That, and I lost the meaning. Mary, go to bed was syllables, not sense. (*Beat.*) Then there were days when the world and its objects separated, disintegrated into their cellular structure, molecular—worse—into their atomic structure. And nothing held its form. The air was the same as the trees and a table was no more substantial than the lady sitting at it . . . Those were . . . not good days.

DELIA: I don't imagine. But you got it together.

JEAN: Oh, yes. Juvenile resilience.

DELIA: And that led one directly into gynecology.

JEAN: That led one directly into an instituition, and contact with some very sick kids. Some of them more physically ill than neurotic—who were not being particularly well cared for; and that led to an interest in medicine. And reading your books and others at an impressionable age led to gynecology. (*Beat.*) Also, living with my grandmother and her cronies, who were preoccupied with illness, kept it pretty much in my curiosity. They were always talking about friends with female troubles, problems with their organs. Of course, the only organ I knew was at church. I developed a theory of musical instruments as families. The cello was the mother, the bass was the father, and all the violins were the children. And the reason the big father organ at Grace Methodist Church made such a mournful sound was that female organs were always having something wrong with them.

DELIA: Round John Virgin.

JEAN: Exactly.

DELIA: Have you seen Dad's book on the eye? Vision, actually?

JEAN: I didn't know he had one. He was a doctor?

DELIA: Physiologist. Hated practicing physicians. Eye, ear, nose, throat.

JEAN: Somewhat different field.

DELIA: I'd guess. The downstairs of the house was his, his consultation room, his office, his examination rooms: big square masculine Victorian rooms with oversized charts of the musculature of the neck and diagrams of the eye with the retina and rods and cones and iris and lens and those lines projected out into space indicating sight. And it appeared to me—still does—that rather than the eye being a muscle that collects light, those beams indicated that the eye projects vision on the outside.

(*Pause.*)

JEAN: The place has changed since last year. I came down a couple of times last summer—weekends—watching their progress. But something odd is happening now—or not happening. There's something . . . I don't think it's the pregnancy, I think it's *here*. Or maybe my eyes are just projecting vision onto the outside.

DELIA: No, I don't think that's quite it.

JEAN: I have an intense desire to turn to the end of the chapter and see how it all comes out. You don't happen to have a deck of tarot on you, do you?

DELIA: No, I just look that way.

JEAN: It's only an anxiety.

DELIA: Generally speaking, Jean, ignore the Ides of March, but beware soothsayers. (JEAN *laughs*.) The old woman in *Dombey and Son* comes upon Edith in a lonely wood and says: "Give me a shilling and I'll tell your fortune." And Edith, of course, cuts her dead and goes on—Edith cuts everyone dead. And the old woman screams: "Give me a shilling or I'll yell your fortune after you."

JEAN: Oh, God. I'd pay. God, would I pay.

DELIA: That's what I thought.

JEAN: Jesus. Would I ever. What was the fortune? (*Pause.*) What was the—

DELIA: Give me a shilling or I'll tell you.

JEAN: Don't! Don't do that. What was the fortune?

DELIA: Uh, someone intervened.

JEAN: The hero.

DELIA: The villain actually.

JEAN: Do you do that? Turn to the end of a book to find out—

DELIA: No, I don't—I don't read any more.

JEAN: You do, of course. What's wrong is this inaction. I'm used to doing things. The university funds a clinic, you can't imagine. Coming off that is like coming off speed.

DELIA: And that's your answer. Why do you want to be a doctor when we get such a kick from diagnosing your own case? What seems to be the problem, Mrs. Blue—"Well, Doctor, I'm afraid I'm going to require twenty-five 300-milligram capsules of Declomycin."

JEAN: Oh, it's true. A gargle and forty Ornade spansules.

DELIA: Jean's only coming down off work and D.K. is frantically beating the bushes for something to believe in. Something with passion to warm up the blood and make her forget where it hurts. Great blinders is believing in and she's a great believer in blinders.

JEAN: Where does it hurt, D.K.?

DELIA: Doctor, it's a pain in the ass.
JEAN: Where does it hurt, D.K.?
DELIA: I thought we agreed not to ask.

Sarita

Maria Irene Fornes

Characters: Sarita (14), Fela (36)
Setting: Fela's living room, New York City, 1939–47
Premiere: INTAR, New York City, 1984
Publisher: Performing Arts Journal Publications (from *Maria Irene Fornes Plays*)

Sarita, a spirited young Hispanic woman, and her mother, Fela, live in the South Bronx. It is 1940. Sarita is fourteen years old.

1940—I'm Pregnant

(FELA's *livingroom.* SARITA *lies on the couch. Her feet are up against the couch's back. Her head touches the floor. She has been crying.* FELA *enters.* SARITA *wears a parochial school uniform.* FELA *wears a house dress.*)

FELA: What's the matter with you?
SARITA: I'm pregnant.
FELA: Don't talk stupid.
SARITA: I'm not talking stupid. I'm pregnant.
FELA: You're a child. You can't be pregnant.
SARITA: I'm serious.
FELA: Would you sit like a normal person? (SARITA *sits up.* FELA *notices her tears.*) Why are you crying?
SARITA: I'm pregnant . . .
(*There is a pause.*)
FELIA: Who says?—You're a child. A baby. Who says!

SARITA: I'm pregnant. No one has to say it.

FELA: You're a kid. Not even in high school. What would your teacher say?

SARITA: My teacher . . . ? I don't care. . . .

FELA: (*Grabbing her by the arm.*) You don't care? (*She looks into her eyes.*) Are you telling the truth? You're lying! It isn't true!

SARITA: It's true.

FELA: How do you know?

SARITA: I missed my period and my breasts hurt. And I know I'm pregnant.

FELA: You're lying!

SARITA: I'm not! Stop saying that! It's true!

FELA: (*Shaking her.*) Why did you do that! To ruin your life! To spend your life on relief. Like a worm on relief, crawling with children. Is that how I raised you? Is that what I taught you? (*Slapping her.*) You embarrass me!

SARITA: Don't!

FELA: What is this! (*Slapping her.*) What is this!

SARITA: Don't, Mami!

FELA: I didn't even start watching you! (*Slapping her.*) I didn't even start!

SARITA: Don't hit me, Mami!

FELA: I didn't think I had to watch you! (*Slapping her.*) You are a kid! (SARITA *runs left, goes around the chair and sits on it wailing.*) You're a kid! (*Raising her arms up in the air.*) I didn't even start watching you! (*Going on her knees. Her arms are raised.*) It's my fault! I didn't watch you! (*Pulling her hair and beating her chest.*) It's my fault!

SARITA: No Mami!

FELA: It's my fault!

SARITA: It's not your fault!

FELA: It's my fault! I let you loose in the street!

SARITA: No, Mami.

FELA: It's my fault! (*She starts to cry.*) It is my fault. . . . It is my fault. . . .

SARITA: Don't cry, Mami.

FELA: (*Starting to stand.*) Where's that kid! Julio!

SARITA: (*Crawls on her knees and grabs* FELA.) It wasn't him!

FELA: Where is he!

SARITA: It wasn't him!

FELA: Who was it!

SARITA: I don't know!

FELA: Somebody raped you!

SARITA: No!

FELIA: Fernando raped you!

SARITA: No, he didn't!

FELA: He's a dirty old man! I knew he was!

SARITA: No!

FELA: Who gave you a baby!

SARITA: Nobody!

FELIA: (*Grabbing her.*) Who did it!

SARITA: I don't know.

FELA: Tell me or I'll kill you.

SARITA: Don't make me tell you.

FELA: Tell me.

SARITA: I went out a lot.

FELIA: Who with?

SARITA: With a lot of guys! I don't know who did it! I went out with a lot of guys!

FELA: You don't know who did it?

SARITA: Mami, I was crying all the time. I was unhappy. I had tears in my eyes all the time. You know how I used to be. Julio left me. I was unhappy. You can't think of anything when you're unhappy like that. I went with boys and I felt better. I didn't care who they were. I was unhappy. You know how I was, Mami. You know I get crazy when he leaves me. You know I was crazy. I didn't know what I was doing. Don't be angry, Mami. It's hard enough . . .

FELA: (*Lowers her head.*). . . I raised you wrong. You didn't have a father. And you didn't have a family. Just me. I didn't teach you right.

SARITA: It's not that, Mami. You taught me right. (*She holds* FELA *tightly.*) It's just that I don't understand . . . I'm a

savage . . . Other people don't have to learn how to be. But
I'm a savage. I have to learn how to lead my life.
(*She cries.* FELA *puts her arms around her.*)

Savage in Limbo
John Patrick Shanley

Characters: Denise Savage (32), Linda Rotunda (32)
Setting: Scales, a bar in the Bronx, New York City
Premiere: Double Image Theatre, New York City, 1985
Publisher: Dramatists Play Service, Inc.

John Patrick Shanley calls *Savage in Limbo* a "concert
play . . . more a series of related emotional and intellectual
events than a conventional story."

A bartender and four neighborhood patrons spend a Monday night together. One of the patrons is Denise Savage. She's
small, wild-haired, and is ready for some action. She tells them
she has energy, and if she sits at home one more second
pwith her mother, who looks "like a dead walrus," she will
die.

Linda Rotunda, "a done-up, attractive, over-ripe Italian
girl" enters and begins to cry. She pronounces her boyfriend's
name Anthony as "Antony," and the word virgin as "version."
Savage recognizes Linda from grammar school and knows her
as a neighborhood joke. "You get knocked up every time you
stop walking. It's stupid to lie about it. Everybody knows.
You're sloppy and you're fertile."

The two women begin to talk.

SAVAGE: So, what's wrong with you? What's the story? Did
you get knocked up again?
LINDA: No. It's Anthony. He's gone crazy.

SAVAGE: Is he hittin you?

LINDA: No.

SAVAGE: What's he doin?

LINDA: He wants to see other women.

SAVAGE: What?

LINDA: He wants to see other women.

SAVAGE: And for this you think he's crazy, huh? You are a pisser.

LINDA: You don't understand.

SAVAGE: I understand that. That's very common.

LINDA: No, no. You don't understand.

SAVAGE: Have it your own way.

LINDA: He wants to see ugly women.

SAVAGE: They may look that way to you, honey, but I guess he sees 'em different.

LINDA: You don't understand. He told me. He says, Linda, I wanna see ugly girls.

SAVAGE: He said that?

LINDA: Yes.

SAVAGE: Well, what did he mean?

LINDA: He meant what he said.

SAVAGE: But that's not possible. Men don't go after women they think are ugly. If they end up with an ugly woman, it's because they made a mistake and they think she's good-lookin. Alright a drunk, a crazy guy, or a loser. But a guy like Tony? A guy like Tony Aronica would never end up with an ugly woman. You know why? He's just got too much dog in 'em He thinks like a dog.

LINDA: What are you tellin me? You're tellin me nothin. I tell you what's goin on, and you tell me it ain't goin on. It's goin on. Anthony wants to see ugly cause I don't know why, but that's the fuckin news and don't tell me otherwise. Every Monday night I go to his place and we spend time together, and this night I go and he's got this look in his eye. Like he knows somethin, and like he never seen me before. I got a scared feelin right away. I touch him but he puts my hand away. He says he wants to talk. What's he wanna talk about

before we go to bed? What's there to talk about? When a
woman wants to talk to a man, it's cause she wants the man
to see her better. When it's the other way, when the man
stops you from touchin to talk, what's there to talk about?
It's gotta be bad. I tried to keep him from talkin. I turned
myself on. But there was somethin in his mind. Even my
mother sees what Anthony's got. Even my mother. She'd
like a taste. She knows where I'm goin on Monday nights. I
don't come home till late, the mornin sometimes, but she
don't say anything. Any other time she would. But she knows
where I go, and she wants it for me. Once I was goin, and
she whispered to me so's my father wouldn't hear, Take it,
Linda. That's all. Take it, Linda. And I did. And now he
don't wanna see me cause he wants to see ugly women. I
said I'd be ugly for him, but he said no. It didn't work that
way. I'm so ashamed. I feel ugly. I feel fat. Anthony don't
want me no more.

SAVAGE: You're not fat. You're almost fat. But you're not fat.
You wanna play some cards?

LINDA: No.

SAVAGE: These cards are disgusting anyway. I left 'em near
the humidifier one night and they got all spongy. I got the
humidifier cause my mother was dryin out. She never goes
anywhere, she can't, and we got so much heat in the that
fuckin apartment—I looked at her one day and she looked
like a dead plant. So I went out and I got the humidifier and
I run it every night. She still looks like freeze-dried shit, but
I feel better cause I did somethin. I didn't just take it. I
didn't just fuckin accept it. I believe in action. Anyway, between the humidity and my sloppy ways, these cards are real
crappy. Some of these Sister Rosita's, you know, these witch-
tellers, they're supposed to be able to see your future inna
pack a cards. I look at these cards, I never see anything about
my future. I just see my fuckin life. I'm gonna go insane.

LINDA: What are you talkin about?

SAVAGE: I'm talkin about tension. I'm talkin about somethin
snappin at your heels, but you can't get away. Bein apart

from everybody else. Bein alone. There's a wall there. Like you're inna glass box, a bee inna jar, dreamin about flowers, smellin your own . . . death. People look at you, it's through somethin. You touch somebody, there's somethin over your hand.

LINDA: I don't get you.

SAVAGE: I'm trying to tell you somethin, but it's not easy.

LINDA: So tell me anyway.

SAVAGE: I'm a virgin.

LINDA: What?

SAVAGE: You heard me. You're just astounded. I'm a virgin.

LINDA: Why you tellin me a lie?

SAVAGE: In the beginnin, it was just bad luck. I'm not like you, and I got a big mouth, and well, it's easy not to lose it at first. You're scared, they're scared, somebody says: Boo, and everybody runs away. At least that's the way it was for me. To start with. But then it became a thing. Most everybody I knew lost it, you know, over a certain period a time, and there I was, still in the wrapper. It woulda been easy to lose it then. But it became a thing, you know? I felt different. I felt like I was holdin out for somethin. Not some guy, not just some guy. I felt like I was holdin out for somethin, sayin no, no, I'm not takin that life just cause it was the first one I was offered. So here I am. I'm thirty-two. And I'm still sayin no, no. And I still only got offered the one life, and I still don't want that one.

LINDA: You're a virgin?

SAVAGE: Yeah.

LINDA: Wow.

SAVAGE: Say somethin.

LINDA: What's it like?

SAVAGE: It's like holding your breath, only you never have to let go. No, that's not what it's like . . .

LINDA: I never knew anybody grown up who never, you know . . . I feel like you know somethin I don't know.

SAVAGE: Well, I know you know somethin I don't know.

LINDA: Yeah, but everybody I know knows what I know.

Except you. It's like common knowledge. But what you know, it's like a secret. How does it feel?

SAVAGE: I feel strong. Like I'm wearin chains and I could snap 'em any time. I feel ready. I go to work and I feel like I could take over the company, but I just type. I go home and I see my mother in her chair and I feel like I could pick her up with one hand and chuck her out the window and roll up the rug and throw a big party. Everybody's invited. I go to the library and I wanna take the books down off the shelves and open all the books on the tables and argue with everybody about ideas. I wanna think out loud with other people. You know what's wrong with everybody? Too smart. I know it sounds crazy. I know. But it's true. Everybody's too smart. It's like everybody knows everything and everybody argued everything and everything got hashed out and settled the day before I was born. It's not fair. They know about gravity so nobody talks about gravity. It's a dead issue. Look at me. My feet are stuck to the fuckin floor. Fantastic. But no. That's gravity. Forget it. It's been done it's been said it's been thought, so fuck it. It's not fair. I've been shut outta everything that mighta been good by a smartness around that won't let me think not one new thing. And it's been like that with love, too. You're a little girl and you see the movies and maybe you talk to your mother and you definitely talk to your friends and then you know, right? So you go ahead and you do love. And somethin a what somebody told ya inna movie or in your ear is what love is. And where the fuck are you then, that's what I wanna know? Where the fuck are you when you've done love, and you can point to love, and you can name it, and love is the same as gravity the same as everything else, and everything else is a totally dead fuckin issue?

LINDA: That's what it's like to be a virgin?

SAVAGE: That's part of it. Maybe that's the good part.

LINDA: You wanna be my friend?

SAVAGE: I don't know how.

LINDA: Me neither.

SAVAGE: Why you want me?

LINDA: Cause I gotta make a change, and you're different.

SAVAGE: What are you gonna do?

LINDA: Things have got to where I got to make a change.

[MURK: Hey, keep it down.

SAVAGE: Back off.]

LINDA: All I had was Monday. I just marked time till Monday. I ain't got Monday no more so I gotta make a change. Everything's doin shit on me an changin on me an lookin different than it was before and now there ain't no Monday and I'm thirty-two and my mother's gonna be on my case again my sucky life and I'll be fucking guys under staircases and I gotta make a change for myself this time no matter how much it hurts, I don't want to, scared, or it's goodbye Linda for sure. You gotta help me.

SAVAGE: How?

LINDA: Don't ask me that. That's the question. I don't know. But I gotta change.

SAVAGE: I gotta ask cause so do I, too.

LINDA: What are we gonna do?

SAVAGE: I don't know.

LINDA: I'm scared. I feel so scared.

SAVAGE: Why?

LINDA: I gotta move outta my whole house.

SAVAGE: So move.

LINDA: Why ain't you moved outta your house? (*No answer.*) Why ain't you moved outta your house?

SAVAGE: I can't do that.

LINDA: Why not?

SAVAGE: My mother's a shut-in. She's trapped. I can't leave her.

LINDA: Ain't we shut-in's, too?

SAVAGE: I gotta good room. I got books there that I read. And I gotta refill the humidifier all the time. My mother, she can only walk on canes. I figured it out. Without me, she'd die in three days.

LINDA: You're scared, too.

SAVAGE: No, I'm not.

LINDA: Yeah, you are.

SAVAGE: Yeah.

LINDA: I thought you weren't.

SAVAGE: I'm scared of everything. I see what could go wrong with everything so I don't do nothin. I got this one thing in me that I hate. I'm a coward.

LINDA: We gotta be friends.

SAVAGE: Alright.

LINDA: I ain't never been friends with a girl. I guess this is it.

SAVAGE: I ain't never been friends with nobody. I ain't had the time. I got my mother. I got the job. I just talk at people, which is lonely. I honestly could just fall down from loneliness.

LINDA: Maybe . . . Maybe we should do somethin together.

SAVAGE: For instance what?

LINDA: I don't know. Maybe we should go dancin together or somethin.

SAVAGE: Dancin?

LINDA: Somethin.

SAVAGE: I don't dance.

LINDA: Somethin.

SAVAGE: Maybe we should, I don't know, getta apartment. Together.

LINDA: Yeah? That'd be a step out, wouldn't it?

SAVAGE: It's an idea.

LINDA: So we're like girlfriends now, right? We're girlfriends, talkin to each other about bein roommates.

A Taste of Honey

Shelagh Delaney

Characters: Jo (nearly 18), Helen (40)
Setting: A comfortless flat in Manchester and the street outside
Premiere: Theatre Royal, Stratford, London, 1958
Publisher: Grove Press

Jo lives with her mother, Helen, a "semi-whore." They move from one ugly flat to another. This time they are running from Peter Smith, a brash car salesman. He tracks Helen down and proposes to her. At first she is reluctant, then accepts his offer. Peter is ten years younger than Helen. It is clear their life together will not include Jo.

When they go away for a week, Jo invites her fiancé, a 22-year-old black sailor, to stay with her. She keeps her relationship with him secret from Helen. She wears her engagement ring hidden on a piece of cord around her neck. She knows she will not see him again once he ships out, but does not care—it is enough for now. They begin sleeping together.

It is Helen's wedding day. Jo has caught her mother's cold.

(*Helen dances with an assortment of fancy boxes, containing her wedding clothes.*)

HELEN: Jo! Jo! Come on. Be sharp now. (JO *comes on in her pyjamas. She has a heavy cold.*) For God's sake give me a hand. I'll never be ready. What time is it? Have a look at the church clock.

JO: A quarter past eleven, and the sun's coming out.

HELEN: Oh! Well, happy the bride the sun shines on.

JO: Yeah, and happy the corpse the rain rains on. You're not getting married in a church, are you?

HELEN: Why, are you coming to throw bricks at us? Of course not. Do I look all right? Pass me my fur. Oh! My fur! Do you like it?

JO: I bet somebody's missing their cat.

HELEN: It's a wedding present from that young man of mine. He spends his money like water, you know, penny wise, pound foolish. Oh! I am excited, I feel twenty-one all over again. Oh! You would have to catch a cold on my wedding day. I was going to ask you to be my bridesmaid too.

JO: Don't talk daft.

HELEN: Where did you put my shoes? Did you clean 'em? Oh! They're on my feet. Don't stand there sniffing, Jo. Use a handkerchief.

JO: I haven't got one.

HELEN: Use this, then. What's the matter with you? What are you trying to hide?

JO: Nothing.

HELEN: Don't try to kid me. What is it? Come on, let's see.

JO: It's nothing. Let go of me. You're hurting.

HELEN: What's this?

JO: A ring.

HELEN: I can see it's a ring. Who give it to you?

JO: A friend of mine.

HELEN: Who? Come on. Tell me.

JO: You're hurting me.

(HELEN *breaks the cord and gets the ring.*)

HELEN: You should have sewn some buttons on your pyjamas if you didn't want me to see. Who give it you?

JO: My boy friend. He asked me to marry him.

HELEN: Well, you silly little bitch. You mean that lad you've been knocking about with while we've been away?

JO: Yes.

HELEN: I could choke you.

JO: You've already had a damn good try.

HELEN: You haven't known him five minutes. Has he really asked you to marry him?

JO: Yes.

HELEN: Well, thank God for the divorce courts! I suppose just because I'm getting married you think you should.

JO: Have you got the monopoly?

HELEN: You stupid little devil! What sort of a wife do you think you'd make? You're useless. It takes you all your time to look after yourself. I suppose you think you're in love. Anybody can fall in love, do you know that? But what do you know about the rest of it?

JO: Ask yourself.

HELEN: You know where that ring should be? In the ashcan with everything else. Oh! I could kill her, I could really.

JO: You don't half knock me about. I hope you suffer for it.

HELEN: I've done my share of suffering if I never do any more. Oh Jo, you're only a kid. Why don't you learn from my mistakes? It takes half your life to learn from your own.

JO: You leave me alone. Can I have my ring back, please?

HELEN: What a thing to happen just when I'm going to enjoy myself for a change.

JO: Nobody's stopping you.

HELEN: Yes, and as soon as my back's turned you'll be off with this sailor boy and ruin yourself for good.

JO: I'm already ruined.

HELEN: Yes, it's just the sort of thing you'd do. You make me sick.

JO: You've no need to worry, Helen. He's gone away. He may be back in six months, but there again, he may . . .

HELEN: Look, you're only young. Enjoy your life. Don't get trapped. Marriage can be hell for a kid.

JO: Can I have your hanky back?

HELEN: Where did you put it?

JO: This is your fault too.

HELEN: Everything's my fault. Show me your tongue.

JO: Breathing your 'flu bugs all over me.

HELEN: Yes, and your neck's red where I pulled that string.

JO: Will you get me a drink of water, Helen?

HELEN: No, have a dose of this. (*Offering whisky.*) It'll do you more good. I might as well have one myself while I'm at it, mightn't I?

JO: You've emptied more bottles down your throat in the last few weeks than I would have thought possible. If you don't watch it, you'll end up an old down-and-out boozer knocking back the meths.

HELEN: It'll never come to that. The devil looks after his own, they say.

JO: He certainly takes good care of you. You look marvellous, considering.

HELEN: Considering what?

JO: The wear and tear on your soul.

HELEN: Oh well, that'll have increased its market value, won't it?

JO: Old Nick'll get you in the end.

HELEN: Thank God for that! Heaven must be the hell of a place. Nothing but repentant sinners up there, isn't it? All the pimps, prostitutes and politicans in creation trying to cash in on eternity and their little tin god. Where's my hat?

JO: Where's your husband?

HELEN: Probably drunk with his pals somewhere. He was going down to the house this morning to let some air in. Have you seen a picture of the house? Yes, you have. Do you like it? (*She peers and primps into mirror.*)

JO: It's all right if you like that sort of thing, and I don't.

HELEN: I'll like it in a few years, when it isn't so new and clean. At the moment it's like my face, unblemished! Oh look at that, every line tells a dirty story, hey?

JO: Will you tell me something before you go?

HELEN: Oh! You can read all about that in books.

JO: What was my father like?

(HELEN *turns away.*)

HELEN: Who?

JO: You heard! My father! What was he like?

HELEN: Oh! Him.

JO: Well, was he so horrible that you can't even tell me about him?

HELEN: He wasn't horrible. He was just a bit stupid, you know. Not very bright.

JO: Be serious, Helen.

HELEN: I am serious.

JO: Are you trying to tell me he was an idiot?

HELEN: He wasn't an idiot, he was just a bit—retarded.

JO: You liar!

HELEN: All right, I'm a liar.

JO: Look at me.

HELEN: Well, am I?

JO: No.

HELEN: Well, now you know.

JO: How could you give me a father like that?

HELEN: I didn't do it on purpose. How was I to know you'd materialize out of a little love affair that lasted five minutes?

JO: You never think. That's your trouble.

HELEN: I know.

JO: Was he like a . . . a real idiot?

HELEN: I've told you once. He was nice though, you know, a nice little feller!

JO: Where is he now, locked up?

HELEN: No, he's dead.

JO: Why?

HELEN: Why? Well, I mean, death's something that comes to us all, and when it does come you haven't usually got time to ask why.

JO: It's hereditary, isn't it?

HELEN: What?

JO: Madness.

HELEN: Sometimes.

JO: Am I mad?

HELEN: Decide for yourself. Oh, Jo, don't be silly. Of course you're not daft. Not more so than anybody else.

JO: Why did you have to tell me that story? Couldn't you have made something up?

HELEN: You asked for the truth and you got it for once. Now be satisfied.

JO: How could you go with a half-wit?

HELEN: He had strange eyes. You've got 'em. Everybody used to laugh at him. Go on, I'll tell you some other time.

JO: Tell me now!

HELEN: Mind my scent!

JO: Please tell me. I want to understand.

HELEN: Do you think I understand? For one night, actually it was the afternoon, I loved him. It was the first time I'd ever really been with a man . . .

JO: You were married.

HELEN: I was married to a puritan—do you know what I mean?

JO: I think so.

HELEN: And when I met your father I was as pure and un-sullied as I fondly, and perhaps mistakenly, imagine you to be. It was the first time and though you can enjoy the second, the third, even the fourth time, there's no time like the first, it's always there. I'm off now. I've got to go and find my husband. Now don't sit here sulking all day.

JO: I was thinking.

HELEN: Well, don't think. It doesn't do you any good. I'll see you when the honeymoon's over. Come on, give us a kiss. You may as well. It's a long time since you kissed me.

JO: Keep it for him.

HELEN: I don't suppose you're sorry to see me go.

JO: I'm not sorry and I'm not glad.

HELEN: You don't know what you do want.

JO: Yes, I do. I've always known what I want.

HELEN: And when it comes your way will you recognize it?

JO: Good luck, Helen.

HELEN: I'll be seeing you. Hey! If he doesn't show up I'll be back.

JO: Good luck, Helen.

(*Exit* HELEN. *"Here Comes the Bride" on the cornet.*)

Top Girls
Caryl Churchill

Characters: Marlene (32), Joyce (late 30s)
Setting: Top Girls Employment Agency, London; Joyce's house, in the provinces
Premiere: Royal Court Theatre, London, 1982
Publisher: Methuen London Ltd.

Marlene has just been made managing director of the Top Girls Employment Agency. The play begins with a surrealistic celebration of this personal milestone, a dinner attended by history-making women: Pope Joan, Lady Nijo of Japan, and the intrepid Scottish traveler Isabella Bird. Marlene then progresses through a series of scenes with her high-flying female colleagues and various women seeking employment through Top Girls.

We also meet Marlene's sister, Joyce, a working-class provincial who never left home, and her fifteen-year-old charge, Angie. Angie is slightly retarded and spends her days playing childish games with her much younger neighbor, Kit. She idolizes the sophisticated "Aunty Marlene," unaware that her "aunt" is the biological mother who had her at seventeen and fled to a fast-lane life in the city. The following scene, at the end of the play, takes place late one night in Joyce's kitchen. The sisters have not seen each other for six years.

Note: Caryl Churchill notes that "when one character starts speaking before the other has finished, the point of interruption is marked with a /."

MARLENE: It's cold tonight.

JOYCE: Will you be all right on the sofa? You can / have my bed.

MARLENE: The sofa's fine.

JOYCE: Yes the forecast said rain tonight but it's held off.

MARLENE: I was going to walk down to the estuary but I've left it a bit late. Is it just the same?

JOYCE: They cut down the hedges a few years back. Is that since you were here?

MARLENE: But it's not changed down the end, all the mud? And the reeds? We used to pick them up when they were bigger than us. Are there still lapwings?

JOYCE: You get strangers walking there on a Sunday. I expect they're looking at the mud and the lapwings, yes.

MARLENE: You could have left.

JOYCE: Who says I wanted to leave?

MARLENE: Stop getting at me then, you're really boring.

JOYCE: How could I have left?

MARLENE: Did you want to?

JOYCE: I said how, how could I.

MARLENE: If you'd wanted to you'd have done it.

JOYCE: Christ.

MARLENE: Are we getting drunk?

JOYCE: Do you want something to eat?

MARLENE: No, I'm getting drunk.

JOYCE: Funny time to visit, Sunday evening.

MARLENE: I came this morning. I spent the day/—

[ANGIE: (*Off.*) Aunty! Aunty Marlene!]

MARLENE: I'd better go.

JOYCE: Go on then.

MARLENE: All right.

[ANGIE: (*Off.*) Aunty! Can you hear me? I'm ready.]

(MARLENE *goes.* JOYCE *sits.* MARLENE *comes back.*)

JOYCE: So what's the secret?

MARLENE: It's a secret.

JOYCE: I know what it is anyway.

MARLENE: I bet you don't. You always say that.

JOYCE: It's her exercise book.

MARLENE: Yes, but you don't know what's in it.

JOYCE: It's some game, some secret society she has with Kit.

MARLENE: You don't know the password. You don't know the code.

JOYCE: You're really in it, aren't you. Can you do the hand-shake?

MARLENE: She didn't mention a handshake.

JOYCE: I thought they'd have a special handshake. She spends hours writing that but she's useless at school. She copies things out of books about black magic, and politicians out of the paper. It's a bit childish.

MARLENE: I think it's a plot to take over the world.

JOYCE: She's been in the remedial class the last two years.

MARLENE: I came up this morning and spent the day in Ips-wich. I went to see Mother.

JOYCE: Did she recognise you?

MARLENE: Are you trying to be funny?

JOYCE: No, she does wander.

MARLENE: She wasn't wandering at all, she was very lucid thank you.

JOYCE: You were very lucky then.

MARLENE: Fucking awful life she's had.

JOYCE: Don't tell me.

MARLENE: Fucking waste.

JOYCE: Don't talk to me.

MARLENE: Why shouldn't I talk? Why shouldn't I talk to you?/ Isn't she my mother too?

JOYCE: Look, you've left, you've gone away,/ we can do with-out you.

MARLENE: I left home, so what, I left home. People do leave home,/ it is normal.

JOYCE: We understand that, we can do without you.

MARLENE: We weren't happy. Were you happy?

JOYCE: Don't come back.

MARLENE: So it's just your mother is it, your child, you never wanted me round.

JOYCE: Here we go.

MARLENE: You were jealous of me because I was the little one and I was clever.

JOYCE: I'm not clever enough for all this psychology,/ if that's what it is.

MARLENE: Why can't I visit my own family/ without all this?

JOYCE: Aah. Just don't go on about Mum's life when you haven't been to see her for how many years./ I go and see her every

MARLENE: It's up to me.

JOYCE: week.

MARLENE: Then don't go and see her every week.

JOYCE: Somebody has to.

MARLENE: No they don't./ Why do they?

JOYCE: How would I feel if I didn't go.

MARLENE: A lot better.

JOYCE: I hope you feel better.

MARLENE: It's up to me.

JOYCE: You couldn't get out of here fast enough.

MARLENE: Of course I couldn't get out of here fast enough. What was I going to do? Marry a dairyman who'd come home pissed?/ Don't you fucking this fucking

JOYCE: Christ.

MARLENE: that fucking bitch fucking tell me what to fucking do fucking.

JOYCE: I don't know how you could leave your own child.

MARLENE: You were quick enough to take her.

JOYCE: What does that mean?

MARLENE: You were quick enough to take her.

JOYCE: Or what? Have her put in a home? Have some stranger/ take her would you rather?

MARLENE: You couldn't have one so you took mine.

JOYCE: I didn't know that then.

MARLENE: Like hell,/ married three years.

JOYCE: I didn't know that. Plenty of people/ take that long.

MARLENE: Well it turned out lucky for you, didn't it.

JOYCE: Turned out all right for you by the look of you. You'd be getting a few less thousand a year.

MARLENE: Not necessarily.

JOYCE: You'd be stuck here/ like you said.

MARLENE: I could have taken her with me.

JOYCE: You didn't want to take her with you. It's no good coming back now, Marlene,/ and saying—

MARLENE: I know a managing director who's got two children, she breast feeds in the boardroom, she pays a hundred pounds a week on domestic help alone and she can afford that because she's an extremely high-powered lady earning a great deal of money.

JOYCE: So what's that got to do with you at the age of seventeen?

MARLENE: Just because you were married and had somewhere to live—

JOYCE: You could have lived at home./

MARLENE: Don't be stupid.

JOYCE: Or live with me and Frank./ You

MARLENE: You never suggested.

JOYCE: said you weren't keeping it. You shouldn't have had it/ if you wasn't

MARLENE: Here we go.

JOYCE: Going to keep it. You was the most stupid, for someone so clever you was the most stupid, get yourself pregnant, not go to the doctor, not tell.

MARLENE: You wanted it, you said you were glad. I remember the day, you said I'm glad you never got rid of it, I'll look after it, you said that down by the river. So what are you saying, sunshine, you don't want her?

JOYCE: Course I'm not saying that.

MARLENE: Because I'll take her,/ wake her up and pack now.

JOYCE: You wouldn't know how to begin to look after her.

MARLENE: Don't you want her?

JOYCE: Course I do, she's my child.

MARLENE: Then what are you going on about/ why did I have her?

JOYCE: You said I got her off you/ when you didn't—

MARLENE: I said you were lucky/ the way it—

JOYCE: Have a child now if you want one. You're not old.

MARLENE: I might do.

JOYCE: Good.

 (*Pause.*)

MARLENE: I've been on the pill so long/ I'm probably sterile.

JOYCE: Listen when Angie was six months I did get pregnant

and I lost it because I was so tired looking after your fucking
baby/ because she cried so much—yes I

MARLENE: You never told me.

JOYCE: did tell you—/and the doctor

MARLENE: Well I forgot.

JOYCE: said if I'd sat down all day with my feet up I'd've kept
it/ and that's the only chance I ever had because after that—

MARLENE: I've had two abortions, are you interested? Shall
I tell you about them? Well I won't, it's boring, it wasn't a
problem. I don't like messy talk about blood/ and what a bad
time we all had. I

JOYCE: If I hadn't had your baby. The doctor said.

MARLENE: don't want a baby. I don't want to talk about gy-
naecology.

JOYCE: Then stop trying to get Angie off of me.

MARLENE: I come down here after six years. All night you've
been saying I don't come often enough. If I don't come for
another six years she'll be twenty-one, will that be OK?

JOYCE: That'll be fine, yes, six years would suit me fine.
   (*Pause.*)

MARLENE: I was afraid of this. I only came because I thought
you wanted . . . I just want . . .
   (MARLENE *cries.*)

JOYCE: Don't grizzle, Marlene, for God's sake. Marly? Come
on, pet. Love you really. Fucking stop it, will you?

MARLENE: No, let me cry. I like it.
   (*They laugh,* MARLENE *begins to stop crying.*)
   I knew I'd cry if I wasn't careful.

JOYCE: Everyone's always crying in this house. Nobody takes
any notice.

MARLENE: You've been wonderful looking after Angie.

JOYCE: Don't get carried away.

MARLENE: I can't write letters but I do think of you.

JOYCE: You're getting drunk. I'm going to make some tea.

MARLENE: Love you.
   (JOYCE *gets up to make tea.*)

JOYCE: I can see why you'd want to leave. It's a dump here.

MARLENE: So what's this about you and Frank?

JOYCE: He was always carrying on, wasn't he. And if I wanted to go out in the evening he'd go mad, even if it was nothing, a class, I was going to go to an evening class. So he had this girlfriend, only twenty-two poor cow, and I said go on, off you go, hoppit. I don't think he even likes her.

MARLENE: So what about money?

JOYCE: I've always said I don't want your money.

MARLENE: No, does he send you money?

JOYCE: I've got four different cleaning jobs. Adds up. There's not a lot round here.

MARLENE: Does Angie miss him?

JOYCE: She doesn't say.

MARLENE: Does she see him?

JOYCE: He was never that fond of her to be honest.

MARLENE: He tried to kiss me once. When you were engaged.

JOYCE: Did you fancy him?

MARLENE: No, he looked like a fish.

JOYCE: He was lovely then.

MARLENE: Ugh.

JOYCE: Well I fancied him. For about three years.

MARLENE: Have you got someone else?

JOYCE: There's not a lot round here. Mind you, the minute you're on your own, you'd be amazed how your friends' husbands drop by. I'd sooner do without.

MARLENE: I don't see why you couldn't take my money.

JOYCE: I do, so don't bother about it.

MARLENE: Only got to ask.

JOYCE: So what about you? Good job?

MARLENE: Good for a laugh./ Got back

JOYCE: Good for more than a laugh I should think.

MARLENE: from the US of A a bit wiped out and slotted into this speedy employment agency and still there.

JOYCE: You can always find yourself work then.

MARLENE: That's right.

JOYCE: And men?

MARLENE: Oh there's always men.

JOYCE: No one special?

MARLENE: There's fellas who like to be seen with a high-flying lady. Shows they've got something really good in their pants. But they can't take the day to day. They're waiting for me to turn into the little woman. Or maybe I'm just horrible of course.

JOYCE: Who needs them.

MARLENE: Who needs them. Well I do. But I need adventures more. So on on into the sunset. I think the eighties are going to be stupendous.

JOYCE: Who for?

MARLENE: For me./ I think I'm going up up up.

JOYCE: Oh for you. Yes, I'm sure they will.

MARLENE: And for the country, come to that. Get the economy back on its feet and whoosh. She's a tough lady, Maggie. I'd give her a job./ She just needs to hang

JOYCE: You voted for them, did you?

MARLENE: in there. This country needs to stop whining./ Monetarism is not

JOYCE: Drink your tea and shut up, pet.

MARLENE: stupid. It takes time, determination. No more slop./ And

JOYCE: Well I think they're filthy bastards.

MARLENE: who's got to drive it on? First woman prime minister. Terrifico. Aces. Right on./ You must admit. Certainly gets my vote.

JOYCE: What good's first woman if it's her? I suppose you'd have liked Hitler if he was a woman. Ms. Hitler. Got a lot done, Hitlerina./ Great adventures.

MARLENE: Bosses still walking on the workers' faces? Still dadda's little parrot? Haven't you learned to think for yourself?/ I believe in the individual. Look at me.

JOYCE: I am looking at you.

MARLENE: Come on, Joyce, we're not going to quarrel over politics.

JOYCE: We are though.

MARLENE: Forget I mentioned it. Not a word about the slimy unions will cross my lips.

(Pause.)

JOYCE: You say Mother had a wasted life.

MARLENE: Yes I do. Married to that bastard.

JOYCE: What sort of life did he have?/

MARLENE: Violent life?

JOYCE: Working in the fields like an animal./ Why wouldn't he want a drink.

MARLENE: Come off it.

JOYCE: You want a drink. He couldn't afford whisky.

MARLENE: I don't want to talk about him.

JOYCE: You started, I was talking about here. She had a rotten life because she had nothing. She went hungry.

MARLENE: She was hungry because he drank the money./ He used to hit her.

JOYCE: It's not all down to him./ Their

MARLENE: She didn't hit him.

JOYCE: lives were rubbish. They were treated like rubbish. He's dead and she'll die soon and what sort of life/ did they have?

MARLENE: I saw him one night. I came down.

JOYCE: Do you think I didn't?/ They

MARLENE: I still have dreams.

JOYCE: didn't get to America and drive across it in a fast car./ Bad nights, they had bad days.

MARLENE: America, America, you're jealous./ I had to get out, I knew when I

JOYCE: Jealous?

MARLENE: was thirteen, out of their house, out of them, never let that happen to me,/ never let him, make my own way, out.

JOYCE: Jealous of what you've done, you're ashamed of me if I came to your office, your smart friends, wouldn't you, I'm ashamed of you, think of nothing but yourself, you've got on, nothing's changed for most people/ has it.

MARLENE: I hate the working class/

JOYCE: Yes you do.

MARLENE: which is what you're going to go on about now, it doesn't exist any more, it means lazy and stupid./ I don't

JOYCE: Come on, now we're getting it.

MARLENE: like the way they talk. I don't like beer guts and football vomit and saucy tits/ and brothers and sisters.—

JOYCE: I spit when I see a Rolls-Royce, scratch it with my ring./ Mercedes it was.

MARLENE: Oh very mature—

JOYCE: I hate the cows I work for/ and their dirty dishes with blanquette of fucking veau.

MARLENE: and I will not be pulled down to their level by a flying picket and I won't be sent to Siberia/ or a loony bin just because

JOYCE: No, you'll be on a yacht, you'll be head of Coca-Cola and you wait, the eighties is going to be stupendous all right because we'll get you lot off our backs—

MARLENE: I'm original and I support Reagan even if he is a lousy movie star because the reds are swarming up his map and I want to be free in a free world—

JOYCE: What?/ What?

MARLENE: I know what I mean/ by that—not shut up here.

JOYCE: So don't be round here when it happens because if someone's kicking you I'll just laugh.

(Silence.)

MARLENE: I don't mean anything personal. I don't believe in class. Anyone can do anything if they've got what it takes.

JOYCE: And if they haven't?

MARLENE: If they're stupid or lazy or frightened, I'm not going to help them get a job, why should I?

JOYCE: What about Angie?

MARLENE: What about Angie?

JOYCE: She's stupid, lazy and frightened, so what about her?

MARLENE: You run her down too much. She'll be all right.

JOYCE: I don't expect so, no. I expect her children will say what a wasted life she had. If she has children. Because nothing's changed and it won't with them in.

MARLENE: Them, them./ Us and them?

JOYCE: And you're one of them.

MARLENE: And you're us, wonderful us, and Angie's us/ and Mum and Dad's us.

JOYCE: Yes, that's right, and you're them.

MARLENE: Come on, Joyce, what a night. You've got what it takes.

JOYCE: I know I have.

MARLENE: I didn't really mean all that.

JOYCE: I did.

MARLENE: But we're friends anyway.

JOYCE: I don't think so, no.

MARLENE: Well it's lovely to be out in the country. I really must make the effort to come more often.

I want to go to sleep.

I want to go to sleep.

(JOYCE *gets blankets for the sofa.*)

JOYCE: Goodnight then. I hope you'll be warm enough.

MARLENE: Goodnight, Joyce—

JOYCE: No, pet. Sorry.

(JOYCE *goes.* MARLENE *sits wrapped in a blanket and has another drink.*)

Waiting for the Parade

John Murrell

Characters: Marta (30s), Janet (late 30s)
Setting: Calgary, Alberta (World War II)
Premiere: Alberta Theatre Projects, Calgary 1977
Publisher: Talonbooks

Waiting for the Parade concerns five Canadian women during World War II. The first, Janet, is extremely patriotic and believes in giving her all for the war effort. This includes working for the Red Cross and being aggressively cheerful. She says her husband desperately wanted to enlist but has remained behind as part of an "essential service." He reads the Texaco News Flashes, afternoons and evenings.

Marta is German and has lived in Canada since she was

nine years old. She owns a men's clothing shop. Her father
has been put in a Canadian camp for being a Nazi—a charge
she refuses to believe.

————————————

(*A Richard Tauber record is heard, softly at first then swell-*
ing.)
VOICE OF TAUBER:
  "Banger Gram, eh's sie kam,
  Hat die Zukunft mir umhüllt,
  Doch mit ihr blühte mir
  Neues Dasein lusterfüllt,"
  Etc.
(JANET *is waiting impatiently, tapping her foot. After a*
moment, MARTA *enters, smoking. She carries a pair of*
men's trousers, with chalk alteration marks, on a wooden
hanger. The Tauber record continues in the background,
rather loud.)
JANET: Good afternoon. I rang the bell on the counter, but
  nobody came.
MARTA: Sometimes I don't hear the bell.
JANET: No? I'm not surprised.
  (*Pause.*)
MARTA: Can I show you something?
JANET: No.
MARTA: Just browsing?
JANET: No. I didn't come in to buy anything.
MARTA: Oh?
  (*Pause.*)
JANET: Look, I'll come straight to the point—if I may?
MARTA: What point?
JANET: We felt it was necessary—at least, I did—I thought
  you and I should—have a little chat.
MARTA: I see. (*Pause.*) Go on then. Chat.
JANET: It's about—about this music of yours.
MARTA: Music?
JANET: On the phonograph.

MARTA: Oh. You don't like it?

JANET: The question is not whether *I* like it—

MARTA: No? What is the question then?

(*Pause.*)

JANET: (*Softly.*) You're not making this any easier. People—a substantial number of people—are bothered by it.

MARTA: By my music?

JANET: Yes.

MARTA: Why?

JANET: Surely I don't have to tell you—Would you mind putting out your cigarette?

MARTA: Yes, I would. Who is it that objects to my music?

JANET: As a matter of fact, I was delegated—unofficially—A substantial number of people have expressed their disapproval. Concern. And I feel it's in your own best interest—

MARTA: Because it's German music, you mean?

JANET: Surely you can understand that.

MARTA: It's not war music. It's a love song.

JANET: I realize that. I am a music lover myself—

MARTA: Are you? Don't you like this song?

JANET: It's—a lovely melody.

MARTA: You want me to translate the words? "Ach, so fromm"—"Oh, so chaste"—"Ach, so traut"—"Oh, so true"—

JANET: Please! You're not making this any easier. There are constant complaints about that noise! That music. It can be heard right out there on Centre Street. You must know that.

MARTA: These old buildings have very thin walls. I wish I could afford a better place. I just like to have some music while I work—

JANET: The point is, nobody wants to hear it!

MARTA: *I* want to hear it!

(*She lights another cigarette.*)

JANET: Look, I came here with every intention of being perfectly pleasant.

MARTA: Oh, you *are* being "perfectly pleasant."

JANET: I can understand that you might feel a bit—resentful. I know all about your father. Where he is. And why. You

have my sympathy. Truly. But it's in your own best interest
to be a little more—discreet. When they asked me to come
here, I told them, "I'm sure she's not a die-hard like her
father. She's been in this country quite a few years now—"

MARTA: Since I was nine years old!

JANET: Don't raise your voice to me! I'm trying to make this
as painless as possible. For your sake!

   (*The Tauber record concludes.*)

[TAUBER:

   "Teile es mit mir!

      Ja! mit mir!"]

MARTA: Get out of my shop.

JANET: Civic authorities can be asked to handle this sort of
thing. But I thought—

MARTA: Get out of my shop.

JANET: —that you'd prefer a more personal approach. Obviously I was—

MARTA: *Get out of my shop.*

   (JANET *totally frustrated, starts to leave, stops, turns back,
crosses swiftly to* MARTA *grabs the trousers from her, rips
them off the hanger, throws the hanger down, violently rum-
ples the trousers and throws them down also, then exits quickly.
Pause.* MARTA *laughs without smiling and stoops to pick up
the trousers.*)

MARTA: (*Singing to herself.*)

   "Banger Gram, eh' sie kam,

      Hat die Zukunft mir umhüllt,

      Doch mit ihr blühte mir

      Neues Dasein—"

      Etc.

TWO MEN

The Blood Knot

Athol Fugard

Characters: Morris, Zachariah (ages not specified)
Setting: One-room shack in the non-white location of Korsten,
near Port Elizabeth, South Africa
Premiere: Rehearsal Room, African Music and Drama Association, Johannesburg, South Africa, 1961
Publisher: Oxford University Press (from *Boesman and Lena
and Other Plays*)

Morris takes off, "a marked man on a long road." After
years, he returns to his brother's shack in a non-white area
and moves in. Zachariah is dark-skinned; Morris, light-skinned.

Morris plans everything. He constantly sets an alarm for
when to eat, sleep, etc. Zachariah's life changes. He no longer
enjoys drinking on Friday nights as his friend Minnie plays
the guitar. Instead, Morris convinces him to save for the future. Zachariah complains, "A whole year of spending tonights
talking, talking. I'm sick of talking." He wants a woman.

Morris comes up with the idea of a pen pal. Through the
paper they write to Ethel Lange. Ethel writes back and sends
a photo. She is white.

Zachariah decides to give his date to his brother, who can
pass as white. Morris objects. (In apartheid South Africa, in-
terracial sex is a crime.) Zachariah convinces him to play along
and uses their year's savings to buy Morris the suit of a gentleman.

Note: The word "swartgat" means "nigger." "Blood knot"
refers to the inseparable tie binding them together . . . "the
bond between brothers."

(MORRIS *is lying on his bed, staring up at the ceiling. There
is a knock at the door.* MORRIS *rises slowly on his bed.*)
MORRIS: Who is there? (*The knock is heard again.*) Speak up.

I can't hear. (*Silence.* MORRIS'*s fear is now apparent. He waits until the knock is heard a third time.*) Ethel . . . I mean, madam . . . no, no! . . . I mean to say Miss Ethel Lange, could that be you? (*In reply there is a raucous burst of laughter, unmistakably Zachariah's.*) What's this? (*Silence.*) What's the meaning of this? (MORRIS *rushes to his bed and looks at the alarm-clock.*) This is all wrong, Zach! It's still only the middle of the day.

ZACHARIAH: (*Outside.*) I know.

MORRIS: Go back to work! At once!

ZACHARIAH: I can't.

MORRIS: Why not?

ZACHARIAH: I took some leave, Morris, and left. Let me in.

MORRIS: What's the matter with you? The door's not locked.

ZACHARIAH: My hands are full. (*Pause.*) I been shopping, Morrie. (MORRIS *rushes to the door, but collects himself before opening it.* ZACHARIAH *comes in, his arms piled high with parcels. He smiles slyly at* MORRIS *who has assumed a pose of indifference.*)

ZACHARIAH: Oh no you don't, this time! I heard you run. So you thought it was maybe our little Miss Ethel, and a bit scared too at that thought, I think I heard? Well, don't worry no more, Morrie, because you know what these is? Your outfit! Number one, and what do we have? A wonderful hat . . . sir. (*Takes it out and holds it up for approval. His manner is exaggerated and suggestive of the shopkeeper who sold him the clothing.*) . . . which is guaranteed to protect the head on Sundays and rainy days. Because! Think for a moment! Who ever knows what the weather will be? It's been bad before. Number two is the shirt, and a grey tie, which is much better taste. Spots are too loud for a gentleman. Next we have—two grey socks, left and right, and a hanky to blow her nose. (*Next parcel.*) Aha! We've come to the suit. Now before I show you the suit, my friend, I want to ask you, what does a man really look for in a good suit? A good cloth. Isn't that so?

MORRIS: What are you talking about?

ZACHARIAH: That's what he said. The fashion might be a season old, but will you please feel the difference. It's lasted for years already. All I can say is, take it or leave it. But remember, only a fool would leave it at that price. So I took it. (*Next parcel.*) Here we have a real ostrich wallet.

MORRIS: What for?

ZACHARIAH: Your inside pocket. *Ja!* You forgot about the inside pocket, he said. A gentleman always got a wallet for the inside pocket. (*Next parcel.*) And a cigarette lighter, and a cigarette case for the outside pocket. Chramonium!

MORRIS: Since when do I smoke?

ZACHARIAH: I know. But Ethel might, he said.

MORRIS: (*Fear.*) You told him?

ZACHARIAH: Don't worry. I just said there was a lady who someone was going to meet. He winked at me and said it was a good thing, now and then, and reminded me that ladies like presents. (*Holds up a scarf.*) A pretty *doek* in case the wind blows her hair away, he said. Here we got a umbrella in case it's sopping wet. And over here . . . (*Last parcel.*) . . . Guess! Come on, Morrie. Guess what's in this box. I'll shake it. Listen.

MORRIS: Shoes.

ZACHARIAH: (*Triumphantly.*) No! It's boots! I got you boots. Ha ha! *Ja!* (*Watching MORRIS's reaction.*) They frighten a *ou*, don't they? (*Happy.*) Satisfied?

MORRIS: (*Looking at the pile of clothing.*) It seems all right.

ZACHARIAH: It wasn't easy. At the first shop, when I asked for the outfit for a gentleman, they said I was a agitator and was going to call the police. I had to get out, man . . . quick! Even this fellow . . . Mr. Moses—"Come again, my friend" . . . "You're drunk," he said. But when I showed him our future he sobered up. You know what he said? Guess.

MORRIS: No.

ZACHARIAH: He said, "Are you the gentleman?" Me! He did. So I said. "Do I look like a gentleman, Mr. Moses?" He said, "My friend, it takes all sorts of different sorts to make this world." "I'm the black sort," I said. So he said, "You don't say." He also said to mention his name and the fair deal to any other gentlemen wanting reasonable outfits. Go ahead, Morrie. (*The clothing.*) Let's see the gentle sort of man.

MORRIS: Okay. Okay. Don't rush me. (*Moves cautiously to the pile of clothing. Flicks an imaginary speck of dust off the hat. Zachariah is waiting.*) Well?

ZACHARIAH: Well, I'm waiting.

MORRIS: Give me time.

ZACHARIAH: What for? You got the clothes.

MORRIS: For God's sake, Zach! This is deep water, I'm not just going to jump right in. Men drown that way. You must paddle around first.

ZACHARIAH: Paddle around?

MORRIS: Try it out!

ZACHARIAH: (*Offering him the hat.*) Try it on.

MORRIS: The idea, man. I got to try it out. There's more to wearing a white skin than just putting on a hat. You've seen white men before without hats, but they're still white men, aren't they?

ZACHARIAH: *Ja.*

MORRIS: And without suits or socks, or shoes . . .

ZACHARIAH: No, Morrie. Never without socks and shoes. Never a barefoot white man.

MORRIS: Well, the suit then. Look, Zach, what I'm trying to say is this. The clothes will help, but only help. They don't maketh the white man. It's that white something inside you, that special meaning and manner of whiteness that I got to find. I know what I'm talking about because—I'll be honest with you now, Zach . . . I've thought about it for a long time. Why do you think I really read the Bible, hey? What do you think I'm thinking about when I'm not saying something? I'm being critical of colour, and the first- fruit of my thought is that this whiteness of theirs is not just in the skin, otherwise . . . well, I mean . . . I'd be one of them, wouldn't I? Because, let me tell you, I seen them that's darker than me. Yes. Really dark, man. Only they had that something I'm telling you about. That's what I got to pin down in here.

ZACHARIAH: What?

MORRIS: White living, man! Like . . . like . . . like let's take looking at things. Haven't you noticed it? They look at things differently. Haven't you seen their eyes when they look at you? (*Pause.*) That snapshot of Ethel. See how she stands there against that brick wall, facing the camera without fear. They're born with that sort of courage. Just suppose, when I'm taking her away to afternoon tea, a man jumps out and points a camera at me! I'm telling you, my first thought will be to run like hell, to protect my face! It's not that I'm a coward. It's what they call instinct, and I was born with it, and now I got to learn to conquer it. Because if I don't, you think that Ethel won't know what it means? I'll be done for, man! . . . again. How else did they know? Because we agree that I'm just as white as some of them. It all boils down to this different thing they got, and, let me tell you, it's even in their way of walking. Something happened to me once which proves it. It was on the road. The first time I had started going.

ZACHARIAH: Where?

MORRIS: Just places. I've got to explain something, Zach, otherwise you won't feel what I mean. A road, Zach, is not a street. It's not just that there isn't houses, or lamp-posts, or hasn't got a name. It's that it doesn't stop. The road goes on and on, passing all the time through nothing. And when a man, a city man, a man used to streets and things, walks out onto it . . . he just doesn't know what he's walking into. You see, you're used to people . . . but there's no people there! You're used to a roof . . . where there is only a sky . . . silence instead of sound. I'm telling you, man, it was nothing instead of something, some any old thing like a donkey, or a dog, or children kicking an empty tin . . . there was nothing, and it was the first time. This is no place for me, I thought, this emptiness! Not even trees. Zach. Only small, dry, little brittle bushes and flat hills in the distance. That, and the road running straight. God, that hurts the eyeball! That staight, never-stopping road! You've reached the end you think, you come to the top, and there . . . t-h-e-r-e it goes again. So the bushes and the hills and the road and nothing else . . . or maybe just a car running away in the dust . . . but only a few of them, and far between, a long way between each one. You see, they never stopped. So all of that and me, there, in the middle for the first time. It hits you when the sun goes. That's when you really know why men build homes, and the meaning of that word "home," because the veld's gone grey and cold with a blind, bad feeling about you being there. (*Pause.*) So there I was on the road. I'd been watching him all day.

ZACHARIAH: Who?

MORRIS: The man ahead of me.

ZACHARIAH: I thought you was alone.

MORRIS: I was feeling alone, but there was this man ahead of me. At first it was enough just to see him there, a spot in the dusty distance. A man! Another man! Another man! There was one other man on that road with me, going my way! But then the item came for the sun to drop, and I found myself walking through the shadows of those white stones on the side of the way. When a man sees shadows he thinks of night, doesn't he? I did. So I began to walk a little faster. I think he began to walk a little slower. I'm sure he also saw the shadows. Now comes the point. The more I walked a little bit faster and faster each time, the more I began to worry. About what, you ask? About him. There was something about him, about the way he walked, the way he went to the top when the road had a hill and stood there against the sky and looked back at me, and then walked on again. And all the time, with this worry in my heart, the loneliness was creeping across the veld and I was hurrying a bit more. In fact, I was going quite quick by then. When the sun went at last, I was trotting you might say, and worried, Zach, really worried, man, because I could see the warm glow of his fire as I ran that last little bit through the dark. When I was even nearer he saw me coming and stood up, but when he saw me clearer he picked up a stick and held it like a hitting stick, stepping back for safety and a good aim . . . so what could I do but pass peacefully. (*Pause.*) Because he was white, Zach. I had been right all along . . . the road . . . since midday. That's what I mean, you see. It's in the way they walk as well.

ZACHARIAH: So you must learn to walk properly then.

MORRIS: Yes.

ZACHARIAH: And to look right at things.

MORRIS: Yes.

ZACHARIAH: And to sound right.

MORRIS: Yes! There's that, as well. The sound of it.

ZACHARIAH: So go on. (*Again offering the hat.*) Try it. For size. Just for the sake of the size. (MORRIS *takes the hat, plays with it for a few seconds, then impulsively puts it on.*) Ha!

MORRIS: Yes?

ZACHARIAH: Aha!

MORRIS: (*Whipping off the hat in embarrassment.*) No.

ZACHARIAH: Yes.

MORRIS: (*Shaking his head.*) Uhuh!

ZACHARIAH: Come.

MORRIS: No, man.

ZACHARIAH: Please, man.

MORRIS: You're teasing.

ZACHARIAH: No, man. I like the look of that on your head.

MORRIS: Really?

ZACHARIAH: 'Strue's God.

MORRIS: It looked right?

ZACHARIAH: I'm telling you.

MORRIS: It seemed to fit.

ZACHARIAH: It did, I know.

MORRIS: (*Using this as an excuse to get it back on his head.*) The brim was just right on the brow . . . and with plenty of room for the brain! I'll try it again, shall I? Just for size.

ZACHARIAH: Just for size. (*Morris puts it on.*) *Ja.* A good fit.

MORRIS: A very good fit, in fact. (*Lifting the hat.*) Good morning!

ZACHARIAH: Very good.

MORRIS: Did it look right? (*Again.*) Good morning . . . Miss Ethel Lange! (*Looks quickly to see* ZACHARIAH'S *reaction. He betrays nothing.*)

ZACHARIAH: Maybe a little bit higher.

MORRIS: (*Again*). Good morning. . . . (*A flourish.*) . . . and how do you do today, Miss Ethel Lange! (*Laughing with delight.*) How about the jacket?

ZACHARIAH: Okay. (*Hands him the jacket. Morris puts it on.*)

MORRIS: (*Preening*). How did you do it?

ZACHARIAH: I said, "The gentleman is smaller than me, Mr. Moses."

MORRIS: It's so smug. Look, Zach, I'm going to that little bit again. Watch me careful. (*Once again lifting his hat.*) Good day, Miss Ethel Lange . . . (*Pleading, servile.*) . . . I beg your pardon, but I do hope you wouldn't mind to take a little walk with . . .

ZACHARIAH Stop!

MORRIS: What's wrong?

ZACHARIAH: Your voice.

MORRIS: What's wrong with it?

ZACHARIAH: Too soft. They don't never sound like that.

MORRIS: To a lady they do! I admit, if it wasn't Ethel I was addressing, it would be different.

ZACHARIAH: Okay. Try me.

MORRIS: How?

ZACHARIAH: You're walking with Ethel. I'm selling monkey-nuts.

MORRIS: So?

ZACHARIAH: So you want some monkey-nuts.

MORRIS: That's a good idea . . . (*His voice trails off.*)

ZACHARIAH: Go on. I'm selling monkey-nuts.

MORRIS: (*After hesitation.*) I can't.

ZACHARIAH: (*Simulated shock.*) What!

MORRIS: (*Frightened.*) What I mean is . . . I don't want any monkey-nuts. I'm not hungry.

ZACHARIAH: Ethel wants some.

MORRIS: Ethel.

ZACHARIAH: *Ja*. And I'm selling them.

MORRIS: This is hard for me, Zach.

ZACHARIAH: You must learn your lesson, Morrie. You want to pass, don't you?

MORRIS: (*Steeling himself.*) Excuse me!

ZACHARIAH: I'll never hear that.

MORRIS: Hey!

ZACHARIAH: Or that.

MORRIS: Boy!

ZACHARIAH: I'm ignoring you, man. I'm a cheeky one.

MORRIS: You're asking for it, Zach!

ZACHARIAH: I am.

MORRIS: I warn you, I will!

ZACHARIAH: Go ahead.

MORRIS: (*With brutality and coarseness.*) Hey, *Swartgat!* (*An immediate reaction from* ZACHARIAH. *His head whips around. He stares at* MORRIS *in disbelief. Morris replies with a weak little laugh, which soon dies on his lips.*) Just a joke! (*Softly.*) Oh, my God! What did I do? Forgive me, Zach. Say it, please. Forgiveness. Don't look at me like that! (*A step to* ZACHARIAH *who backs away.*) Say something. For God's sake say anything! I didn't mean it now. I didn't do it then. Truly. I came back. I'm your brother

ZACHARIAH: (*Disbelief.*) My brother?

MORRIS: Me, Zach, Morris!

ZACHARIAH: Morris?

> (MORRIS *at last realizes what has happened. He tears off the jacket and hat in a frenzy.*)

MORRIS: Now do you see?

ZACHARIAH: It's you.

MORRIS: Yes!

ZACHARIAH: That's funny. I thought . . .

MORRIS: I know. I saw it again.

ZACHARIAH: What?

MORRIS: The pain, man. The pity of it all and the pain in your eyes.

ZACHARIAH: I was looking, I thought, at a different sort of man.

MORRIS: But don't you see, Zach? It was me! That different sort of man you saw was me. It's happened, man! And I'll swear, I'll take God's name in vain that I no longer wanted it. That's why I came back. I didn't want it any more. I turned around on the road and came back here because I couldn't stand that look in your eyes any more. Those bright, brotherly eyes in my dreams at night, always wet with love, full of pity and pain . . . God, such lonely eyes they were! . . . watching and sad and asking me, why? softly, why? sorrowfully, why? . . . Why did I do it? . . . Why try to deny it? Because . . . because . . . I'll tell you the whole truth now. . . . Because I did try it! It didn't seem a sin. If a man was born with a chance at a change, why not take it, I thought . . . thinking of worms lying warm in their silk, to come out one day with wings and things! Why not a man? If his dreams are soft and keep him warm at night, why not stand up the next morning, Different . . . Beautiful! It's the natural law! The long arm of the real law frightened me—but I might have been lucky. We all know that some are not caught, so . . . so . . . so what was worrying me? You. Yes, in my dreams at night, there was you, as well. What about you? My own brother. What sort of a thing was that to do to a *ou's* own flesh-and-blood brother? Because he is, you know. There was only one mother, and she's what counts. And watch out! She will, too, up in heaven, her two little chickens down here and find one missing. She'll know what you've done! If you don't mind about hell, all right, go ahead . . . but even so there was still you, because it wasn't that next life but this old, worn out, and wicked one, and I was tired because there was still you. Anywhere, any place or road, there was still you. So I came back. (*Pause.*) It's not been too hard. A little uneasy at times, but not too hard. And I've proved

I'm no Judas. Gentle Jesus, meek and mild, I'm no Judas!
(*The alarm rings. Neither responds.*)

The Colored Museum
George C. Wolfe

Characters: Man (20s–30s), Kid (his former self)
Setting: A museum where the myths and madness of black/
Negro/colored Americans are stored
Premiere: Crossroads Theatre Company, New Brunswick, New
Jersey, 1986
Publisher: Broadway Play Publishing, Inc.

The Colored Museum consists of a series of sketches or
"exhibits" that examine the lives of black Americans. This
scene is entitled "Symbiosis."

(*The Temptations singing "My Girl" is heard as lights reveal
a black* MAN *in corporate dress standing before a trash bin
throwing objects from a Saks Fifth Avenue bag into it.
Circling around him with his every emotion on his face is*
THE KID, *who is dressed in a late sixties street style. His
moves are slightly heightened. As the scene begins the music
fades.*)

MAN: (*With contained emotions.*) My first pair of Converse
All-Stars. Gone. My first Afro comb. Gone. My first dashiki.
Gone. My autographed pictures of Stokely Carmichael, Jomo
Kenyatta and Donna Summer. Gone.

KID: (*Near tears, totally upset.*) This shit's not fair man. Damn!
Hell! Shit! Shit! It's not fair!

MAN: My first jar of Murray's Pomade. My first can of Afro-
Sheen. My first box of curl relaxer. Gone! Gone! Gone! Eld-
rige Cleaver's *Soul on Ice.*

KID: Not *Soul on Ice*!

MAN: It's been replaced on my bookshelf by *The Color Purple*.

KID: (*Horrified.*) No!

MAN: Gone!

KID: But—

MAN: Jimi Hendrix's *Purple Haze*. Gone. Sly Stone's *There's a Riot Goin On*. Gone. The Jackson Five's *I Want You Back*.

KID: Man you can't throw that away. It's living proof Michael had a black nose.

MAN: It's all going. Anything and everything that connects me to you, to who I was, to what we were, is out of my life.

KID: You've got to give me another chance.

MAN: *Fingertips Part 2*.

KID: Man how can you do that? That's vintage Stevie Wonder.

MAN: You want to know how kid? You want to know how? Because my survival depends on it. Whether you know it or not, the ice age is upon us.

KID: (*Playfully.*) What the hell you talkin about. It's ninety-five damn degrees.

MAN: The climate is changing kid and either you adjust or you end up extinct. A sociological dinosaur. Do you understand what I'm trying to tell you? King Kong would have made it to the top if only he had taken the elevator. Instead he brought attention to his struggle and ended up dead.

KID: (*Pleading.*) I'll change. I swear I'll change. I'll maintain a low profile. You won't even know I'm around.

MAN: If I'm to become what I'm to become then you've got to go. I have no history. I have no past.

KID: Just like that?

MAN: (*Throwing away a series of buttons.*) Free Angela! Free Bobby! Free Huey, Dewey and Louie! U.S. out of Vietnam. U.S. out of Cambodia. U.S. out of Harlem, Detroit and Newark. Gone!

(*He holds up the last object.*) "The Temptations' Greatest Hits!"

KID: (*Grabbing the album.*) No!!!

MAN: Give it back kid.

KID: No.

MAN: I said give it back!

KID: No. I can't let you trash this. Johnny man it contains fourteen classic cuts by the tempting Temptations. We're talking "Ain't Too Proud to Beg," "Papa Was a Rolling Stone," "My Girl."

MAN: (*Warning.*) I don't have all day.

KID: For God's sake Johnny man "My Girl" is the jam to end all jams. It's what we are. Who we are. It's a way of life. Come on man, for old times' sake. (*He sings.*)

I got sunshine on a cloudy day
Dum-da-dum-da-dum-da-dum
And when it's cold outside
(*Speaking.*) Come on Johnny man sing.
I got the mouth of May
(*Speaking.*) Here comes your favorite part.
Come on Johnny man sing.
I guess you say
What can make me feel this way
My girl, my girl, my girl
Talkin 'bout—

MAN: (*Exploding.*) I said give it back!

KID: (*Angry.*) I ain't givin you a muthafuckin thing!

MAN: Now you listen to me!

KID: No, you listen to me. This is the Kid you're dealin with so don't fuck with me!

(*The* KID *smacks his fist into his other hand, and the* MAN *grabs for his heart. The* KID *repeats the action twice, causing the* MAN *to drop to the ground clutching his chest.*)

KID: Jai! Jai! Jai!

MAN: Kid please.

KID: Yeah. Yeah. Now who's begging who. Well, well, well, look at Mr. Cream-of-the-Crop, Mr. Colored-Man-on-Top. Now that he's making it, he no longer wants anything to do with the Kid. Well you may put all kinds of silk ties round your neck and white lines up your nose, but the Kid is here to stay. You may change your women as often as you change

your underwear, but the Kid is here to stay. And regardless
of how much of your past that you trash, I ain't goin no damn
where. Is that clear? Is that clear?

MAN: (*Regaining his strength, beginning to stand.*) Yeah.

KID: Good. (*After a beat, playfully.*) You all right man? You
all right? I don't want to hurt you, but when you start all
that talk about getting rid of me, well it gets me kind of crazy.
We need each other. We are one . . .

(*Before the* KID *can complete his sentence, the* MAN *starts
to choke him violently.*)

MAN: (*As he strangles the* KID.) The . . . ice . . . age . . .
is . . . upon us . . . and either we adjust . . . or we end
up . . . extinct.

(*The* KID *hangs limp in the* MAN'*s arms.*)

MAN: (*Laughing.*) Man kills his own rage. Film at eleven.

(*The* MAN *dumps the* KID *into the trash bin, and closes the
lid.*)

MAN: (*In a contained voice.*) I have no history. I have no past.
I can't. It's too much. It's much too much. I must be able to
smile on cue. And watch the news with an impersonal eye.
I have no stake in the madness.

Being black is too emotionally taxing therefore I will be
black only on weekends and holidays.

(*The* MAN *turns to go, but sees the Temptations album lying
on the ground. He picks it up and sings quietly to himself.*)

MAN: I guess you say

What can make me feel this way

(*The* MAN *pauses, then crosses to the trash bin and lifts
the lid. Just as he is about to toss the album in, a hand
reaches from inside the bin and grabs hold of the* MAN'*s
arm. The* KID *emerges from the bin with a death grip on
the* MAN'*s arm.*)

KID: (*Smiling.*) What's happenin?

(*Blackout.*)

The Dance and the Railroad

David Henry Hwang

Characters: Lone (20), Ma (18)
Setting: A mountaintop near a construction site on the Transcontinental Railroad, 1867
Premiere: New Federal Theatre, New York City, 1981
Publisher: Bard/Avon (from *Broken Promises*)

It is 1867, and the Transcontinental Railroad is inching across the Sierra Nevadas. A group of Chinese laborers stage a strike to protest the long hours and low pay of their backbreaking jobs.

One of the men, Lone, had studied for eight years with the Peking Opera before his family shipped him off to work on "Gold Mountain." A haughty and disciplined man, Lone has worked on the railroad for two years without making friends. Instead, he goes to a mountaintop every night to practice his stylized opera steps: "I look at the other Chinamen and think, 'They are dead. Their muscles work only because the white man forces them. I live because I can still force my muscles to work for me.'"

One night, Ma, a brash young worker, steals up to the mountaintop to watch Lone practice. Ma thinks the "stuff" Lone does is beautiful, and wants him to perform for the guys at camp. Lone calls him an insect and tells him to fly away. Ma matches his insults and leaves. The next day, Ma returns.

(*Mountaintop.* LONE *is practicing.* MA *enters.*)
MA: Hey.
LONE: You? Again?
MA: I forgive you.
LONE: You . . . what?
MA: For making fun of me yesterday. I forgive you.
LONE: You can't—

MA: No. Don't thank me.

LONE: You can't forgive me.

MA: No. Don't mention it.

LONE: You—! I never asked for your forgiveness.

MA: I know. That's just the kinda guy I am.

LONE: This is ridiculous. Why don't you leave? Go down to your friends and play soldiers, sing songs, tell stories.

MA: Ah! See? That's just it. I got other ways I wanna spend my time. Will you teach me the opera?

LONE: What?

MA: I wanna learn it. I dreamt about it all last night.

LONE: No.

MA: The dance, the opera—I can do it.

LONE: You think so?

MA: Yeah. When I get outa here, I wanna go back to China and perform.

LONE: You want to become an actor?

MA: Well, I wanna perform.

LONE: Don't you remember the story about the three sons whose parents send them away to learn a trade? After three years, they return. The first one says, "I have become a coppersmith." The parents say, "Good. Second son, what have you become?" "I've become a silversmith." "Good— and youngest son, what about you?" "I have become an actor." When the parents hear that their son has become only an actor, they are very sad. The mother beats her head against the ground until the ground, out of pity, opens up and swallows her. The father is so angry he can't even speak, and the anger anger builds up inside him until it blows his body to pieces—little bits of his skin are found hanging from trees days later. You don't know how you endanger your relatives by becoming an actor.

MA: Well, I don't wanna become an "actor." That sounds terrible. I just wanna perform. Look, I'll be rich by the time I get out of here, right?

LONE: Oh?

MA: Sure. By the time I go back to China, I'll ride in gold sedan chairs, with twenty wives fanning me all around.

LONE: Twenty wives? This boy is ambitious.

MA: I'll give out pigs on New Year's and keep a stable of small birds to give to any woman who pleases me. And in my spare time, I'll perform.

LONE: Between your twenty wives and your birds, where will you find a free moment?

MA: I'll play Gwan Gung and tell stories of what life was like on the Gold Mountain.

LONE: Ma, just how long have you been in "America"?

MA: Huh? About four weeks.

LONE: You are a big dreamer.

MA: Well, all us ChinaMen here are—right? Men with little dreams—have little brains to match. They walk with their eyes down, trying to find extra grains of rice on the ground.

LONE: So, you know all about "America"? Tell me, what kind of stories will you tell?

MA: I'll say, "We laid tracks like soldiers. Mountains? We hung from cliffs in baskets and the winds blew us like birds. Snow? We lived underground like moles for days at a time. Deserts? We—"

LONE: Wait. Wait. How do you know these things after only four weeks?

MA: They told me—the other ChinaMen on the gang. We've been telling stories ever since the strike began.

LONE: They make it sound like it's very enjoyable.

MA: They said it is.

LONE: Oh? And you believe them?

MA: They're my friends. Living underground in winter—sounds exciting, huh?

LONE: Did they say anything about the cold?

MA: Oh, I already know about that. They told me about the mild winters and the warm snow.

LONE: Warm snow?

MA: When I go home, I'll bring some back to show my brothers.

LONE: Bring some—? On the boat?

MA: They'll be shocked—they never seen American snow before.

LONE: You can't. By the time you get snow to the boat, it'll have melted, evaporated, and returned as rain already.

MA: No.

LONE: No?

MA: Stupid.

LONE: Me?

MA: You been here awhile, haven't you?

LONE: Yes. Two years.

MA: Then how come you're so stupid? This is the Gold Mountain. The snow here doesn't melt. It's not wet.

LONE: That's what they told you?

MA: Yeah. It's true.

LONE: Did anyone show you any of this snow?

MA: No. It's not winter.

LONE: So where does it go?

MA: Huh?

LONE: Where does it go, if it doesn't melt? What happens to it?

MA: The snow? I dunno. I guess it just stays around.

LONE: So where is it? Do you see any?

MA: Here? Well, no, but . . . (*Pause.*) This is probably one of those places where it doesn't snow—even in winter.

LONE: Oh.

MA: Anyway, what's the use of me telling you what you already know? Hey, c'mon—teach me some of that stuff. Look—I've been practicing the walk—how's this? (*Demonstrates.*)

LONE: You look like a duck in heat.

MA: Hey—it's a start, isn't it?

LONE: Tell you what—you want to play some *die siu?*

MA: *Die siu?* Sure.

LONE: You know, I'm pretty good.

MA: Hey, I play with the guys at camp. You can't be any better than Lee—he's really got it down.

(LONE *pulls out a case with two dice.*)

LONE: I used to play till morning.

MA: Hey, us too. We see the sun start to rise, and say, "Hey, if we go to sleep now, we'll never get up for work." So we just keep playing.

LONE: (*Holding out dice.*) *Die* or *siu*?

MA: *Siu.*

LONE: You sure?

MA: Yeah!

LONE: All right. (*He rolls.*) *Die!*

MA: *Siu!*

(*They see the result.*)

MA: Not bad.

(*They continue taking turns rolling through the following section; MA always loses.*)

LONE: I haven't touched these in two years.

MA: I gotta practice more.

LONE: Have you lost much money?

MA: Huh? So what?

LONE: Oh, you have gold hidden in all your shirt linings, huh?

MA: Here in "America"—losing is no problem. You know—End of the Year Bonus?

LONE: Oh, right.

MA: After I get that, I'll laugh at what I lost.

LONE: Lee told you there was a bonus, right?

MA: How'd you know?

LONE: When I arrived here, Lee told me there was a bonus, too.

MA: Lee teach you how to play?

LONE: Him? He talked to me a lot.

MA: Look, why don't you come down and start playing with the guys again?

LONE: "The guys."

MA: Before we start playing, Lee uses a stick to write "Kill!" in the dirt.

LONE: You seem to live for your nights with "the guys."

MA: What's life without friends, huh?

LONE: Well, why do *you* think I stopped playing?

MA: Hey, maybe you were the one getting killed, huh?

LONE: What?

MA: Hey, just kidding.

LONE: Who's getting killed here?

MA: Just a joke.

LONE: That's not a joke, it's blasphemy.

MA: Look, obviously you stopped playing 'cause you wanted to practice the opera.

LONE: Do you understand that discipline?

MA: But, I mean, you don't have to overdo it either. You don't have to treat 'em like dirt. I mean, who are you trying to impress?

(*Pause.* LONE *throws dice into the bushes.*)

LONE: Oooops. Better go see who won.

MA: Hey! C'mon! Help me look!

LONE: If you find them, they are yours.

MA: You serious?

LONE: Yes.

MA: Here. (*Finds the dice.*)

LONE: Who won?

MA: I didn't check.

LONE: Well, no matter. Keep the dice. Take them and go play with your friends.

MA: Here. (*He offers them to* LONE.) A present.

LONE: A present? This isn't a present!

MA: They're mine, aren't they? You gave them to me, right?

LONE: Well, yes, but—

MA: So now I'm giving them to you.

LONE: You can't give me a present. I don't want them.

MA: You wanted them enough to keep them two years.

LONE: I'd forgotten I had them.

MA: See, I know, Lone. You wanna get rid of me. But you can't. I'm paying for lessons.

LONE: With my dice.

MA: Mine now. (*He offers them again.*) Here.

(*Pause.* LONE *runs* MA's *hand across his forehead.*)

LONE: Feel this.

MA: Hey!

LONE: Pretty wet, huh?

MA: Big deal.

LONE: Well, it's not from playing *die siu*.

MA: I know how to sweat. I wouldn't be here if I didn't.

LONE: Yes, but are you willing to sweat after you've finished sweating? Are you willing to come up after you've spent the whole day chipping half an inch off a rock, and punish your body some more?

MA: Yeah. Even after work, I still—

LONE: No, you don't. You want to gamble, and tell dirty stories, and dress up like women to do shows.

MA: Hey, I never did that.

LONE: You've only been here a month. (*Pause.*) And what about "the guys"? They're not going to treat you so well once you stop playing with them. Are you willing to work all day listening to them whisper, "That one—let's put spiders in his soup"?

MA: They won't do that to me. With you, it's different.

LONE: Is it?

MA: You don't have to act that way.

LONE: What way?

MA: Like you're so much better than them.

LONE: No. You haven't even begun to understand. To practice every day, you must have a fear to force you up here.

MA: A fear? No—it's 'cause what you're doing is beautiful.

LONE: No.

MA: I've seen it.

LONE: It's ugly to practice when the mountain has turned your muscles to ice. When my body hurts too much to come here, I look at the other ChinaMen and think, "They are dead. Their muscles work only because the white man forces them. I live because I can still force my muscles to work for me." Say it. "They are dead."

MA: No. They're my friends.

LONE: Well, then, take your dice down to your friends.

MA: But I want to learn—

LONE: This is your first lesson.

MA: Look, it shouldn't matter—

LONE: It does.

MA: It shouldn't matter what I think.

LONE: Attitude is everything.

MA: But as long as I come up, do the exercises—

LONE: I'm not going to waste time on a quitter.

MA: I'm not!

LONE: Then say it.—"They are dead men."

MA: I can't.

LONE: Then you will never have the dedication.

MA: That doesn't prove anything.

LONE: I will not teach a dead man.

MA: What?

LONE: If you can't see it, then you're dead too.

MA: Don't start pinning—

LONE: Say it!

MA: All right.

LONE: What?

MA: All right. I'm one of them. I'm a dead man too.

   (*Pause.*)

LONE: I thought as much. So, go. You have your friends.

MA: But I don't have a teacher.

LONE: I don't think you need both.

MA: Are you sure?

LONE: I'm being questioned by a child.

   (LONE *returns to practicing. Silence.*)

MA: Look, Lone, I'll come up here every night—after work—
   I'll spend my time practicing, okay? (*Pause.*) But I'm not
   gonna say that they're dead. Look at them. They're on strike;
   dead men don't go on strike, Lone. The white devils—they
   try and stick us with a ten-hour day. We want a return to
   eight hours and also a fourteen-dollar-a-month raise. I learned
   the demon English—listen: "Eight hour a day good for white
   man, alla same good for ChinaMan." These are the demands
   of live ChinaMen, Lone. Dead men don't complain.

LONE: All right, this is something new. But no one can judge
   the ChinaMen till after the strike.

MA: They say we'll hold out for months if we have to. The
   smart men will live on what we've hoarded.

LONE: A ChinaMan's mouth can swallow the earth. (*He takes
   the dice.*) While the strike is on, I'll teach you.

MA: And afterwards?

LONE: Afterwards—we'll decide then whether these are dead or live men.

MA: When can we start?

LONE: We've already begun. Give me your hand.

Father Dreams

Mary Gallagher

Characters: Paul Hogan (30s), Dad (old)
Setting: Hogan family living room; Paul's mind
Premiere: Loretto-Hilton Repertory Theatre, St. Louis, 1980
Publisher: Dramatists Play Service, Inc.

Mary Gallagher describes the play as "a series of waking and sleeping Dreams—dreams, myths, memories, and fantasies—within a 'real' structure consisting of a period of about an hour on a Sunday afternoon in the Hogan household. The 'real' scenes, which are the opening and the end of the Sixth Dream, take place in the living room of the house. The rest of the play—the Dreams—takes place in the mind of Paul Hogan, the oldest son of the family. Through the Dreams, Paul makes an imaginative and emotional journey toward his father . . . Paul has not seen his father in twelve years, since Dad was first institutionalized and his parents separated. Since that time, increasingly, he has withdrawn from the world, living in his own head, struggling to define himself . . . We never see Dad as he really is. We see Paul's imagined version of him as the great guy, the perfect father . . . It is not till the end of the play, in the Seventh Dream, that Paul allows himself to see Dad as he probably is: a broken and frightened old man."

This is the first Dream. Dad wears green state-issued pajamas, a cheap cotton robe, and scuffy slippers. He has an old battered leather accordion-type briefcase with him. He has put on a brand-new tie and some aftershave and is eagerly looking forward to Paul's visit. Paul sits in "Area 5"—reality. "It is both Paul's prison and his refuge."

(*In Area 5,* PAUL *sits on the couch, thinking. Torn.* DAD *is now sitting on the module, eating ice cream from a carton with a spoon. He sees* PAUL, *beams and rises.*)

DAD: Hello, son!

PAUL: Hi, Dad.

DAD: Glad you could make it out here to the hospital today. It's such a beautiful sunny day, I wouldn't have blamed you for playing hookey. Sneaking away to the golf course.

PAUL: (*Taken aback.*) Golf?

DAD: How's your mother?

PAUL: Fine. (*He assumes an air of good-humored detachment, as if he is talking to a TV set, until he enters Area 2, when the dream takes over and becomes real.*)

DAD: Did she get the box of candy I sent her?

PAUL: You got me. She doesn't tell me what she gets.

DAD: Chocolate-covered turtles. That's the only kind of candy your mother likes. The kind with the peanuts.

PAUL: She doesn't eat candy.

DAD: I had my sweetheart, Mrs. Yallich, in the commissary, send your mother a box of those turtles. It was sort of a late anniversary present, and an apology, in case the phone calls upset her. Later, we'll go down to the commissary and I'll show you off to Mrs. Yallich. I've been mouthing off all over the hospital about my brilliant son. (DAD *is relaxed, exuberant, throughout the dream. Only* PAUL *shows strain, which increases as the dream goes on.*)

PAUL: (*Laughs.*) For Chrissake!

DAD: I can't eat those turtles because of my teeth. Remember when I was having all that trouble with my teeth? I had to go into the hospital, and to have six teeth pulled.

PAUL: Mom says it wasn't your teeth.

DAD: I never knew an Irishman that had good teeth. Your mother's teeth are worse than mine.

PAUL: (*Cheerful.*) Mom says you flipped out. She says they had to take you away in a shopping cart.

DAD: How are your teeth, son?

PAUL: Terrific, Pop.

DAD: Good teeth is the same as money in the bank! (*Takes a box of Junior Mints from robe pocket, eats some; to* PAUL *confidentially.*) I eat a lot of candy here on the ward. The food is pretty awful.

PAUL: All I ever saw you eat was fudge ripple ice cream. You used to eat it in bed. That's all I remember now . . . watching you nod off into the fudge ripple . . .

DAD: Your mother's done a wonderful job, raising you kids by herself. Six kids! How are the little guys? And Katie and Therese?

PAUL: The little guys are in high school. (*Almost unwillingly, he is drawn into Area 2 by* DAD's *ease and charm. Lights fade in Area 5.*)

DAD: And Joan? I thought she might come out with you today.

PAUL: Not with me. Not good old Joan.

DAD: Have a mint, Paulie?

PAUL: (*Recoiling slightly.*) No, thanks. I don't eat sugar. (DAD *keeps eating mints till the box is empty.*)

DAD: Are you keeping up with your music? You know, son, it makes me proud . . . having another musician in the family. You must have gotten that from me . . . I used to play the piano.

PAUL: (*Annoyed.*) I'm not a musician. I used to mess around on guitar, that's all. I hardly even . . .

DAD: We'll have to get you out here to play a concert on the ward. I'd like to do a little something to show my appreciation to the doctors and nurses and the staff, like Mr. Johnson, he's the big fella in white that let you in . . . for twelve years of consideration. They've been awfully good to your old man out here.

PAUL: How many times did they shock you?

DAD: (*Smiling, serene.*) Our family has a lot to be thankful for.

PAUL: How about if we get out of here?

DAD: We'll have to ask Mr. Johnson about that. This is a locked ward, you know, son. That's why you had to ring the bell and Mr. Johnson had to let you in.

PAUL: But they give you passes, don't they? When you have visitors? At St. Jude's, they gave us passes . . .

DAD: (*Sits on module, indicates an invisible chair.*) Sit down, son. These plastic chairs are goddamn uncomfortable. There's no room for long legs like yours when they attach them to the table like this. (PAUL *almost sits, then jumps up, stares at the invisible chair. Shaken, he says:*)

PAUL: If we could just go out in the grounds and walk . . .

DAD: You've seen the grounds, son. A six-acre parking lot. Looks like the drive-in movie.

PAUL: Don't they ever let you go outside?

DAD: Here, I'll buy you a Coke. (DAD *gets up, turns to D. invisible Coke machine, mimes taking dime from pocket, putting in machine. Sound: coin falling, machine noises, Coke pouring, etc.* DAD *takes Coke cup from pocket, hands it to* PAUL.)

PAUL: (*Suspicious.*) What's in it?

DAD: It's Coca-Cola. The pause that refreshes.

PAUL: I won't drink it till you tell me what's in it.

DAD: Just sugar and water and bubbles, son. Good for what ails you.

PAUL: I don't eat sugar. Sugar makes you crazy. (*Then* PAUL *laughs, embarrassed. But* DAD *hasn't heard this. As the scene continues,* DAD *in his exuberance leads* PAUL *from area to area, using the whole stage except for Area 5, and the light follows them.*)

DAD: Maybe I can charm Mr. Johnson into letting us go down to the rec room. I'll take you on at Ping-Pong. Around here, I'm considered a major threat with a Ping-Pong paddle. You didn't know that about your old man, did you?

PAUL: Sure, you're the Ping-Pong king . . . bouncing up,

bouncing down, bouncing from Grandmother Hogan's house to the nut house . . .

DAD: I've played a lot of Ping-Pong over the years. (*Sees invisible patient approaching in another area, leads* PAUL *over there.*) Hello, Phil! This is my son, Paul Hogan. Francis Paul the Third. He's a big strapping guy compared to his old man, isn't he? Paul's a musician, Phil. He's one of the finest guitar players in the city.

PAUL: I haven't touched the fucking thing in three years.

DAD: (*To* PAUL.) Remember when I gave you that guitar for Christmas? (*To the invisible patient.*) I've got the pictures somewhere. Hold on a minute, Phil. (*Hands Coke cup to* PAUL, *searches robe pockets. Absently,* PAUL *drains the cup; then, revolted, he crumples it.* DAD *as invisible patient walks away.*) PHIL, CAN I BUY YOU A COKE? . . . OKAY, SEE YOU IN THE TV ROOM FOR "WIDE WORLD OF SPORTS"! (*Turns to* PAUL, *confidentially:*) That guy Phil is a neurosurgeon. Has three degrees, helluva bright guy. One of the wealthiest men in this town. But here he is on the ward, with junkies and alkies and poor screwy bastards like me. You know why? He tried to kill himself. He ate razor blades. Took him a long time to do it, too. You know those slots in bathroom walls where you drop the razor blades? He had to rip away the tiles to get at them! But he's like you and me, Paulie. He's a stubborn son of a bitch! Dugout over a hundred razor blades, and ate 'em! But it didn't kill him! So here he is on the ward. I'll tell you, son, money isn't the whole story. (PAUL *tosses his Coke cup on the floor;* DAD *picks it up, hands it to him.*) Let me get that, son. They're pretty gung ho on neatness here on the ward. I feel like I'm back in the army! You know, they transferred me to this ward last month . . . a locked ward and a different doctor—and they wouldn't even tell me why, the dirty bastards. You know they've changed my medication four times this year.

PAUL: Four times?

DAD: Four times! Half the time I can't wake up, and the other half I'm swinging from the chandeliers! And these snotty little nurses . . . one of 'em has braids. Looks like one of you kids. She wouldn't give me my sleeping pill last night because the doctor didn't write it on my chart. I told her, "Call the doctor and ask him!" I said, "I need that pill! I can get through the days, but at night I have to sleep." But she wouldn't call him. "I can't disturb him," she said. Real snotty. So I was up all night.

PAUL: What did you think about?

DAD: They think they can make it up to us with bingo on Friday night. But bingo isn't much fun for a manic depressive . . . I told Father John, "I'd like to burn this place to the ground with everybody in it." You know what he said? He said, "Francis, crosses are made for those who are strong enough to bear them."

PAUL: Good old God.

DAD: Father John's a great guy. He's going to say a Mass for all the members of our family who have passed away. Your Grandmother Hogan, and Grandpa, and Aunt Louise, and Aunt Therese, and Uncle Dinny . . . and Father Chuck . . .

PAUL: (*Overlapping this.*) They're all dead, aren't they? Everyone who gave a shit what happened to you kicked the bucket. They won't even let you out for Christmas any more. Nobody wants you, Dad. (*Unconsciously,* PAUL *is tearing up the paper cup, dropping pieces on the floor; absently,* DAD *picks them up, puts them in his pocket.*)

DAD: I'd like all you kids to come out here for the family Mass. Maybe your mother would like to come. She's never been out here, you know.

PAUL: We don't go to Mass anymore.

DAD: We had some great times, didn't we, Paulie? Remember how I used to take all you kids out to breakfast after Mass? Pancakes and sausage and chocolate milk! The waitresses always came up after to tell me what beautiful children I had. How well-behaved! I said, "That's their mother's work, not mine!" Remember that, Paulie? They had a trunk with prizes in it for children who cleaned their plates? And you signed up on cards for the birthday club?

PAUL: Were you crazy then?

DAD: I'll take you down and introduce you to the ladies in the cafeteria. They're all my sweethearts. They save me raisin bread. I've made some valuable contacts out here. It's all in who you know.

PAUL: (*With rising panic.*) Could we open a window?

DAD: The windows don't open, son. Ask your mother. She'll back me up on that. (DAD *takes out his briefcase again, starts hunting in it.*)

PAUL: Did they shock you? She won't tell me, but I know goddamn well they did.

DAD: I want you to think about law school, son. Hogan and Hogan! Right?

PAUL: How many times? You remember it, don't you? Every separate time.

DAD: Let me make some phone calls . . . (*Takes from brief-case a tattered old address book.*) I've still got a lot of friends in this town . . .

PAUL: Do they make you bite on a wooden spoon? . . . Did she come and watch? (*Meanwhile, DAD is leafing through address book. One page falls out. DAD picks it up, looks at it.*)

DAD: Abbott . . . is he dead?

PAUL: I don't think I can do this. (DAD *starts rooting in brief-case again, taking out large stiff pieces of raisin bread, piling them in Paul's arm.*)

DAD: We can go down to the social hall. That's where we'll have your concert. I figure you could do a few family-type folk songs, you know, nothing rabble-rousing. Some of the fellas out here are in pretty bad shape, Paulie . . .

PAUL: (*Stuffing bread back in briefcase.*) I'm sorry. I can't do this. (PAUL *retreats to Area 5.* DAD *returns briefcase to module.*)

DAD: But I always make a point of speaking to everybody here in the hospital. And I always keep some change in my pocket, so I can buy a fella a Coke. Contacts, son. They'll pay off when I'm back in practice. (DAD *strolls into Area 4, as if*

PAUL *is beside him, and they are chatting. Light follows* DAD.)

PAUL: That time on the highway . . . that night we drove home from Detroit . . . that's when I knew you were crazy.

DAD: I can take those Cokes off my income tax. Business expenses.

PAUL: We lay in the dark, with the trucks roaring down on us, blasting the whole car with light . . . and I thought, "My father's crazy."

DAD: You don't understand business, son. Your mother never did either. (*Points to an invisible sign between them.*) You see that sign? It says, "Visitors are not allowed to cross this line." (DAD *draws a line from upstage to out front, dividing him from* PAUL. *As he does, a narrow line of light appears along the stage floor.*) You don't ever want to cross this line, Paulie.

PAUL: Dad . . .

DAD: After your mother threw me out, I was living at Grandmother Hogan's house, and I came out here for treatment. Just a change in medication, that's what they told me. And I never crossed that line, Paul, no matter what they told you. I never crossed it. They moved it on me, the dirty bastards. I'm warning you, son. She crossed me off, and she'll cross you off if you give her half a chance. You've got to watch her every minute.

PAUL: (*Sitting on the couch.*) Okay, Dad.

DAD: (*Takes Hershey bar out of his pocket, unwraps it.*) I'll tell you, son . . . I've made some wonderful friends out here over the years.

PAUL: Sure, Dad.

DAD: I would have gone crazy if I hadn't.

(*Takes a bit of candy. Blackout.*)

Fences

August Wilson

Characters: Troy Maxson (53), Cory Maxson (18)
Setting: The yard and porch of the Maxson household in Pittsburgh, 1957–65
Premiere: Yale Repertory Theatre, New Haven, Connecticut, 1985
Publisher: Plume

Troy Maxson is "fifty-three years old, a large man with thick heavy hands; it is this largeness that he strives to fill out and make an accommodation with. Together with his blackness, his largeness informs his sensibilities and the choices he has made in his life."

Troy works as a garbage collector in Pittsburgh. An ex-con with a talent for baseball, he firmly believes that he could have played in the big leagues had they not been segregated. Troy's younger son, Cory, plays high school football. He has been recruited for an athletic scholarship, but Troy will hear none of it. He refuses to believe that times might have changed for black athletes—or that his son might get something he didn't.

TROY: (*Calling.*) Cory! Get your butt out here, boy!
  (TROY *goes over to the pile of wood, picks up a board, and starts sawing.* CORY *enters from the house.*)
TROY: You just now coming in here from leaving this morning?
CORY: Yeah, I had to go to football practice.
TROY: Yeah, what? What kind of talk is that?
CORY: Yessir.
TROY: I ain't but two seconds off you noway. The garbage sitting in there overflowing . . . you ain't done none of your chores . . . and you come in here talking about, "Yeah."
CORY: I was just getting ready to do my chores now.

TROY: Your first chore is to help me with this fence on Saturday. Everything else come after that. Now get that saw and cut them boards.

(CORY *takes the saw and begins cutting the boards.* TROY *continues working. There is a long pause.*)

CORY: The Pirates done won five in a row.

TROY: I ain't thinking about the Pirates. Got an all-white team. Got that boy . . . that Puerto Rican boy . . . Clemente. Don't even half-play him. That boy could be something if they give him a chance. Play him one day and sit him on the bench the next.

CORY: He gets a lot of chances to play.

TROY: I'm talking about playing regular. Playing every day so you can get your timing. That's what I'm talking about.

CORY: They got some white guys on the team that don't play every day. You can't play everybody at the same time.

TROY: If they got a white fellow sitting on the bench, you can bet your last dollar he can't play! The colored guy got to be twice as good before he get on the team. That's why I don't want you to get all tied up in them sports. Man on the team and what it get him? They got colored on the team and don't play them. Same as not having them. All them teams the same.

CORY: The Braves got Hank Aaron and Wes Covington. Hank Aaron hit two home runs today. That makes forty-three.

TROY: Hank Aaron ain't nobody. That's the way you supposed to do. That's how you supposed to play the game. Ain't nothing to it. It's just a matter of timing . . . getting the right follow-through. Hell, I can hit forty-three home runs right now!

CORY: Not off no major-league pitching you couldn't.

TROY: We had better pitching in the Negro League. I hit seven home runs off of Satchel Paige. You can't get no better than that!

CORY: Sandy Koufax. He's leading the league in strikeouts.

TROY: I ain't thinking of no Sandy Koufax nothing.

CORY: You got Warren Spahn and Lew Burdette. I bet you couldn't hit no home runs off of Warren Spahn.

TROY: I'm through with it now. You go on and get them boards cut.

(*Pause.*)

Your mama tells me you got recruited by a college football team? Is that right?

CORY: Yeah. Coach Zellman say the recruiter gonna be coming by to talk to you. Get you to sign the permission papers.

TROY: I thought you supposed to be working down there at the A&P. Ain't you supposed to be working down there after school?

CORY: Mr. Stawicki say he gonna hold my job for me until after the football season. Say starting next week I can work weekends.

TROY: I thought we had an understanding about this football stuff? You suppose to keep up with your chores and hold that job down at the A&P. Ain't been around here all day on a Saturday. Ain't none of your chores done . . . and now you telling me you done quite your job.

CORY: I'm gonna be working weekends.

TROY: You damn right you are! Ain't no need for nobody coming around here to talk to me about signing nothing.

CORY: Hey, Pop, you can't do that. He's coming all the way from North Carolina.

TROY: I don't care where he coming from. The white man ain't gonna let you get nowhere with that football no way. You go and get your book-learning where you can learn to do something besides carrying people's garbage.

CORY: I get good grades, Pop. That's why the recruiter wants to talk with you. You got to keep up your grades to get recruited. This way I'll be going to college. I'll get a chance—

TROY: You gonna get your butt down there to the A&P and get your job back.

CORY: Mr. Stawicki done already hired somebody else 'cause I told him I was playing football.

TROY: You a bigger fool than I thought . . . to let somebody take away your job so you can play some football. That's downright foolishness. Where you gonna get your money to

take out your girlfriend and whatnot? What kind of foolishness is that to let somebody take away your job?

CORY: I'm still gonna be working weekends.

TROY: Naw . . . naw. You getting your butt out of here and
finding you another job.

CORY: Come on, Pop! I got to practice. I can't work after
school and play football too. Coach Zellman say the team
needs me—say—

TROY: I don't care what nobody else say, I'm the boss . . . you
understand? I'm the boss around here. I do the only saying
what counts.

CORY: Come on, Pop!

TROY: I asked you. Did you understand?

CORY: Yeah . . . Yessir.

TROY: You do down there to that A&P and see if you can get
your job back. If you can't do both, then you quit the football
team. You've got to take the crooked with the straights.

CORY: Yessir.

   (*Pause.*)

Can I ask you a question?

TROY: What the hell you wanna ask me? Mr. Stawicki the one
you got the questions for.

CORY: How come you ain't never liked me?

TROY: Liked you? Who the hell say I got to like you? What
law is there say I got to like you? Wanna stand up in my face
and ask a damn fool-ass question like that. Talking about
liking somebody. Come here, boy, when I talk to you.

   (CORY *comes over to where* TROY *is working. He stands
   slouched over and* TROY *shoves him on his shoulder.*)

Straighten up, goddammit! I asked you a question. What law
is there say I got to like you?

CORY: None.

TROY: Well, all right then! Don't you eat every day?

   (*Pause.*)

Answer me when I talk to you! Don't you eat every day?

CORY: Yeah.

TROY: Nigger, as long as you in my house you put that sir on
the end of it when you talk to me!

CORY: Yes . . . sir.

TROY: You eat every day. Got a roof over your head. Got clothes on your back.

CORY: Yessir.

TROY: Why you think that is?

CORY: 'Cause of you.

TROY: Aw, hell I know it's 'cause of me . . . but why do you think that is?

CORY: (*Hesitant.*) 'Cause you like me.

TROY: Like you? I go out of here every morning, bust my butt, putting up with them crackers every day . . . 'cause I like you? You about the biggest fool I ever saw.

(*Pause.*)

It's my job. It's my responsibility! You understand that? A man got to take care of his family. You live in my house, sleep you behind on my bedclothes, fill you belly up with my food . . . 'cause you my son. You my flesh and blood. Not 'cause I like you! 'Cause I owe a responsibility to you! 'Cause it's my duty to take care of you. Let's get this straight right here—before it go along any further—I ain't got to like you. Mr. Rand don't give me my money come payday 'cause he likes me. He gives me 'cause he owe me. I done give you everything I had to give you. I gave you your life! Me and your mama worked that out between us. And liking your black ass wasn't part of the bargain. Don't you try and go through life worrying about if somebody like you or not. You best be making sure they doing right by you. You understand what I'm saying, boy?

CORY: Yessir.

TROY: Then get the hell out of my face, and get on down to that A&P.

(CORY *exits.*)

Highest Standard of Living

Keith Reddin

Characters: Bob (28), Gary (28)
Setting: U.S.S.R.; U.S.A.
Premiere: Playwrights Horizons, New York City, 1986
Publisher: Broadway Play Publishing, Inc.

Bob is a graduate student in Soviet literature at Columbia University. He goes to Moscow to research his thesis. While in the U.S.S.R., he gets food poisoning and lands in the hospital. In his fever, he is visited by his Mother, Uncle Tom, and Aunt Lottie (who is dressed as a bear and pretending to be with the Moscow Circus). He is attacked by a pack of little children with hammers, wears out his welcome, and is told to leave. His paranoid nightmare continues.

Bob returns to America to find he is on the "shit list." His "un-American" statements while in the U.S.S.R., as well as his entire history, are chronicled on the computer. He is interrogated at Kennedy Airport and then, once sufficiently scared, is told he can re-enter the U.S.

Bob and Gary were friends in college. They meet in a restaurant.

(GARY *waits at table.* BOB *enters. Nose bandaged.*)
GARY: Hey Bob . . .
BOB: Look, I can't really afford this place . . .
GARY: No problem I got it. Sit down.
  (BOB *sits.*)
BOB: Okay. Thanks.
GARY: Bob, what happened?
BOB: With the nose? Hit by a hammer.
GARY: Fuck.
BOB: Absolutely.
  (WAITER *brings menus, exits.* BOB *and* GARY *study menus.*)

GARY: Got great salmon steak here. I recommend it.

BOB: Uh huh.

GARY: Still working on the thesis, huh?

BOB: That's right.

GARY: Always chained to those library stacks. I remember your nose buried in those bummer books. Tolstoy, Dostoyevsky, had to be at least 2,000 pages.

BOB: Turgenev, Pushkin, Gorky, Lermontov.

GARY: All those greats. Hey, remember the track team.

BOB: Uh huh.

GARY: Remember what they called you? Remember your nickname on the track team?

BOB: Not really.

GARY: Leadboots. Ha. They called you Leadboots. Remember your nickname on the tennis team, huh?

BOB: Spaz.

GARY: Right. Ol' Spaz. Great time on that team. You, me, and Doug. What a group.

BOB: Uh huh. Great.

GARY: So you're probably wondering why I called.

BOB: Thought you called to see how I was.

GARY: Oh, sure, yeah, that too. But more importantly, to touch base and say, Where have we come from where are we going, you know?

(WAITER *crosses stage with flaming skewer of meat.*)

BOB: Well, I'm almost done with my thesis . . .

GARY: Listen, it's great to get nostalgic and all, but when I tell you the news, I think everything's gonna change.

BOB: What news?

GARY: The new job.

BOB: Job?

GARY: It's gonna blow your mind, really.

(WAITER *crosses stage without the flaming skewer.*)

GARY: You remember in college, I was taking those political science courses.

BOB: Pre-law stuff.

GARY: We all believed that at the time.

(WAITER *crosses the stage with fire extinguisher and exits.*)

GARY: It was understood to be pre-law courses, like the minor in history. It was all carefully planned out under their guidance. See, I was approached early on. I don't want you to think it was the money, that is not what we are discussing. But by working my way through law, then politics, then hooking up with the re-election juggernaut, I'm helping them, looking towards the future. Then this new thing happened. The nod. The phone call. The pitch was tossed, because my record speaks, Bob. The work, the work I've done and that was for real, sure it was. But the pitch was what I was looking for all along. And I dangled it in front of them. I made the right hints and they bit. The phone call from the White House. From the special counsel to the fucking president, Bob. From Ron to his staff to me. And we make it official. The Pitch. I got the slot I go in I get the office down the hall from him, from the fucking president. And we know what that means. For them. What it means now for down the road.

BOB: Excuse me, but what are we talking about?

GARY: It's okay, and I think for our conversations about your interests and the recent visit and the hopeful results of that visit, we can talk turkey.

BOB: Turkey?

GARY: When I was approached I thought I could never reveal what I was into to anyone. But Bob, welcome home. Here's my phone number, okay, this is the new office number. You let them know this is only the beginning, there is a lot on the horizon. I'm in now Bob. I'm working for the bastards on the inside, that's what we've been pushing for all these years and by Christ it's touchdown all the way and go for the gold, Bob.

BOB: Gary, uh . . . Congratulations on the new job.

GARY: Thank you and remember the lunch is on me, that's understood, right?

BOB: Right.

GARY: You about ready to order?

BOB: Oh, yeah, sure. Look, Gary, maybe I'm a bit off here, I'm back a few weeks and I don't know, I'm still kind of out of it but what the fuck is happening here?

GARY: Here at the restaurant?

BOB: Here, now, you and me. I'm not connecting I'm sorry.

GARY: They told me after you got back from there to make contact. The way I figure you can make these trips every couple of months, and okay we'll have lunch before you go, and you just bring in what I get you. It's perfect, anyway you look at it. Your profile is excellent, so I know you from school that makes it easier, we have lunch, we make contact, I tell you where I stand and it's a deal.

BOB: What?

GARY: Comrades, huh, Bob? Helping the cause. Doing our part. For the future. And of course the money does not hurt, not at all.

BOB: I think you made a mistake here.

GARY: I don't think so, Bob, your profile is excellent. Don't be nervous, it'll be fine, I'm the one in the hot seat, I'm the one passing the shit. You just have to slip it in one of your magazines or journals or whatever and that's it.

BOB: You're from us, right? You're telling me you're from them but you're really from us, trying to trap me and say, yes, I'll work for them.

GARY: Now I'm lost here, Bob.

BOB: You're CIA, right?

GARY: Very funny, Bob, order your lunch.

BOB: Oh come on, this was very obvious, using you, asking me to lunch, but it just won't work, and I won't fall for it. You guys tried tripping me up at the airport but no fucking way, and the idea that you, Gary, a friend of mine, would use that friendship, turns my stomach. Well, if that's what you think of me, just fuck and fuck them and fuck us.

GARY: What are you talking about?

BOB: I'm not sure, but I am so incredibly pissed off.

GARY: Sit down, Bob.

BOB: NO I WILL NOT SIT DOWN. I will not be a tool and

you can tell your bosses TO EAT SHIT AND LEAVE ME
ALONE.

   (BOB *exits.*)

GARY: Check, please . . .

   (*Lights dim.*)

The House of Ramon Iglesia

Jose Rivera

Characters: Javier (22), Julio (19)

Setting: The Iglesia family home in Holbrook, Long Island

Premiere: Ensemble Studio Theatre, New York City, 1983

Publisher: Samuel French, Inc.

Ramon and Dolores Iglesia have raised their three sons in
America, and now they are packing to move back home to
Puerto Rico—if they can manage to straighten out the deed
to their house. To Dolores, who's never learned English, the
move back home is a dream come true. To Javier, the oldest
son, it smacks of failure.

Javier has a college degree and an Anglo girlfriend named
Caroline. His condescending attitude toward his family has
created a lot of friction between him and his two younger
brothers, Julio "The Beast" and Charlie ("Carlos to you, bro").
Here, Javier accompanies Julio to the Marine Corps recruiting
office.

(*Outside in front of the Marine Corps recruiting office in
Holtsville, New York. It's 4:00 A.M. It's very cold. JULIO
and JAVIER enter, carrying bags.*)

JAVIER: God, Julio.

JULIO: This is it.

JAVIER: God, Julio.

JULIO: Stop being a pussy.

JAVIER: *God*, Julio.

JULIO: Go stay in the car if you're so cold.

JAVIER: You had to pick the coldest damn night of the millennium, didn't you?

JULIO: Go back in the car if you're so cold.

JAVIER: I don't want to sit in there by myself—

JULIO: I don't want to miss anybody—

JAVIER: No one's stupid enough to be out here this early, in this freezing weather . . .

JULIO: Well, you wanted to come out with me—

JAVIER: I thought you would have the good sense to stay in the *car*.

JULIO: A Marine's got to get used to the cold, wimp!

JAVIER: Oh, Mother of God, spare me. (JULIO *puts his bags down and looks around. He checks his watch.*)

JULIO: Nobody.

JAVIER: Who's supposed to come?

JULIO: Sergeant Overbaby.

JAVIER: Who?

JULIO: Overbaby.

JAVIER: You're giving your future to a man named *Overbaby*?

JULIO: (*Looking into the office.*) It's not quite four; I'm early . . .

JAVIER: He's probably in a snowbank doing pushups in the nude . . .

JULIO: I think he told me he has to come in from Hempstead.

JAVIER: "I sing of Olaf, glad and big." Do you know that poem?

JULIO: Maybe I should give him a call . . .

JAVIER: "I sing of Olaf, glad and big."

JULIO: Who's Olaf, your boyfriend?

JAVIER: He was a Swede, a pacifist, and got the life kicked out of him in a poem because he would not kiss your fucking flag.

JULIO: (*Looking at* JAVIER.) Sometimes I think you have the basic mentality of a handball.

JAVIER: I'm going to give your recruiting officer a copy of it . . .

JULIO: Great. They'll have me shot for having a flake for an older brother. Why don't you stop living in the 60's? Be like me! Adjust to the times! Be a beast!

JAVIER: I'd rather be in bed, thank you. (JAVIER *walks over to the recruiting office and looks inside the window.*) That's interesting. Hmmmmmmmmmm. That's very, *very* interesting. Wow.

JULIO: What is it?

JAVIER: Well. Up against the wall. In there. Are all these little boxes . . .

JULIO: I sense something profoundly stupid coming on.

JAVIER: . . . *and* above each of the little boxes is a name, rank, and serial number . . . and inside each of the little boxes— let me make sure—(*He looks into the window.*) Yep! Inside each of the little boxes is a pair . . . of human testicles . . . little Marine testicles.

JULIO: Har. Har. Har. Yuck. Yuck.

JAVIER: Isn't that part of the Deal? You give Uncle Sam your balls, and what's left of your nervous system, and they zap you and turn you into a grunt!

JULIO: I'm not going to be a grunt—I'm going to be a technician, asshole, a hydraulics *technician.*

JAVIER: Right. Exactly like the ads. "High school dropout? Can't read English or do long division? Join the Marines and become a neutron physicist!" Ha!

JULIO: It's not like that, Bolshevik!

JAVIER: "Learn bio-warfare and global defoliation!"

JULIO: Hey, at least I didn't waste four years in some obscure little college, learning political science, just so I can come home and hang my brain on the loading dock of a warehouse! *That's* good! That's real progress!

JAVIER: Leave me alone.

JULIO: I, howsoever, am getting my brain together in a big way, with a future, and a job, out in the world where the real power is.

JAVIER: *Nuts!*

JULIO: True!

JAVIER: The real world? You're going right from Mommy's bosom to Uncle Sam's! Fed, clothed, and told what to do. *And* you might get killed in the process. Might get mistaken for a Southeast Asian and blown to bits—.

JULIO: Javier, for Chrissakes, it's 1980, it's *peacetime*!

JAVIER: Accidents can happen in peacetime!

JULIO: Accidents *don't* happen in peacetime! Not to Marines!

JAVIER: And promise me you won't develop a drug habit, or go to Iran.

JULIO: Promise me you'll never run for public office! You're so hopeless! What a mother hen! I can't believe you! Javier, you're such an old nurse . . .

JAVIER: I am not.

JULIO: You are. You're an old nurse. You're a den mother.

JAVIER: I am *not*.

JULIO: I know the real Javier. Nonviolent, nonalcoholic, boring, abnormal . . .

JAVIER: Listen, have a great military career. I'll see you later.

JULIO: Javier the Saint. The unhappy Javier.

JAVIER: Leave me alone.

JULIO: Awwwww, I know one of the things he's unhappy about. I know why he broods. What does Caroline want from your ass this time? What is the evil woman doing to our hero now?

JAVIER: Nothing. She's . . . been looking for furniture that's all. (*Beat.*) Do you think Overbaby will let me join the Corps?

JULIO: The Corps don't take the mentally ill . . . the castrated . . . or the pussy-whipped, and you, dear bro, show signs of becoming all three. (JULIO *walks away from* JAVIER.)

JAVIER: (*Lost in thought.*) Don't call me bro. (*Looking at* JULIO.) Do you remember *Patton*? (*Takes* JULIO*'s arm, imitates George C. Scott.*) "When you put your hand into a mess of goo that ten seconds ago was your best friend's face, you'll know what to do!"

JULIO: (*Smiling.*) And the line from *Apocalypse Now*?

TOGETHER: (*Imitating Robert Duvall.*) "I love the smell of napalm in the morning. It smells like victory!" (*They laugh.*)

JULIO: (*Beat.*) So. What are you going to do about Dad?

JAVIER: I don't know. He told me he wants to start a restaurant down in Arecibo—but he hasn't even found a place to live yet. He hasn't even sold the house.

JULIO: Listen, don't fuck with his dreams. When I'm gone you have to keep that house together. That's the only thing I can tell you. It's your *job*.

JAVIER: I don't want that job. I want to solve my problems— not Dad's, not Mom's, not Caroline's: mine. I always used you to protect myself—(*A car can be heard pulling up.*) Wait; listen—(JULIO *looks out into the distance.*) Yep. The Marines have landed.

JULIO: Already? Really? (*Getting his stuff together.*) This is it, my friend.

JAVIER: Dammit. I had—so many things I wanted to tell you. Ideas and advice—all sorts of things.

JULIO: Well unless you can say them in ten words or less you better just say good-bye. I can feel myself turning into government property even as we speak.

JAVIER: I'm going to miss you.

JULIO: I'm going to miss you too. Hey, the truth—doesn't that Overbaby look like a grim guy?

JAVIER: Terrifying. Awesome.

JULIO: You take care of everybody—and make sure they write— and keep Mom from getting too excited—and for Godsakes, why don't you make it big already? I mean, doesn't that Overbaby look like a *really grim guy?* (JULIO *salutes* JAVIER *and exits.* JAVIER *waves to* JULIO. JULIO *re-enters the stage and embraces* JAVIER. *Blackout.*)

How I Got That Story

Amlin Gray

Characters: Reporter (late 20s), the Historical Event (older)
Setting: Am-bo Land

Premiere: Milwaukee Repertory Theater, 1979
Publisher: Dramatists Play Service, Inc.

How I Got That Story takes place in the fictionalized Asian Country Am-bo Land and is written for two actors. The first plays the Reporter; the second portrays the Historical Event, comprising twenty characters, including Mme. Ing (the tyrannical ruler of Am-bo Land), an American G.I., Li (a prostitute), a Guerrilla, and a Nun. Over the course of the play, the Reporter moves from being an outside observer to being an integral participant in the Event.

The Reporter begins his new job wide-eyed, seeing Am-bo Land as Everywhere: "If I can just keep my eyes wide open I can understand the whole world." Many things happen. He becomes disgusted by Am-bo Land and plans to leave. He misses his plane, then gets on a bomber, which is shot down. Guerrillas hold him hostage. When the news agency pays $100,000 ransom, he is released. Now planning to stay in Am-bo Land forever, he asks Li, a prostitute, to marry him. She refuses unless he will take her to America.

The Reporter decides to adopt an Ambonese child. This scene takes place toward the end of the play. The Event plays the Nun.

Note: Every sound effect in the play is made, live or on tape, by the Event actor. Where possible the audience should be able to recognize his voice. A series of slides announcing the titles of scenes, etc., is also used in production.

(*The taped crying of babies is heard. Lights come up on an* AMBONESE NUN *tending children who are imagined to be in a long row of cribs between her and the audience. The* REPORTER *comes in left.*)

REPORTER: Excuse me, Sister.

NUN: Yes?

REPORTER: The Mother Superior told me to come up here.

NUN: Yes?

REPORTER: I'm going to adopt a child.

NUN: (*Scanning his garments; gently.*) Adopt a child?

REPORTER: Yes.

NUN: Have you been interviewed?

REPORTER: Not yet. I have to get a bit more settled first. But the Mother Superior said I could come upstairs and if I chose a child she would keep it for me.

NUN: Ah. How old a child would you want?

REPORTER: He should probably not be very young. And tough. He should be tough. I don't have lots of money.

NUN: You said "he."

REPORTER: A girl would be all right. A girl would be nice.

NUN: It must be a girl. The Government has a law that only girls may be adopted. The boys are wards of the State. When they are older, they will go into the army.

REPORTER: Well, a girl is fine.

NUN: (*Starting down the line with him, moving left.*) This girl is healthy.

REPORTER: Hello. You're very pretty. You have cheekbones like a grownup, like your mommy must have had. Look. If I pull back my skin as tight as I can, I still don't have skin as tight as you. (*He pulls his skin back toward his temples. One effect is that this gives him slanted eyes.*) Why won't you look at me?

NUN: She is looking at you.

REPORTER: She doesn't trust me. (*To the child.*) I won't hurt you. I just want to have a child of your country. Will you be my child? (*To the* NUN.) She doesn't like me. Do you see that child down the line there? (*Pointing right.*) That one's looking at me. Let's go talk to that child.

NUN: That section is boys. This way. (*She leads him to the next crib to the left.*)

REPORTER: She's asleep but, look, her little fists are clenched. She wouldn't like me. I don't want to wake her up.

NUN: Here is another.

REPORTER: (*To the third child.*) Do you like me? I'll take care of you. I understand that you need food, and I'll try and be a friend to you. (*To the* NUN.) She doesn't even hear my voice.

NUN: Here.

REPORTER: These aren't children! These are ancient people, shrunken down! Look at their eyes! They've looked at everything! They'll never look at me!

NUN: You're upsetting the children.

REPORTER: (*Pointing toward the boys' section.*) That child sees me. He's been looking at me since I came in the room. I want that child.

NUN: I've told you that you cannot have a boy—Wait. Which child?

REPORTER: The one who's standing up and looking at me.

NUN: The child in green?

REPORTER: Yes.

NUN: You can have the child in green. The Government will not object to that. The boy is blind.

REPORTER: Blind?

NUN: Yes.

REPORTER: He's looking at me.

NUN: He can't see you.

REPORTER: Yes he can.

NUN: You'd better go now. Come back when you have made an application and have been approved. The boy will be here.

REPORTER: He can see. He's looking at me.

NUN: Come away now.

REPORTER: Is he blind?

NUN: Yes.

REPORTER: Yes. I'm going to go now. (*He doesn't move.*)

NUN: Yes, please go now.

REPORTER: Yes. He's blind. (*He starts out the way he came.*)

NUN: God be with you.

(*Blackout.*)

A Lie of the Mind

Sam Shepard

Characters: Jake (20s–30s), Frankie (20s–30s)

Setting: Highway, hospital room, motel room, Jake's mother's house, Beth's parents' house. The American West.

Premiere: Promenade Theatre, New York City, 1985

Publishers: Dramatists Play Service, Inc.

As the play opens Jake is calling his brother, Frankie, from somewhere out on Highway 2—he's not sure what state. He has beaten his wife, Beth, and thinks she may be dead. They meet in a motel room, and Jake tries to explain to Frankie why he did it.

(*Soft orange light up on Stage Right platform, revealing small ragged motel couch with a floor lamp beside it. Main light source emanating from lamp. A wooden chair opposite couch. Jake's suitcase on floor with clothes spilled out of it. Jake sits in middle of couch, legs apart, slouched forward, holding his head in his hands. Frankie stands behind couch with a plastic bag full of ice, trying to apply it to the back of Jake's neck. Jake keeps pushing the ice away.*)

JAKE: (*Shoving ice away.*) I don't want any goddamn ice! It's cold!

FRANKIE: I thought it might help.

JAKE: Well, it don't. It's cold.

FRANKIE: I know it's cold. It's ice. It's supposed to be cold. (*Pause. Frankie goes to chair. Sits. Silence between them for a while.*) You didn't actually kill her, did ya', Jake? (*Jake stays seated. Starts slow, low, deliberate.*)

JAKE: She was goin' to these goddamn rehearsals every day. Every day. Every single day. Hardly ever see her. I saw enough though. Believe you me. Saw enough to know somethin' was goin' on.

FRANKIE: But you didn't really kill her, did ya?

JAKE: (*Builds.*) I'm no dummy. Doesn't take much to put it together. Woman starts dressin' more and more skimpy every time she goes out. Starts puttin' on more and more smells. Oils. She was always oiling herself before she went out. Every morning. Smell would wake me up. Coconut or Butterscotch or some goddamn thing. Sweet stuff. Youda' thought she was an ice cream sundae. I'd watch her oiling herself while I pretended to be asleep. She was in a dream, the way she did it. Like she was imagining someone else touching her. Not me. Never me. Someone else.

FRANKIE: Who?

JAKE: (*Stands, moves around space, gains momentum.*) Some guy. I don't know. Some actor-jerk. I knew she was gettin' herself ready for him. I could tell. Got worse and worse. When I finally called her on it she denied it flat. I knew she was lying too. Could tell it right away. The way she took it so light. Tried to cast it off like it was nothin'. Then she starts tellin' me it's all in *my* head. Some imaginary deal I'd cooked up in *my* head. Had nothin' to do with her, she said. Made me try to believe I was crazy. She's all innocent and I'm crazy. So I told her—I told her—I laid it on the line to her. Square business. I says—no more high heels! No more wearin' them high spikey high heels to rehearsals. No more a' that shit. And she laughs. Right to my face. She laughs. Kept puttin' 'em on. Every mornin'. Puttin' 'em back on. She says it's right for the part. Made her feel like the character she says. Then I told her she had to wear a bra and she paid no attention to that either. You could see right through her damn blouse. Right clean through it. And she never wore underpants either. That's what really got me. No underpants. You could see everything.

FRANKIE: Well, she never wore underpants anyway, did she? (*Jake stops, turns to Frankie. Frankie stays in chair. Pause.*)

JAKE: How do you know?

FRANKIE: No, I mean—I think you told me once.

JAKE: (*Moving slowly toward Frankie.*) I never told you that.

I never woulda' told you a thing like that. That's personal.

FRANKIE: (*Backing up.*) No, I think you did once—when you were drunk or somethin'.

JAKE: (*Close to Frankie.*) I never woulda' told you that!

FRANKIE: All right. (*Pause.*)

JAKE: I never talked about her that way to anybody.

FRANKIE: Okay. Forget it. Just forget it.

JAKE: You always liked her, didn't you, Frankie? Don't think I overlooked that.

FRANKIE: Are you gonna' finish tellin' me what happened? 'Cause if you're not I'm gonna' take a walk right outa' here. (*Pause. Jake considers, then launches back into the story.*)

JAKE: (*Returns to speed, moves.*) Okay. Then she starts readin' the lines with me, at night. In bed. Readin' the lines. I'm helpin' her out, right? Helpin' her memorize the damn lines so she can run off every morning and say 'em to some other guy. Day after day. Same lines. And these lines are all about how she's bound and determined to get this guy back in the sack with her after all these years he's been ignoring her. How she still loves him even though he hates her. How she's saving her body up for him and him only.

FRANKIE: Well, it was just a play, wasn't it?

JAKE: Yeah, a play. That's right. Just a play. "Pretend." That's what she said. "Just pretend." I know what they were doing! I know damn well what they were doin'! I know what that acting shit is all about. They try to "believe" they're the person. Right? Try to believe so hard they're the person that they actually think they become the person. So you know what that means don't ya'?

FRANKIE: What?

JAKE: They start doin' all the same stuff the person does!

FRANKIE: What person?

JAKE: The person! The—whad'ya' call it? The—

FRANKIE: Character?

JAKE: Yeah. The character. That's right. They start acting that way in real life. Just like the character. Walkin' around— talkin' that way. You shoulda' seen the way she started to walk and talk. I couldn't believe it. Changed her hair and everything. Put a wig on. Changed her clothes. Everything changed. She was unrecognizable. I didn't even know who I was with anymore. I told her. I told her, look—"I don't know who you think you are now but I'd just as soon you come on back to the real world here." And you know what she tells me?

FRANKIE: What?

JAKE: She tells me this is the real world. This acting shit is more real than the real world to her. Can you believe that? And she was tryin' to convince me that *I* was crazy? (*Pause.*)

FRANKIE: So you think she was sleeping with this guy just because she was playing a part in a play?

JAKE: Yeah. She was real dedicated.

FRANKIE: Are you sure? I mean when would she have time to do that in rehearsals?

JAKE: On her lunch break.

FRANKIE: (*Stands.*) Oh, come on, Jake.

JAKE: Sit down! Sit back down. I got more to tell you.

FRANKIE: No! I'm not gonna' sit down! I came to try to help you out and all you're tellin' me is a bunch of bullshit about Beth screwing around with some other guy on her lunch break?

JAKE: She was! It's easy to tell when a woman gets obsessed with somethin' else. When she moves away from you. They don't hide it as easy as men.

FRANKIE: She was just trying to do a good job.

JAKE: That's no job! I've had jobs before. I know what a job is. A job is where you work. A job is where you don't have fun. You don't dick around tryin' to pretend you're somebody else. You work. Work is work!

FRANKIE: It's a different kind of a job.

JAKE: It's an excuse to fool around! That's was it is. That's why she wanted to become an actress in the first place. So she could get away from me.

FRANKIE: You can't jump to that kind of conclusion just because she was—

JAKE: I didn't jump to nothing'! I knew what she was up to even if she didn't.

FRANKIE: So, you mean you're accusing her of somethin' she wasn't even aware of?

JAKE: She was aware all right. She was tryin' to hide it from me but she wasn't that good an actress. (*Pause.*)

FRANKIE: So you beat her up again. Boy, I'm tellin' you—

JAKE: I killed her. (*Pause.*)

FRANKIE: You killed her.

JAKE: That's right.

FRANKIE: She stopped breathing?

JAKE: Everything stopped.

FRANKIE: You checked.

JAKE: I didn't have to check.

FRANKIE: She might've just been unconscious or something.

JAKE: No.

FRANKIE: Well, what'd you do? Did you tell the police?

JAKE: Why would I do that? She was already dead. What could they do about it?

FRANKIE: That's what you're supposed to do when somebody dies. You report it to the police.

JAKE: Even when you kill 'em?

FRANKIE: Yeah! Even when you kill them. Especially when you kill them!

JAKE: I never heard a' that. (*Pause.*)

FRANKIE: Well, somebody should check up on it. I mean this is pretty serious stuff, Jake.

JAKE: I done my time for her. I already done my time.

FRANKIE: She had nothin' to do with that. She never did.

JAKE: She got me in trouble more'n once. She did it on purpose too. Always flirtin' around. Always carryin' on.

FRANKIE: She had nothin' to do with it! You lost your temper.

JAKE: She provoked it!

FRANKIE: You've always lost your temper and blamed it on somebody else. Even when you were a kid you blamed it on somebody else. One time you even blamed it on a goat. I remember that. (*Pause. Jake stops.*)

JAKE: What goat?

FRANKIE: That milk goat we had.

JAKE: What was her name?

FRANKIE: I forget.

JAKE: What was that goat's name?

FRANKIE: You remember that goat?

JAKE: Yeah, I remember that goat. I loved that goat.

FRANKIE: Well you kicked the shit out of that goat you loved so much when she stepped on your bare feet while you were tryin' to milk her. You remember that? Broke her ribs.

JAKE: I never kicked that goat!

FRANKIE: Oh, you don't remember that huh? You broke your damn foot you kicked her so hard.

JAKE: What was that goat's name? (*Jake suddenly falls to the floor, collapses. Frankie goes to him. Tries to help him.*) Get away from me!

FRANKIE: What happened?

JAKE: Just get away!

FRANKIE: You all right?

JAKE: Somethin's wrong. My head's funny.

FRANKIE: (*Trying to help Jake up.*) Come on, let's get you back on the couch.

JAKE: (*Pushing Frankie away, crawls on knees toward couch.*) I don't need any help!

FRANKIE: You feel dizzy or something?

JAKE: (*Crawling to couch.*) Yeah. All of a sudden. Everything's—

FRANKIE: You want me to get you something?

JAKE: (*Climbing up on couch and lying on his belly.*) No. I don't need nothin'.

FRANKIE: You want me to get a doctor for you?

JAKE: I'm gonna' die without her. I know I'm gonna' die. (*Pause.*)

FRANKIE: I could go to her folks' place. They'd know what happened to her.

JAKE: No! You stay away from there! Don't go anywhere near there. I'm through chasin' after her.

FRANKIE: Somebody's gotta' find out, Jake. Sooner or later. (*Pause. Jake speaks in a whisper, almost to himself. His whole tone changes. Very vulnerable, as though questioning a ghost.*)

JAKE: Now. Why now? Why am I missing her now, Frankie? Why not then? When she was there? Why am I afraid I'm gonna' lose her when she's already gone? And this fear—this fear swarms through me—floods my whole body 'til there's nothing left. Nothing left of me. And then it turns—It turns to a fear for my whole life. Like my whole life is lost from losing her. Gone. That I'll die like this. Lost. Just lost.

FRANKIE: It's okay, Jake.

JAKE: You liked her too, didn't you, Frankie?

FRANKIE: Yeah, I liked her. (*Pause.*)

JAKE: My back's like ice. How come my back's so cold?

FRANKIE: (*Moves right.*) I'll get you a blanket.

JAKE: No! Don't leave.

FRANKIE: (*Stops.*) All right. (*Pause.*) You okay?

JAKE: Yeah. Just sit with me for a while. Stay here.

FRANKIE: (*Goes to chair, pulls it near couch.*) Okay. (FRANKIE *sits in chair next to couch.* JAKE *stays on his belly, arm hanging limply over the side of couch, hand touching the floor.*)

JAKE: Don't leave.

FRANKIE: I won't.

(*Lights dim to black.*)

The Mound Builders

Lanford Wilson

Characters: Dan Loggins (29), Chad Jasker (25)

Setting: A farmhouse near an archaeological dig in Blue Shoals, Illinois

Premiere: Circle Repertory Company, New York City, 1975

Publisher: A Mermaid Dramabook (Hill and Wang)

Archaeologist August Howe stands in his office trying to organize what is left of the wreckage of last summer's expedition. As he searches through slides he dictates his notes into a tape machine, and the play flashes back to the previous summer.

August, his partner Dan Loggins, and several students are excavating a Mississippian Indian mound site in southern Illinois. Their overstuffed house includes both their wives, August's eleven-year-old daughter, and his sister D.K. (Delia) Eriksen, a brilliant but dissipated novelist. They are visited often by Chad Jasker, whose father owns the house and land the excavation site stands on. Chad is in love with Dan's wife Jean. He is also having an affair with August's wife. He is an American dreamer—very physical, not an intellectual. He and Dan are stoned. They have been fishing and have polished off five six-packs.

(CHAD *and* DAN *are noisily divesting themselves of rods, reels, creels, etc. Enjoying the noise; oblivious of the silence of the house.* DAN *goes to the refrigerator.*)

DAN: Nothing!

CHAD: Nothing?

DAN: Nothing to drink. Do you want to eat?

CHAD: God, no—

DAN: Food?

CHAD: Never again in my life. (*He has found a bottle of Scotch.*)

DAN: Well, then there's nothing.

CHAD: You call that nothing?

DAN: Are you crazy; you want to kill yourself?

CHAD: No—you go. "Beer on whiskey—mightly." Mightly?

DAN: Mightly?

CHAD: What is it? You say it.

DAN: You're saying it. I don't know what—

CHAD: I'm telling you, it's an old wives' tale—there's a *thing*— a saying that tells you how to judge.

DAN: A what? What's the thing?

CHAD: A thing. You're the educated member of the family—
you're supposed—

DAN: But not in FOLKLORE! Not in—

CHAD: I'm not talking—

DAN: —Absolute blind spot in folklore!

CHAD: I'm talking words—it's a epigram or epitaph or aphorism or anagram.

DAN: Axiom.

CHAD: It's not an axiom.

DAN: Well, what is it? Is it—

CHAD: It's not a goddamned axiom. It's an easy word—it's a
word! It's a saying—a truth!

DAN: That's the word. It's a truth.

CHAD: It's a truth, but that's not the word—ANYWAY!

DAN: Anyway. How does it go? Tell us! Are we safe? Will we
survive?

CHAD: It goes . . .
   (*Pauses, trying to frame it.*)

DAN: (*Under.*) How does . . .

CHAD: (*Under.*) Just cool it a minute, will you? It goes: (*Head-
line.*) "BEER. ON WHISKEY."

DAN: Sounds bad.

CHAD: "MIGHTY RISKY . . . WHISKEY, ON BEER, NEVER FEAR."

DAN: (*Pause.*) It's an aphorism.

CHAD: So. (*Pours a glass each.*) Whiskey on beer—
   (*Toast.*)

DAN: Cheers.

CHAD: WHISKEY ON BEER . . .

DAN: That's what I said: "Never fear."

CHAD: Cheers.
   (*They drink.*)

DAN: This will probably kill us.

CHAD: Hey! Have you ever seen anything as beautiful as that
moon?

DAN: Never.

CHAD: As big?

DAN: Never. When's the harvest moon?

CHAD: October.

DAN: Only the harvest moon.

CHAD: November.

DAN: Only the harvest moon.

CHAD: October.

DAN: Only the harvest moon.

CHAD: September.

DAN: As golden?

CHAD: Never.

DAN: What is it? June 21, 23—that's the summer solstice—moon.

CHAD: (*Simple.*) It's a full moon.

DAN: It's a full moon.

CHAD: And you're full of shit.

DAN: I'm fulla beer.

CHAD: I gotta piss.

   (*He goes out the door.*)

DAN: (*Alone.*) What'd we do?

CHAD: (*Off.*) Twelve.

DAN: Twelve's ass. I caught five and you caught what?

CHAD: (*Off.*) You caught five, I caught seven.

DAN: They be all right out in that tub?

CHAD: (*Off.*) You want to clean 'em?

DAN: Hell, I couldn't clean me.

CHAD: (*Off.*) You better manage it; Jean'll kick your ass out on the floor.

DAN: Hell she will. (*He stands, miming rod: casting, catch.*) Strike! Shitfire! Strike! Get the net!

CHAD: (*Off.*) What?

DAN: Get the net, goddamnit, I got another one!

CHAD: (*Off.*) Get your own damn net; I got a seven-pounder out here.

DAN: (*Dropping it.*) He who brags about size of meat—I forget what it was, but Confucius said something very appropriate to that. What'll it weigh? The big one. Five pounds?

CHAD: Six.

DAN: Was that one motherfuckin' fish? Was that a *fight*? To the *death*?

CHAD: (*Entering.*) That was a fight to the death.

DAN: Was that the biggest bass you ever saw in your life?

CHAD: No.

DAN: Shit.

CHAD: No.

DAN: You've seen a bigger bass?

CHAD: I've seen a bigger bass.

DAN: Drink your beer.

CHAD: I gotta get my ass home.

DAN: Would you drink your damn beer?

CHAD: You better get your duds off; get up to that warm bed, you're gonna be diggin' tomorrow.

DAN: Terrific. You know why? Cause what's happening is, it's all gone wrong. And that's always very terrific.

CHAD: Get up and have your girl give you a rubdown, huh?

DAN: Everything's looking like a typical village, right? And all of a sudden it's not typical anymore. They got something under the roundhouse.

CHAD: Isn't that right?

DAN: We don't know what yet. What?

CHAD: You gotta get up to your girl.

DAN: She's beautiful, isn't she?

CHAD: She is that.

DAN: And bright—you wouldn't believe it.

CHAD: No, I'm counting on it. Let's take you up, put you to bed.

DAN: And sweet; you wouldn't believe it.

CHAD: No, I'm a believer.

DAN: You better believe it.

CHAD: Let's get you up to bed, come on.

DAN: I'm all wet.

CHAD: Come on.

DAN: I'm all wet, come on.

CHAD: Well, you said it.

DAN: Drink your—Scotch.

CHAD: Wore your life preserver, didn't you? That's nice out there, just you and me, huh?

DAN: Beautiful.

CHAD: Wouldn't be right with no one else, huh?

DAN: No way.

CHAD: You gettin' warm?

DAN: I'm fine.

CHAD: (*Very close to him.*) You gonna be O.K.?

DAN: I am.

CHAD: (*Pulling him closer.*) You sure? You sure?

DAN: Yeah, well, I didn't drown, I can survive without mouth-to-mouth resuscitation.

CHAD: Huh?

DAN: I'm fine.

CHAD: You know why you didn't drown—because you got a cork head!

The Nerd

Larry Shue

Characters: Willum Cubbert (34), Rick Steadman (30s)
Setting: Willum's home in Terre Haute, Indiana
Premiere: Milwaukee Repertory Theater, 1981
Publisher: Dramatists Play Service, Inc.

Willum Cubbert, an architect, is the nicest guy in the world. He's *too* nice. He is unrequitedly in love with a woman named Tansy, who describes him as "wonderful; he's talented, he's the gentlest man I've ever known, he's—he could use a little gumption." She is about to move to Washington to become a television weather girl. Willum is already pining, but too shy to make his move. Their friend Axel, a cynical drama critic, decides to play Cupid.

Willum was wounded in Vietnam, and his life was saved by a grunt named Rick Steadman, who dragged him a mile and a half through the jungle. Willum has not seen him since, but still sends him Christmas cards promising, "As long as I'm *alive,* you will have someone on this earth who will do *anything* for you." The week before Tansy is scheduled to leave, Rick Steadman shows up at Willum's—and stays.

Rick, the nerd of the title, is as abrasive as Willum is docile: the world's worst guest. He tells long-winded stories about his job as a chalk-factory inspector, plays terrible party games, erases the message machine to tape-record "The Rick Steadman Show," and starts to drop hints about staying through Christmas. Finally, Willum determines to challenge his guest.

Note: At the end of the play, the audience learns—although Willum does not—that "Rick Steadman" is Axel's actor friend Kemp, in a performance designed to prod Willum to action. It works.

————————————

(WILLUM *starts to set up his drawing materials, then starts pacing back and forth in front of the couch, speaking objectively, maturely, to an imaginary* RICK.)

WILLUM: Now, Rick. Rick, sit down. (*Pause.*) Put down your tambourine. Now, as you know, there's a kind of—chemistry between any two people, which can affect both people in very different ways. Now, just as there's some chemistry in you which allows you to like my company—there's some chemistry in me that just always makes me want to scratch your face off. (*Abandoning that.*) No, um—(*Trying again— the no-nonsense approach.*) Rick, I'm not going to mince words. It's time for you to leave. We needn't go into all the reasons; let's just say it's something I've thought about and have decided on. Now, I realize that you saved my life. I owe you my life. I acknowledge that. And I realize that I promised—promised in writing—that as long as I was alive, you could come to me for anything, and that you would always have a place that you could—. (*Breaking off again.*) Oh, God. (*He picks up a large T-square.*) Rick, do you know what this is? This is a crossbow. (*Dispatching the imaginary Rick with an arrow.*) Thhhkkk! (*Turning the T-square on himself.*) Thhhkkk! (*He drops, slain, to the sofa. Presently he opens*

his eyes again.) Oh, me. Oh, well. (*Getting back to work.*)
Okay. Concentrate. If I just—concentrate. (WILLUM *works,
clenching a pencil far back in his teeth like a bit. Momen-
tarily, in comes* RICK, *hands in pockets, head to one side—
in a word, depressed. He sighs.* WILLUM *works. He sighs
again, more loudly.* WILLUM *looks up grimly, the pencil still
clenched in his teeth.*)

RICK: What are *you* smileen' about? (WILLUM *takes the pencil
from his mouth, goes back to work.*) I'm not smileen'. 'Cause
you wanta know *why*? (*No answer.*) Huh? (*No answer.*) You
wanta know *why* I'm not smileen'? (*No answer.*) Huh?

WILLUM: (*Stopping work.*) All right. What's the problem?

RICK: You really want to know?

WILLUM: Sure.

RICK: Really?

WILLUM: Rick.

RICK: (*Sighs.*) Well—you know my brother Bob?

WILLUM: Brother Bob, yes.

RICK: I called him up this morneen', and you know what?

WILLUM: What?

RICK: He moved.

WILLUM: He—he *moved*?

RICK: Yep.

WILLUM: Moved where?

RICK: That was the thing. He didn't leave any forwardeen'
address. It was so strange.

WILLUM: (*Hoping he is right.*) Well, surely—if he really has
moved, surely he'll get in touch.

RICK: I don't know. I hope he at least sends my things.

WILLUM: Your things? What things?

RICK: My clothes? My chemistry set?

WILLUM: Uh—.

RICK: My chihuahua?

WILLUM: Your Chihuahua?

RICK: Yeah. Oh, you should see him. He's really lifelike.

WILLUM: Rick, wait. Where—where would Bob send your
things?

RICK: (*Shrugs.*) Here, right?

WILLUM: Uh—here?

RICK: This is where I am, right?

WILLUM: Rick—? (*He tries to go on, but can only manage to repeat.*) Rick—?

RICK: (*Giving him his full attention.*) What?

WILLUM: Rick—there's something I have to say. (RICK *watches him with his all-purpose expression.*) All right. Here goes. Now—you're here. And I'm here. (*Stalling to think.*) Um . . . okay. Are you with me so far?

RICK: I'm a little bit lost.

WILLUM: Rick, all I said was, "You're here and I'm here."

RICK: Oh.

WILLUM: (*Exhales audibly.*) All right. Now—when—when two people are together a lot of the time, they can't help influencing each other, and influencing each other's ability to function. You—are you still with me?

RICK: (*Nods.*) You're here and I'm here.

WILLUM: (*Uncertainly.*) Rrright. (*Should he go back? He decides to press on.*) So. What we're talking about, really, is personality, isn't it? Uh—(*Telling a joke on himself.*) I mean, I know there are qualities in me that make it hard for some people to have me around—I'm sloppy, I lose things, I'm always getting lost. Some people aren't able to deal with that; it's not their fault, it's not my fault, it's just—personality. You see what I'm driving at? (*Rick gives a more or less affirmative shrug.*) Okay . . . So, we all have these character traits. So, what if, just out of curiosity—(*Trying to sound hypothetical.*) what if somebody were to say to you—oh— "Get out of here and don't ever come back"—something like that. I mean, I know it's hard, but if you stood back, do you think you could see what might lead a person to say that to you?

RICK: Oh, sure.

WILLUM: *Really?*

RICK: Oh, sure.

WILLUM: Oh, Rick. That's great.

RICK: Sure. Like if he hated me because I believed in God?

WILLUM: Oh, Rick.

RICK: Or believed in God, or—(*Getting into it like a game.*) or maybe he hates people 'cause they work in a factory?

WILLUM: (*A quiet moan.*) Ahhhhh. . . .

RICK: And he hates me because my hands are all rough, and stained with honest chalk? Y'know?

WILLUM: Rick. No. No decent person would hate you for—

RICK: Or, what else? Oh! (*The best yet.*) How 'bout because I was in the war? And this guy hates people with Purple Hearts?

WILLUM: Oh, God.

RICK: What?

WILLUM: Nothing. Nothing. All right, just—let me ask you this. What would you say are the main differences between you—and me?

RICK: (*Shrugs.*) None.

WILLUM: None? You mean you and I are—are—?

RICK: The same. Sure. (*Willum looks at him a long moment, then picks up his T-square.*)

WILLUM: Rick, do you know what this is? (RICK *shrugs.* WIL-LUM *gives up both his campaign and his fantasy.*) It's a T-square. I've got to get back to work.

RICK: 'Kay. That was fun.

WILLUM: (*Shakily lighting a cigarette.*) Great.

RICK: You smoke cigarettes?

WILLUM: Yeah.

RICK: Since when?

WILLUM: Since the airport. (*He is searching for something.*)

RICK: Oh, that reminds me, hey. I bet you don't think I don't know what you're lookeen' for, right?

WILLUM: What?

RICK: Right?

WILLUM: What?

RICK: (*Who suddenly is in high spirits.*) Wait, don't even answer that.

WILLUM: Answer what?

RICK: Or—you wanna guess?

WILLUM: Guess *what*?

RICK: Huh?

WILLUM: Guess *what*?

RICK: I give up. (RICK *waits expectantly*. WILLUM *slumps into a chair. It would not surprise us to see him crumble into dust.*) What? Anything? Okay. I got one for *you*. You know your picture of that hotel?

WILLUM: (*Suddenly alert.*) That's what I was *look*ing for.

RICK: I know, 'cause you said you were afraid it was like *miss*een' some*theen*', right?

WILLUM: I may have; Rick, if you've seen that—that's my final color rendering—.

RICK: No, I know, so this morn*een*' I to-o-ook it out, and I he-e-eld it up to the light—.

WILLUM: (*Barely audible.*) Rick—.

RICK: And I loo-o-ooked at it this way awhile, then I looked at it that way, then this way again—.

WILLUM: Rick, don't tell me you—.

RICK: No, wait. So guess what? You know what I finally realized it needed? So simple. (*He pulls the rendering from beneath the couch.*) A chimney! (*Imposed on the roof of a careful watercolor of the Regency is an immense, hideous, black square, boldly executed in some less refined medium— Crayola, perhaps, or laundry-marker. A second square, on the opposite side of the roof, has been begun, then cancelled with a large "X."* RICK *points to the crossed-out mistake.*) Not this one. That was just a goof. (*He puts his hand over it.*) But see?

WILLUM: Uh . . . Rick . . . ?

RICK: I don't know where I got the idea.

WILLUM: Rick—.

RICK: God, I guess.

WILLUM: (*Looking closer, hoping that the drawing can somehow be saved.*) Rick, you—did you put a hole in this?

RICK: Oh, right, that's why I remembered. Here, look. (*He takes WILLUM's burning cigarette from the ashtray, gets a mouthful of smoke, and blows it slowly through the chimney-hole from behind. The effect is made a little surreal by the presence of* RICK's *eyes, which peer expectantly over the top of the drawing during the demonstration.*) See? (*He snorts happily.*) Y'know, I thought I was a lot of things, but I sure never knew I was an architect!

WILLUM: (*Who really doesn't.*) Rick—I—I don't know what to say—

RICK: That's okay. But, so—what would I do next, if I were—me?

WILLUM: (*Clutching a pencil-box.*) What?

RICK: I mean, you know, in the architect business. Could you like show me the ropes, and introduce me around, and that?

WILLUM: Uh—.

RICK: Or, wait a minute! *Hey!* We could be *part*ners! (*The box in* WILLUM's *hand suddenly shatters, crushed by his clenched fist. He grabs his wrist, pained.*)

WILLUM: Aah!

RICK: (*Running to him.*) What happened?

WILLUM: (*Nursing his hand.*) Nothing, it's—.

RICK: Hey, you're *bleed*een'! (*Grabbing the wounded hand.*) Lemme look at that.

WILLUM: Ow!

RICK: You sit there, I know just the thing for that.

WILLUM: I'll take care of it.

RICK: Sit *there*. This is my mom's kitchen remedy, you just rub it into the cut.

WILLUM: Rick—I'm—don't.

RICK: Sit *there*, now—and don't *move*. I'll be in here heateen' up the salt!

(*He disappears into the kitchen.*)

The Normal Heart

Larry Kramer

Characters: Ned Weeks (late 30s), Felix Turner (30s)
Setting: New York City
Premiere: Public Theatre, New York Shakespeare Festival, New York City, 1985
Publisher: Samuel French, Inc.

The Normal Heart deals with the onset of the AIDS epidemic and the inadequate response by the media and the Koch administration.

When a friend is stricken with AIDS, Ned Weeks is approached by his friend's doctor, Emma Brockner. She has heard he is scared and has a big mouth. She wants Ned, a writer, to spread the word: "Tell gay men to stop having sex." At first, Ned thinks her request is preposterous. Then as he hears the dimensions of the approaching epidemic and, through his friend Craig, sees how devastating AIDS can be, he starts an organization to raise money and spread information.

Ned goes to *The New York Times*, which is ignoring the epidemic. He speaks to Felix Turner, a conservatively dressed, outgoing, and completely masculine *Times* reporter. Ned has heard through the grapevine that Felix is gay, and hopes he will help. Felix refuses. "I just write about gay designers and gay discos and gay chefs and gay rock stars and gay photographers and gay models and gay celebrities and gay everything. I just don't call them gay. Isn't that enough for doing my bit?" Ned tells Felix, "Guys like you give me a pain in the ass," and starts out. Felix asks if Ned's in the phone book, to which Ned responds, "Yes." This is their first date.

(NED's *apartment. It is stark, modern, all black and white.* FELIX *comes walking in from another room with a beer, and* NED *follows, carrying one, too.*)

FELIX: That's quite a library in there. You read all those books?

NED: Why does everybody ask that?

FELIX: You have a whole room of 'em, you must want to get asked.

NED: I never thought of it that way. Maybe I do. Thank you. But no, of course I haven't. They go out of print and then you can't find them, so I buy them right away.

FELIX: I think you're going to have to face the fact you won't be able to read them all before you die.

NED: I think you're right.

FELIX: You know, I really used to like high tech, but I'm tired of it now. I think I want chintz back again. Don't be insulted.

NED: I'm not. I want chintz back again, too.

FELIX: So here we are—two fellows who want chintz back again. Excuse me for saying so, but you are stiff as starch.

NED: It's been a long time since I've had a date. This is a date, isn't it? (FELIX *nods*.) And on the rare occasion, I was usually the asker.

FELIX: That's what's thrown you off your style: I called and asked.

NED: Some style. Before any second date I usually receive a phone call that starts with "Now I don't know what you had in mind, but can't we just be friends?"

FELIX: No. Are you glad I'm here?

NED: Oh, I'm pleased as punch you're here. You're very good-looking. What are you doing here?

FELIX: I'll let that tiny bit of self-pity pass for the moment.

NED: It's not self-pity, it's nervousness.

FELIX: It's definitely self-pity. Do you think you're bad-looking?

NED: Where are you from?

FELIX: I'm from Oklahoma. I left home at eighteen and put myself through college. My folks are dead. My dad worked at the refinery in West Tulsa and my mom was a waitress at a luncheonette in Walgreen's.

NED: Isn't it amazing how a kid can come out of all that and wind up on the *Times* dictating taste and style and fashion to the entire world?

FELIX: And we were talking so nicely.

NED: Talking is not my problem. Shutting up is my problem. And keeping my hands off you.

FELIX: You don't have to keep your hands off me. You have very nice hands. Do you have any awkward sexual tendencies you want to tell me about, too? That I'm not already familiar with?

NED: What are you familiar with?

FELIX: I have found myself pursuing men who hurt me. Before minor therapy. You're not one of those?

NED: No, I'm the runner. I *was* the runner. Until major therapy. After people who didn't want me and away from people who do.

FELIX: Isn't it amazing how a kid can come out of all that analyzing everything incessantly down to the most infinitesimal neurosis and still be all alone?

NED: I'm sorry you don't like my Dr. Freud. Another aging Jew who couldn't get laid.

FELIX: Just relax. You'll get laid.

NED: I try being laid-back, assertive, funny, butch . . . What's the point? I don't think there are many gay relationships that work out anyway.

FELIX: It's difficult to imagine you being laid-back. I know a lot of gay relationships that are working out very well.

NED: I guess I never see them.

FELIX: That's because you're a basket case.

NED: Fuck off.

FELIX: What's the matter? Don't you think you're attractive? Don't you like your body?

NED: I don't think anybody really likes their body. I read that somewhere.

FELIX: You know my fantasy has always been to go away and live by the ocean and write twenty-four novels, living with someone just like you with all these books who of course will be right there beside me writing your own twenty-four novels.

NED: (*After a beat.*) Me, too.

FELIX: Harold Robbins marries James Michener.

NED: How about Tolstoy and Charles Dickens?

FELIX: As long as Kafka doesn't marry Dostoevsky.

NED: Dostoevsky is my favorite writer.

FELIX: I'll have to try him again.

NED: If you really feel that way, why do you write all that society and party and fancy-ball-gown bullshit?

FELIX: Here we go again. I'll bet you gobble it up every day.

NED: I do. I also know six people who've died. When I came to you a few weeks ago, it was only one.

FELIX: I'm sorry. Is that why you agreed to this date?

NED: Do you know that when Hitler's Final Solution to eliminate the Polish Jews was first mentioned in the *Times* it was on page twenty-eight. And on page six of the *Washington Post*. And the *Times* and the *Post* were owned by Jews. What causes silence like that? Why didn't the American Jews help the German Jews get out? Their very own people! Scholars are finally writing honestly about this—I've been doing some research—and it's damning to everyone who was here then: Jewish leadership for being totally ineffective; Jewish organizations for constantly fighting among themselves, unable to cooperate even in the face of death: Zionists versus non-Zionists, Rabbi Wise against Rabbi Silver . . .

FELIX: Is this some sort of special way you talk when you don't want to talk? We were doing so nicely.

NED: We were?

FELIX: Wasn't there an awful lot of anti-Semitism in those days? Weren't Jews afraid of rubbing people's noses in too much shit?

NED: Yes, everybody has a million excuses for not getting involved. But aren't there moral obligations, moral commandments to try everything possible? Where were the Christian churches, the Pope, Churchill? And don't get me started on Roosevelt . . . How I was brought up to worship him, all Jews were. A clear statement from him would have put everything on the front pages, would have put Hitler on notice. But his administration did its best to stifle publicity at the same time as they clamped down immigration laws forbidding entry, and this famous haven for the oppressed became as inaccessible as Tibet. The title of Treasury Secretary Morgenthau's report to Roosevelt was "Acquiescence of This Government in the Murder of the Jews," which he wrote in 1944. Dachau was opened in 1933. Where was everybody for eleven years? And then it was too late.

FELIX: This is turning out to be a very romantic evening.

NED: And don't tell me how much you can accomplish working from the inside. Jewish leaders, relying on their contacts with people in high places, were still, quietly, from the inside, attempting to persuade them when the war was over.

FELIX: What do you want me to say? Do you ever take a vacation?

NED: A vacation. I forgot. That's the great goal, isn't it. A constant Fire Island vacation. Party, party; fuck, fuck. Maybe you can give me a few trendy pointers on what to wear.

FELIX: Boy, you really have a bug up your ass. Look, I'm not going to tell them I'm gay and could I write about the few cases of a mysterious disease that seems to be standing in the way of your kissing me even though there must be half a million gay men in this city who are fine and healthy. Let us please acknowledge the law of averages. And this is not World War Two. The numbers are nowhere remotely comparable. And all analogies to the Holocaust are tired, overworked, boring, probably insulting, possibly true, and a major turnoff.

NED: Are they?

FELIX: Boy, I think I've found myself a real live weird one. I had no idea. (*Pause.*) Hey, I just called you weird.

NED: You are not the first.

FELIX: You've never had a lover, have you?

NED: Where did you get that from?

FELIX: Have you? Wow.

NED: I suppose you've had quite a few.

FELIX: I had a very good one for a number of years, thank you. He was older than I was and he found someone younger.

NED: So you like them older. You looking for a father?

FELIX: No, I am not looking for a father! God, you are re-
lentless. And as cheery as Typhoid Mary. (NED *comes over
to* FELIX *and sits beside him. Then he leans over and kisses
him. The kiss becomes quite intense. Then* NED *breaks away,
jumps up, and begins to walk around nervously.*)

NED: The American Jews knew exactly what was happening,
but everything was downplayed and stifled. Can you imagine
how effective it would have been if every Jew in America
had marched on Washington? Proudly! Who says I want a
lover? Huh!? I mean, why doesn't anybody believe me when
I say I do not want a lover?

FELIX: You are fucking crazy. Jews, Dachau, Final Solution—
what kind of date is this! I don't believe anyone in the whole
wide world doesn't want to be loved. Ned, you don't remember me, do you? We've been in bed together. We made
love. We talked. We kissed. We cuddled. We made love
again. I keep waiting for you to remember, something, anything. But you don't!

NED: How could I not remember you?

FELIX: I don't know.

NED: Maybe if I saw you naked.

FELIX: It's okay as long as we treat each other like whores. It
was at the baths a few years ago. You were busy cruising
some blond number and I stood outside your door waiting
for you to come back and when you did you gave me such
an inspection up and down you would have thought I was
applying for the CIA.

NED: And then what?

FELIX: I just told you. We made love twice. I thought it was
lovely. You told me your name was Ned, that when you were
a child you read a Philip Barry play called *Holiday* where
there was a Ned, and you immediately switched
from . . . Alexander? I teased you for taking such a Wasp,
up-in-Connecticut-for-the-weekend-name, and I asked what
you did, and you answered something like you'd tried a number of things, and I asked you if that had included love, which

is when you said you had to get up early in the morning. That's when I left. But I tossed you my favorite go-fuck-yourself yourself when you told me "I really am not in the market for a lover"—men do not just naturally not love—they learn not to. I am not a whore. I just sometimes make mistakes and look for love in the wrong places. And I think you're a bluffer. Your novel was all about a man desperate for love and and a relationship, in a world filled with nothing but casual sex.

NED: Do you think we could start over?

FELIX: Maybe.

Not About Heroes

Stephen MacDonald

Characters: Wilfred Owen (24), Siegfried Sassoon (31)

Setting: Craiglockhart War Hospital for Nervous Disorders, Sassoon's Country House, etc.

Premiere: Dundee Theatre Company at the Edinburgh Festival, 1982

Publisher: Samuel French, Inc.

In his notes on *Not About Heroes,* Stephen MacDonald writes: "When Wilfred Owen was sent to Craiglockhart War Hospital for Nervous Disorders in June, 1917, he was suffering from shell-shock after four months in the trenches in France. It seems that his Commanding Officer equated shell-shock with cowardice. Owen was completely unknown. He aspired to be a poet, but had achieved nothing of note. He was killed in November, 1918. He had won the Military Cross a month before his death. He is now widely recognized as the greatest of the many British poets of the First World War. *Not About Heroes* is concerned with this transformation and how it might have happened.

"The crucial event was the meeting with Siegfried Sassoon. He was a well-known, acclaimed poet and a soldier of remarkable courage, who had achieved notoriety by publishing a protest against the 'evil and unjust' conduct of the war. He was sent to Craiglockhart Hospital at the end of July, 1917, possibly to undermine the strength of his protest by questioning his sanity. Wilfred Owen nervously introduced himself about two weeks later. They had little in common, but a warm and loving friendship developed. . . . The friendship seems to have been the key which unlocked Owen's genius as a poet. I also believe, from the tone of Owen's subsequent letters, that it liberated the man."

The following scene depicts the first meeting of Owen and Sassoon.

———————————

(OWEN, *timidly, knocks.* SASSOON *does not welcome the intrusion. He quickly takes a golf club and a polishing rag from the golf bag, then moves away.* SASSOON *speaks sharply and does not look at* OWEN *when he enters the space which is* SASSOON's *hospital room.*)

SASSOON: Yes? Come! (OWEN *comes forward.*)

OWEN: Lieutenant Sassoon?

SASSOON: For the moment—yes.

OWEN: Oh . . .

SASSOON: I *am* Sassoon. Is there something you want?

OWEN: I've d-disturbed you. I'm very sorry.

SASSOON: *Having* disturbed me, could you not at least tell me why?

OWEN: It's . . . these . . .

SASSOON: What are they?

OWEN: Copies of your b-book. Your l-latest book, I mean. "The Old Huntsman." (SASSOON *is surprised, but will not let* OWEN *see it.*)

SASSOON: Mmm . . . Not wise to go around in public with those under your arm. Unless you *want* to stay in this place until the end of the war.

OWEN: No.

SASSOON: No?

OWEN: No—I don't want to stay in this p-place until the end of the war.

SASSOON: Then you'd be safer even with Shelley. And positively impregnable with Rupert Brooke.

OWEN: I really have disturbed you. F-forgive me. Sorry. (OWEN *smiles apologetically and turns to go.*)

SASSOON: No, stay . . . ! I don't *mean* to be rude.

OWEN: Oh, it's not rude. I understand.

SASSOON: You do?

OWEN: Oh, yes.

SASSOON: It's just that—in this place, you never know who's going to come in next.

OWEN: Or what m-may be wrong with him.

SASSOON: Exactly. (*A truce seems to be established.* OWEN *ventures further in.*)

OWEN: Actually, I like Shelley.

SASSOON: (*With no memory of having mentioned him.*) Shelley?

OWEN: Almost as much as Keats.

SASSOON: (*Blank.*) Oh?

OWEN: I'm sorry—I thought—er, I'm sorry.

SASSOON: What, for liking Shelley and Keats?

OWEN: For d-disagreeing with you.

SASSOON: You think I *don't* like Shelley and Keats.

OWEN: Well, I thought you said . . . (*Thinks.*) I'm *sure* you said . . . (SASSOON *puts down the golf club, turns to* OWEN *and challenges him.*)

SASSOON:

"He is made one with Nature . . .
  He is a presence to be felt and known
  In darkness and in light, from herb and stone . . .
  He is a portion of the loveliness
  Which once he made more lovely . . ."

OWEN: Yes . . . "Adonaïs."

SASSOON: Yes, now give me—just *one*—copy of that, for a

moment. (OWEN, *bewildered, hands him a copy of "The Old Huntsman."* SASSOON *reads from "The Last Meeting," making points unemotionally.*)

"He was beside me now, as swift as light.
I knew him crushed to earth in scentless flowers,
And lifted in the rapture of dark pines.
'For now,' he said, 'my spirit has more eyes
Than heaven has stars; and they are lit by love.
My body is the magic of the world,
And dawn and sunset flame with my spilt blood . . .' "
(SASSOON *stops. Emotionally unable to go on, he looks and sounds impassive.*)

OWEN: "The Last Meeting" . . . (SASSOON *nods, expressionless.*) I should have seen that. Of course. Will you go on?

SASSOON: No.

OWEN: I think it is profoundly . . . It's among the finest in the book.

SASSOON: Oh, I've written worse—very often.

OWEN: *Won't* you finish reading it?

SASSOON: There's no need. The point is surely made. Still think I don't like Shelley?

OWEN: That was very stupid of me, I should have known. With "Adonaïs" above all.

SASSOON: You weren't being at all stupid. It is just possible that I was being aggressive.

OWEN: (*Mildly, defending him.*) Or defensive.

SASSOON: (*Surprised.*) Or—that—as you say. Whatever else it was, it was rudeness. I . . . I hope you'll forgive me. (SASSOON *returns the golf club to the bag and takes out another. Returning, he risks a glance at* OWEN, *who is smiling slyly but reassuringly at him.*) Now, I don't want to pry, but are you going to tell me why you're carrying all those copies of my book about with you? Are you delivering them to the patients? Has it been made recommended reading? If it has, the staff must be madder than the inmates. (OWEN, *enjoying the sense of humour, shakes his head in response.*) Then why?

OWEN: I wondered if you might inscribe them for me.

SASSOON: What, all of them?

OWEN: Oh, if it's too much trouble . . .

SASSOON: No, it's not that. You've contributed at least two shillings' worth of royalties there. But all of them—for you?

OWEN: Oh, no. For friends. And my mother.

SASSOON: I see.

OWEN: And *one* for me.

SASSOON: Good.

OWEN: Then you will?

SASSOON: I'm very flattered. Of course I will.

OWEN: Thank you.

SASSOON: Well, hand them over. (OWEN *does so, then starts searching his pockets.*)

OWEN: I've made a list. (SASSOON *has opened a book and seen "Absolution."*)

SASSOON: Oh, dear God . . .

OWEN: Sorry . . . ?

SASSOON: This thing:
"War is our scourge, yet war has made us wise
And fighting for our freedom, we are free . . ."

OWEN: Er . . . "Absolution"?

SASSOON: You know, I think if *I* read this one first, I'd be sick all over it then throw it into the fire.

OWEN: Well, I did wonder if you really meant it.

SASSOON: Oh, I meant it when I wrote it, God help me. The truth was revealed a bit more gradually.

OWEN: But you decided to publish it . . . ?

SASSOON: Yes. Bait them with this, and the "Huntsman." Hook them with the rest.

OWEN: Sorry . . . ?

SASSOON: (*Patiently.*) It's called tactics. They'll never take it in if I just call them fools. But they might if I admit how much of a fool I was myself.

OWEN: Oh, yes I see. It's much harder to win the medal than to throw it away. (SASSOON *is surprised—and suspicious of how much* OWEN *knows, he demands harshly:*)

SASSOON: What makes you say that?

OWEN: (*His nervousness returning.*) It's just that you have to win the m-medal, first—before you have the right to say anything . . . (*Struggling.*) You have to try to write a poem before you can say "any fool can write poetry." That's all.

SASSOON: Mmm . . .

OWEN: About the next one—'To My Brother' . . . (SASSOON *turns the page and does not like what he sees.*) When did he—? I hope you won't mind me asking—but when was he killed?

SASSOON: Two years ago. Exactly two years ago. Gallipoli.

OWEN: Oh . . . I suppose that was when most of us began to doubt.

SASSOON: But not me, it would seem . . . It was on that peninsula that Hecuba, after the fall of Troy, blinded King Polymestor, slaughtered his children, and was turned into a dog for her pains. Did you know that?

OWEN: No, I didn't.

SASSOON: It could have been an omen—if only they'd known. Elementary Greek should be a compulsory qualification for Ministers of War. (OWEN *is about to laugh, then wonders if* SASSOON *means it to be funny.*) *And*, when we crept, humiliated, off that sorry place, at the end of the year—in the middle of the night—the bedraggled remnants were packed off for a fresh chance to be slaughtered on the Somme. (*Trying to lighten the mood.*) Are you sending one of these to your Colonel, by any chance? (*But* OWEN *does not respond to the attempt. His reflex is a sudden tension, turning his head away as if ashamed. It is his turn to wonder how much* SASSOON *knows.*) What is it? . . . I've said something tactless. Something that hurt? (*No reply.*) About your Colonel? . . . Was it your Colonel who had you sent here?

OWEN: (*Mumbling.*) Yes . . . It . . . it's not important. (SAS-SOON *is angry with himself, but then asks for the list of names with surprising gentleness.*)

SASSOON: Let me see, then. (*Takes the list from* OWEN.) Who's this? A relation?

OWEN: That's . . . S-Susan is my m-m-mother. (SASSOON *starts to write.*)

SASSOON: That's good. But you surprise me. These puny at-

tempts at enlightening the civilians—won't they worry her?
Perhaps frighten her.

OWEN: You've said n-nothing there that I've not already told
her in my letters.

SASSOON: Really? You've told her? Was that a good idea, do
you think?

OWEN: She wants the truth. She doesn't want me to protect
her from it. And I certainly couldn't lie to her.

SASSOON: A civilian who wants the truth? Is there such an
animal? Even—(*He finds "They" in the book.*) *this* sort of
truth?

> "The Bishop tells us when the boys come back
> They will not be the same: for they'll have fought
> In a just cause . . .
> We're none of us the same! the boys reply.
> For George lost both his legs; and Bill's stone blind;
> Poor Jim's shot through the lungs and like to die;
> And Bert's gone syphilitic: you'll not find
> A chap who's served that hasn't found *some* change.
> And the Bishop said: The ways of God are strange!"

OWEN: That's brilliant. And it's true.

SASSOON: Well, it's true. But for your mother?

OWEN: Yes.

SASSOON: You can trust her with knowing all that?

OWEN: *She* must not be taken in by the lies.

SASSOON: I see. And would you risk telling her about yourself?
That, in the end, every one of us can kill and go on killing,
if it means saving our own lives?

OWEN: If you love someone, that person has to know *all* that
you are. The worst, the most horrific . . . And the most
shameful.

SASSOON: Everything the war calls out of us, in fact.

OWEN: You know. Of course you do. Better than anybody, I
think. It's your poems that will help me to make her understand. Sometime, she will have to know who I really am.

SASSOON: But most of the people at home don't want to know—
and they don't even try to imagine.

OWEN: I told you, I wrote to her—even about winter at the

Front. Last February. You remember? The cold that makes your brain ache with it? When you're afraid that your eyes will freeze over? I told her about No Man's Land under snow—like the face of the moon, a chaos. I called it a place of madness, where nothing lived—not an insect, not a blade of grass. Only the shadows of the hawks across the sky, when they scent carrion. I said that we were the carrion. The "Glorious Dead," lying unburied day after day, until their putrefied bodies explode in our faces. We know that we'll die like that, filthy and terrified. And that *is* how we die. And it's all for lies. Their Justice and Liberation are *lies*. We really die because no one *cares* to save us. No one dares to imagine how it really is.

SASSOON: We are the only ones who can help them to imagine. If they know the truth, the killing will have to stop!

OWEN: Will you . . . Will you teach me the words? (SASSOON, *having got so near, reacts in character by ducking away.*)

SASSOON: Jingles, that's all I can write . . . But until there's something better, let the jingles ring out.

OWEN: You know that's not true. Your poems have too much of yourself in them.

SASSOON: (*Surprised, wary.*) I'm not sure I want to know what you mean.

OWEN: Compassion is the most important thing.

SASSOON: You can't be serious.

OWEN: It's true. It's here. (OWEN *takes a book from* SASSOON's *hands. He finds* "The Death Bed," *which he knows by heart, and starts it, as a challenge.* SASSOON, *uneasily, moves away from him.*)

"He drowsed and was aware of silence heaped
   Round him, unshaken as the steadfast walls;
   Aqueous like floating rays of amber light,
   Soaring and quivering in the wings of sleep.
   Silence and safety; and his mortal shore.
   Lipped by the inward, moonless waves of death.

Someone was holding water to his mouth.
He swallowed, unresisting; moaned and dropped

Through crimson gloom to darkness; and forgot
The opiate throb and ache that was his wound . . .

SASSOON: (*Remembering the event, relives it.*)

He stirred, shifting his body; then the pain
Leapt like a prowling beast, and gripped and tore
His groping dreams with grinding claws and fangs.
     But someone was beside him; soon he lay
     Shuddering because the evil thing had passed.
     And death, who'd stepped toward him, paused and
     stared.
Light many lamps and gather round his bed.
Lend him your eyes, warm blood, and will to live.
Speak to him; rouse him; you may save him yet.
He's young; he hated War; how should he die
When cruel old campaigners win safe through?
But death replied: 'I choose him.' So he went,
And there was silence in the summer night;
Silence and safety; and the veils of sleep.
Then, far away, the thudding of the guns."

OWEN: I've been trying for three years to . . . Nothing. Well, never mind . . . Would you call that a "jingle"?

SASSOON: (*A reluctant concession.*) There's always one exception. Sometimes two . . . but now, one last book. (SASSOON *takes the book* OWEN *is holding, and looks at the list.*) Who is this one for?

OWEN: For me.

SASSOON: Of course. (*About to write, then:*) I'm sorry, I don't know your name.

OWEN: Owen. W.E.S. Owen.

SASSOON: (*Writing.*) W.E.S. Owen . . . from . . . Well. There you are. (SASSOON *hands over the pile of books.*)

OWEN: (*Suddenly formal.*) Thank you for doing that. But thank you more for what's in the book.

SASSOON: The pleasure was mine. The . . . astonishment was mine, also. (OWEN *starts to go.*) Lieutenant Owen!

OWEN: Sir?

SASSOON: Who are you?

OWEN: . . . Sir?
SASSOON: *What* are you? What do you do?
OWEN: Nothing, now. But I shall be a poet.
  (OWEN *leaves him.*)

A Prayer for My Daughter

Thomas Babe

Characters: Kelly (40), Sean (40s)
Setting: Dilapidated squad room of a New York police precinct
Premiere: New York Shakespeare Festival, 1978
Publisher: Samuel French, Inc.

It is 1:00 A.M. after the Fourth of July. Two lowlife cops haul in two lowlife crooks to be interrogated about a brutal murder. The younger crook, Jimmy Rosehips, is "a kid, that's all, pure punk but with the aspect of a choirboy." He is a drug addict. So is one of the cops, Jack, who gives him a fix to speed along his confession. The second crook, Simon Cohn (a.k.a. Sean de Kahn), is a "weird" with a lengthy police record.

Both cops are cynical rule-breakers. In private, they make a cash bet on which crook pulled the trigger, and talk about whether to go with the good cop/bad cop "psychological crap" or "hurt 'em a little, physically." The older cop, Kelly, wants a quick conviction. His crazy daughter Margie has called him and threatened to kill herself, and Kelly wants to "straighten her." He is mentally and physically exhausted; as he puts it, "fuckin fucked out." The two cops split up and interrogate the prisoners one-on-one. Kelly interrogates Sean.

KELLY: Yeah, Sean.
SEAN: Simon.

KELLY: Sean de Kahn.

SEAN: Simon Cohn.

KELLY: You really let some nice hardworking Hebraic parents down when you embarked on this life of crime, didn't you?

SEAN: If you please. . . .

KELLY: I don't care, see, we all let somebody down somewheres. Your folks still living?

SEAN: I want to call my attorney.

KELLY: What do you want to call him, your attorney, courageous?

SEAN: I don't have to—

KELLY: You don't have to do anything, right? (*Picks up phone book.*) It's Brooklyn, if memory serves.

SEAN: What?

KELLY: Your folks. (*Looking.*) A lotta you in Brooklyn, Cohns. But I remember, Flatbush Avenue, right? Didn't I have to bust you there once. Yeah, used goods, here.

SEAN: I want to call my attorney.

KELLY: He's in bed.

SEAN: So are my parents.

KELLY: I know . . . the same bed, fifty years now. Where the fuck do you sleep?

SEAN: Really . . .

KELLY: All over town, I know. Well, Sean . . .

SEAN: You're a bum, officer. Of all the low-grade moron operatives in the various departments of your department, you have the odor, officer, of a bum.

KELLY: (*Unruffled.*) And you're just a ponce. So it's 682-7738, is that right?

SEAN: I want to see my attorney.

KELLY: I'm gonna have your father call one. He probably knows a good one, family friend, who'll work cheap.

SEAN: I—want to see my attorney, now!

KELLY: Yeah, well your father, Abraham, I see by the entry in the book here, Abraham Cohn, he must know somebody. (*Pause.* KELLY *dials the phone.*)

SEAN: Hang up. I'll talk to you.

KELLY: Yeah?

SEAN: I'LL TALK.

KELLY: (*Hanging up; a pause.*) So, I'm waiting, Sean, I'm all ears for the talk.

SEAN: Obviously.

KELLY: Obviously you are not quite making music yet.

SEAN: Obviously. (KELLY *picks up the phone again.*) What I wanted to tell you, at the outset . . . (KELLY *puts down the phone.*)

KELLY: Was?

SEAN: That boy I was arrested with in there . . .

KELLY: Jimmy?

SEAN: Is a very disturbed, very disturbing young man, do you know what I mean, very deeply disturbing?

KELLY: He don't bother me none.

SEAN: I mean, he's very difficult young man to get a line on, if you see what I mean, that's what's disturbing.

KELLY: Is this by way of saying you're gonna let him take the fall for this, the little druggie?

SEAN: (*Contemptuous.*) You're silly. That wasn't my point at all.

KELLY: No, Sean?

SEAN: Simon, Mr. Cohn.

KELLY: I figure either of you two could've actually blown Mrs. Linowitz away. Old cons like you got icewater for blood, but young guys like Jimmy, they can be very impetuous.

SEAN: I know.

KELLY: I know you know.

SEAN: You're silly. We'll beat it.

KELLY: I know. That's why we do this.

SEAN: What's "this"?

KELLY: We try and sneak in a little punishment before the court has a chance to decide you don't deserve it on a technicality, like you were born incurable homo, or I didn't read you your rights Shakespeare-perfect.

SEAN: No one's read me my rights.

KELLY: I don't read 'em to homos.

SEAN: Then what you're doing here is a dreadful farce.

KELLY: You wanna talk Miranda and Escobedo with me, Sean, okay. You're entitled to a lawyer, except you're not really entitled to a lawyer, because you got blood on your hands and it stinks. Now this is my house, Sean, I make the rules. That's your warning, you have the right to be very careful around me, okay?

SEAN: You're worse than silly. You're . . . insane.

KELLY: I'm tired, Sean. Got this daughter who's got her head wedged up in trouble, you know, family stuff, I stake a dry cleaning establishment all day, my ass is sore, you and your friend treat me to an old woman, her head half off—I'm just not as used to shit like that, like you imagine I am: I get tired, edgy. (*Pause.*) You got any kids? No, you wouldn't, otherwise you'd be home, in bed fifty years, I'd have to call you, say, Mr. Cohn, your son, your daughter just stiffed somebody just like you, got bail money? Hear the tears on the phone, yours, Simon. How old are you?

SEAN: I am entitled to one phone call.

KELLY: You know, we ain't gonna squeeze a fly turd out of this if you don't tell me what I can readily discern from your rap sheet. Forty . . . uh . . . one. Gettin on.

SEAN: I don't know why you do this, if you don't mind my saying so. You're silly. Everything you're doing is silly. That other detective in there will have Jimmy crying and signing anything he wants in ten minutes, and you and I can sit here until you drop dead, officer, which frankly doesn't seem to me too far in the distance.

KELLY: Forty-one, you got no job at all, no profession, nothin, you got to turn little old lady dry cleaners into hamburger. Hunh? What are you? I mean, talk.

SEAN: Everything.

KELLY: Name it.

SEAN: I'm a teacher, in fact. I'm Jimmy's teacher.

KELLY: What do you teach him?

SEAN: A way of life.

KELLY: What way of life?

SEAN: Eclectic spiritualism.

KELLY: Don't say. And you *do* like him, right, the kid?

SEAN: Jimmy.

KELLY: Too much to come right out here and pin the wrap on him?

SEAN: He's my son.

KELLY: No kidding.

SEAN: And my daughter.

KELLY: That sounds more like it.

SEAN: They're all my children, who need me.

KELLY: You been in his pants, then, is that the teaching part?

SEAN: You're silly, I'm a celibate.

KELLY: Or a masturbate.

SEAN: No, officer, the things that detain you don't bother me, don't concern me at all. Hard for you to believe, I can understand that.

KELLY: Me, naw, I'm easy, I'll believe anything. I can appreciate your predatory streak, Sean, stalk and catch and like that, and move on. I've never been longtime attached to any of the garbage I've put away, but for the moment, you're everything, baby, you're all I want.

SEAN: I can see that.

KELLY: A drink?

SEAN: You drink on the job?

KELLY: Sometimes, when I wanna mellow out, when I understand everything perfectly and feel entitled to swallow one or two for a guiltless reward.

SEAN: It's against regulations for you to drink on duty. You're armed.

KELLY: Tell you what we're gonna do. In a few minutes, I'm gonna be slightly drunk and I'm gonna get up and beat the holy shit out of you. I mean, there's gonna be very little you can do to influence that decision, I mean, if you confessed now, you don't confess, you tell me to fuck off, you kiss my ass—so before it gets unpleasant, which won't be wholly your fault, if you'd like to tell me was it you or was it Jimmy Rosehips who blasted Mrs. Linowitz, then I'll be able to think

while I'm tap-dancing on your forehead—hey, this is a killer,
or hey, this is just an accomplice. (*Pause.*) I may be. (*Pause.*)
Insane. (*Pause.*)

SEAN: I don't want anything to happen to Jimmy, I don't want
anything to happen to me.

KELLY: Sure.

SEAN: Protect him, protect myself.

KELLY: I follow.

SEAN: That's all I wanted to say.

KELLY: You wanted to say more, didn't you, one motherfuckall
of a lot more.

SEAN: Maybe I did, or didn't.

KELLY: Okay, I'm gonna beat you up a little bit now because
that's gonna make me feel better there and then we can get
back to this nice talk.

SEAN: Don't hit my face.

KELLY: I never hit faces. I'm not sadistic.

Principia Scriptoriae

Richard Nelson

Characters: Bill Howell (early 20s), Ernesto Pico (early 20s)
Setting: Latin America, 1970 and 1985
Premiere: Manhattan Theatre Club, New York City, 1986
Publisher: Broadway Play Publishing, Inc.

It is 1970. Bill Howell and Ernesto Pico are in jail, having
been arrested earlier in the day for handing out leaflets crit-
icizing the local government. A journalist shares their cell. He
knows Ernesto's rich, right-wing father, but will not talk about
him.

Ernesto, who is deeply committed to political change, has
written the leaflets they were distributing. He refuses to call

this country home. "If anything made me not call this home, it's my going to school in England. You wouldn't believe how ignorant people here are."

Bill, an American, has flown down on standby from Kennedy. He would have gone to Cuba, but that would have meant a flight from Paris, "And it just didn't seem to be the time for Paris, you know what I mean?" He considers himself a writer, but seems to lack any deep political commitment. He also speaks no Spanish. Asked how he could hand out leaflets not knowing what they said, he responds, "I know what they said. You don't have to know the language to know what they said—generally."

———————————

(ERNESTO *and* BILL *are on the floor, trying to sleep. Pause. From off we hear a round of automatic gunfire. Pause.*)

BILL: He'll be back. They'll bring him back. He's a journalist, right? (*Beat.*) He said he was a journalist, right? They're not about to . . . (*Beat.*) . . . to a journalist, Ernesto. (*Pause.*)

ERNESTO: They fake shooting you. To frighten you. I read that somewhere.

BILL: Right. So that's what they're doing. I get it. (*Pause.*) I cannot believe this is happening to me. I can't believe I am experiencing this.

(BILL *gets up and goes to a small faucet in the wall, with a bucket under it. He turns the faucet on and sticks his head under the water.* ERNESTO *watches, then stands up.*)

ERNESTO: Good idea.

BILL: Sticky in here. I think it's night out, don't you?

ERNESTO: Yes. I do. (*He puts his head under the faucet.*) It feels like night. (*Beat.*) I can't sleep. Can't you?

BILL: (*Lying down again.*) It takes me awhile. Even—in college, it would usually take me awhile.

(ERNESTO *sits in one of the lawn chairs. Pause.*)

ERNESTO: (*Pointing to the other chair.*) Bill, mind if I . . .

BILL: What? (*Looks up at Ernesto pointing.*) Mind if you what?

ERNESTO: The chair.

BILL: (*Turning over.*) What are you asking me for?

ERNESTO: It's your chair.

BILL: Do whatever you want.

(ERNESTO *takes the other chair, sets it in front of him and uses it as a footrest.*)

BILL: (*Quietly.*) It's not my chair.

(*Pause.*)

ERNESTO: My father does some journalism too. I don't mean "too" like—(*Points toward the door.*) I wasn't talking about him. I mean—as well as being a lawyer. He does both. Though he tries to keep those two careers separate. When he can. (*Short pause.*) When he can. You'll meet him.

BILL: Yeh. I guess I will.

(ERNESTO *rubs his face. Pause.* BILL *rolls over and watches* ERNESTO.)

BILL: What that guy said about your father, it hasn't—, you're not upset, are you?

ERNESTO: No, of course not.

BILL: Good. (*Rolls over.*)

ERNESTO: If it weren't for my father—I'd have never been a writer. You didn't know that, did you? You couldn't know that. (*Pause.*) Bill . . . ?

BILL: (*Still turned away.*) I'm listening.

ERNESTO: You know it really takes that kind of immediate encouragement—like I got from my father—to do anything here, something different here. It is almost impossible to fight your own family's wishes here. Oh you can try. My father tried. But it is hard here, Bill.

BILL: (*Turns, sits up.*) Ernesto . . .

ERNESTO: He didn't upset me!! (*Stands and walks to one side.*) My father would never have anything to do with the government. I know this. He has told me this. He wants nothing to do with it. He says—because he doesn't want to end up retiring to Miami. (*He laughs.* Bill *smiles.*) My grandmother wanted him to go into the government. She said, that's where the money is made. I don't think she's ever forgiven him, really. She still pressures him I think. (*He lifts his shirt and dries his face. Pause. He uses his shirt to fan his face.*) He wanted to go to Europe to university. His family had the money. We know they had the money. It wasn't the money. It cost a lot and they weren't rich but they could have gotten up the money. That's what Father always said. So he didn't go to Europe. Not for twenty years. (*Beat.*) Twenty years later I meet him at Heathrow. I think that's why he sent me to school in England, so I could meet him at Heathrow. (*Beat.*) In fact, from the time I was . . . there was never even a question. I was going. Not from anyone. Not from my sisters. (*Beat.*) My father screamed with joy when he saw me at Heathrow. (*Beat. He is fighting back tears.*) We fed the ducks. I knew he'd want to do something like that. Something English like that. (*Trying to laugh.*) When he first got off the plane, he looked to me like a bus conductor. But he was my father. (*Beat.*) A good man. Who'd have shit to do with the government. Shit! (*Beat.*) That's how he raised me.

(*Pause.*)

BILL: Obviously the guy just didn't know what he was talking about.

ERNESTO: Obviously.

(*Long pause.*)

BILL: Look, even if he did meet . . .

ERNESTO: He didn't!!!! (*Stands and moves to one side.*) He couldn't.

BILL: Right. I know that. (*Beat. Quietly.*) But even if he did, what is so wrong about being seen meeting Manuel Rosa? Rosa's a pretty well-known poet after all.

ERNESTO: He's the government's ambassador to Franco. (*Beat.*) My father would know what anyone would think if they saw him meeting with Rosa. Poet or not, he's this government's ambassador to Spain. It's clear to anyone what meeting with him means.

(*Pause.*)

BILL: Then, the guy's wrong. It's that simple.

(*Slowly* ERNESTO *goes back and sits in the chair. Pause.*)

ERNESTO: Read much of Rosa?

BILL: Maybe a couple of things in an anthology.

ERNESTO: He doesn't translate well. If you knew his love poems especially, there's little else like them in Spanish. (*Short pause.*) Incredible how you'd never guess Rosa's thinking from his poetry. He doesn't put any of that right-wing shit into his poetry (*Short pause.*) You're right, Bill—the guy's simply wrong about my father. (*Long pause.*) Tell me about yours. Your father.

BILL: Ernesto . . .

ERNESTO: Please. I'd like to know.

BILL: (*Sits up again.*) He—teaches chemistry in a college. I grew up on a college campus. He doesn't read much. At least he doesn't read what I read. He reads a lot of journals. (*Pause.*) They must be very upset. My parents. My father becomes pathetic when there is nothing he can do. There is nothing he can do.

> (*Suddenly another round of automatic fire. Pause.* ERNESTO *begins to sob.* BILL *gets up and pats him on the shoulder,* ERNESTO *hugs him. They hug. Finally* BILL *pulls away.*)

BILL: Hey, watch that hugging stuff. Remember, I know what kind of school you went to.

> (ERNESTO *smiles,* BILL *smiles.*)

Ties

Jeffrey Sweet

Characters: Walker, Francis (both mid- to late 40s)
Setting: Taylor Ridge, a college town in Ohio
Premiere: Victory Gardens Theatre, Chicago, 1981
Publisher: Dramatists Play Service, Inc.

Walker Davies, a New York director, is on the skids. Haunted by guilt from a drunk-driving accident which killed his girl-friend, he has "retreated behind an antic posture." Walker's old friend Francis, a theatre professor at Spencer University, invites him to Ohio to direct a student play—what Walker terms "a working rest cure." He is surprised and moved to find himself "gradually falling in love with the town, with the kids under his charge, with the idea of living as an accepted part of this cozy community, and with Carol."

Carol is Francis's sister. She has been through a rocky divorce and is every bit as wary as Walker. Gingerly, they get involved. Walker blossoms, and Francis is unexpectedly jealous and threatened.

WALKER: Did you know that you can get an educational discount on a subscriptior to *Astrology Today*? I didn't know astrology was an academic field.

FRANCIS: Sure, how do you think we decide who gets tenure?

WALKER: How ridiculous do you think I'd look on a bicycle?

FRANCIS: Is that what you're looking for?

WALKER: I'm getting a little tired of shnorring rides from people. Besides, it might be a good investment. In the long run. Or the long ride.

FRANCIS: Does that mean you're thinking about staying?

WALKER: The idea has a definite appeal, yes.

FRANCIS: Glad to hear it.

WALKER: There doesn't seem to be anything in here.

FRANCIS: Hunh?

WALKER: By way of bikes.

FRANCIS: I'll keep my eyes open for you.

WALKER: I've got a rehearsal starting in a couple minutes. Want to sit in?

FRANCIS: Can't do it today. But soon, I promise.

WALKER: Things to do?

FRANCIS: Always and forever.

WALKER: Something wrong?

FRANCIS: Well, not wrong exactly . . .

WALKER: Anything you'd care to . . . ?

FRANCIS: Carol.

WALKER: Oh?

FRANCIS: I'm a little concerned about her.

WALKER: Why?

FRANCIS: She's been gone a lot lately.

WALKER: Gone?

FRANCIS: Out. At night. Sometimes all night.

WALKER: You're worried about this.

FRANCIS: Not worried. Concerned.

WALKER: Why?

FRANCIS: Well, I mean, I don't know where she goes.

WALKER: You haven't asked her?

FRANCIS: She hasn't told me.

WALKER: What does she say?

FRANCIS: That it's personal.

WALKER: And you think?

FRANCIS: Well, it's obvious, isn't it? She's seeing someone. Some guy.

WALKER: Any reason why she shouldn't?

FRANCIS: Well, no, not in general. But who knows who he is? What kind of person? If he's good for her.

WALKER: She's a smart lady. Don't you think she can judge for herself?

FRANCIS: Marrying Ted was not such a terrific move.

WALKER: But she got out of it OK.

FRANCIS: That's a matter of opinion. And then there's whatever happened with Philip. You saw how stable he is.

WALKER: He'd had a little too much to drink.

FRANCIS: I don't think it was just a little too much to drink. He impresses me as a volatile, immature, unstable personality.

WALKER: Of course, he has some bad points, too.

FRANCIS: I don't know what she ever saw in him.

WALKER: Whatever it was, it's not something to be concerned about now. Not according to her.

FRANCIS: She told you this?

WALKER: The night of the party, driving me back, she explained. I really don't think you have anything to worry about.

FRANCIS: I'd worry less if I knew who he is.

WALKER: You could hire a detective.

FRANCIS: A detective?

WALKER: Have him trail her. Follow her car. Take down license plate numbers. Maybe shoot grainy photos of a clandestine rendezvous.

FRANCIS: There are occasions when you are not funny.

WALKER: I just don't think it's something for you to get upset over.

FRANCIS: Is she afraid I wouldn't approve?

WALKER: Do you have to approve?

FRANCIS: No, but I'd like to at least . . . I mean, she's my younger sister. She lives in my house, and I have a responsibility to see that . . .

WALKER: (Interrupting.) That she doesn't sleep with anybody you don't want her to?

FRANCIS: That's not what I'm saying.

WALKER: I've misinterpreted.

FRANCIS: You have.

WALKER: Sorry.

FRANCIS: I have a right to be concerned. I do.

WALKER: You have the right.

FRANCIS: If I think she's doing something self-destructive.

WALKER: Self-destructive.

FRANCIS: Getting involved with the wrong person.

WALKER: Maybe she's involved with the right person.

FRANCIS: Wouldn't she tell me if she were?

WALKER: That's not for me to say.

FRANCIS: I mean, if it were somebody that she knew I would . . . (A beat.)

WALKER: Approve of?

FRANCIS: I said no.

WALKER: Do you tell her everything?

FRANCIS: How do you mean?

WALKER: About your personal life. Your private affairs. Do you answer to her?

FRANCIS: She doesn't answer to me.

WALKER: Say if you were to bed down with one of your students.

FRANCIS: I don't.

WALKER: One of your protégés.

FRANCIS: I don't do that.

WALKER: I'm not saying you do.

FRANCIS: Has someone been spreading rumors?

WALKER: Not that I know of. All I'm saying is—whatever you may or may not choose to do in the privacy of your own whatever, it's your business. And what she does is hers. Don't you think?

[(CHRIS *and* GRAHAM *enter*.)

GRAHAM: Hi, Dr. Madden.

FRANCIS: Good morning, Graham.

GRAHAM: You going to visit rehearsal?

FRANCIS: Uh, not today no. But Walker tells me that it's coming along well. That's what he was just saying, weren't you?

WALKER: Very well.

GRAHAM: Do you know Chris? She's in the cast.

FRANCIS: Are you a student here?

CHRIS: In the school of ed.

FRANCIS: Then you must know Dr. Kreeger.

CHRIS: I have him on Tuesdays.

FRANCIS: He's a very good teacher.

CHRIS: Yes. (*A beat.*)

WALKER: (*To Chris.*) The costume designer wants to see you in the dressing room.

CHRIS: (*To Francis.*) Nice meeting you.

FRANCIS: Nice to meet you. (*Graham and Chris exit.*)

WALKER: First love. Kind of touching, hunh? (*A beat.*)] Well, I've got a rehearsal. That's what you're paying me for.

FRANCIS: Walker.

WALKER: Yes, Francis?

FRANCIS: First, just for the record, I don't bed down with my students.

WALKER: OK. Second?

FRANCIS: I would take it as a great personal . . .

WALKER: What?

FRANCIS: I want you to let her alone. (*A beat.*)

WALKER: I like the way you put that.

FRANCIS: Look, she's barely gotten over a lousy marriage. She's still very rocky. I don't think that getting emotionally involved with someone who is also emotionally unstable— pardon me for saying it, but you know it's true—I don't think that it's in her best interests.

WALKER: I see.

FRANCIS: Do you?

WALKER: Yes.

FRANCIS: Then will you leave her be?

WALKER: I don't drag her to bed.

FRANCIS: I'm not saying you do.

WALKER: Strange as it may seem, she likes me.

FRANCIS: It doesn't seem strange to me.

WALKER: Maybe that's the real issue.

FRANCIS: What? I don't follow you. (*A beat.*)

WALKER: Never mind.

FRANCIS: Never mind what?

WALKER: Just never mind. (*A beat.*)

FRANCIS: When I set it up for you to come here, I thought— a quiet town, a circle of friends, students to look up to you. I thought, "This will be good for Walker." Maybe help you get over the accident. I don't guess that's something you get over exactly. But at least find something to . . . engage yourself. In a positive way. This wasn't what I had in mind.

WALKER: You do love me.

FRANCIS: Much good that does either of us.

WALKER: It does good.

FRANCIS: Then don't you think you owe me? Just a little?

WALKER: More than a little, Francis.

FRANCIS: But not enough.

WALKER: She's not negotiable currency. (*A beat.*)

FRANCIS: If I were you, I wouldn't look too hard for a bicycle.

WALKER: Oh, come on now, Francis . . .

FRANCIS: I don't think you'll get much use out of it.

(FRANCIS *exits*.)

━━━━━━━━━━━━━━━━━━

Victoria Station

(from *Other Places*)

Harold Pinter

Characters: Controller, Driver (ages not specified)
Setting: Controller's office/Cab
Premiere: National Theatre, London, 1982
Publisher: Dramatists Play Service, Inc.

Other Places is a triple bill of plays by Harold Pinter. *Victoria Station*, a dialogue via short-wave radio between a cabbie and a dispatcher, is printed in its entirety.

─────────────────

(*Lights up on office.* CONTROLLER *sitting at microphone.*)

CONTROLLER: 274? Where are you? (*Lights up on* DRIVER *in car.*) 274? Where are you? (*Pause.*)

DRIVER: Hullo?

CONTROLLER: 274?

DRIVER: Hullo?

CONTROLLER: Is that 274?

DRIVER: That's me.

CONTROLLER: Where are you?

DRIVER: What? (*Pause.*)

CONTROLLER: I'm talking to 274? Right?

DRIVER: Yes. That's me. I'm 274. Who are you? (*Pause.*)

CONTROLLER: Who am I?

DRIVER: Yes.

CONTROLLER: Who do you think I am? I'm your office.

DRIVER: Oh yes.

CONTROLLER: Where are you?

DRIVER: I'm cruising.

CONTROLLER: What do you mean? (*Pause.*) Listen son. I've got a job for you. If you're in the area I think you're in. Where are you?

DRIVER: I'm just cruising about.

CONTROLLER: Don't cruise. Stop cruising. Nobody's asking you to cruise about. What the fuck are you cruising about for? (*Pause.*) 274?

DRIVER: Hullo. Yes. That's me.

CONTROLLER: I want you to go to Victoria Station. I want you to pick up a customer coming from Boulogne. That is what I want you to do. Do you follow me? Now the question I want to ask you is this. Where are you? And don't say you're just cruising about. Just tell me if you're anywhere near Victoria Station.

DRIVER: Victoria what? (*Pause.*)

CONTROLLER: Station. (*Pause.*) Can you help me on this?

DRIVER: Sorry?

CONTROLLER: Can you help me on this? Can you come to my aid on this? (*Pause.*) You see, 274, I've got no one else in the area, you see. I've only got you in the area. I think. Do you follow me?

DRIVER: I follow you, yes.

CONTROLLER: And this is a good job, 274. He wants you to take him to Cuckfield.

DRIVER: Eh?

CONTROLLER: He wants you to take him to Cuckfield. You're meeting the 10:22 from Boulogne. The European Special. His name's MacRooney. He's a little bloke with a limp. I've known him for years. You pick him up under the clock. You'll know him by his hat. He'll have a hat on with a feather in it. He'll be carrying fishing tackle. 274?

DRIVER: Hullo?

CONTROLLER: Are you hearing me?

DRIVER: Yes. (*Pause.*)

CONTROLLER: What are you doing?

DRIVER: I'm not doing anything.

CONTROLLER: How's your motor? Is your motor working?

DRIVER: Oh yes.

CONTROLLER: Your ignition's not on the blink?

DRIVER: No.

CONTROLLER: So you're sitting in a capable car?

DRIVER: I'm sitting in it, yes.

CONTROLLER: Are you in the driving seat? (*Pause.*) Do you understand what I mean? (*Pause.*) Do you have a driving wheel in front of you? (*Pause.*) Because I haven't, 274. I'm just talking into this machine, trying to make some sense out of our lives. That's my function. God gave me this job. He asked me to do this job, personally. I'm your local monk, 274. I'm a monk. You follow? I lead a restricted life. I haven't got a choke and a gear lever in front of me. I haven't got a cooling system and four wheels. I'm not sitting here with wing mirrors and a jack in the boot. And if I did have a jack in the boot I'd stick it right up your arse. (*Pause.*) Listen, 274. I've got every reason to believe that you're driving a Ford Cortina. I would very much like you to go to Victoria Station. *In* it. That means I don't want you to walk down there. I want you to drive down there. Right?

DRIVER: Everything you say is correct. This is a Ford Cortina.

CONTROLLER: Good. That's right. And you're sitting in it while we're having this conversation, aren't you?

DRIVER: That's right.

CONTROLLER: Where?

DRIVER: By the side of a park.

CONTROLLER: By the side of a park?

DRIVER: Yes.

CONTROLLER: What park?

DRIVER: A dark park.

CONTROLLER: Why is it dark? (*Pause.*)

DRIVER: That's not an easy question. (*Pause.*)

CONTROLLER: Isn't it?

DRIVER: No. (*Pause.*)

CONTROLLER: You remember this customer I was talking to you about? The one who's coming in to Victoria Station? Well, he's very keen for you to take him down to Cuckfield. He's got an old aunt down there. I've got a funny feeling she's going to leave him all her plunder. He's going down to pay his respects. He'll be in a good mood. If you play your cards right you might come out in front. Get me? (*Pause.*) 274?

DRIVER: Yes? I'm here.

CONTROLLER: Go to Victoria Station.

DRIVER: I don't know it.

CONTROLLER: You don't know it?

DRIVER: No. What is it? (*Silence.*)

CONTROLLER: It's a station, 274. (*Pause.*) Haven't you heard of it?

DRIVER: No. Never. What kind of place is it? (*Pause.*)

CONTROLLER: You've never heard of Victoria Station?

DRIVER: Never. No.

CONTROLLER: It's a famous station.

DRIVER: Well, I honestly don't know what I've been doing all these years.

CONTROLLER: What have you been doing all these years?

DRIVER: Well, I honestly don't know. (*Pause.*)

CONTROLLER: All right 274. Report to the office in the morning. 135? Where are you? 135? Where are you?

DRIVER: Don't leave me.

CONTROLLER: What? Who's that?

DRIVER: It's me. 274. Please. Don't leave me.

CONTROLLER: 135? Where are you?

DRIVER: Don't have anything to do with 135. He's not your man. He'll lead you into blind alleys by the dozen. They all will. Don't leave me. I'm your man. I'm the only one you can trust. (*Pause.*)

CONTROLLER: Do I know you, 274? Have we met? (*Pause.*) Well, it'll be nice to meet you in the morning. I'm really looking forward to it. I'll be sitting here with my cat o'nine tails, son. And you know what I'm going to do with it? I'm going to tie you up bollock naked to a butcher's table and

I'm going to flog you to death all the way to Crystal Palace.

DRIVER: That's where I am! I knew I knew the place. (*Pause.*) I'm sitting by a little dark park underneath Crystal Palace. I can see the Palace. It's silhouetted against the sky. It's a wonderful edifice, isn't it? (*Pause.*) My wife's in bed. Probably asleep. And I've got a little daughter.

CONTROLLER: Oh, you've got a little daughter? (*Pause.*)

DRIVER: Yes, I think that's what she is.

CONTROLLER: Report to the office at 9:00 A.M. 135? Where are you? Where the fuck is 135? 246? 178? 101? Will somebody help me? Where's everyone gone? I've got a good job going down to Cuckfield. Can anyone hear me?

DRIVER: I can hear you.

CONTROLLER: Who's that?

DRIVER: 274. Here. Waiting. What do you want me to do?

CONTROLLER: You want to know what I want you to do?

DRIVER: Oh by the way, there's something I forgot to tell you.

CONTROLLER: What is it?

DRIVER: I've got a P.O.B.

CONTROLLER: You've got a P.O.B.?

DRIVER: Yes. That means passenger on board.

CONTROLLER: I know what it means, 274. It means you've got a passenger on board.

DRIVER: That's right.

CONTROLLER: You've got a passenger on board sitting by the side of a park?

DRIVER: That's right.

CONTROLLER: Did I book this job?

DRIVER: No, I don't think you came into it.

CONTROLLER: Well, where does he want to go?

DRIVER: He doesn't want to go anywhere. We just cruised about for a bit and then we came to rest.

CONTROLLER: In Crystal Palace?

DRIVER: Not *in* the Palace.

CONTROLLER: Oh, you're not *in* the Palace?

DRIVER: No. I'm not right inside it.

CONTROLLER: I think you'll find the Crystal Palace burnt

down years ago, old son. It burnt down in the Great Fire of
London. (*Pause.*)

DRIVER: Did it?

CONTROLLER: 274?

DRIVER: Yes. I'm here.

CONTROLLER: Drop your passenger. Drop your passenger at
his chosen destination and proceed to Victoria Station. Otherwise I'll destroy you bone by bone. I'll chew your stomach
out with my own teeth. I'll eat all the hair off your body.
You'll end up looking like a pipe cleaner. Get me? (*Pause.*)
274? (*Pause.*) You're beginning to obsess me. I think I'm going
to die, I'm alone in this miserable freezing fucking office and
nobody loves me. Listen, pukeface—

DRIVER: Yes? (*Pause.*)

CONTROLLER: 135? 135? Where are you?

DRIVER: Don't have anything to do with 135. They're all blood-
suckers. I'm the only one you can trust. (*Pause.*)

CONTROLLER: You know what I've always dreamed of doing?
I've always had this dream of having a holiday in sunny Barbados. I'm thinking of taking this holiday at the end of this
year, 274. I'd like you to come with me. To Barbados. Just
the two of us. I'll take you snorkelling. We can swim together
in the blue Caribbean. (*Pause.*) In the meantime, though,
why don't you just pop back to the office now and I'll make
you a nice cup of tea? You can tell me something about your
background, about your ambitions and aspirations. You can
tell me all about your little hobbies and pastimes. Come over
and have a nice cup of tea, 274.

DRIVER: I'd love to but I've got a passenger on board.

CONTROLLER: Put your passenger on to me. Let me have a
word with him.

DRIVER: I can't. She's asleep on the back seat.

CONTROLLER: She?

DRIVER: Can I tell you a secret?

CONTROLLER: Please do.

DRIVER: I think I've fallen in love. For the first time in my
life.

CONTROLLER: Who have you fallen in love with?

DRIVER: With this girl on the back seat. I think I'm going to keep her for the rest of my life. I'm going to stay in this car with her for the rest of my life. I'm going to marry her in this car. We'll die together in this car. (*Pause.*)

CONTROLLER: So you've found true love at last, eh, 274?

DRIVER: Yes. I've found true love at last.

CONTROLLER: So you're a happy man now then, are you?

DRIVER: I'm very happy. I've never known such happiness.

CONTROLLER: Well, I'd like to be the first to congratulate you, 274. I'd like to extend my sincere felicitations to you.

DRIVER: Thank you very much.

CONTROLLER: Don't mention it. I'll have to make a note in my diary not to forget your Golden Wedding, won't I? I'll bring along some of the boys to drink your health. Yes, I'll bring along some of the boys. We'll all have a few jars and a bit of a singsong. (*Pause.*) 274? (*Pause.*)

DRIVER: Hullo. Yes. It's me.

CONTROLLER: Listen. I've been thinking. I've decided that what I'd like to do now is to come down there and shake you by the hand straightaway. I'm going to shut this little office and I'm going to jump into my old car and I'm going to pop down to see you, to shake you by the hand. All right?

DRIVER: Fine. But what about this man coming off the train at Victoria Station—the 10:22 from Boulogne?

CONTROLLER: He can go and fuck himself.

DRIVER: I see.

CONTROLLER: No, I'd like to meet your lady friend, you see. And we can have a nice celebration. Can't we? So just stay where you are. Right? (*Pause.*) Right? (*Pause.*) 274?

DRIVER: Yes?

CONTROLLER: Don't move. Stay exactly where you are. I'll be right with you.

DRIVER: No, I won't move. (*Silence.*) I'll be here.

(*Light out in office. The* DRIVER *sits still. Light out in car.*)

Vivien

Percy Granger

Characters: Vivien Howard (around 60), Paul Howard (mid-30s)
Setting: A bench outside a mental institution
Premiere: Ensemble Studio Theatre, New York City, 1979
Publisher: Samuel French, Inc.

Paul is a high-strung, self-centered theatrical director. He has directed a production of Chekhov's *The Seagull*, and has come to take his father, Vivien, to the opening night. Vivien has spent the past thirty years in a mental institution, on heavy medication. Paul does not know his father at all. He finds Vivien seated on a bench outside the institution.

(*Lights up. A man sits on a bench, his mouth is slack and his eyes are glazed. There is a trace of a deep anger nestled in his brow, the impression is that of a slumbering violence. He is a large man with massive shoulders. He wears a white shirt, yellowed with age; grey work pants held up by suspenders and a garrison belt outside and below the belt loops; and a shabby car coat. His black work shoes are scuffed and his thin white socks are bunched down below his ankles. An old tie protrudes from one pocket. No movement. After a long moment he rocks slightly. He stops. No movement. A younger man enters. He is fashionably dressed in sports jacket, tie, slacks and a smart new raincoat with belt and epaulets. He stops and peers at the seated figure.*)

PAUL: Dad? (*No response; the man does not look at him.*) Dad? It's Paul. (*No response.*) Dad . . . Mr. Howard . . . Vivien? (VIVIEN *looks at him.*)

PAUL: Hi. (*No response.*) You been waiting long? (*No response.*) I'm sorry about the rain.

VIVIEN: (*Looking away.*) Weather doesn't bother me.

PAUL: Are you all set to go? (*No response.* PAUL *takes a step forward.*) Can I give you a hand?

VIVIEN: Keep your distance.

PAUL: What's the matter?

VIVIEN: I'm not going with you.

PAUL: What?

VIVIEN: You're not Paul.

PAUL: Yes I am. It's Paul. (VIVIEN *begins to tremble slightly.*) Are you cold? Should we get in the car?

VIVIEN: I'm not getting in your car.

PAUL: Why not?

VIVIEN: You're not Paul.

PAUL: Sure I'm Paul. Of course I'm Paul. It's me. Who else would I be?

VIVIEN: That's your problem.

PAUL: Are you Vivien Howard?

VIVIEN: Yes.

PAUL: I'm Paul Howard, I'm your son. (*No response.*) I know it's been a long time; I'm just grown up now. It's still me. (*No response.*) Norristown, you remember? It was just like today, it was raining. We sat in the parking lot. Mom went in and got you. You sat in the backseat. You stared at me, do you remember that? It was 1955, I was ten, I was just ten.

VIVIEN: Everyone I know is dead.

PAUL: I spoke to—Mrs. Tendesco is it?

VIVIEN: Yes.

PAUL: She said you were very excited.

VIVIEN: I'm all right.

PAUL: I mean we made all the arrangements. She said you wanted to go out. (*No response.*) You want me to get her?

VIVIEN: You can get her if you want.

PAUL: What should I tell her's the matter?

VIVIEN: You're not Paul.

PAUL: What are you doing out here then?

VIVIEN: Waiting for Paul.

PAUL: (*Gestures.*) You got'im. (*Beat.*) Look, it's starting to rain again, let's get in the car okay?

VIVIEN: No.

PAUL: It's right over there—

VIVIEN: No.

PAUL: Dad, it's after twelve, we've got to go.

VIVIEN: You go on.

PAUL: What about you?

VIVIEN: I'm sorry you drove all this way for nothing.

PAUL: (*Taking out his wallet.*) I can prove I'm Paul. There's my driver's license, there's my picture and my name. (VIVIEN *won't look.*) Look—I've got credit cards, union cards—I've got identification coming out of my ears!

VIVIEN: Don't show me your private property.

PAUL: Look for yourself.

VIVIEN: Don't show me your private property! (*Pause.*)

PAUL: Can I sit down?

VIVIEN: It's a free country. (PAUL *sits next to him.*)

PAUL: Paulie? Po? Pooh? I don't remember, what did you call me? (*No response.*) How are you?

VIVIEN: I can't complain.

PAUL: You look terrific.

VIVIEN: You're not Paul.

PAUL: I am Paul! Why else would I be here?

VIVIEN: I'm supposed to meet Paul here.

PAUL: Okay—here, right? At the bus stop?

VIVIEN: Yes.

PAUL: In front of the buildings?

VIVIEN: Yes.

PAUL: On the bench?

VIVIEN: Yes.

PAUL: Okay, so here we are.

VIVIEN: Here we are.

PAUL: I'm your son.

VIVIEN: Go away.

PAUL: Didn't Mrs. Tendesco tell you who I was?

VIVIEN: You don't know her.

PAUL: Do you want to go talk to her?

VIVIEN: No.

PAUL: Why don't we go see her?

VIVIEN: No.

PAUL: All right, we won't. Look, could we start over?

VIVIEN: He's late.

PAUL: It's only twelve-fifteen.

VIVIEN: Late! There's going to be hell to pay. You stick around if you want to see some fireworks, mister. When he sees this son of his there's going to be hell to pay! He won't stand for it—he doesn't have to. He's got other recourses. He knows the score. There's a worm of truth there, you don't think so by your expression? You think he's just free?

PAUL: I didn't know were you where, all right. I had to fight with Mom to get her to tell me. I told her I had a right to know.

VIVIEN: I'm sure you're very busy.

PAUL: (*In a frenzy.*) I rented a car, you want to see the papers? Here—see?—that's my signature! That's my handwriting! And look here, I got a letter from my wife, see? It's addressed to me! What else do you want? I know I'm Paul Howard, I paid a lot of money to an analyst to establish that fact! (VIVIEN *looks at him.*)

VIVIEN: You ever make a basket? (*Pause.*)

PAUL: No. So what I hear you saying is you don't want to come with me.

VIVIEN: I'm going to wait for Paul.

PAUL: Well he won't come because that's me!

VIVIEN: Go away.

PAUL: We were supposed to spend the day together!

VIVIEN: (*Rising, advancing on* PAUL.) Go away! Scat!

PAUL: Dad—

VIVIEN: Shoo!

PAUL: (*Backing up, frightened.*) Hey Dad, come on, okay?

VIVIEN: Sssss!

PAUL: Take it easy—

VIVIEN: (*Makes a large gesture with his arms; roars.*) Aaaaaaaah! (*He turns and walks off with a jerky, stiff-legged stride.*)

PAUL: (*Angry.*) Why'd you say yes then if you didn't want to come? Why'd you make me rent a car and drive all the way down here? Why'd you make me come?! (*Beat.*) I thought you'd enjoy this!

What's Wrong with This Picture?
Donald Margulies

Characters: Mort (about 50), Artie (17)
Setting: Middle-class Jewish apartment in Brooklyn
Premiere: Manhattan Theatre Club, New York City, 1984
Publisher: Broadway Play Publishing, Inc.

Mort's wife, Shirley, choked to death on a piece of moo shu pork in a Chinese restaurant. The family has just completed the Jewish mourning ritual of sitting *shiva*. The mirrors are covered, the mourners are unshaven and barefoot, a memorial candle is burning, the whole place is covered with food. To add to the chaos, there are two complete sets of living room furniture. Before Shirley died, she ordered a living room set. Mort will neither part with the old set ("she sat in this sofa, your mother") nor send back the new ("this is what she wanted"). His mother, Bella, and sister, Ceil, are eager to clear out Shirley's belongings and start sorting through her clothes; his teenage son, Artie, just wants the whole thing to be over. This scene takes place right after the rest of the relatives go, leaving father and son alone for the first time.

Note: The doorbell at the end of the scene is rung by the dead Shirley, who comes in wearing a muddy shroud, says "I don't even want to talk about it," and jumps in the shower, where she proceeds to sing "Send in the Clowns."

(ARTIE *is alone in the living room, silently surveys the room. In a few beats,* MORT *shuffles back into the apartment and closes the door behind him. Long silence.*)

ARTIE: Dad?

MORT: (*Picks up one of Shirley's garments.*) What am I gonna do with all that closet space?

(*Pause.*)

ARTIE: Some week, huh? (*Pause.*) Pretty quiet *now*, though. (*Pause.*) Dad? (*Pause.*) Hey, I thought of something today. (*Pause.*) Something I haven't thought about in a long time. This game Mommy used to play with me at the beach. See, we're at Coney Island. Me and Mommy. And she's in the ocean, playing this game with me.

MORT: Your mother was funny. (*Begins laughing to himself.*)

ARTIE: Yeah. I'm a little-little boy, maybe four, and she's out in the ocean playing this game with me.

MORT: She always made me laugh, your mother. What a sense of humor.

ARTIE: Uh huh. So, I see her way out in the ocean where the water's too deep, I'm not allowed to go out that far, and I see her face . . .

MORT: What a face . . .

ARTIE: That young-Mommy face? Wet and shiny, smiling at me, getting smaller and smaller, rising away on a wave . . . and she teaches me . . .

MORT: (*Interrupting.*) What a sense of humor. We were in the supermarket once, must've been Waldbaum's, in the aisle with all the cereals . . . and I was pushing the cart . . . and your mother said to me . . . (HE *can't remember.*)

ARTIE: Dad, she teases me, she calls to me—

MORT: She said something . . .

ARTIE: Dad, wait, let me finish.

MORT: Something funny. Something so funny, it cracked me up.

ARTIE: Dad?

MORT: You could be sure if it was coming out of her mouth, it was funny. She had a real talent with words. She would put together sentences of all kinds, your mother. I wish I could remember some of the stuff she said. I should've written it down.

(*Pause.*) Ya know? I get the feeling your mother's gonna come walking through that door any minute. (*Pause.*)

ARTIE: Dad, we really should do something about the house.

MORT: What's wrong with it?

ARTIE: Maybe if we piled some of the furniture on top of each other. (MORT *is looking through Shirley's garments left on the sofa;* HE *holds one to his face and sniffs it.* ARTIE *attempts to lift a coffee table himself.*) Help me with this. Dad? Help me. (ARTIE *struggles with it, but manages to set it down and attempt to move more furniture during the following.*)

MORT: What class your mother had! What flair! The way she filled these things out with that body of hers! God, she was something else in the love department, your mother, Artie.

ARTIE: That's great news, Dad, thanks for telling me.

MORT: (*Looking at another dress.*) Oh, your mother got pizza juice on this. She made me open up the store on a Sunday morning to dryclean it. You see a stain?

ARTIE: Nope.

MORT: Of course not. I'm a professional. (HE *comes across a red-sequined dress.*) Oh! Remember this?! Hm? I'll bet you don't remember when your mother . . .

ARTIE: (*Overlap.*) She wore that to my bar mitzvah.

MORT: That's right! I'll never forget how she looked that night: chandelier earrings . . . high-heeled shoes . . . her hair in a French flip . . . and this dress. God, she was a vision. I watched her on the dance floor doing the "Alley Cat." She shimmered! Like fire she was! (*Hums a few bars of the "Alley Cat" song while holding the dress to his chest, then holds it over his face, smelling it.*) That's your mother all right. You can't give something like this away.

ARTIE: You can't save souvenirs either.

MORT: Never mind, you. You're too young. You don't know what love is. You know how much this thing cost? Cost me a fortune. Whatever your mother wanted, she got: this dress, shoes that had to be dyed to match perfect, a beaded bag she *hocked me a chinik* for, I doubt she used it more than once. Look at this construction. Look how it's stitched. Even dry cleaning couldn't hurt it. Let's see how it held up. Try it on.

ARTIE: What?

MORT: Just slip it on over your head a minute.

ARTIE: Why?

MORT: I'm curious.

ARTIE: You want me to wear this?

MORT: Why are you getting so touchy? Who's asking you to wear it? I just want you to try it on.

ARTIE: This is crazy. (*Grabs the dress. Holds it up against him.*) Here, how does it look?

MORT: (*Humoring him.*) No, no, that's no way to see how something looks, how well it hangs. That's the trouble with beading of any kind: the garment loses shape.

ARTIE: So *you* put it on.

MORT: You gotta be kidding. Me? I couldn't fit into this, I'm too broad. Believe me, if I could, I would. You're lucky. You it would fit.

ARTIE: What are you talking about?!

MORT: When do I ever ask you for a goddamn thing? Hm? I ask you one simple thing . . .

ARTIE: I'm not gonna put on my mother's dress just because you want me to.

MORT: It would give your dad such pleasure, Artie, such a kick.

ARTIE: To see me in a dress?!

MORT: Oh, not just any dress. Your mother's spitfire dress! She wore this to your bar mitzvah, Artie, to your bar mitzvah! We're not talking *schmatte* here, we're talking something I would give my eye teeth to see shimmering again. Your mother wore this dress, Artie. On her body. She sweated in this dress. She danced in this dress. She shook and shimmered in it. This dress was your mother, Artie. (ARTIE *considers it for a moment, then takes the dress back from* MORT.) Thatta boy.

ARTIE: For one minute.

MORT: That's all I'm asking. (ARTIE *begins to pull the dress over his head.*)

ARTIE: It's not gonna fit.

MORT: So I'll have it taken in.

ARTIE: (*Adjusting the dress.*) I don't know, Dad . . . (MORT *looks on, enthralled.*) Well? How does it look?

MORT: Fabulous!

ARTIE: You're just saying that.

MORT: Sweetheart, you look exquisite . . .

ARTIE: Zip me up?

(MORT *does.*)

MORT: Turn around.

ARTIE: Do I have to?

MORT: Come on . . . (ARTIE *does.*) Oh yes! Beautiful! Again! (ARTIE *turns and, beginning to revel in the dress, spins around again and again.* HE *and* MORT *are almost giddy.*) Shimmer! That's right, shimmer! (MORT *puts his hands on* ARTIE's *hips and sings the "Alley Cat" song as* HE *and* ARTIE *go through the dance steps. Sings.*) "Left foot, left foot, right foot, right . . . "

(*Etc. They continue dancing for several beats,* MORT *behind* ARTIE, *winding their way through the living room, until* THEY *collapse, laughing, on the sofa.* THEY *compose themselves.*)

ARTIE: (*Meaning the dress.*) This thing is heavy. It's pulling a little bit in the shoulders.

MORT: I can let that out. Whatever you want. (*Settling in,* MORT *leans over and turns on the television set.* ARTIE *prepares to stand.*) Sit here with me a minute?

ARTIE: (*A beat.*) Okay. (HE *settles back into the sofa, watching TV.* MORT *slips his arm over* ARTIE's *shoulders. Pause.* MORT *laughs at something on the TV. Pause.* ARTIE *gets up.*)

MORT: Where you going? We're just getting comfortable.

ARTIE: I thought I'd make us something to eat.

MORT: Now there's an idea . . . (ARTIE, *still wearing the dress, exits to the kitchen.* MORT, *humming, making himself more comfortable, takes off his trousers, lays them over a chair.* ARTIE *enters, carrying paper plates, silverware, paper napkins, and several aluminum foil–wrapped packages of food.*) Wow . . . look at all that stuff! (ARTIE *sets everything down, then exits to the kitchen.* MORT *has approached the table, and picks at the food, sampling with his fingers.*) Mm . . . lox . . . and cole slaw . . . potato salad . . . macaroni salad . . .

(ARTIE *returns with bagels, pickles, and other wrapped items.*)

ARTIE: (*Setting down the food.*) Use a fork.

MORT: . . . pickled herring in cream sauce . . . mmmm . . .

ARTIE: Come on, sit down and use a fork. Here's a plate. Help yourself.

MORT: (*Sits, surveys the food.*) I don't know what to have— (ARTIE, *unwrapping food, sniffs for freshness.*) Your mother always did that. One whiff, she could tell you what day it was gonna go sour.

ARTIE: How about something to drink?

(ARTIE *exits to kitchen.*)

ARTIE: (*Off.*) There's a Tab. You want a Tab?

MORT: What else you got?

ARTIE: (*Off.*) There's some tomato juice. Wait, it smells funny, I'm spilling it out . . . I'm giving you a Tab.

MORT: Okay, sweetheart, a Tab. With ice. (ARTIE *reenters with a glass, an ice tray, and a can of Tab, sets it all on the table and prepares a drink for* MORT.) What should I eat? How about you?

ARTIE: I'm gonna have white fish on a bagel.

(*Starts to slice himself a bagel.*)

MORT: No, don't do that. You'll cut yourself. (*Takes the bagel and knife from* ARTIE *and slices it.*) I don't want you to cut yourself.

ARTIE: I can do it.

MORT: Your mother was always cutting herself. (*Returns the sliced bagel to* ARTIE, *who proceeds to prepare a sandwich as* MORT *watches.*) What do you do? You just smear the fish on the bagel?

ARTIE: That's right.

MORT: What about the bones?

ARTIE: You pick out the bones.

MORT: One by one?

ARTIE: That's right.

MORT: They're so tiny. Hey, you do that good.

ARTIE: (*Passes the fish and a bagel.*)

Here. Help yourself.

MORT: Isn't that funny? I never knew what happened to the bones. You see how good she was to me? (*Having sliced a bagel.*) Now I have to smear on the fish and pick out the bones. Right? Boy she was some cook, wasn't she.

ARTIE: Yeah.

MORT: Oh, what an imagination on her. How about that meat loaf?

ARTIE: Yeah.

MORT: She'd throw in things you'd never in a million years expect to taste good together and they'd come out spectacular. Like a can of peas she'd throw in. Who would've thought of that? That's a talent, isn't it? To throw things together and have them come out like a gourmet meal? Remember she'd throw together all those different things and put it in the oven?

ARTIE: Yeah . . .

MORT: Remember those casseroles she made?

ARTIE: Yeah . . .

MORT: What did she call them?

ARTIE: The casseroles?

MORT: Yeah, she had a name for them.

ARTIE: "Casseroles."

MORT: Right, what did she call them?

ARTIE: She called the casseroles "casseroles."

(*A beat.* MORT *is annoyed at* ARTIE.)

MORT: Always the wiseguy.

ARTIE: What's the matter?

MORT: Always with the smart answers.

ARTIE: That's what she called her casseroles: "casseroles."

MORT: (*Overlap.*) You talk to your teachers like this? Hm? Is this how you talk to your teachers, or just to your father you talk like this?

ARTIE: (*Overlap.*) She called them "casseroles"!

MORT: Never mind, you little bastard. I ask you a question and I don't want any of that wiseguy shit.

ARTIE: I answered your question!

MORT: Look, you've been blasé about this whole thing—

ARTIE: What?!

MORT: (*Continuing.*)—from the very beginning.

ARTIE: What are you talking about?!

MORT: The little jokes, the comments. Don't think I wasn't paying attention. You don't give a damn what happened.

ARTIE: How can you say that?!

MORT: I can and I do.

ARTIE: I was the one who made the phone calls, who picked out the box, who made the arrangements. I held *you* up at the cemetery . . .

MORT: I haven't seen you cry once all week.

ARTIE: Is that what you want? Well, I haven't gotten around to that yet. I'm new at this, okay?!

MORT: If somebody's hungry, they eat. If somebody's sad, they cry.

ARTIE: You're saying I'm not sad?!

MORT: I don't know. (ARTIE *looks at him frustrated, in disbelief. Doorbell.*) Your father's a very simple man, Artie. (ARTIE *continues looking at him and realizes he is right.*)

ARTIE: Yeah, I guess *so*.

MORT: (*Doorbell. Calls to the door.*) Coming. (*To* ARTIE.) Get the door.

ARTIE: Why don't you?

MORT: I'm wearing underwear.

ARTIE: So what? I'm wearing a dress.

   (*Doorbell.*)

MORT: You're closer.

FOR THE BEST IN PAPERBACKS, LOOK FOR THE 🐧

☐ **A SPORT OF NATURE**
Nadine Gordimer

Hillela, Nadine Gordimer's "sport of nature," is seductive and intuitively gifted at life. Casting herself adrift from her family at seventeen, she lives among political exiles on an East African beach, marries a black revolutionary, and ultimately plays a heroic role in the overthrow of apartheid.

354 pages   ISBN: 0-14-008470-3   **$7.95**

☐ **THE COUNTERLIFE**
Philip Roth

By far Philip Roth's most radical work of fiction, *The Counterlife* is a book of conflicting perspectives and points of view about people living out dreams of renewal and escape. Illuminating these lives is the skeptical, enveloping intelligence of the novelist Nathan Zuckerman, who calculates the price and examines the results of his characters' struggles for a change of personal fortune.

372 pages   ISBN: 0-14-009769-4   **$4.95**

☐ **THE MONKEY'S WRENCH**
Primo Levi

Through the mesmerizing tales told by two characters—one, a construction worker/philosopher who has built towers and bridges in India and Alaska; the other, a writer/chemist, rigger of words and molecules—Primo Levi celebrates the joys of work and the art of storytelling.

174 pages   ISBN: 0-14-010357-0   **$6.95**

☐ **IRONWEED**
William Kennedy

"Riding up the winding road of Saint Agnes Cemetery in the back of the rattling old truck, Francis Phelan became aware that the dead, even more than the living, settled down in neighborhoods." So begins William Kennedy's Pulitzer-Prize winning novel about an ex-ballplayer, part-time gravedigger, and full-time drunk, whose return to the haunts of his youth arouses the ghosts of his past and present.   228 pages   ISBN: 0-14-007020-6   **$6.95**

☐ **THE COMEDIANS**
Graham Greene

Set in Haiti under Duvalier's dictatorship, *The Comedians* is a story about the committed and the uncommitted. Actors with no control over their destiny, they play their parts in the foreground; experience love affairs rather than love; have enthusiasms but not faith; and if they die, they die like Mr. Jones, by accident.

288 pages   ISBN: 0-14-002766-1   **$4.95**

☐ THE LAST SONG OF MANUEL SENDERO
Ariel Dorfman

In an unnamed country, in a time that might be now, the son of Manuel Sendero refuses to be born, beginning a revolution where generations of the future wait for a world without victims or oppressors.

464 pages   ISBN: 0-14-008896-2   **$7.95**

☐ THE BOOK OF LAUGHTER AND FORGETTING
Milan Kundera

In this collection of stories and sketches, Kundera addresses themes including sex and love, poetry and music, sadness and the power of laughter. "*The Book of Laughter and Forgetting* calls itself a novel," writes John Leonard of *The New York Times*, "although it is part fairly tale, part literary criticism, part political tract, part musicology, part autobiography. It can call itself whatever it wants to, because the whole is genius."

240 pages   ISBN: 0-14-009693-0   **$6.95**

☐ TIRRA LIRRA BY THE RIVER
Jessica Anderson

Winner of the Miles Franklin Award, Australia's most prestigious literary prize, *Tirra Lirra by the River* is the story of a woman's seventy-year search for the place where she truly belongs. Nora Porteous's series of escapes takes her from a small Australia town to the suburbs of Sydney to London, where she seems finally to become the woman she always wanted to be.

142 pages   ISBN: 0-14-006945-3   **$4.95**

☐ LOVE UNKNOWN
A. N. Wilson

In their sweetly wild youth, Monica, Belinda, and Richeldis shared a bachelor-girl flat and became friends for life. Now, twenty years later, A. N. Wilson charts the intersecting lives of the three women through the perilous waters of love, marriage, and adultery in this wry and moving modern comedy of manners.

202 pages   ISBN: 0-14-010190-X   **$6.95**

☐ THE WELL
Elizabeth Jolley

Against the stark beauty of the Australian farmlands, Elizabeth Jolley portrays an eccentric, affectionate relationship between the two women—Hester, a lonely spinster, and Katherine, a young orphan. Their pleasant, satisfyingly simple life is nearly perfect until a dark stranger invades their world in a most horrifying way.

176 pages   ISBN: 0-14-008901-2   **$6.95**